A Single Star and Bloody Knuckles

The Texas Bookshelf

The publication of this book was made possible
by the generous support of the following:

Christine and Charles Aubrey
Roger W. Fullington
Jeanne and Mickey Klein
Marsha and John Kleinheinz
Lowell H. Lebermann Jr.
Joyce and Harvey Mitchell
Brad and Michele Moore
Office of UT President William Powers Jr.
Ellen and Ed Randall
Jean and Dan Rather
Tocker Foundation
Judith Willcott and Laurence Miller
Suzanne and Marc Winkelman

A Single Star and Bloody Knuckles

A History of Politics and Race in Texas

BILL MINUTAGLIO

University of Texas Press ⌄ *Austin*

The Texas Bookshelf

Requests for permission to reproduce material from this work should be sent to:
   Permissions
   University of Texas Press
   P.O. Box 7819
   Austin, TX 78713-7819
   utpress.utexas.edu/rp-form

♾ The paper used in this book meets the minimum requirements of ANSI/NISO
z39.48-1992 (R1997) (Permanence of Paper).

Library of Congress Cataloging-in-Publication Data
Names: Minutaglio, Bill, author.
Title: A single star and bloody knuckles : a history of politics and race in Texas /
Bill Minutaglio.
Other titles: Texas bookshelf.
Description: First edition. | Austin : University of Texas Press, 2021. |
Series: The Texas bookshelf | Includes index.
Identifiers: LCCN 2020033064
    ISBN 978-1-4773-1036-6 (cloth)
    ISBN 978-1-4773-2189-8 (library ebook)
    ISBN 978-1-4773-2190-4 (non-library ebook)
Subjects: LCSH: Minorities—Political activity—Texas—History. | Women—
Political activity—Texas—History. | Minorities—Violence against—Texas—
History. | Texas—Politics and government. | Texas—Race relations—History.
Classification: LCC JK4816 .M56 2021 | DDC 976.4/06—dc23
LC record available at https://lccn.loc.gov/2020033064

doi:10.7560/310366

To Tessie, Francesco, Robert, Tom, Frank, and John
To Nicholas, Rose, and Holly
To Steven L. Davis
To Bob Compton

TEXAS HILL COUNTRY, 1938—Over some of the graves towered huge, richly ornamented monuments of marble and granite, while others had only simple weather-worn wooden crosses; and since the rich dead are forgotten as quickly and conveniently as the poor dead, weeds and tall clumps of uncut grass crowded as tightly around the huge hulks of stone as around the tiniest, most humble wooden cross.

TEXAS WRITER CLAUDE STANUSH, FROM HIS SHORT STORY "PEACE AND JOY"

Contents

A Single Star and Bloody Knuckles

Prologue

FOR SEVERAL DECADES IN TEXAS, a wry theory was batted about that only one person would be able to rally state residents from every political persuasion. The thought was that just Willie Nelson could pull together all the disparate forces in Texas—the ones forever shaped by the inherited history tied to Native Americans, white settlers, Mexicans, enslaved people, Tejanos, ranchers, cotton farmers, freedmen, industrialists, oil barons, and twenty-first-century high-tech entrepreneurs. Wags speculated that the legendary musician would win a gubernatorial race with the biggest landslide ever—and that he would appeal to Democrats and Republicans, liberals and conservatives, and a wide variety of ethnic and racial groups.

Some T-shirts were made, and a few "Willie Nelson for President" stickers showed up on car bumpers (I had one on my auto for a few years), but perhaps he was too busy touring and splitting time between his smoky lairs near the Texas Hill Country town of Spicewood and the north shore of Maui. The "Draft Willie" movement never took off, though many wished it had. Maybe, in the end, it was just that Nelson was being guided by a personal philosophy akin to the one often attributed to Groucho Marx, who allegedly said he would refuse to "join any club that would have me as a member." Or, maybe it was the fact that Nelson knew governing his home state would always be an inherently elusive process.

He once said: "I'm from Texas, and one of the reasons I like Texas is because there's no one in control."[1]

Choosing the exact starting point for any examination of Texas political history is a matter of debate. Some zero in on the internal dynamics and confederacies of those earliest Native Americans before the genocidal erasure by white settlers who hunted them, introduced deadly diseases like smallpox, and embarked on the total elimination of the lifeblood buffalo herds. The buffalo, like the Comanche, had roamed free, and the natives relied on them for sustenance and their cosmology. For many of the white invaders, there was no difference—the Comanche and the buffalo were both beasts that needed to die. For another starting point for a look at Texas politics, some focus on the governing principles introduced during the Spanish and Mexican dominations, or to the fitful and controversial ways Anglo colonists tried to organize as they began thudding across Old Mexico and New Texas—battling over land, coastlines, water, and what they hoped were boundless natural treasures.

Some settle, maybe for the sake of fate and poetry, on the Battle of the Alamo as the best launching pad for political history—thinking that the famous conflict was the perfect symbol for the passionate, even feral ambitions of white politicians hell-bent on securing homesteads and fortunes. Others suggest starting the political history later in 1836, when the hard-fighting, nimble guerrilla armies subdued the Mexican military, and a few dozen men, most pro-slavery, met at Washington-on-the-Brazos to form a country and draft a constitution. The latter was put together hastily, with some of its signatories no doubt surprised that they had defeated Mexico and now had to turn their full attention to outlining a system of governance.

Their two-volume *Laws of the Republic of Texas* was terse, little more than 6,500 words, with elements derived from Spanish and Mexican laws, other states, and the US Constitution.[2]

Separate authorities were granted to the governor's office, to a judicial system (with city, county, district, and Texas Supreme courts), and to a two-body state legislature (a senate and a house of representatives). Of course, key provisions to protect landownership were included—a nod to the fact that land was the very reason for the invasions, battles, and wars.

The leaders of the new Texas nation were also anxious for Anglo primacy—to have even more white Protestant settlers joining them and becoming a permanent firmament against Mexico or even slave revolts. Section 9 of the General Provisions of that early attempt at a constitution made a point to legalize slavery in uncompromising terms. It is one of the founding principles of Texas politics, and it would inspire laws, bills, elections, and debates at the city, county, and state levels—and pit Texas lawmakers against the federal government until the twenty-first century:

> All persons of color who were slaves for life previous to their emigration to Texas, and who are now held in bondage, shall remain in the like state of servitude, provide the said slave shall be the bona fide property of the person so holding said slave as aforesaid. Congress shall pass no laws to prohibit emigrants from the United States of America from bringing their slaves into the Republic with them, and holding them by the same tenure by which such slaves were held in the United States; nor shall Congress have power to emancipate slaves; nor shall any slave-holder be allowed to emancipate his or her slave or slaves, without the consent of Congress, unless he or she shall send his or her slave or slaves without the limits of the Republic. No free person of African descent, either in whole or in part, shall be permitted to reside permanently in the Republic, without the consent of Congress, and the importation or admission of Africans or negroes into this Republic, excepting from the United States of America, is forever prohibited, and declared to be piracy.[3]

If someone intended to embark for the wide-open spaces of Texas, they were welcome to bring slaves either purchased or inherited. Once in Texas, you couldn't free the slaves unless lawmakers agreed. If permission was granted, then any freed Black men, women, and children would have to leave Texas. There would be no freed slaves in the Republic of Texas. Africans and Native Americans would not be considered "persons" who were guaranteed basic rights. No Texas political history can be considered complete unless one weighs the lingering, brutal impact of slavery—and then the subsequent ways state leaders wrote and enforced laws deliberately designed to keep minorities segregated and forcibly excluded from the democratic process.

Texans willingly accepted annexation into the United States in 1845—and then the very next year America's expansionist impulses ignited another war. Mexico hadn't rested easily with surrendering the land north of the Rio Grande. And the men in Washington wanted Texas protected. The

Mexican-American War lasted for two years, and when the marching US armies moved deep into Mexico, some said expansionism was really just cold, domineering imperialism—that the US was ramrodding what it believed to be its military, religious, and economic superiority. The bloody war touched on so many things, including whether America was really guided by an ordained blessing from God—that it really was America's Manifest Destiny to permanently occupy land from one ocean to another. In a few years, one thing was going to be clear: the same Americans who together invaded Mexico would take up guns against one another in the Civil War.

Into the mid-1800s, Texas remained a hurly-burly promised land for white newcomers, including hardy groups of German settlers aiming for the beautiful springs and unclaimed acres for anyone brave enough to venture into the loping shoulders of the Hill Country. The hunt for any roaming Native Americans was carried out by federal troops coming to places like a small hilltop in Mason County, where soldiers, including Robert E. Lee, watched for Comanche bands camping near the Llano River. If you survived the confrontations with the master horsemen, those "lords of the plains," Texas had boundless land. It was where you might be able to let your cattle roam free and where you could take the law into your own hands.

In 1861, it was almost an easy segue for slave-owning Texas leaders to cast their lot with the Confederacy. Thousands fought in the Civil War, even beyond the Texas boundaries. Some carried weapons to the very official end, and maybe beyond in the form of roving, unrepentant enemies of the Union. But the defeated Texans were left to wrestle with the bitter fact that the tables had been turned—the conquerors had been conquered. They had seized Texas from Mexico, but now they were under the heel of another invading army—one ordering them to dissolve the slave system that had attracted them in the first place.

Still, there was something that kept calling Confederates to Texas: after the war, waves of ex-rebels left North Carolina, Alabama, and other defeated states and headed west. More and more men steeped in the buying and bartering of Blacks were crossing the Sabine River—like the bearded, angular-faced, and hawkeyed Col. Alfred Horatio Belo, who had a sense that Texas would always be more receptive to "Southern customs." It was on the outer edge of America, as far away as could be from federal regulation. Belo was from a prominent slave-owning family in North Carolina, and he would eventually oversee the *Dallas Morning News*, which would become one of the state's most reactionary and politically influential newspapers. (This newspaper, in fact, would be run a century later by a publisher named Ted Dealey, who loathed federal officials so much that he would call Washington "nigger town.")[4]

As Col. Belo and other restless Confederates looked to Texas as a welcoming outpost where Blacks and Latinos would be aggressively barred from power, the state was building toward a political blueprint that would last for the next 150 years—and maybe well beyond.

An uncompromising Union soldier, Edmund Jackson Davis, was installed as governor in 1870, with the full blessing of the powers-that-be in Washington. Immediately, his ascension was anathema to so many that it led to a fierce, galvanizing resistance—and a new Texas constitution.

As that political playbook was being debated in the 1870s, state lawmakers were surrounded by the shadows, echoes, and ghosts from the Battle of the Alamo—the slave traders like Jim Bowie; frontiersmen like Davy Crockett; and, really, all those renegades, Mexican soldiers, and opportunists who once found themselves fighting at a mission along the narrow, twisting arms of a small Texas river in San Antonio. The state's sense of itself, another key to how politics would be practiced, was being written and burnished. Selectively culled nods to the past—nostalgic, romantic, and inspiring versions of Texas history—would be handed down. Then taught in schools. And then celebrated in countless books, hagiographies, and articles.

In time, there was a parade of breathless odes to a state forged by singularly heroic men and protected by heaven's blessed hand. "God Bless Texas" became a kind of defining mantra, an easy way of saying that white men and the Creator had moved in sync to shape the state's destiny. It really was an endless horizon luring people with the fortitude to occupy it. Texas had once beaten a large and heavily armed Mexico—and become its own country. It really had stared down Comanche "savages" and blind Northern leaders who had no clue as to what it had ever meant to survive in the dangerous hollows of East Texas or the granite hills west of the Colorado River. Yes, it had lost to the antislavery Union, but it never got on its knees.

As the chroniclers began scripting the preferred history, and as the men in Austin mapped out the state's rules and regulations, a guiding impulse evolved: to always insist on letting Texas pursue its own path—federal or centralized control be damned—and to cling, in either subtle or glaring fashion, to many of the core principles of the Confederacy.

Today, the myths and the realities of Texas history are still being mulled over by voters, elected officials, activists, organizers, and the darting consultants and lobbyists who mingle at the exclusive, once-segregated Austin Club in the heart of the state capital. Or by the people whispering in the echoing hallways of the Henderson County Courthouse. Or who huddle under the old ceilings of San Antonio City Hall. Or who confer inside the hushed Petroleum Club in Midland. Or who sit under the ancient mesquite trees in Roma, overlooking the green-gray river that some from Mexico still cross on their way to whatever is waiting for them in Texas. Or, perhaps, who gather at the small South Dallas bungalow of a widow named Juanita Craft and remember how she had tried to register Black voters, especially after someone in the city threatened to kill Martin Luther King Jr.

One veteran political insider, an Austin suburbanite who began sporting cowboy hats late in life, said he was able to boil down what Texas was all about: "limited government, low taxes, controlled spending and debt, and a restrained regulatory environment make Texas work," said Mark McKinnon, a plugged-in political advertising man.[5] He had helped run George W. Bush's campaigns. And in the twenty-first century, he was maybe even inadvertently describing some of the old anti-regulatory, anti-Washington impulses from the Confederates who laid the foundation for Texas politics.

They had headed west and used thousands of enslaved families, tenant farmers, sharecroppers, and even leased prisoners to move mountains of earth for massive cotton plantations, or to fell the looming pines in the forests bordering Louisiana. And then they were followed by hard-charging white men punching holes in the deserts and tapping into oceans of oil, or forcing water into the Mexico borderlands and turning them into an Eden of citrus groves.

In some ways, it wasn't dissimilar to what was happening elsewhere around America. Settlers, explorers, and entrepreneurs were forever driving the expansion of the nation. They headed toward the billion-dollar California gold rush. Or to Oregon, where moguls like John Jacob Astor made a fortune in the fur trade. The Bush dynasty, so tied to Texas, was present at every expansionist thunderclap in the nation—selling food and supplies along the railroad lines uniting the American coasts, and making millions along the way. Texas certainly wasn't the only place promising economic possibilities. But it was forged by that often far more complicated history featuring Comanche, bartered humans, nationhood, and the uneasy dance with Mexico. And then Texas simply leaned especially hard into its sense of itself, into its curated, sanitized mythology, into its particular devotion to what others called "states' rights."

It was, then and now, a magnet. Willie Nelson's family moved to Texas from Arkansas in 1929, seeking work at a time when almost one out of every four Texans eked out a meager existence on plots of land they rented from big farmers. The Nelson clan joined the millions who drilled the wells around Beaumont, stooped in the cotton fields outside Mexia, or thudded pickaxes into the caked earth of McAllen. Migrants were going from one West Texas onion field to another to earn a few cents a day, or into cramped and dangerous pecan-shelling plants in San Antonio. Texas was initially built by enslaved workers—and then it always seemed able to draw more foot soldiers for the grand plans mapped out by politicians, investors, and industrialists.

It was true in 1870, as the modern Texas political system was born, and it remains true today: the process of governance in Texas has been defined by who and what can be conquered, extracted, owned, and built. Again, that's not something isolated to the state. It's just that Texas seemed to conquer, extract, own, and build in especially spectacular, unbridled, and sometimes unhinged and bloody ways.

Today it's impossible to even remotely grasp what it must have been like to feel the heat and rage of cheering mobs, sometimes with ten thousand people, gathering in East Texas for the most horrifying public murders in American history—ones so hellish, so gruesome, so condemnable that they achieved a crazed level of celebration. Travel to some Black communities in that part of the state and it's still not difficult to have people point to trees where Blacks were hung and tortured to death. In the mid-1990s, I went to Mexia to work on a story for a national magazine about Ray Rhodes, a local man who had become a trailblazer as a Black coach in the National Football League. While researching his life with the help of the kind archivists at the local library, I saw hints about the possibility that his uncle had been lynched near the sluggish, muddy Navasota River. I left the library, and on a blindingly rainy afternoon, I knocked on a shack where one of Rhodes's elderly aunts lived. She didn't blink when I asked her if there was truth to the lynching story, and if she knew where the hanging tree was. She opened her falling-down screen door and pointed a finger down a narrow country road. I found a looming tree in a very isolated area that had some pieces of wood nailed high up on a sturdy limb—maybe it was a kind of scaffolding or support system that could hold a rope and a swaying body.

Years later, I ran into a lauded Texas writer who told me she had been to a party with white liberals in Austin who argued that "Texas was a part of the Confederacy, but wasn't a slave-owning state." We wondered if they were folks who had been raised on that narrow, celebratory sense of Texas that many chroniclers had produced while deeming slavery and lynchings to be road bumps in the way of that heroic, rosy legend. The slave machine, with tens of thousands exiled as human chattel, stretched from the Red River to the Sabine, from Rusk County to the very halls of political power in Austin. But long after it was outlawed, its story often never seemed to fit alongside the sanguine and marketable histories Texans were required to learn in public schools. For generations of politicians and writers selling a shinier version of the state ("Top Ten Barbecue" or "Top Ten Swimming Holes"), it was an inconvenient truth. But, unequivocally, cruelties remained rampant for decades and decades after the Civil War ended. They persisted after slavery was ostensibly outlawed—through carefully legislated Jim Crow segregation, gerrymandering, voter suppression, and a cauldron of other politically mandated schemes. The racism, the exclusion, seemed to bleed deep into the muscle memory of the state.

In the mid-1990s, I heard about a very old restaurant nestled near the railroad tracks in Taylor, Texas. I was told the place was still segregated. Not by the enforcement of the owner, but by the habits of the customers. When I found the place, I realized there were two entrances. By accident or luck, I happened to pick the one that white diners used. The restaurant had another door, one that Black men and women were using to enter. A long counter divided the dining room, with white people eating on one side and Black customers eating on the other side. The white part of the room had a jukebox with country music records by George Jones from Saratoga, Texas. The Black side of the room had a jukebox with blues tunes by Freddie King from Gilmer, Texas.

I talked to the elderly owner, and he told me that he harbored grudges against no man, but that old habits die hard in Texas. He said people came in the doors that they had always used. They sat on the side of the restaurant where they had always sat. It was, he seemed to suggest, a habit born out of history, out of habit in Texas.

It made me think of a bundle of things that I had once seen but never fathomed. In San Antonio in March 1980, I went to the Alamo to watch as police and glowering Texas Rangers moved in on some young Latino protesters who were racing across the roof and shouting that they had "retaken" the mission. In Houston, I watched lines of Black parishioners, in their Sunday best, headed down West Dallas Street toward their old, historic church. It was now surrounded by downtown office buildings past the highway, and it was a symbol of how leaders in almost every major Texas city had deliberately splintered, carved up, historic neighborhoods where freed slaves were "allowed" to live. The people in Houston's Fourth Ward had their church separated from them by towers and highways, but they were going to walk to it every Sunday morning. And they'd be marching not far from what someone in Houston later told me was the "hanging tree"—the big oak used to lynch Blacks, just outside the Old City Cemetery where the white men who helped found Houston were buried.

Later, in the early 1980s, I moved to Dallas to work on a newspaper, and the first week I was there, I walked down a street that I eventually learned had been named to honor the Confederate general who created the Ku Klux Klan. I stopped in a community fixture, a long-standing dry-cleaning business, introduced myself, and said I was interested in local history. The owner of the store, a Black man, chased me out of his place—and he called my newspaper to see if I really was a reporter. I assumed he thought I was a white policeman ferreting out information on his neighborhood.

In Dallas, I met a wonderfully erudite student of history named Donald Payton. One day he took me to Old City Park, a collection of older preserved homes. He pointed to one of the finer buildings on display and said, matter-of-factly, "That's the house of the people who owned my family." After we left the slavemaster's residence, Payton took me on a trip to the library in my Oak Cliff neighborhood, not far from where Jack Ruby and Lee Harvey Oswald had once lived. He pointed to an exterior wall, where I could see two small, shadow-like rectangles. Payton told me that there had been signs there, taken down years ago, that indicated the water fountains were segregated: one for whites, one for coloreds. He said that older people knew what the shadows once held.

Payton also told me there were similar shadows everywhere in Texas, but you had to be willing to find them and to move beyond the easier, less troubling depictions. He said to look beyond the ginned-up tales of heroic Texas, the ones peddled by magazine and newspaper editors, and that was how you would find the real political history of the Lone Star State.

Starting with the 1870s and then moving decade by decade, this work will tell a story of politics through the prism of thorny issues and influential Texans. At times it will also tell the story through my own window—through some people and events I encountered over the last four decades. It is my hope that the reader won't be put off by my very occasional appearance, or think it the height of ego. I decided that maybe it would be worth including a few of my own stories, if only to illustrate how little I, or maybe anyone, can ever really see the true face of policies and politics in Texas.

Working on this book brought back a flood of memories—especially of those echoes from the past that Donald Payton had told me to listen and look for. I suddenly remembered that when I moved to Abilene in the 1970s, a new Latino friend had said that his family was "owned by John Connally"—and that they were "raised" on a South Texas ranch run by the formidable governor and secretary of the treasury. It went far beyond what I had been reading in the "horse race coverage" of elections or in the deep-dive analysis of this or that subcommittee hearing and legislative bill in the statehouse. It certainly was well beyond the hats-off-hooray stories I had been reading in the publications that wanted to hawk their version of Texas to the millions of newcomers relocating to the state in the 1970s and 1980s. Only two Black people were featured alone on the cover of *Texas Monthly* magazine in the 1970s: U.S. congresswoman Barbara Jordan and a heroin addict who was described as a "boss man" in "the ghetto" of Houston's Fifth Ward. Two other Black faces appeared on 1970s covers—both were maids attending to white women. There were no Black Texans featured alone on the cover in the 1980s, and there were only a handful more, often athletes, over subsequent decades.

Given all these tangled, enormous complexities, this book makes what might be seen as a simplistic attempt to corral the evolution of the state's politics. The work is structured by decades, but the themes ebb and flow far beyond my ten-year boundaries. The decade-by-decade design is intended to frame a fraction of the enormous history and to also find some influential folks amid the thunderclaps. The stories are told, heaven help the reader, through an admittedly subjective selection of people, policies, and events.

This work is intended for general-interest audiences, including readers who might be introduced to Texans they haven't heard about before—and might find compelling. Readers will also notice that there are some visits to the final resting places of a few major characters in the book. This is not an outgrowth of morbid fascination. It is an attempt to point to how some Texans are honored and remembered—or forgotten and maybe overlooked. From San Antonio to Austin, from Waco to the Rio Grande Valley, a few of those resting places can be quite telling.

Too, this work will linger at times on fits of public violence against minorities in Texas—horrifying spasms of inhumanity that might lead a reader to ask why state and local lawmakers allowed them to happen in the first place. They were, no matter your political persuasion, shocking moments that could define a place and its elected officials. Slavery was outlawed in Texas, but cruelties persisted—and were often insisted upon by political leaders.

Finally, some powerful figures and policies are left out of this work. Choices had to be made. Mark Twain put it this way: "The very ink with which history is written is merely fluid prejudice."[6]

I have had the careening fortune to visit several Texas luminaries from different sides of the political aisle. I sat in John Connally's office one afternoon and listened to him reminisce about almost dying from an assassin's bullet in Dallas. I sat with George W. Bush as he put his custom-made eel-skin boots on the governor's desk—and I stared at the collection of autographed baseballs he kept in his office. I walked with Maury Maverick Jr. through Brackenridge Park in San Antonio and listened to him talk about how people had thought he and his father, a congressman and mayor, were Texas communists. I took a car ride with Henry Cisneros from Capitol Hill to Baltimore, and we talked about his rise to power from the poor West Side of San Antonio. I sat at Bob Bullock's bedside, listening as the dying but still intimidating lieutenant governor of Texas talked about his role in getting Bush elected president of the United States. There were others, especially ones less known: D. B. Hardeman, who reshaped the Democratic Party in Texas in the 1950s; and Hudson Griffin, a Black Republican who exerted power from his tiny tailoring and dry-cleaning storefront not far from a vine-covered Confederate cemetery in South Dallas.

My sanctimonious goal is to draw from those encounters, from the five Texas cities I've lived in, from the four Texas newspapers I worked for, and from several books I've done about Texas history, politics, and race. And then, to push my piety to another level, to aim for what the *Abilene Reporter-News*—where I worked as a cub reporter almost forty-five years ago—inscribes on its front page as a guiding motto: "With or without offense to friends and foes, we sketch your world exactly as it goes." As far as I can tell, it is the only newspaper in the nation using a lofty quote from Lord Byron, and it serves as a tip of the hat to the fact that it tried (or claimed) to find an accurate version of things.

To help in that endeavor, this work relies on thousands of pages of hard-earned research done by many brilliant people in their definitive books, dissertations, master's theses, and articles, including the ones that sought to remedy the fact that some prescribed works, assigned in classrooms and handed down through the generations, had enormous gaps when it came to slavery, the Confederacy, and racism. Ross Ramsey, an editor for the *Texas Tribune*, once told me that what scared him the most about covering politics in Texas was the "stories that we don't know about."

A team of research assistants helped cull thousands of documents, essays, online entries, family chronicles, and a fair share of out-of-print tomes. I reminded my assistants that the political writer David Broder had once reviewed a book I wrote about the Bush dynasty and its political emergence in Texas. Broder, sort of a dean of Washington observers, said the book was "neither adulatory nor cynical." Whether that is true of this book remains to be seen.

This work will have mistakes, and they will be mine. There will be sins of inclusion and omission, and they will be mine.

If not for his deep affection for the church and the roots music he heard as a young man in the Texas hamlet of Abbott—and his deep-seated populist belief that no one is ever really in control—maybe we would have had ... Governor Willie Nelson. I once spent several interesting hours talking with him about farm and tax policies at his hideaway near the waterfalls of Krause Springs and the meandering, shaded Cypress Creek. I also spoke to him inside his hushed tour bus in the parking lot of the cavernous Billy Bob's nightclub in Fort Worth. (I remember writing that outside the bus there were many middle-aged women wearing dollops of "hopeful rouge." I was later told that you are not considered a real writer in Texas until you have "survived" a long interview session on Willie Nelson's tour bus.)

Maybe it's best to go back to the Hill Country Sage for another word about politics, especially as the 2020s dawned with spiraling uncertainties. The state was gripped by a marauding virus—and then by roiling unrest tied to wicked, ceaseless racism and injustice. Some said it was a kind of reckoning, and that Texas and other places were finally facing the accumulated pains that flowed straight from slavery to modern-day lynchings. There were marches to demand that Texas acknowledge its deliberately hidden history. But there were also communities rallying to protect memorials to Confederates who had fought for the right to enslave other Texans.

Just yards from the state capitol and the governor's mansion, artists painted "Black Austin Matters" in giant letters on Congress Avenue. On the sidewalk, aiming directly at the word "Black," was a statue that had been installed years ago. It depicts Angelina Eberly, a slavemaster who had achieved a kind of heroic status among some Texans for firing a cannon against "invaders" who wanted to have a city other than Austin become the state capital. The image of the slavemaster alongside a slogan on a street leading to the front door of the statehouse was a perfect distillation of how the real and imagined versions of Texas were colliding.

Meanwhile, through the long, complicated days of 2020, Willie Nelson was lingering as a kind of Texas Diogenes—a bard with a guitar who was forever in search of honesty. Through the smoke and mirrors of politics, he had decided to rely on his instincts to tell him whom to trust.

He once said this: "I'm just an ole redneck from Texas who ain't a Democrat or Republican, but I can look at a guy and tell whether I like him or not."[7]

CHAPTER 1

Remain Quietly: The 1870s

BOB BULLOCK, ONCE THE VERY powerful lieutenant governor of Texas, was rumored to have whipped out a handgun in restaurants and fired away at rats or bugs—real or imagined. One evening, in his bare feet, he jumped out the rear window of a motel, perhaps another Texas politician scrambling to perdition or from infidelity. He once drank so much that he fell asleep on the back floor of a car that was not his, and scared the holy hell out of the unsuspecting owner by popping up as the driver cruised down a Lone Star highway ... and then listened as Bullock cheerfully introduced himself as the driver's faithful public servant. He once attended a formal banquet in Austin and shook the hands of newspaper representatives (one was me) who had come from Dallas—while hissing in their ears that he wanted to "fuck" the woman who ran their editorial pages.

Bullock was arguably the apotheosis of political evolution in Texas and proof positive that urgent personalities often dominated state affairs. Through the 1980s and 1990s, he perfected a special Texas version of per-suading legislation, the kind that saw major policy moves being charted by businessmen and government officials who gathered at mansions, pri-vate dinners, and members-only clubs—or who joined together for guided trips to hunt imported African animals on sprawling Texas ranches. Bul-lock loved his version of Texas as a place of iron-willed independence, and one Texas writer observed that he also enjoyed hopping over the fence at the Texas State Cemetery. When he padded through the graveyard, in a part of Austin where minority residents had once been exiled but then supplanted by an avalanche of high-priced gentrification, he'd linger by the endless monuments to the men who had shaped the state. He no doubt could see, nestled among the many monuments to Confederate soldiers and allies, a singular marble anomaly—the resting place of a feisty Union general who had been tasked with bringing Texas to heel, with making Texas bow to Washington. That general's name has been a bit lost to history—perhaps written out of some books because he was so reviled by the men who replaced him. His very existence, as a conquering general and then a governor told to tame a wayward state, had led a wave of single-minded Texans to construct and enforce the political process that would rule the state for more than a century.[1]

On Monday, June 19, 1865, the balding, broad-faced Union Army general Gordon Granger arrived at the humid port of Galveston along with 2,000 federal troops. He was war-seasoned, a native New Yorker, and a graduate of West Point—and now he was occupying Texas on behalf of the federal government. He read aloud from "General Order No. 3," which announced the emancipation of what one historian would estimate to be as many as 250,000 slaves in Texas:[2]

> The people of Texas are informed that, in accordance with a proclamation from the Executive of the United States, all slaves are free. This involves an absolute equality of personal rights and rights of property between former masters and slaves, and the connection heretofore existing between them becomes that between employer and hired labor. The freed are advised to remain quietly at their present homes, and work for wages. They are informed that they will not be allowed to collect at military posts, and that they will not be supported in idleness either there or elsewhere.[3]

It was a moment meant to trumpet a new reality for Texas after the Great War, and it would be commemorated for years as the "Juneteenth" holiday. In what some would say was a prophetic act of symbolism, Blacks in Texas had not been notified about emancipation until almost two years after slaves elsewhere around the nation had. Thirty miles north, in Houston, the *Tri-Weekly Telegraph* was writing that the federal government could still allow some form of forced labor; the *Republican* published in Marshall was urging slave owners not to let their human property loose.[4] Still, "slaves cried and danced for hours. Many shouted to the heavens … Thousands had no idea what freedom meant or how to experience it, but they knew it had to be better than eating hog scraps, wearing tattered clothes, living in slave quarters, and working for zero dollars."[5]

Even with Granger's decree, Confederate soldiers from around the battered South were still planning to come to Texas, hoping or assuming they would be honored and could make economic inroads in an unsettled place that was dealing with the lingering, nettlesome presence of Native Americans or the constant and uncertain relationship with Mexico. And at least one Union loyalist was also weighing his own ambitious opportunities.

Edmund Jackson Davis, a native of St. Augustine, Florida, and the son of a lawyer, had relocated with his parents to Galveston in 1848. He had roots in American history and was proud of the fact that his grandfather had given his life during the Revolutionary War. In Texas, the tall, bearded, and gaunt Davis also became a lawyer. He settled in Corpus Christi, and then Laredo, until he became a district attorney in Brownsville. He married into a family close to General Sam Houston's and climbed into the upper reaches of a still-forming Texas hierarchy. By the 1860s, he was a state judge—and increasingly opposed to the rumblings that Texas should join the secessionist movement.

When Texas officially joined the rebellion, Davis refused to swear allegiance. He had a sincere aversion to slavery—and perhaps a welling fear that leaders he had befriended in Texas legal circles would look the other way if people came gunning for him. In May 1862, Davis fled to New Orleans and then to Washington, DC, where he was given an audience with President Lincoln in August. He convinced Lincoln there was a solid core of loyalists in Texas. Davis was made a commander of the 1st Texas Cavalry, and he traveled back to New Orleans and then to Mexico to put together a guerrilla army. He took out advertisements seeking soldiers and suggested there would be sturdy horses waiting for any man. Davis and his troops fought in Galveston in the winter of 1863, unsuccessfully trying to keep the city from being commandeered by rebels. He roamed south, across the Rio Grande, but was captured by Confederate outfits not far from the Mexican city of Matamoros. He weighed the very real possibility that he'd be executed—and he learned that he had narrowly avoided being lynched, but only after his wife and Mexican officials had begged for his life. Confederate officers, anxious to avoid confrontations with Mexico,

Edmund J. Davis, a Florida native who served as a Union brigadier general
(as pictured) in the Civil War, became governor of Texas in 1870. His grandfather
gave his life in the American Revolution.

finally decided to release him, and by the end of 1863, Davis was fighting
again in South Texas. In 1864 he was promoted to brigadier general, and
in the summer of 1865, Davis was back in Galveston to watch the surren-
der of one of the last remaining Confederate armies.

Texas, like most of the South, was in a churning state of confusion and uncertainty. One thing was clear: some roaming rebels were refusing to put down their arms. There was one more final flare-up in the unforgiving heat of South Texas—the Battle of Palmito Ranch. Some quibble over whether it was the "official" last battle of the Civil War. Others say it was only a dustup between federal troops and a few restless ex-Confederates, ones who knew the war had ended but were not ready to give up. Maybe the fight suggested an embedded resistance, that predilection to never submit to Washington. For defeated Confederates around the South, Texas was a beacon of defiance. A few weeks after the guns were silenced at Palmito, the Union troops finally raised their flag at the Texas State Capitol in Austin. That day, more than one bitter Confederate was watching and vowing some sort of perpetual political resistance.

Davis knew Texas would never thaw that easily, but he decided to throw himself into state politics, including the rapid, tangled attempts after the war to mold a permanent Texas constitution. He had been a Democrat but was now a pro-Lincoln Republican, and at the state constitutional convention in 1868, Davis delivered a thunderbolt to the wary listeners: "In my judgment, the great mass of the conservatives in the state, with their views and feelings towards the government of the country, are not fit to govern."[6]

His condemnation settled on the gaggle of ex-Confederates like black ash from a fire—and it came at a time when both conservative Democrats and liberal Republicans were hearing frightening news from all corners of Texas: there were still some violent spasms between Native Americans and settlers pushing west of Austin, west of the Colorado River, and into the oak-covered hills by Packsaddle Mountain. And now there was rumbling about Mexico eying a fragile Texas—and about armed ex-rebels and itinerant gunslingers roaming all the way from Louisiana and Arkansas, into the woods of East Texas and the frontier lands of the Texas Hill Country. Texas was seemingly more wide open, for good and bad reasons, than ever before.

The war had splintered dozens of relatively new city governments and law enforcement agencies, ones trying to establish a cohesive political process. Meanwhile, some slave owners were moving slowly to divest their "property." Others were adapting instantly to legal forms of indenture. Sharecropping and tenant farming involved renting small plots of land to freed slaves, often the very same fields the freedmen had worked in before. The rents were paid with the cotton, corn, and wheat the sharecroppers grew, and seeds, plows, and hoes were borrowed or purchased from the bigger plantation owners—or through credit from white merchants and bankers. Those repayments, too, were made with crops. And, of course, if there was a withered harvest caused by a drought or a plague of insects, the freedmen would be locked deeper and deeper into an economic prison. It was a grinding, cruel, unending cycle—and one that was so pervasive and successful it lured more ex-Confederates rushing in from other defeated states.

Along the caramel-colored Trinity River and back into the kudzu-blanketed woods near the Big Thicket, there were more and more rootless men with guns and horses: some plain criminals, some rallying around vestiges of the Old South, some affixed to white "citizens' groups" that were offshoots of what would be called the Ku Klux Klan (KKK). Into the 1870s, families, cowboys, dry-goods salesmen, and clergy were told to travel in pairs or in groups, and with armed escorts—from the Sabine River and Texarkana and well to the west.

Texas was trying to reestablish itself as a politically cohesive place, in all the big and little towns, but the lack of centralized authority was making many places as lurching and unpredictable as the wicked late-summer storms coming from the Gulf of Mexico. Roving gangs were criss-crossing near the Sabine River and as far west as Burnet and the areas where the Pedernales River flowed into the Colorado, where white settlers were still trying to attack or fend off Comanche—but were now also worrying about outlaws waiting for them if they traveled thirty miles from Llano to Mason. Nominally, Davis and the Republicans were in control of Texas. But on the ground, on the unpaved streets of Austin and Seguin and Mexia, vigilantes, Union soldiers, Dixie warriors, and bandits were all vying for an advantage.

With the uncertain, scary swirl, it wasn't hard for many people to believe that the occupying federal government had engendered the chaos; that Washington had brought the troubles and was incapable or unwilling to restore order; that the fumbling, distant Union overseers and their minions in Texas had stripped the state of both its dignity and its economic bedrock. In Austin, Davis heard the rumblings on an almost daily basis. When he was alone, he kept circling back to the idea that he needed to never bend: that Texas had been beaten on the battlefield, and now it had to be broken and rebuilt—politically and economically. He assumed that he would always have the greatest, most powerful ally to bring Texas into line: President Ulysses S. Grant, along with others in Washington who were watching and waiting for some kind of order and allegiance in Texas.

Davis ran for governor, won by eight hundred votes, and took office in January 1870. Conservative Democrats howled that the entire election was a sham, that it was rigged, that white voters had been prevented from casting ballots—and that registration rolls had been doctored to exclude ex-Confederates. Meanwhile, Grant still hadn't signed a decree allowing Texas to be officially readmitted to the Union, and to rein in the federal military oversight of the state. And now Texas had the conqueror's agent— the former Union general Edmund Davis—deciding its fate.

All over the state, hundreds of thousands of slaves were nominally freed, and some simply began to trudge miles down the wagon-wheel paths denting the black, loamy earth on the plantations outside of Lufkin, Palestine, and other places in East Texas. They were following news about the formation of small communities of fellow freed slaves, about clapboard churches built for Black people, about jobs in the city for servants and maids— anything better than bending over in the unforgiving cotton fields. They moved into small towns in East and Central Texas, and then to Houston and Dallas. And with them came a dizzying jumble of fresh upheavals, including, with the support of Lincoln's Republican Party in Washington, startling appointments and eventually the election of a few Black officials.

With segregation aggressively enforced, "freedmen's towns" began to take shape on unclaimed, flood-prone land near the brown waters of Buffalo Bayou and the Trinity, Colorado, Navasota, and Brazos Rivers. Water wells were dug, stick houses or log cabins were built, and the semblance of communities would emerge in Joppa, Elmo, Sand Branch, and other hidden pockets around the state.

It was a wholesale shift, one that angered and scared the holy hell out of people in Austin who were trying to buck Edmund Davis and his liberal Republicans. At hastily called meetings around the state, white Texans and conservative Democrats argued about the best ways to keep the economic underpinnings of the old order intact. All over the defeated South, landowners and businessmen were desperate for a workforce. And they were also desperate to keep freed slaves out of polling places and in the fields.

At night, families would crouch behind locked doors, clutching their children, as they listened to gunshots, yelps from the woods, or the labored breathing of horses pounding across the dirt roads. It was, in some places, complete anarchy. Some of it was tied to the roving outlaws who had sniffed a weakened, fragile Texas. Some of it was aimed at the freed slaves, in part as vengeance but often just as a matter of forcing them back to work in the fields. Hundreds of Black Texans were hunted down, tortured, and murdered—and an overwhelmed official with the Freedmen's Bureau, the federal agency responsible for assisting ex-slaves with adjusting to the new economic and political realities, sent an alarming telegram to Washington: "The State is utterly unmanageable for bureau purposes. Its vast extent places it beyond the reach of any ordinary mechanism of centralized government."[7]

The roiling troubles were there on the frontier, on the prairies, and deep in the biggest cities, from Galveston to San Antonio. Years later, many historians would scramble to find the right way to characterize the postwar convulsions and the crimes committed by racists and self-appointed police—or to describe the sporadic uprisings by armed freedmen against unrepentant Confederates in firm control of newspapers, stores, and farms.

One frantic ex-rebel in Houston sent a Western Union telegram to some friendly state lawmakers in Austin: "Negroes in armed force at Sandy Point in superior numbers to the whites." The missive then begged, "Give me orders to use troops to disperse the rioters."[8] The telegram was signed by Will Lambert, who had succeeded in controlling several news outlets in Central and East Texas, as well as becoming a commissioned colonel in the Texas State Guard.[9]

And with each bit of news coming in about recalcitrant Negroes abandoning plantations, and maybe moving into the cities, there was also that incessant stream of shootings and hangings and robberies. It became even easier for the racists and ex-rebels to trace the ugliness to the liberal occupiers and federal sympathizers.

On a bitterly cold winter day in early 1870, an aide told Edmund Davis that a crowd of torchbearers was marching over the hard mud streets of Austin. The governor stepped onto his balcony, stared down at the bobbing flames, and was relieved to realize that it was a small but boisterous crowd of about fifty Black supporters. Davis walked outside, shook hands with the freed slaves, and expressed his appreciation for the solidarity. It was an invigorating moment, one that might have hardened his resolve to push back against anyone who wanted to buck his and Washington's wishes. He had fought to drag an unwilling Texas back into the national order—and Texas would need to bend, much more, to the greater good.[10]

The governor's public solidarity with freedmen didn't go unnoticed. News spread about Davis giving Black Texans attention and prominence they had never enjoyed. Davis also quickly recommended something else to state lawmakers: one of his first moves at the statehouse was to try to prohibit handguns—except on the restless frontier lands. He put it this way: "We are the most lawless people on the face of the earth. In New York City, with about the same population as Texas, there were 75 or 80 homicides last year [1869]. Here in Texas there were up to 800."[11]

In Austin and plenty of other parts of the state, it was seen as a clear sign that Davis was trying to smash some inalienable rights—and that he was doing it under orders from Washington. His anti-gun move failed, but Davis quickly moved on to other matters, including pressuring state lawmakers to embrace the "Civil War Amendments"—the Thirteenth, Fourteenth, and Fifteenth Amendments that forbade slavery and codified rights for Black Americans. In Austin, the loathing was palpable—and people were meeting to talk about what could only be called a coup. Davis didn't stop. He pushed for more powers to be given to the governor's office, including the ability to appoint the secretary of state, the attorney general, and state justices. He asked for his own broad law enforcement authority around the state. He called for restrictions on gambling and the sale of alcohol—thinking that it would tamp down the recklessness, the flare-ups ... and the people who might come for him or for freed Blacks.

To his close friends, Davis was usually a self-aware man, someone who knew what he was getting into when he first decided to join the Union forces in Texas. He had heard the whispers and then the outright accusations from some fellow Republicans that he had gone too far, too soon. They demanded to see him in his office, and they complained that he didn't understand just how fractured Texas was. Davis listened as they told him he had strayed too much from the principle of local governing in Texas; that he had moved too fast to protect Black men; that people were howling that he was going to tax and regulate Texans to death; and that he had been foolish to try to legislate guns, gambling, and alcohol.

Davis, of course, had no way of knowing it—but every Texas governor for the next 150 years would wrestle with the same issues and acidic accusations.

The original state capitol building in Austin, built in 1839 from lumber felled in the pine forests of Bastrop, was placed on a small rise of land west of today's Congress Avenue. It was a modest log structure surrounded by an eight-foot-high stockade barrier. In 1853 it was replaced by a blocky-looking state capitol, topped with a small dome and made of limestone, that was erected near the site of the present state capitol. It cost $150,000 and peered, some said inelegantly, down the main city street. It had an aura of impermanence, perhaps a nod to the fact that Austin had not been cemented as the seat of political power. An election in 1850 had indicated that Austin was to be the capital for twenty years, at which time Texans would revisit the matter—and there had been strong suggestions that the capital be relocated to other cities, perhaps Waco or Houston.

On April 28, 1870, Davis walked from the governor's mansion to the capitol and then stepped before the brooding members of the state legislature. He was talking directly to the lawmakers for the first time as the narrowly, controversially elected leader of Texas:

> My fellow citizens of Texas: This day the government of your State and the control of your destinies is handed over to you. What may fairly be termed the second annexation of Texas is now consummated; but, a Texas very different from that of 1845 is found assuming her functions as a State. That Texas brought with her single star also her thousands of slaves, this Texas knows no bondmen on her soil. We may differ in our opinion of the manner of bringing about this great change, and the necessity for it. We live too near (in time) the scene of this struggle to ever agree that Providence may have directed the issue as part of the great work of improvement and progress of the human race.... It may be said that the American Revolution, opening in 1776, with the proclamation "that all men are created equal," had its verification, and made its promise good only in 1870.[12]

His words, and the wicked skepticism from his listeners, reverberated inside the chambers—and then around the state. "Fellow citizens," Davis went on, "the disease under which our political system labored was a severe one, and required a sharp remedy. It unquestionably could only be cured by the application of the national sword."

The state senators and representatives absorbed his scolding. He had just compared the American Revolution with 1870, the year Texas was finally going to try to ratify the Civil War amendments, the year that Texas was officially going to be readmitted to the Union. They listened glumly as he announced that the "national sword" had come down to eradicate the "disease" eating the state alive. And now he was linking the "great change" in Texas with the great change that birthed the United States.

For many in the room, it was as if Davis were still an enemy general—especially as he thundered that Texas had been set on fire by its own people. "Local despotisms often flourished," he said, but those days were going to end. Regulation, supervision, were coming:

> While local self-government still remains, it is within the just bounds that there is a supervisory power over all, far withdrawn from local prejudice and bias.[13]

Two of every three Texas workers were involved in growing cotton, and without slavery, tenant farming and sharecropping spread more quickly and widely. The new forms of subjugation were being unleashed at the same time that Texas was giving away swaths of land to settlers through homestead grants.[14] More farmers, settlers, and ranchers were arriving, and the population doubled, from 818,000 in 1870 to 1.6 million in 1880.[15] With close to 14,000 residents, Galveston was the biggest city, and its wooden docks were bustling with commerce and immigration. San Antonio, with 13,000 residents, was the state's cultural center, its biggest window to Mexico, and always in clear view of the evolving *patrón* political systems close to the Rio Grande—where white landowners were busy acquiring thousands of acres and controlling the flow of jobs, housing, and voting patterns among Tejanos and Mexican Americans.[16] As they began sculpting enormous farming and ranching enterprises, they grew accustomed to traveling to Austin—to tell the governor and lawmakers that they needed to send state police to protect the border, and to make sure that there was no unrest among the thousands of Latino field hands being conscripted to build irrigation canals or string up miles of fence lines in the Rio Grande Valley.

From his office on the ground floor of the capitol, Davis could sense Texas being yanked in a dozen different directions: it remained a "frontier" state; it was still defining its marriage with Mexico; and it was overrun by unleashed entrepreneurs, ex-soldiers, freed slaves, homesteaders, carpetbaggers, and political kingmakers jockeying for either survival or a seat at the power table. Davis decided to focus on the bloodiest and most overt symptoms he could see.

In the hot summer of 1870, in direct response to the violence in East Texas, he told his aides and then lawmakers that he was going to create a state police force—and that it would include freed Black men. News raced around the state: having ex-slaves wielding weapons and law enforcement power was beyond staggering. Thousands of former Confederates were aggressively trying to assert political control in towns across Texas. Some had led reigns of terror aimed at the freedmen. Hundreds of former slaves— perhaps as many as one thousand—had been murdered since the Civil War ended. And now Davis was creating a state police force with dozens of freed slaves and Union loyalists. For ex-rebels and Democrats plotting against him, it was as if the war had never truly ended.

John Wesley Hardin—a cold-eyed gunslinger, a former Confederate, and one of the most dangerous men in the nation—was blunt: he called the Texas state police "carpetbaggers, scalawags from the North, with ignorant Negroes."[17] In the early 1870s, the rangy and intimidating Hardin killed at least two of the state policemen—one who was Black and another who was part Black and part Mexican. In Austin, the governor heard the news about the murders.

To some friends, Davis appeared to be a proud but increasingly politically lonely figure, sometimes burrowed in the statehouse and weighing just how to make wayward Texas submit to a greater good. Maybe, he decided, Texas could be educated to be tolerant or to weave itself more willingly into the national fabric. In his second year as governor, he promoted an even bigger taxpayer-funded public education system. Conservative Democrats immediately feared that someone in Austin would be deciding what version of Texas history would be taught to their children—that Texans would be forced to pay for some sort of a cultural conversion beyond their local control.

More angry meetings were held around the state, and in 1871, the conservative Democrats seized control of the Texas legislature. In September, they gathered at a combustible Tax-Payers' Convention at the state capitol, and the meeting became far more than a gathering of businessmen fighting higher taxes—it turned into an angry and racist rally to finally oust Davis. One observer put it this way: "Conservative businessmen who wanted to avoid taxes and planters who wanted to avoid turmoil in their Black workforce joined the small farmers, who, destroyed by the war, turned all of their anger into hatred of freed Blacks, the cause, it seemed, of all their woes."[18]

Davis knew that his enemies were more rabid and organized than ever, but it was as if he had embarked on a zealous mission that he would never abandon. In 1872, he called out state police to guard Black voters going to the polls in midterm elections. Democrats immediately voted to disband the integrated state force. The battle boiled into 1873, just as North America and Europe were rocked by a financial panic—and plantation owners and diehard segregationists believed, more than ever, that Davis was putting Texas in danger of an utter economic collapse.

In Austin, a handful of Davis's supporters assumed that he was going to be consumed by forces and fates beyond his control. Davis continued to hope that the freed slaves, progressives, and what he believed were reasonable men in Texas would reelect him. He was dead wrong: Davis was defeated by a two-to-one margin in his 1873 bid. He went immediately to the Texas Supreme Court, arguing that the polls had closed too early and that some of his supporters had been denied the right to vote. In private, Davis told friends and family that he was not going to leave the statehouse quietly. He actually believed what the Democrats had been saying: Texas was corrupt and riddled with rigged elections.

Davis barricaded himself in his office at the capitol and called for armed supporters to guard him. He sent frantic messages to the White House and waited for help from Ulysses Grant. Surely the president and Washington would do all they could to keep him as governor. Surely they would send troops, at least as a nod to the dangerous work he had been doing dragging Texas back into the United States—and then fighting to enforce the Republican Reconstruction; to allow Black Texans to be free; and to cobble together all the fractured pieces of the state.

President Grant sent a terse reply. It had a faint air of resignation, with the implication that Washington felt that Texas was permanently inscrutable and insubordinate: "Would it not be prudent, as well as right, to yield to the verdict of the people as expressed by their ballots?"[19]

Davis was stunned. He had once directly petitioned Abraham Lincoln for guidance and aid. Confederate soldiers in Mexico had almost hanged him. Aides had told him that, like Lincoln, he could be assassinated. He worked his way through a dozen possible outcomes, machinations, but he finally decided to give up and take down the barricades holding back his enemies at the capitol. Surrounded by his careful guards, Davis emerged from his office, contemplating the fact that he would be handing over the governorship to a former Confederate soldier.[20] That day, and for the rest of his life, he would wonder why Washington didn't want to exert more might in Texas.

As he left the governor's mansion for the last time, his wife took down a portrait of President Grant that had hung on a wall and jammed her foot through it.[21]

During his last days in office, Davis had to have thought about whether he had been bucking something that he could never fully fathom. Maybe there was something in the state firmament, something as hard as the rocks in Marble Falls, something as unforgiving as the hurricanes that would batter Texas towns like Velasco and Indianola and erase them from some maps.

For years after being hounded out of power, Davis remained affixed to some of the most progressive tendencies of the Lincoln Republicans. He continued to harbor the belief that there would be a political evolution over time, maybe a pattern of slow but steady inclusion. He kept waiting for it to happen, he kept steering his version of the Republican Party, and he would even try, unsuccessfully, to win back the governor's office.

Davis died in Austin at the age of fifty-five, nine years after his frustrated wife destroyed that oil painting of the president's face. He was buried in the Texas State Cemetery, where his brother erected an imposing, impressive monument in his honor. At thirty-one feet, it is the tallest in the cemetery and was once described by a writer as a "mutant stalk of gray granite."[22] As the sun dips and the shadows grow, the monument can appear to grow even taller. At night, if one were predisposed to wander among the ghosts, as Lt. Governor Bob Bullock liked to do, it really would be hard to escape the looming loneliness.

Edmund Davis embodied, for generations of Texas politicians, the very elements they would resist for the next century and beyond. For others, his resting place would be an aching symbol of roads not traveled.

Not far from the waterfront in Galveston is a small city park with basketball courts and, in the warm-weather months, a splash pad for children. It's not uncommon to see pickup basketball games being played, with teams of Black and white players playing alongside one another. In the summer, the celebration of the emancipation of slaves—the Juneteenth holiday—is held at this place named for a pioneering figure in Texas history—Norris Wright Cuney. An activist, lawyer, and union organizer, Cuney had once

Norris Wright Cuney of Galveston, whose activism and reputation for integrity led him to become a national liberal Republican committee man for Texas, was deemed a "friend of law and public tranquility" by the pro-Democratic *Galveston Daily News* and was ranked among the South's shrewdest political operatives by the *New York Times*. In Cuney's day, nine in ten Black Texans were Republicans.

steered nineteenth-century Texas in ways that it had never experienced—and at a time when the very idea of integration seemed as remote and difficult as traveling by foot from the port city to the distant mountains of West Texas.

Cuney's father was a prominent plantation owner who had established a sprawling operation with over one hundred slaves in the loamy, fertile Brazos River valley near the town of Hempstead. Cuney's mother was a slave, and she and her white master had eight children. A light-skinned, mixed-race man, Cuney was afforded opportunities other Blacks were denied, and he was sent to a school for Negroes in Pennsylvania. He eventually settled in Galveston, studied to be a lawyer, and immersed himself in politics.

Almost one of every four residents in Galveston, the state's largest city, was Black. It was the epicenter of the state's liberal Republican Party as well as the Texas headquarters for the Freedmen's Bureau, still struggling to grant Blacks equal access to jobs, loans, housing, and voting rights. Galveston was also home to the Union League, which was attempting to recruit Blacks into the Republican Party. During Reconstruction, forty-two Black men were elected to the state legislature, and one of them, Senator George T. Ruby from Galveston, took Cuney on as his energetic and eloquent protégé.

Cuney became the first assistant to the sergeant-at-arms of the 12th Legislature. It was a profile-raising move for a minority Texan, and then he was named a delegate to the Republican National Convention. In 1872,

Cuney ascended to the powerful position of federal customs inspector in Galveston. The next year, the ambitious and confident Cuney helped organize the Convention of Colored Citizens in Texas—held in Brenham in the summer of 1873—and issued a powerful statement:

> We appeal to the law-abiding and honest people of Texas, of whatever political party, to join with us in deprecating the outrages and wrongs perpetrated upon the colored people in various sections of our State ... and we ask that all acts of violence towards us, from whatever source, shall be condemned by the public sentiment of the community in such unequivocal terms as that law and order shall be enforced.... We cannot close this address without the strongest expression of our confidence in and regard for President Grant and reiterate our thanks to him for his efforts to ameliorate our condition and obtain our civil rights. We also express our confidence in the Federal government and reaffirm our allegiance to the National Republican party.[23]

Cuney and his group boldly condemned the spasms of Klan violence and praised Grant and the federal "occupiers" of Texas. Cuney was voted president of the convention and was increasingly emerging as a rallying figure for more disenfranchised liberal Republicans. In reaction, some leaders in Galveston tried to boot him from his position as customs inspector.[24] But several Democrats in Galveston put the brakes on Cuney's dismissal, perhaps in a fit of enlightened self-interest, and as a way of soothing the Black dockworkers that made Galveston's economic engine hum. The *Galveston Daily News*, the first newspaper in the state, was fiercely conservative, but it said, "Cuney has shown himself to be above the average of his race—a friend of law and public tranquility."[25]

Cuney became the national Republican Party's committeeman from Texas, arguably among the most important political positions given to a Southern Black man in the nineteenth century.[26] He caught the attention of the *New York Times*, which called him "one of the shrewdest political 'workers' in all the South"—while adding that he was the richest Black man in Texas.[27]

Cuney had no exact statewide portfolio, no specific control over legislative matters, but through the late nineteenth century he often met with national Republicans who wondered what to do in Texas. Davis had counseled Cuney about Republican strategies, and once Davis was ramrodded out of office, Cuney was often essentially representing the Republican

Party. Some political observers hoped he would be able to generate more Black votes—by the late 1870s, almost one out of every three Texans was Black. As many as nine out of ten Republicans were Black. Cuney became more of a public presence, and he was known, for lack of a better term, as an "urban Negro"—someone who hadn't emerged from the cotton fields. He was always a city dweller, an educated, well-traveled lawyer who mingled comfortably in the hustle and bustle of Galveston, negotiating with white political leaders about the issues of the day.

At the Republican state convention in 1876, Cuney decided to argue for resolutions attacking the Klan and began spearheading efforts to remove federally appointed conservative Republicans—neo-Democrats—from offices in Texas. He wanted to have some sway over the new state constitution Democrats were pushing into existence. Cuney bravely offered his own platform: a clear end to school segregation, inclusion of minorities on juries, and consideration of minorities for publicly funded jobs.[28]

He organized his Colored Men's Convention, and, in 1875, also his Most Worshipful Grand Lodge, Free and Accepted Ancient York Masons of the State of Texas—a group he hoped could foster economic opportunities and even community-based activism. Right-wing Democrats were watching and worrying that Cuney was leaning on a system of fraternal organizations as a way to convince more Blacks to join the Republican Party—and that he was subversively stealing a page from the white "fraternal" groups, including the Klan, that had political control as part of their agenda.

Back in Galveston, Cuney was also using his influence to unionize Black dockworkers through the Colored Screwmen's Benevolent Association, which argued for higher wages and better working conditions. In 1889, he was promoted to the position of head federal customs collector in Galveston, maybe the one minority person with the most public authority in the South. Cuney served as a symbol of possibilities, and his very presence, his elegant and erudite aura, served as a constant rebuff to racist characterizations aimed at Black Texans. He knew how to swim with the white overseers, and he had a preternatural ability to navigate his way around the shifting, scary storms in Texas—where lynchings and murders fed the smothering, constant dread.

Cuney remained a liberal Republican stalwart to the end of his life in San Antonio, where he died in 1898. Today, if you travel along the narrow streets near Texas Southern University, the historically Black academy in Houston, you'll be close to Cuney Homes, a public housing complex named in his honor. He once called himself a "son of Texas" and said that he always knew who was in charge of his state—but that he dreamed of change: "Because an oligarchy now governs the South, doesn't mean it always will, it is contrary to the genius of our constitution and laws."

He added wistfully, "It is true, the clouds are lower over our Southland ... yet I do know that we are not without hope."[29]

In Block 1, Lot 66, in Oakwood Cemetery in Waco, you can see an obelisk flanked by two sculpted busts. The dead eyes in the faces stare above and beyond anyone standing before them. On the monument is a triangle of granite marked with a large letter "C"—a letter that's an obvious salute to the man buried here, but perhaps an unsubtle reminder that he was an especially loyal son of the Confederacy. Underneath the triangle and on a slab between the two stone faces, it reads, "RICHARD COKE— Characterized By A Splendid Manhood—The Brave Soldier—The Able And Impartial Judge—The Enlightened And Patriotic Governor—The Distinguished Senator In Congress For Eighteen Years—Always True To The People And Faithful To Every Trust."

In 1916, close to two decades after Coke was laid to rest and the memorial placed over his grave, the Texas state archivist Sinclair Moreland sang the praises of the man who became the role model for generations of Texas politicians. Moreland took glowing note of Coke's repudiation of people exactly like Norris Cuney:

> Governor Coke had faith in his people. He believed in the supremacy of the Anglo-Saxon race—he prided in the rich red blood of the Southern people. As their leader he fought back the tide of tyranny that was about to engulf them in the murky water of mulatto domination. He was a constructive statesman; he served his people with true fidelity and left Texas to rich heritage of a fruitful and useful like. His name is engraved on the scroll of immortals, and his footprints are in the sands of time.[30]

In the Central Texas Baptist churches, the dry-goods stores springing up near railroad stops, and even the informal drinking sheds where farmers shared some home-brewed corn liquor, it was easy to hear stories about the burly, bearded Richard Coke, with his dark, deep-set eyes and his rugged face that looked like it had seen a few things. He had grown up in Waco, had become a lawyer, and had developed a reputation for driving any remaining Comanche out of the state. Coke owned fifteen slaves and voted for Texas to break away during the Secession Convention in Austin. He joined the Fifteenth Texas Infantry; was wounded at Bayou Bourbeau near Opelousas, Louisiana; and settled back in Texas as a war hero. As conservative Democrats seized control of the legislature and took aim at Edmund Davis, Coke emerged as a perfectly electable symbol and savior—someone who had conquered the savages, fought for slavery, and shed blood for Dixie.

On a frigid Thursday in January 1874, with Austin waking to a rare dusting of snow, the forty-four-year-old Coke took the oath of office. He had come, more or less, to bury Davis, his legacy and his policies. Coke was hell-bent on reassuring Texas that it was now in the hands of a white supremacist, backed by a conservative legislature that would work each day to rebuff unwanted incursions from Washington. Coke decided to issue a Texas political clarion call that would echo into the twenty-first century:

> Today, for the first time since she emerged from the ruin and disaster of the great civil war, Texas sees the inauguration in her Capitol of a government chosen by the free and untrammeled suffrage of her people ... the ancient liberties of the people of Texas re-established. ... How indispensable to the liberty of the citizen it is that the government which thus controls and deals with his person and property should be near him and directly accountable to him. On the other hand, to the Federal government, which is more remote, inaccessible, and therefore not so directly accountable to the people, is delegated power over matters that do not so nearly concern the people ... The genius, tastes, sentiments, feelings, and will of the great mass of the people of Texas will find expression in the administration of their State government, and the destiny of Texas, her glory and her history, will be the work of her own people.[31]

Coke had to have smiled as he paused, patted his flowing beard, and then leaned into his war cry. Texas, he thundered, would "preserve the right of local self-government ... from the dangers which menace it in the constantly growing process of centralization."[32]

After the financial Panic of 1873 a conservative farmer's organization known as the Grange emerged and argued hard for a new state constitution—one that Coke and the anti-Davis, anti-Washington forces would all agree on. The Texas power structure was neatly detailed in the final proposed constitution. There would be seven governing officials at the heart of government: the governor, lieutenant governor, secretary of state, attorney general, comptroller of public accounts, treasurer, and land commissioner. The governor's powers over county, city, and state officials were scaled down, but he was going to be able to ask for special legislative sessions to address emergency measures. The new constitution called for voting precincts, and it reinforced segregation in both subtle and unsubtle ways. Poll taxes would remain in place; segregated schools would be controlled at a local level. A higher education system known as the University of Texas would be created to supervise several branches, including Texas A&M.

There was a sense among giddy Democrats that under Coke's reign, and with the revised constitution, Texas was finally going to have its destiny back in its own hands—and that much of what had transpired during Davis's hated tenure was not worth memorializing. It was a full-on effort to rewrite Texas history, to pass one version of it down through the ages. The plan was simple but sweeping: historians would praise Coke while downplaying or erasing Davis, Cuney, and liberal Republicans from the articles, chronicles, and textbooks.[33]

Coke was more than pleased at the wide mandate he assumed he enjoyed. He had the support of the people and the lawmakers, and it was emboldening.

As Coke was overseeing the movers who were hauling his clothing trunks and books into the governor's mansion, he stopped to study some flowering bushes. They were ones that Edmund Davis and his family had planted.

Coke raised his booted foot and stomped them down until each of the damned liberal bushes snapped under his considerable weight.[34]

CHAPTER 2

Our Defective Plan: The 1880s

CONSTRUCTION WORKERS WERE BUSY digging into the moist earth of Sugar Land in the winter of 2018, preparing to build a technical center for a local school district in Fort Bend County. As the sweat-stained workers pushed the dirt, they were stunned to unearth piles of human remains—and some chains and pieces of metal that could perhaps serve as handcuffs or leg cuffs. Archaeologists and state historians were quickly summoned, and their consensus was that the shovels and bulldozers had uncovered a mass burial site for ninety-four men and one woman. They ranged in age from fourteen to perhaps seventy.

Once widespread across the South, convict leasing was a form of legalized slavery, of intentional bondage, which engendered horrific stories about Black citizens being falsely arrested and imprisoned in order to provide a steady labor force that could be leased to white farmers and businessmen. Apologists said it was a boon for the state, a way to ease the financial burdens of an overcrowded prison system and a way to build roads, docks, bridges, and railroad tracks and to keep the sugar, cotton, and rice fields alive—especially, they argued, at a time when Texas was finding its way back to fiscal solvency and back to some form of independence apart from Washington. It was a conveniently attained workforce. And it was a conveniently disposed-of workforce. When the workers were too frail to till the cotton fields, to cut the sugarcane, they were left un-treated—and then, when they died, disposed of in mass graves. The one in Sugar Land was no doubt not the only one. That kind of tale was never routinely entered into the annals of Texas history.

If one believes that the story of the United States cannot be understood without a full accounting of slavery, then the socioeconomic and socio-political history of late nineteenth-century Texas cannot be understood un-less convict leasing and the way it was promoted and protected are mea-sured. "These were crimes against humanity," the activist and historian Reginald Moore has said. "They had been dehumanized, victimized and tortured, and it was sanctioned by the state."[1] The unmarked burial site the construction workers uncovered was near miles of land where sugarcane farms had prospered—and it was not just a symbol of how human leasing was once a cog in the Texas economy. The fact that its practice flourished points to the way political leaders—at the state, county, and local levels— were almost always guided by strict fidelity to economic imperatives.

Into the 1880s, the nation was again expanding, and miles of rail-road lines were stabbing into the prairies and the heartland, aiming as far into the American West as imaginable. The giant economic engines were primed, going to full throttle, and in Austin clear decisions were being made to make sure that the state was getting its piece of the railroad growth, the economic boons, and doing all it could to provide land, access, deregulation, friendly oversight ... and a cheap and seemingly inexhaust-ible supply of workers with pickaxes, hoes, and shovels. Texas once had as many as a quarter of a million slaves. It could easily conscript thousands of Black Texans to serve the railroad operators, the road builders, and, yes, the miles of sugar fields.

A lonely roadside marker in Tahoka, Texas, suggests that the very last skirmish between cowboys and Native Americans in the state occurred near alkaline Double Lakes in Lynn County. There might have been small battles and encounters elsewhere, but that West Texas moment in 1879 was certainly symbolic. The new decade in Texas was going to witness both the true waning of the frontier days but also the hearty unveiling of what affectionate historians would gently call "the Restoration"—the celebra-tion and reclamation of Confederate traditions, memories, and ideologies.

The process was real, unyielding, and fueled, as always, by that perva-sive belief that Texas was at its best when it marched to its own destiny. In the 1880s, ex-rebels were firmly staked in hundreds of local and state offices across the state, and each fresh election served as a lure to even more men who saw Texas as one of the most committed havens for states' rights and muscularly enforced segregation.

Coke had left the governor's office in 1876 and moved to the US Senate, hoping to go right into the heart of the Republican beast. He had been replaced by Richard Hubbard, another Democratic officer in the Confederacy. One Texas observer once noted that if you wanted to be in politics in early Texas, you'd stand the best chance possible if you had worn the rebel gray. Monuments to the Confederacy were springing up in Vega in Oldham County; Snyder in Scurry County; San Angelo in Tom Green County; Perryton in Ochiltree County; Pecos in Reeves County; Miami in Roberts County; Longview in Gregg County; Granbury in Hood County; Giddings in Lee County; Fort Davis in Jeff Davis County; Cleburne in Johnson County; Clarendon in Donley County; Canyon in Randall County; Canadian in Hemphill County; and Aspermont in Stonewall County.[2]

In the 1880s, chain gangs laid down more railroad tracks, and several of the unsteady cotton and sugar plantations began prospering again with the work provided by those leased prisoners. More and more newspapers were also emerging across the state, many owned or supported by hard-core conservative Democrats. The newspapers served as exceedingly useful political platforms reinforcing the post-Confederacy base and promoting that warm nostalgia for the slavery and secessionist days.

The Confederate officer Alfred Horatio Belo, who came from a slave-owning family in North Carolina, created the *Dallas Morning News* in 1885 after helping run the *Galveston News*. He was a popular figure in the burgeoning newspaper industry in Texas, largely because of his personal history, including his deep ties to the Confederate general Nathan Bedford Forrest. During the waning days of the Civil War, Belo had heeded a plea from Forrest for rogue units to keep fighting for slavery in Texas:

> In 1865, when General Robert E. Lee surrendered at Appomattox, Nathan Bedford Forrest, who would later become one of the founders of the Ku Klux Klan, sent out a call for all Confederate diehards to join General Kirby Smith, who was still fighting in Texas, where they would continue the war, possibly as a guerrilla struggle. Alfred Horatio Belo answered the call.[3]

In a day when newspapers, and their influence, are on the wane, it's hard to imagine how enormously influential they were in a state as vast as Texas. They were the only source of news in most regions, and they had a powerful role in deciding who would get elected — and what issues, policies, crimes, and machinations would be covered ... or not. Belo's papers, like others in Texas, would help catapult conservative Democrats into office and paint a rosy picture of past and present Texas, while routinely avoiding mention of the lynchings and tortures suffered by Black and Latino Texans.

Texas Ranger John Barclay Armstrong, who finally captured the outlaw John Wesley Hardin, is buried in Austin's Oakwood Cemetery. Susanna Dickinson, who, along with her daughter Angelina, had survived the crushing victory in 1836 by the Mexican army at the Alamo, is also buried there. (General Antonio López de Santa Anna had interviewed Dickinson, given her $2 and a blanket, and allowed her to go free — perhaps to spread the word of his benevolence and invincibility.)

Also in the cemetery you will find Oran Roberts, whose gravesite is testimony to his priorities. The pink granite marker, mined from the same Hill Country quarries that provided the rocks for the Texas statehouse, says that he was "President of the Secession Convention" and "Colonel of Infantry in the Confederate Army" — and, lastly, it is noted that he was a governor of Texas as well as a professor of law at the University of Texas.

Roberts, born in South Carolina, enrolled in the University of Alabama and served in the Alabama legislature. He moved to San Augustine, Texas, to open a law practice and went on to serve as a district attorney, district judge, and Texas Supreme Court justice — and one of the most persuasive of all Texas secessionists. He helped organize the Eleventh Texas Infantry, and after the war he settled into the upper ranks of those disenchanted, restless Confederates jockeying for higher office. A man with a kind, well-creased face and a wave of silver hair, he struck people as dignified. His allies knew that he was harder than he looked: he was elected to the US Senate but was denied his seat by pro-Union Republicans in Washington who were banning entire delegations from the breakaway states. It was a bitter turn that Roberts would never forget or forgive.

A livid Roberts decided to move to Gilmer to practice law and wait for the tide to turn. When he became governor in 1879, he prepared an inaugural address that was aimed right at the men who had once denied a Texan a place in Washington. He railed against the "powerful influences operating upon the country," and then he lashed out at both freed slaves and immigrants pushing onto the nation's shores: "The large emigration from other countries, . . . the extension of our frontier and the changed condition of a large colored population, have all contributed to generate and exhibit an amount and character of crime and civil wrong entirely unprecedented in this country."[4]

Roberts forcefully added that Texas leaders would be looking at ways to hammer down the aliens and the coloreds, and also to keep the lucrative convict leasing programs intact:

> It may be doubted whether our plan of leasing and working the convicts outside of the penitentiary is favorable to reform any more than whipping and hanging. Still the other ground holds good even under our defective plan, and it would be contrary to the spirit of the age not to continue in the effort to perfect it. . . . This should be done as far as practicable in such way as would incur as little expense to the State as possible.[5]

Almost more than anyone before him, an angry Roberts portrayed Washington as an octopus, a beast spreading its tentacles across the nation, holding each state hostage: "The government of the United States has grown to gigantic proportions, reaching out in all directions."[6]

In all parts of the state, the balance between economic and political realities was being worked out: in South Texas, ranchers and large landowners were in control of almost every aspect of local government, and many were effectively binding Mexican immigrants into a patronage system—one that ensured the same kinds of steady workforces and absurdly predictable political elections occurring around the state. In parts of East Texas, the same patterns were in full swing and accomplishing the same immutable outcome: local businessmen, plantation owners, and landowners deciding who among them was going to be promoted by the local newspaper and then elected.

In Austin, Roberts was comfortable knowing that he had all but buried the progressive political impulses of Davis and the Republicans. He had other problems to confront, including how to fund state government. Roberts was among the brashest Texas politicians demanding fiscal conservatism—a pay-as-you-go platform—but he still had to figure out how to pay the state's bills and fund public schools. He resorted to a low-hanging-fruit option: he pushed for Texas to sell off giant chunks of public land. As ranchers scooped up thousands of acres, it signaled that the political machine in Texas could always be modified to serve business interests. And Roberts's approach to antitax, anti-regulatory fiscal conservatism would be aped for decades and feed almost every new industrial advance in Texas—from the railroads to the oil and petrochemical firms, from Fortune 500 companies in the 1980s to high-tech startups in the twenty-first century.

Even if they weren't aware of how Roberts had once willingly sold pieces of Texas to private entities, generations of elected officials became predisposed to find ways to allow big business to prosper. It's not a new fact or one that is isolated to Texas, but in the 1880s, the state had pro-business conservatives firmly in charge, along with a state constitution designed deliberately to limit centralized regulation and oversight.

Things were working hand in glove to put Texas in a position to become one of the most powerful places on planet earth.

In the early 1880s, workers in Austin began extending railroad tracks toward the quarries of pink granite west of the city. Now it would be easier to bring in tons of shimmering stone to build the towering state capitol. In 1883, hundreds of workers were scrambling around the construction site, not far from the governor's mansion, eventually including almost ninety expert stonecutters summoned from Europe. The goal was to have the cornerstone placed on Texas Independence Day in March 1885.[7]

Roberts's successor as governor was John Ireland, a Kentucky-born lawyer who had moved to Seguin and entered local politics. He was yet another Confederate soldier, but one who had an especially odious mission unique to Texas: he wanted to hunt down slaves who had somehow tried to escape to Mexico. During the war, he saw action close to the Rio Grande—where he knew full well that his Union military nemesis, future governor Edmund Davis, had roamed.

After the war ended, a humiliated Ireland was ordered by Union officers and Republicans to step down from his position as a district judge. Like countless others, he wanted to extract some measure of revenge—or at least not allow the Republicans to exile the Confederacy to dim, forgotten history. As governor, he raced to solidify affection for what nostalgic Confederates were now calling the "Lost Cause." His battles to preserve the rebel legacy were in many ways the perfect precursor for the next Lone Star governor.

Lawrence Sullivan "Sul" Ross was a native of Iowa whose family moved to Milam County before relocating to Austin and then finally Waco. Ross

arrived in Texas in the late 1830s, and his personality and political trajectory were defined by his family's insistent battles in those areas pressing
hard against Indian country. His uncle was captured by Native Americans,
and it inspired Ross to become a latter-day Andrew Jackson, hell-bent on
combating the "savages." Ross skipped educational or business opportunities to join raids into the countryside. And in the winter of 1860, he helped
attack a Native American encampment along Mule Creek in Pease County.
One of the captured was Cynthia Ann Parker, an Anglo woman who had
been taken by the Comanche a quarter century earlier and who had lived
most of her life as a Native American. During the Civil War, Ross served
as a brigadier general with the Texas Cavalry Brigade.

Ross, an oval-faced man with a bushy goatee and abnormally large
forehead, was elected governor with 73 percent of the vote. He took office
in January 1887 as the nineteenth leader of Texas and someone who would
oversee the official dedication of the new statehouse the following year.
Like Andrew Jackson, his political career was gusted forward by his well-
chronicled exploits as an Indian fighter. And his rise to political power
stemmed in part from a persuasive form of narrative sculpting—the very
pervasive Texas-mythmaking in the news accounts and history books.

Along with the lingering affection for the Lost Cause, there were clearly
warm feelings for the Lost Republic of Texas. For many, Ross was a living
embodiment of the long, bruising heritage: he was a cowboy, a gunslinger,
a Texas Ranger, an Indian fighter, and a defender of the state's selected
memories of nationhood, of slavery, of conquering the Wild West.

For sure, Ross was also clearly unafraid to use force when necessary:
in the late 1880s, he ordered state troops to shut down what is now a
long-forgotten "war" in East Texas that pitted Black residents and white
sympathizers against a group of white Democrats in Fort Bend County.
"Yesterday evening Gov. Ross received a dispatch . . . saying that a fight
had occurred between . . . rival political factions . . . and that troops were
needed."[8] The white Democrats were nicknamed the "Jaybirds," and the
Black-white coalition was called the "Woodpeckers." Ross wanted armed
men to enforce a whites-only political primary, and his priorities needed
no further explanation.

Meanwhile, Ross was also hearing from anxious white farmers who
had traveled to Austin to complain to him that they were being price-
gouged by robber-baron railroad operators from outside Texas. Ross had
always remained chronically predisposed to fight regulatory interference.
But he hadn't counted on the modern realities of industrial monopolies

in the United States, and the demands from the farmers were a reminder that Texas might want elected officials willing to fight economic intruders as well as federal interference.

The handful of men who owned the burgeoning rail system in Texas had colluded and agreed to levy the same exorbitant, price-gouging shipping rates. Across the state, more farmers and ranchers bucked the usual anti-regulatory feelings and begged Ross and state lawmakers to do something. In 1885, six hundred influential businessmen attended a convention aimed at hitting back at the price-fixing. It wasn't lost on many of the Texans that the railroads that had a stranglehold on the state were in large part run by the New Yorker Jay Gould. He owned endless expanses of railroad, including a tight grip on the Texas and Pacific line. For farmers—the ex-Confederates with big cotton plantations near the Louisiana border, or the ones who used former slaves and leased convicts to load sugar onto freight cars outside Houston—Gould was a consummate Northern carpetbagger. And the price-gouging was a tipping point that led to a push for some sort of state control and supervision—as well as an early nod to a strain of populist politics that would spark up for years and even become an unpredictable undercurrent that future candidates in Texas would have to think hard about.

As he listened to the angry farmers, Ross had other urgencies on his mind, ones that he could more easily wrap his hands around. Some ranchers were hounding him about the establishment of grazing boundaries, and about who owned what land in Texas, and who got access to precious water sources. The expansionist fervor coursing through the nation raged full-on in Texas, and thousands more people were crossing the Red River, disembarking in Galveston, fording the Sabine River. Small towns were popping up all over the state, and free or cheap land and water were often the lures—and now both older and newer residents were fighting range wars, trying to seize control of the millions of acres. Ross knew the frontier days were ending in earnest, but as he studied the state, he also understood that Texas was being wildly reconfigured and divvied up.

Something, anything, had to be done to harness the frantic scramble for water and land. Under Ross's watch as governor, the legislature broadened the powers of the Land Office Commissioner in a desperate attempt to corral or at least arbitrate the flare-ups around Texas.

Baked more and more into the careful stories constructed about the life and times in the 1870s and 1880s was the sense of a special Texas superiority—of people pulling themselves up by the bootstraps, embracing adventure and danger in pursuit of freedom, independence, and self-reliance. Often left out of the narratives were sobering examinations of the way the land was acquired, or how the social "norms" were enforced, or how racist abuses led to so much blood seeping into the soil. Through the decade, the sense of exceptionalism was packaged and perpetuated, and the state's early political histories skirted the horrors of intimidation and racism endorsed and carried out by Texas officials. It's not an insignificant development, if only because the narratives would persist and then define Texas for many decades.

Without a doubt, the evolution of politics in Texas is inextricably bound to the way journalists, writers, and historians were aggressively shaping views of the state's leaders in the 1880s—and how politicians quickly learned to capitalize on the symbiotic relationship. The late nineteenth-century chroniclers began earnestly offering heroic nods to the grand myths that would have special appeal to newly arrived white settlers, entrepreneurs, and former Confederates searching for a sense of place. (Almost a century later, the state's most prominent magazine, *Texas Monthly*, was crafted in part to serve larger-than-life mythologies to anxious white arrivals hoping to establish roots.) The acquiescent political reporting apparatus continued to flourish through the 1880s, selectively covering events and issues and rarely challenging local or state political leaders. Sul Ross, for one, was saluted as a hardworking visionary and a conqueror of Texas demons.

The enduring images of what it meant to be a "real Texan" began to multiply in the 1880s, in large part because of the statewide promotion and popularity of Ross. Directly and indirectly, every politician after him would have to weigh "how Texan" they wanted to be and, really, what parts of Texas history they wanted to embrace or ignore.

Even if it wasn't written in the contemporary accounts, it was no secret that many Black Texans were terrified to venture into parts of the state heading east from Austin, Dallas, and San Antonio. It was an aching fear that would linger as lynchings, castrations, and other tortures snaked through the woods or slithered into plain view in town squares, at county courthouses, or in front of city halls. More white Texans were organizing in the guise of "social" and "cultural" associations, and domestic terrorism was controlling who could go to a polling place or register to vote. Black

Convict leasing—the cruel practice that put many Black citizens in government-sanctioned bondage—helped fund state government. Here, guards and prisoners pause at the Imperial Farm.

Texans were watching as homes, farms, or small businesses were set ablaze or attacked as a form of voter intimidation. The warnings came at all hours and even in broad daylight. The codified manifestations had already arrived when the Texas legislature outlawed mixed marriages in Article 2843: "It shall not be lawful for any person of European blood or their descendants to intermarry with Africans or the descendants of Africans."[9]

At the State Convention of Colored Men of Texas in 1883, Norris Cuney and others had tried to address the economic underpinnings that fed the rampant racism. He had singled out convict leasing, which state leaders had essentially endorsed: "When a fresh convict is carried to the farms, he is taken down by the other convicts and beaten, at the command of the guard ... in a few days he is hauled out of his sick quarters and put to work, whether he is physically able to do it or not.... In many cases sick convicts are made to toil until they drop dead in their tracks.... Others are maltreated by being placed in the pillory or stocks until they are dead or nearly so."[10]

Cuney had to know he was facing a fierce rising tide of enforced racism: in 1889, lawmakers gave railroad operators in Texas the freedom to exile Blacks to separate compartments on public trains. Two years later the legislature made separate railroad cars mandatory. Cuney was driven to political despair: "It is uncalled for, unwise ... a brutal invasion of the rights of a people whose consciences will feel keenly the wrong done them by the New South in its effort to reverse fate and check the growth of a broader and better humanity."[11]

Cuney had to wonder if anyone really knew the real Texas. And he had to wonder what the rest of the country thought of the state he had labored in for so many years.

John Henninger Reagan was born in Tennessee, moved to Texas in search of a fortune, and, like so many others, took up arms against Native Americans. Even after he became a lawyer, the barrel-chested Reagan continued to seize his gun and horse whenever there was news about Indians near Nacogdoches or Palestine, or along the Trinity River. A man with dark flowing hair and narrow eyes, he became the Confederacy's postmaster general and served as the head of its Treasury Department in the waning days of the Civil War.

Reagan never really needed to prove his allegiances to anyone—he had named his son after Confederate president Jefferson Davis. He and Davis were both captured in the spring of 1865 in Georgia, and Reagan was shipped to Boston and put in solitary confinement. Three months into his term, he sent out a missive that seemed to be on bended knee to the Union, calling for Texans to think twice about giving freedmen the right to vote.[12]

After the war, Reagan raced to repair his image among the Democratic ex-rebels in Texas, and he joined the populist groups of farmers who were demanding some action against the Northern-run railroad monopolies. It took almost a decade to reassure his former Dixie allies that he was still committed to core Confederate ideals before he was elected to Congress in 1875. He served until 1887, and then his pro-farmer stances helped him win a US Senate seat.

Later in life, Reagan reflected on the role of the Negro in the United States. He had time to turn his attention to his memoirs, and in them he suggested that the "elevation of the slaves to all the dignities of citizenship" was an "evil." He pondered the best ways to prevent Blacks from entering a voting booth, including literacy tests designed to bar minorities from participating in elections.[13]

Around Texas, Reagan's return to political prominence had been

Tennessee native John Henninger Reagan, formerly postmaster general of the Confederacy, rode pro-farmer sentiments and opposition to wealthy railroads to a US Senate seat before resigning to become the first chairman of the Texas Railroad Commission. He ultimately secured a reputation as a racist defender of the Old South.

honored with pomp and circumstance. He was heralded as a Texas icon who had been captured and imprisoned by the federal government—and later worked hard to protect the state against Washington's empowerment of Blacks. It's best left to others to interpret what exactly inspired the widespread adulation of a racist like Reagan in Texas. What's evident is that he possessed an extraordinary cunning by seeming to initially accept the principles of the conquering party of Abraham Lincoln but then going back to Texas to keep the embers of the Confederacy's Lost Cause and its Restoration alive.

As his own reputation was revived, and as he rode the wave of rural populism that raged against those Northern railroad "marauders," Reagan became increasingly treasured in Texas. He was a living icon of the Old South. He was someone who knew Jefferson Davis. He was a former cabinet member in the Confederacy—and someone with enough political gravitas to fathom bigger national schemes designed to ensnare Texas.

In Washington, DC, his crowning achievement was working on the Interstate Commerce Act, an attempt to regulate the national railroad industry. Reagan was asked by state leaders to head the first Texas Railroad Commission. He nursed it to life and then put it on the path toward being one of the most powerful political entities in state history—it was nominally in charge of regulating railroads, but it would eventually become the tightly forged link between big business and politics in Texas. It set tariffs to protect Texas companies, and it kept an eye on federal intrusions. And when Texas moved into the age of Big Oil, the railroad commission's powers multiplied and it became a carefully watched political prize. It was the perfect entity to demonstrate how business often regulates politics in Texas—and not the other way around. Reagan built it, and politics was never the same once big business had what amounted to a state office of its own.

In appreciation, in ensuing decades, schools and state government buildings would be named in honor of Reagan. Despite his autobiography being an unblinking ode to slavery, a multi-ton statue of Reagan sculpted by the artist Pompeo Coppini was erected on the campus of the University of Texas at Austin in 1919 though a review of Reagan's history, and that of other Texas Confederates, led to its removal to a barely visited location in the city almost a century after it was installed. An impressive-looking State of Texas office building, just north of the capitol, still bears his name.

CHAPTER 3

Elites and Aliens: The 1890s

AROUND THE NATION, ANTICIPATION was running high for the World's Columbian Exposition in Chicago. The massive undertaking was being heralded as one of the grandest gatherings in United States history. It was going to be a celebration of the American way of life—and a trumpeting announcement that the country was at the forefront of innovation as well as being a welcoming home for both democracy and enlightened thought.

Dozens of nations were invited to participate. Throngs were expected to marvel at Nikola Tesla's electrical devices and performances by the Mormon Tabernacle Choir and composer Antonin Dvorak. American artists—John Singer Sargent and Mary Cassatt—were preparing works for display. There would be exhibits devoted to the latest architecture, anthropological advances, and inventions like moving sidewalks and a "third rail" that would power trains. Additionally, in a nod to how many people in the United States had seemingly embraced equal treatment of all races, influential Black cultural figures would arrive, including Joseph Douglass (grandson of the abolitionist and civil rights leader Frederick Douglass, and the first Black American to tour as a concert violinist) and the opera singer Sissieretta Jones.

Another pioneering Black artist, one from Texas, decided that he would travel to Chicago and try to be heard: Scott Joplin, from Texarkana, was perfecting what would be called ragtime, a sound that directly influenced the evolution of blues, country, jazz, and rock. He and his family had labored in the East Texas fields and even helped build the railroads occupying the minds of the state's political leaders. He had, in all senses, traveled a long way to the World's Fair—to that exquisite display, the shining pinnacle, of how far America had evolved. Maybe Joplin, from the woods of Texas, was a symbol of how the humane side of the state could encourage legacies of lasting beauty.

In the weeks building to the much-anticipated 1893 exposition, Governor Jim ("Big Jim") Hogg, who had entered office a year earlier, was studying a story splashing across Texas newspapers, knowing full well that similar accounts were appearing around the nation. The front page of the February 3, 1893, edition of the *New York Times* had this headline: "Another Negro Burned—Henry Smith Dies at the Stake." An additional, smaller headline added: "Drawn through the streets on a cart—tortured for nearly an hour with hot irons and then burned—awful vengeance of a Paris (Texas) mob."

The story said that Smith was a "brute" and "burly Negro" who had committed "the most atrocious murder and outrage in Texas history." According to the *Times*, Smith had lured a four-year-old white girl with candy and then torn her "asunder" and covered her body with leaves and brush. Smith was reported to have fled Paris; walked seventeen miles east to Detroit, Texas; and then jumped onto a freight train headed to Arkansas—where he was captured twenty miles north of the city of Hope. On February 1, under a cold, sleeting rain, he was brought to Texarkana, back to the place where the great Scott Joplin had been born. There was an angry, screaming crowd of five thousand waiting for him.

The day Smith arrived in Texarkana, Hogg wired messages to county officials and sheriffs in Lamar and Bowie Counties, praising them for capturing Smith—but telling them that the Negro had to be protected. "Mobs must not be permitted to try prisoners in Texas," Hogg wrote.[1]

In Texarkana, a contingent of restless residents from Paris, ninety miles west, demanded that Smith be handed over to them. The argument was that "justice" was best delivered in Paris, where he had allegedly killed the girl. There was no call for an investigation or trial. No prosecution and no defense was necessary, even though some people who knew Smith believed he suffered from serious mental health issues.

In Paris, locals waited in the damp cold, eventually dragging pieces of wood through the mud and hastily building a lynching platform. Finally, Smith was shoved back on a train stationed in Texarkana, held down, and shipped off. As the train pulled into the Paris station, he could see an even bigger mob, as many as ten thousand people. Word about a public execution had been spreading in the newspapers, in churches, and by telegrams. It was impossible that Hogg and the lawmakers in Austin didn't know about the impending violence in East Texas.

Smith was hurled off the train; hands grabbed at him; and his clothes were ripped, torn off, and thrown in the air. Children scrambled to get pieces as souvenirs. Smith began begging anyone who would listen that he would prefer to be shot. He was shackled, paraded down Main Street on a chair atop a carnival float, and brought back to a spot near the Texas and Pacific railroad station. Smith tried to bolt, but the crowd, including many who had come from other Texas cities, closed in. Smith tried to break away again, and this time he felt a thick rope dropping over him. He was pulled to the ground, moaning and thrashing, and dragged to a ten-foot-high wooden scaffold.

Several men began dipping iron rods into a roaring furnace and stabbing them into Smith's feet. Slowly, methodically, and as he screamed for mercy, the torturers rolled the white-hot irons up his ankles and legs. Children and other onlooker stared, mesmerized, as Smith's flesh sizzled and then peeled from his bones. As another iron was applied, his moans were drowned out by thundering cheers. The torturers then began pressing their irons on his back, arms, and stomach—then on his genitals. Finally, the burning metal rods were forced into his eyes. Somehow, with his eye sockets melting and smoking, Smith continued to pray and beg until his mouth was forced open and another thick piece of glowing metal was shoved onto his tongue.

Smith's body seemed to cease quivering, and "kerosene was poured upon him, cottonseed hulls placed beneath him, and he was set on fire." Some in the crowd looked away, some grew quiet, some continued to yelp. Blue flames and smoke rose up, and suddenly, Smith raised his burning stumps to his face and let out a whimper. The fire must have burned his ropes loose, and the burning figure staggered and bumped against the scaffold railing. He wobbled for a second and then slid into the flames licking at the wood.

When it was clear he was dead, some in the crowd pushed to scoop up slivers of his clothing and whatever else was in the ash.[2]

Smith's torture and execution was one of the most openly savage moments of mob rage in US history—and in Texas it served as a warning to liberal Republicans, anti-segregationists, and anyone else pushing for minority participation in the political process. Nascent movements to organize anti-Democrats in East Texas, Houston, and Galveston were on full alert in the wake of the murder and the lack of immediate, comprehensive response from the state capitol. The Democratic governor and lawmakers hadn't stopped what many knew was going to happen under the dark clouds blanketing East Texas—and most likely no one would ever be prosecuted, even though the torturers had been identified. The hellish murder was written about in the Northeast and elsewhere.

In the statehouse, Hogg had been busy preparing for trips around the nation, trying to drum up investment in Texas, touting the benefits of doing business in a low-taxation and anti-regulation state. He was going to go to New York, where he now had to wonder if investors and bankers had read about the way hot pieces of iron had been forced into the eyes and mouth of a Negro.

Hogg might not have been aware that this particular horror in Texas served as the first "spectacle" lynching in US history—a reference to vigilante executions being captured by roaming photographers planning to sell grisly postcards commemorating the killings. That sensationalist phenomenon was born in Texas, and it spread across the country. It was a wicked extension of how local rule was allowed to run free, and even the way "voter suppression" could be enforced. What was obvious was the image Texas sent beyond its borders.

The crusading national journalist Ida B. Wells focused her attention on the incident: "Never in the history of civilization has any Christian people stooped to such shocking brutality and indescribable barbarism as that which characterized the people of Paris, Texas." Wells's investigation is comprehensive and staggering—and she suggests that Smith suffered from mental illnesses and had needed treatment. Given the numbing viciousness, it seems incomprehensible that any caretaker of history would not return to this moment as a defining one in the state's legacy—and then make the easy connection to a lack of response from Texas lawmakers.

No one keeps the record of the most grisly lynching, but Wells—one of the icons of early American investigative journalism—paints the incident as a true nadir. Her report is one of the most condemning portraits ever painted of behavior inside the state: "News flashed across the country that the white Christian people of Paris, Texas and the communities thereabout had deliberately determined to lay aside all forms of law and inaugurate an entirely new form of punishment for the murder. They absolutely refused to make any inquiry as to the sanity or insanity of their prisoner, but set the day and hour when in the presence of assembled thousands they put their helpless victim to the stake, tortured him, and then burned him to death for the delectation and satisfaction of Christian people."[3]

The nightmare in Texas knew no bounds: "According to some accounts, his [Smith's] agonized screams were recorded on a primitive 'graphophone' and later played before audiences as images of his killing were projected on a screen."[4]

Hogg, the first governor born in the state (near Rusk, Texas), realized the full value of public image, especially in the last decade of the nineteenth century, when news outlets were connecting the once-disparate sections of the country. Hogg, whose father was a Confederate general, had gone into the newspaper business, eventually running two small Texas papers. If the *New York Times* was running stories immediately in the wake of a heinous public ritual in Texas, it might give investors pause—and, maybe worse, bring federal outsiders to scrutinize the way the state was being governed.

In a way, the arching concept of states' rights might have become a bridge too far in Texas—to the point where Hogg and others in Austin wondered if they had been too preoccupied with making sure that the state was utterly committed to allowing local officials maximum control over their affairs. Hogg decided to make an announcement a few days after Smith's death, and the governor's message came in the form of an open letter to state lawmakers: "Our civilization stands aghast, a helpless witness to the most revolting execution of the age, in which large numbers of citizens openly, in broad day, publicly became murderers by methods revolting to humanity."[5]

Cynics would say that Hogg was putting only a small bit of balm on the open wounds in East Texas; his supporters would say that he was truly staggered by what had unfolded in the bitter cold in Texas—that even Hogg, as committed as anyone to the Confederate legacy, had a humanistic revulsion. According to most of the final accounts, no one was ever arrested, charged, or brought to trial in the death of Henry Smith.

Meanwhile, hundreds of miles away in Chicago, Scott Joplin was eagerly trying to export his version of Texas beauty. He was from the same part of the state as the doomed Henry Smith—and Joplin would be playing his Texas-inspired music and serenading folks coming and going from the grand international exposition. He would also spend his spare time soaking up other eclectic sounds in and around the World's Fair. Joplin was a true musical polyglot, a genius inspired by the boundless American promise on display in Chicago. The man from Texarkana would go on to create and shape music native to the nation—all while opening doors for the practice and appreciation of "Negro" artistry around the world, far from Texas.

"Big Jim" Hogg had taken office with the support of the angry cotton plantation owners and farmers who had targeted non-Texas interlopers—those wealthy railroad and banking moguls—as the source of so many problems. Throughout his time in office in the 1890s, Hogg pushed the state legislature to pass laws limiting the rights of "aliens" to own land in Texas.[6]

Hogg had successfully sold himself as a man of the people, a grassroots fighter for the commoner—someone on the side of Texans who believed they were victims of "foreign" forces. It was a bit of political protectionism, and it would help reinforce and extend, for decades, the us-versus-them mindset in the corridors of power. It would become deep-rooted, part of the political soul of Texas, and it reinforced the idea that an ambitious politician would be well served to agree that Texas was coveted and often under invasion. It was intentionally crafted political paranoia and an old-fashioned closing of ranks. Clearly, Hogg saw the sense of victimization and the way that many felt federal agencies and non-Texas power brokers were exploiting them.

He watched as a group called the Texas People's Party formed in Dallas in the early 1890s. Its creation sent strong signals to every politician in the state: there was a growing alliance of farmers, ranchers, and local businessmen who wanted the national bankers reined in, lower taxes, protections for the agriculture sector, and tighter restrictions on immigration.[7] "Populist camp meetings"—gatherings featuring a mix of religion and politics—began to pop up. Tying the Bible to public policy wasn't just persuasive, it was beginning to be required, and the camp meetings underscored the connections that lawmakers needed to have to a higher power. One observer described a Texas camp meeting this way: "The opening address was given by Reverend A. W. Dumas, a Presbyterian with a reputa-

East Texan James Stephen "Big Jim" Hogg was the state's first native-son governor after initially serving as attorney general. He ran on a platform calling for a body that would regulate wealthy out-of-state railroad companies—the Texas Railroad Commission. Hogg, the son of a Confederate general, sold himself as a grassroots fighter for the commoner—a white supremacist on the side of Texans who believed they were victims of "foreign" forces.

tion as one who preaches politics from the Bible and who uses the good book in every one of his speeches to prove that the Populist platform is the voice of universal Christianity."[8]

The camp meetings, which could pass as a form of local entertainment, almost like a traveling show, forged the communal sense that God wanted Lone Star politics practiced a certain way—and that a good politician was able to hear the Lord advocate for the heartland workers in Texas. Political anthems in the guise of hymns were heard, including "The People's Jubilee" and other tunes:

> The working people are getting tired of having no home nor land—
> so now, they say, to run this government, they are going to try their hand.
>
> There's gold and silver in the White House cellar, and the workers all want some—for they know it will be all counted out if the people's party comes.[9]

One more Texas pioneer was in Chicago attending the World's Columbian Exposition in 1893. Ellen Lawson Dabbs appeared at a special event at the fair—the World's Congress of Representative Women—along with the national activist Susan B. Anthony. Dabbs was serving as another emissary from Texas, someone who could tell the rest of the nation about both the strides made and the setbacks in the state. Dabbs, born in Rusk County,

Ellen Lawson Dabbs, the only daughter of a Confederate colonel, forged her own way after an inequitable divorce to work as a Fort Worth physician, before emerging as one of the nation's leading women's rights activists. Dabbs helped found the state's first women's suffragist group, the Texas Equal Rights Association.

was rising to prominence as one of the earliest, most important figures arguing that women deserved a greater role in Texas politics.

One of eight children, and the only girl in the house, Dabbs grew up in the plantation home of a slave-owning family that had arrived from Georgia and settled a few miles east of the town of Mount Enterprise. Her father became a Confederate colonel and then served in the state legislature, where he was dead set on rebuking Reconstruction regulations. She received a rudimentary education in one-room country schools and then was sent by her parents to the Furlow Masonic Female College in Georgia. Skilled at mathematics, she graduated with honors, returned to East Texas, and spent several years teaching in Nacogdoches.

Dabbs loved music and art and sometimes traveled to Galveston, the state's most sophisticated city.[10] On the coast, she met Joseph Wilkes Dabbs, a dry goods merchant from Sulphur Springs and a widower with four boys. He was twenty years older, and they married after a yearlong courtship. Dabbs worked in her husband's store, keeping his financial records, but after having five daughters with him, she quietly began to revisit what an equitable marriage really meant in the late nineteenth century. She decided to resort to abstinence to avoid any more pregnancies. Her husband grew enraged, began beating her, and then deeded his business and money to the boys he had with his first wife.

Afraid for her life, Dabbs planned to divorce him and then try to find some way to make a living. She filed the paperwork in Sulphur Springs, citing her husband's domestic abuse, and also asked for a share of the family fortune and full custody of the girls. She decided she would try to become a doctor, a profession she knew would transfer to cities around the nation (but at a time when women were hardly encouraged to study medicine). She moved to Iowa to attend the College of Physicians and Surgeons and kept hoping to have her marriage officially declared dead. She wound up missing a key divorce court date in Texas, and some speculated that her husband had bribed local officials to keep her in the dark about the hearing. In the end, she was granted a divorce, but her request for a fair share of the family business was thrown out. She retained custody of the girls, opened a medical practice in Dallas, and eventually went back to Sulphur Springs, where she served as a doctor and also invested in a local newspaper.

In the early 1890s, Dabbs relocated to Fort Worth, working as a single mother of five—and in a city defined by its frontier and cattle-driving heritage. She began writing about women's rights for national publications and organizations, including the National Farmers' Alliance. She helped found the first women's suffragist organization in the state, the Texas Equal Rights Association. And when Dabbs traveled to Chicago in 1893 to confer with Susan B. Anthony and others leading the fight for rights—women from a variety of backgrounds and impulses, including academia and the temperance movements—it empowered her: after she returned to Texas, Dabbs began advocating for changes that had never been a priority in the male-dominated statehouse, including the creation of a technical school that would eventually become Texas Woman's University. She co-created the Texas Women's Council to unite organizations and link women around the state to the broader efforts of the National Council of Women, and she also helped form the Texas Women's Press Association.

As the twentieth century loomed, Dabbs increasingly heard from other organizers around the nation, people asking her to define Texas for them, and she moved into another gear. She called for a reexamination of school curricula, including ones that would open young women to myriad possibilities that hadn't previously been encouraged: science, math, and engineering. She advocated for dialogue about birth control and what the legal age for sexual consent should be. One of her chroniclers put it this way: "Remembering the violence in her own marriage, Dabbs felt strongly that a woman should be in charge of her own sexuality and have the option to prevent unwanted pregnancies."[11]

During the Spanish-American War, she volunteered as a nurse but came back to Fort Worth after contracting tuberculosis. She lost her house to a fire, and then closed a fateful circle when she decided to return to Rusk County, back to the area around her family's old slave plantation. It's difficult to determine if her attempts to remedy the plight of women corresponded with a clear rejection of her family's racist past, as no evidence shows her vigorously denouncing the way her family had made its money with slaves in Texas.

Well into the 1890s, Dabbs argued that economic progress needed to precede political participation for women.[12] Those close to her knew that it was deeply personal: she was forced into a livelihood, as a doctor, that was hard for women to enter—and she did it because she needed to support her disenfranchised daughters. Her travels and her stances made Dabbs a subject of both admiration and revulsion around Texas, and for most of her adult life she remained an insistent anomaly: the only woman in the room. As the male lawmakers who ran the statehouse were closing ranks around socially and economically conservative platforms, they were forced to keep an occasional eye on the persistent woman asking for the right to vote.

Her tuberculosis lingered for years, and Dabbs began looking for a place where she could stabilize her health, or maybe even improve it. She went to Oklahoma and finally to a New Mexico ranch near the town of Logan, but her health deteriorated for years. She summoned her daughters to her bedside in the summer of 1908, bid them farewell, and committed suicide by using chloroform, a substance she knew very well from her days as a doctor. She was laid to rest in an anonymous ranch grave on the side of the state that hugged the Texas border. Astute historians noted that "the inequitable results of the Dabbs divorce case, particularly the disinheritance of her daughters in favor of their brothers, spurred Ellen Dabbs to battle for equality for women. Her evolution as a radical was typical of the small number of women who pursued women's rights in Texas during the 1890s."[13]

Toward the end of her life, Dabbs had a telling moment of self-reflection, a sense that enormous shifts were coming for Texans—ones so big that even the usually unyielding state leaders would have to confront them; ones so fundamental that they would shatter the often reflexive, ingrained resistance to outside pressures: "What a spirit of unrest, a changing of ideals, and, associated with this, a new seeking after truth and its relation to man's welfare—mentally, physically, spiritually."[14]

Word began spreading through Waco in 2016 that the fence was finally coming down. Since the 1870s, the quarter-mile-long stretch had served as a powerful, enduring symbol of racism, the metal line separating the Blacks from the whites buried in Greenwood Cemetery. For decades, Black volunteers worked on one side of the fence, propping up fallen tombstones and clearing weeds, while white volunteers toiled on the other side, planting flowers and picking up bottles left by vandals. (Another major city cemetery, Oakwood, sits just a little more than three miles to the south, and some wondered if that cemetery was historically afforded more attention. Several prominent Texans are buried there: Confederate generals Thomas Harrison and Felix Robertson, and former governors Sul Ross, Richard Coke, and Patrick Neff.)

Greenwood has its share of important figures: veterans from the War of 1812 and the Civil War—and in the once-segregated section, Vivienne Malone-Mayes, the first Black professor at Baylor and one of the first Black women in the nation with a doctorate in mathematics. It is also the resting place for Andy Cooper, a superstar in the Negro League and the only person from Waco enshrined in the Baseball Hall of Fame. As you wander the "Black" section of the cemetery, a small marker stands out, one with musical notes and bars stretching across the front, along with the words "Ol' Man River—he just keeps rolling along." It is the grave of the singer and composer Jules Bledsoe, known around the planet for playing the role of "Joe" and singing "Ol' Man River" in the film *Show Boat*. Bledsoe, in addition to studying at Columbia University—one of the earliest Ivy League universities to openly encourage minority attendance—became the first Black performer to appear at the Metropolitan Opera House and the first Black artist to work continuously at a Broadway theater. He toured the world, performed with major symphonies, appeared in several movies, and wrote an orchestral piece entitled "African Suite"—as well as creating an opera called *Bondage* based on Harriet Beecher Stowe's *Uncle Tom's Cabin*.

A short walk from Bledsoe's grave you'll find an even more understated marker for Robert Lloyd Smith, noting only that he lived from 1861 to 1942 and that he was "the founder of the Farmers Improvement Society of Texas." Smith in many ways is lost to history, though some local residents still know him, often because his name eventually graced a segregated elementary school for Blacks that first opened in the early 1900s as the Fifth Ward School in Waco. When it was renamed R. L. Smith Elementary, it was to honor his groundbreaking attempts to bring political, civil, and educational rights to Blacks across Texas. As history marched on, the Smith school was abandoned in the 1970s. It became an eyesore and was finally razed in 2013 with a plan to use the land to provide new housing for nearby Black residents. The school had served as a proud, visible connection to the courageous way Smith and his colleagues labored at a time when lynchings like the one in Paris, Texas, were always more than possible. Now, all that is visibly left of his legacy is a tombstone that barely hints at his role in changing his home state.

Robert Lloyd Smith was born in South Carolina, into a family of freedmen, in the winter of 1861. He was never a slave. Neither, apparently, were his parents. They believed in education as a route to any form of independence, and he was sent to several schools, including the University of South Carolina until it was closed to Blacks in the late 1870s. He graduated from Atlanta University and then taught in segregated public schools in different Southern states. In a nod to the complicated, frustrating, and intimidating sociocultural and racial undercurrents, he was forced to flee South Carolina after he married a woman with an especially dark complexion.

Smith decided there might be job openings in East Texas, which had thousands of Black children in need of a public education.[15] He settled in Colorado County in a part of the state that had originally been granted to James Bowie—the soldier, mercenary, and wicked slave trader (taught by his father how to buy and sell slaves, Bowie made money purchasing slaves from the pirate Jean Lafitte, who ran human-bartering operations in Louisiana and Galveston). The town of Oakland needed someone to run a segregated facility. The Oakland Normal School had opened in 1882, and it was one of the last vestiges of the Freedmen's Bureau efforts to provide public education for freed Blacks. The school was designed to educate teachers who would then move into other areas in East Texas. Smith was more than qualified to coordinate that new network, and by 1885 he was overseeing the school.

Smith, a student of history, knew where he was headed, and he must have hoped that racism had abated a bit. Colorado County was the epicenter of the Texas cotton plantation economy, and just twenty years before he arrived—at a place where newly freed people lived in flimsy stick houses—there had been at least three hundred slaveholders, including four cotton farmers who owned a minimum of one hundred slaves each.[16] For a while, the population in the county was almost evenly divided be-

YOURS TRULY
R. L. SMITH.

Robert Lloyd Smith, a Black activist who was never a slave, founded the Farmers' Improvement Society of Texas with the goal of steering freedmen away from tenant farming and sharecropping. Smith, who lived in Colorado County and then Waco, served as a member of the Texas House, where he championed education for Blacks.

tween whites and enslaved Blacks. Colorado County had also been the scene of one of the few recorded slave insurrections in Texas—but like any uprising led by Blacks and Latinos, the one in Colorado County was viciously, violently stamped out. As many as four hundred slaves had plotted to escape to Mexico, but many of them were captured, hung, or whipped to death.

Colorado County, like many other places in Texas, had been mired in postslavery economic confusion. The fears, the threats of violence, were constant. But Smith felt a modicum of protection provided by the federal government, a hint that something profound was changing in Texas. Perhaps time and numbers were on his side—perhaps the creation of the Oakland Normal School, with its mission to train Blacks to be teachers, was a sign that true economic and political inclusion was coming.

As he traveled the narrow, soggy lanes near the Colorado River, Smith was moving through areas where the first organized group of white settlers in Texas—part of Stephen F. Austin's slave-owning colony—had arrived a few decades earlier. He was at the heart of deep-rooted history and habits. Smith knew very well that he was a highly educated Black man in postwar plantation Texas—someone who was preparing an army of teachers for impoverished and vulnerable former slaves. The Freedmen's Bureau had set up an office in the county, in Columbus, to attend to thousands of nearby freedmen, one of the largest concentrations in Texas.

Smith had many moments to ponder being at the center of a historical overhaul: he had lived and traveled in Georgia and South Carolina. He
knew racism, segregation, and slavery across the South, and then he had
washed ashore in a part of the United States that was so isolated, so hidden, that its true racist nature was often never as evident as it might have
been in other areas of the Deep South. Perhaps it was the remote nature
of his part of Texas—or because the state had that cauldron of hidebound
slave masters, Confederate soldiers, and others determined not to call it a
Lost Cause but more of an Ongoing Cause. For Smith, it was a given that
Texas had kept its massive subjugation of uneducated Blacks more hidden than other states. Keep the freed slaves uneducated and they would
never access power, let alone know how to write their name at the election booths.

Five years after he was named head of Oakland Normal School, Smith
was in touch with the extraordinary national leader Booker T. Washington
and talking about their belief that the key to minority advancement was
in the economic wheelhouse. In East Texas, that meant helping freedmen
farm, but this time it needed to be on their own terms, so they could buck
the almost instant economic oppression that erupted after Emancipation,
with freedmen forced to survive as sharecroppers and tenant farmers.

It was a radical task, basically threatening the way politicians and landowners had adapted to the end of slavery—including the use of rented-out
prisoners to plow the earth. In 1890, Smith formed the Farmers' Home
Improvement Society, with an ambitious plan to steer desperately poor
freed slaves out of their exile in the tenant and sharecropping cycles. He
knew that Black farmers were never going to receive loans to buy their
own land, and that they would be facing retailers who were going to favor
white farmers when it came to pricing, shipping, and support—white
farmers who were bristling at the idea of losing their field hands. Smith's
idea was to build an offshoot of the populist alliances that had begun in
Texas in the 1880s and were birthing local political movements.

His Farmers' Home Improvement Society helped struggling sharecroppers manage their own acreage and create a mutual aid network
advocating for easier credit and better prices when the farmers loaded up
wagons and brought sweet potatoes, greens, corn, peanuts, and even cotton to the big wholesalers and exporters in Dallas. Smith, without question, was inspired by Booker T. Washington's advocacy for economic independence and cultural pride as preludes to political equality. Make money,

establish economic alliances, and then figure out ways to send minorities to the election booths and to the statehouse in Austin.

In 1894, with some Republicans still holding sway in a place with so many freed slaves—and with some Democrats fleeing their party for the white populist factions—Smith decided to run for the state legislature. He won, and that fact alone would be extraordinary, given the insistent specter of clandestine "whites' rights" groups huddling at lodges, halls, homes, or cabins in the woods and talking about using guns and whips to maintain supremacy. But Smith's election was especially breathtaking, since it came just months after the harrowing news about another Smith—Henry Smith, the Black man tortured in front of thousands of howling white people deep in the heart of Texas.

As he traveled the bumpy lanes from Columbus to Austin, past the majestic pine forests around Bastrop and Smithville, the freshly elected lawmaker had time to review what Booker T. Washington was preaching. Washington said that "the Negro problem" was "to teach him how to live and how to take hold of the things around him."[17] Even before he arrived at the statehouse, Smith had mapped out a very careful agenda, one that might serve Washington's credo—and one that, in subtle fashion, might seem nonconfrontational: making sure Blacks were attending their segregated schools; trying to enforce socially conservative measures to thwart "non-Christian" behaviors; and trying to urge freedmen to improve their homes, farms, churches, cemeteries, stores, and neighborhoods.

When he returned to Colorado County, Smith religiously pressed his neighbors to repair old places and build new ones. He told people that he didn't want to give local white leaders, police, and sheriffs more excuses to hound any freed families. As he went door to door around the newly formed freedmen's towns, Smith could tell he was trusted. People came to his meetings, preachers spread the word, and a semblance of community and neighborhood sprang up. In another era, Smith might have been called a sellout, since the things he was pushing for clearly soothed the reactionary Texas Democrats. They saw a Black elected official calling for temperance, and for self-improvement without the need for government assistance. It seemed benign, nonthreatening. And maybe it would keep Blacks with their own kind.

When he returned to Austin, Smith was alone in many ways. He had wrestled with how to push—and how hard to push—for change. In the statehouse, "Smith was surrounded by whites, some helpful, some malevolent, but most indifferent to the concerns of blacks," wrote one historian many years later. "Smith knew the realities of Southern race politics, as well as the boundary beyond which he would be considered dangerous," and so he chose "the accommodationist approach."[18]

Almost every day inside the statehouse, Smith concentrated his legislative efforts on education, including support for Prairie View Normal School, which would evolve into Prairie View A&M, one of the important historically Black colleges in the nation. He served two terms, the only Black man in the lair of the white lawmaker, and then decided to move to the Waco area and go into business for himself. He had two adopted children with his wife, Ruby, and they started a clothing company that made farmer's overalls. Still, Smith kept his hand in organizing. At one point, his Farmers' Improvement Society had 21,000 members, including many from outside Texas. The group held fairs and festivals to promote small farmers. It provided health insurance and guided people to friendly banks. Smith also became head of the National Negro Business League's office in Texas. Finally, convinced that county farm agencies in Texas remained hopelessly racist, he created the Negro Extension Division. His small home in Central Texas was a gathering place for community leaders, including some who came from other cities to learn how he had been able to survive and organize.

As he grew older, Smith would walk the Black neighborhoods of Waco, including the ones near the often capricious Brazos River. People would step from their front doors to shake his hand and thank him. But by the 1930s, the Farmers' Improvement Society had disbanded. Even Smith couldn't stare down a national economic collapse—and one of the untold stories of Texas is how the Great Depression slammed Blacks and Latinos who were just beginning to win some kind of economic independence.

Smith passed away in 1942, with the nation focused on war and not so much on the plight of independent Black farmers in Palestine, Mexia, Lufkin, and the cloistered pockets along the Bosque and Angelina rivers and the Cedar, Chambers, and Richland creeks. The members of his Methodist church laid Smith to rest in Waco, and his grave was adorned with a simple marker noting only that he had founded something called the Farmers' Improvement Society.

Smith's passing merited little coverage, though long after he died, his name emerged as a footnote in stories celebrating other Texas pioneers—especially ones about a woman whose name now graces several schools around the state, a woman memorialized in a suitably impressive statue that greets visitors to the Austin airport. The main terminal there is named after her.

Smith was the last Black person to serve in the Texas legislature until Barbara Jordan in 1966.

CHAPTER 4

The Bosses: The 1900s

ISAAC CLINE, A STUDIOUS AND meticulous meteorologist in Galveston, rose from the bed where his pregnant wife was sleeping. He stepped out into the quiet streets of the prosperous city, watching the shopkeepers slowly beginning to open their stores. He headed for the waterfront. He stared out over the bay, studying the choppy rows of waves, looking at the sky. He was a man of science, but he seemed to sense that ominous forces were headed toward Texas.

His city was home to almost forty thousand residents and remained a financial beating heart for the state. Galveston was still a place that drew investors, cotton brokers, and dockworkers, and it had also been the port of entry for a stream of hardy German immigrants anxious to settle along Hickory Creek, Lang Creek, and the clear streams and springs of the Hill Country. Parts of outlying Galveston were bucolic, with families living in homes ringing the inlets and marshes—and accustomed to dining on oysters scraped from the rocks or on bounties of crabs plucked from the reedy shallows where the salt water met the fresh water.

Cline returned home to his family and braced for something awful. And on September 8, the Great Hurricane of 1900 roared into the Gulf of Mexico and took aim at Galveston. Winds and water flattened building after building, collapsing one atop the other, until the city was a mangled heap of splintered wood. Every inch of the two-hundred-square-mile island was covered by water. As rescuers tried to trudge over the wreckage, they found hundreds of bodies. Maybe hundreds more were washed out to sea. The greatest natural disaster in US history took eight thousand to twelve thousand lives.

The impact would last for generations, and Galveston would take years to rebuild. In Austin, lawmakers scrambled to deal with the damage to the state economy. In Galveston, leaders who had escaped the storm wondered how to revive the city—and whether or not to beg for assistance from Washington. A decision was made to ask state lawmakers to form a five-person commission to oversee the emergency reconstruction. Critics immediately barked that Galveston—let alone any town in Texas—shouldn't be subject to state dictates, to some sort of state-appointed control.[1] And then the legislature passed a measure requiring that the Galveston city commission members be elected and not appointed. That emphasis on local control, the formation of more local governing bodies and agencies, was emulated around the state. By the end of the decade, Dallas, Fort Worth, Houston, El Paso, Denison, and Greenville would also adopt elected commissioner systems.[2]

A nightmare storm had put its imprint on local politics in Texas.

In certain cloistered Houston circles, some people still call Glenwood Cemetery the "River Oaks of the dead"—a nod to its proximity to the neighborhood where many of the most influential, wealthy Texans have lived. Apart from the Texas State Cemetery, it contains the largest collection of politically and economically powerful people in state history.

Among them are Howard Hughes, who had become a film and aircraft mogul, internationally famous for dating Hollywood starlets before turning into an unkempt recluse inside a penthouse on the ninth floor of the Desert Inn in Las Vegas. There is Anson Jones, the former president of the Republic of Texas, who shot himself to death after finishing dinner at the Capitol Hotel in Houston—where he had temporarily relocated in the wake of several bitter setbacks (state lawmakers had refused to support his dream of being a US senator, he had been forced to sell his farm at a loss, and then he had lost the full use of one of his arms after fallng from a horse).

And there are Texas governor and Humble Oil cofounder Ross Sterling; Texas governor William Hobby; and Oveta Culp Hobby, once the secretary of health, education, and welfare. Wander about and you will find a gaggle of mayors, ambassadors, more oil company founders, and university presidents.

Nestled among the people whose names are affixed to airports and buildings is a modest-looking site dedicated to Edward M. House, a primogenitor for a political way of life in Texas. Today, if you are a lobbyist meeting at the Austin Club (in an old opera house, from which Black lawmakers were once excluded) or other hushed places where money and power are bartered, where public policy is hammered together outside public view, then you owe a debt to House. He was the earliest of the great backroom influencers in Texas—someone who created the script for latter-day political strategists like Karl Rove who would meet and decide who would be elected and what issues were going to dominate legislative sessions.

House's father was a former Houston mayor and a merchant banker who worked hard to provide financial aid to the Confederacy. The family had begun acquiring large chunks of land in the mid-1800s, including a seventy-thousand-acre ranch in LaSalle County. They diversified into cotton and then a sprawling sugarcane operation in Fort Bend County. The House sugar mill—and the acres of other nearby farmland—were defined by slavery and convict leasing. One nearby plantation, in an area known as Arcola, was run by the Waters family, who had a reputation for especially cruel treatment of their more than two hundred slaves.

Growing up, the angular and soft-spoken House always knew that his family was grooming him for a bigger role, and he was sent to schools in Virginia and Connecticut, and then to Cornell University in bucolic upstate New York. When his father grew ill, House returned to Texas and assumed control of the family's vast fortune. He decided he wanted to be in Austin, where he could meet face-to-face with any lawmakers who had a say in the pricing, shipping, and regulating of his cotton, cattle, and sugar inheritances.

In the city, House was seemingly everywhere, dressed in impeccable suits and shined shoes. He was slim and clean-shaven, without the flowing beard worn by so many of the Confederate heirs in political power. To some, House looked like a Philadelphia lawyer or a banker from the Northeast, someone who had a diplomatic, even suave, aura. He built one of the grandest mansions in the city, not far from the capitol, and held parties and dinners for politicians and businessmen from around the state. It was clear to power brokers in Austin that even if he wasn't appointed to any office, he was designing his own role as a plugged-in advisor, consultant, and chess player. As House settled into the upper tiers of power in Austin, more political candidates began to seek out the calm, stately man. He had mounds of money, plenty of connections, and a built-in army of business partners around the state—and, perhaps best of all, he had little personal desire to run for office.

When visitors arrived, House ordered bourbon and branch water brought by his servants and said he only wanted to advise, to be a political consigliere. Conservative Democrats were comfortably in control, and House told people that his only goal was to lubricate the corridors of power, to broker introductions between the unelected bosses and the lawmakers of Texas. He explained that if there were any outside disturbances—populists complaining about bankers, or progressives trying to peel back segregation, or women clamoring for the right to vote—he had ideas about how to take care of them all.

Suitors gathering in his parlor knew very well that the ambassadorial House had already bonded with Big Jim Hogg, the portly, bearded lawyer who had clambered his way into the governor's office. House was the cardinal behind the throne and willing to surround Hogg and anyone else in power in Texas with a tight, connected network. "House acquired a deftness in intrigue and showed a talent for subterranean manipulation," wrote one astute chronicler. "Fascinated with the machinery of politics, House developed a taste for efficient organization and a disdain for divisive opposition. He was careful to see that the governors he supported distributed key state offices to loyal members of his network."[3]

House was building a Wizard of Oz world of Texas politics where key figures worked behind the curtain to orchestrate events and elections. And it wasn't only about a sense of civic duty or protecting the old Southern order; it was a way to line his pockets. "His zest for the political game did not extend to the substance of legislation, and he rarely risked prestige to support a proposed law. House wished to use politics to perpetuate his own reputation."[4]

At his stately home on West Avenue in Austin, House welcomed more and more petitioners, including Joseph Sayers, S. W. T. Lanham, and Thomas Campbell—all destined to be governors of Texas. House traveled by private railroad cars around the state and the nation, and also sailed to Europe, drumming up investments for Texas. House was a negotiator, a strategist, and he was creating an Austin-centric haven for socially conservative, affluent industry leaders who would gather for balls, booze, and debates about who would be allowed to serve in the Texas capitol—and who would then be sent to Washington, DC.

In the often harsh and seemingly endless flatlands stretching from San Antonio to Laredo, from Corpus Christi to Brownsville, a handful of hard-charging white men were dreaming up an almost unimaginable plan. It was, really, part of the Texas ethos: to conquer, extract, and carve something out of what others saw as a brutal, unforgiving landscape. They wanted to remake the boundless horizon of arid, parched border-lands—and soak it with millions of gallons of water piped in from the Rio Grande.

The "Valley miracle" was coming, with a cornucopia of onions, spinach, and citrus—and with it another perfectly Texan system of vicious economic and political control. The *patrón* would conscript thousands of Mexican immigrants to crack open the caked fields, inch by inch, and then build the enormous irrigation system that would turn the barren land green. Then the boss would provide jobs in the fields—and sell food, housing, clothes, and goods to the workers and their familes. It was just another form of indentured servitude, not really distinct from the bruising sharecropping and tenant farming in East Texas. The bosses did what they knew how to do: they looked south, across the sluggish river, and waited for the Mexi-can workers to come to them.

The South Texas landowners, elected or not, also exerted maximum control over elections, deciding who could vote and who could run. It was a system that Edward House understood, and it was a process that Big Jim Hogg and so many others who emerged from East Texas endorsed.

Their biggest prize was John Nance Garner from Uvalde, someone the *patrones* were going to gift with an absurdly drawn congressional district that stretched across the belly of the state.

Garner was born in November 1868 in the tiny settler's hamlet of Blos-som Prairie, in the northeastern part of the state, not far from the slug-gish Red River. One legend had it that Davy Crockett, the frontiersman who died at the Alamo and whose legend was now being taught to Texas children, had first come to Texas through Blossom Prairie. Growing up, Garner quickly fell in love with the sagas and the oft-told stories about the final fading of the Republic of Texas, the echoes of the Confederate rebel-lion, and even the last eruptions of what some still called the "Indian depredations"—and what others referred to gingerly as the "troubles" between the white men and the Native Americans.

In his early twenties, Garner moved to Uvalde, closer to what was left of the Old Southwest, closer to Mexico. Garner thought the breezier, drier climate in Uvalde would be better for his health—but he also believed that the wide-open, unregulated landscape would yield untapped opportunities for a young man with political ambitions. He explored the territories stretching from San Antonio and Corpus Christi south to the Mexico border, into a part of the state governed by that *patrón* system. Garner traveled the borderlands and courted the bosses, hoping they'd repay his loyalty if he ever threw his hat in the ring. They liked his pugnacious style, his salty language, and his ability to drink hard and often. And they loved the fact that he believed Texans needed to roam free, unfettered by outside control. (The provenance is hard to determine, perhaps because it is another bit of drummed-up Texas mythology, but years later it would be easy to find online a quote attributed to Garner: "The trouble today is that we have too many laws.")[5]

Supported by the money, blessings, and controlled voting booths in South Texas, Garner served in Congress into the early 1930s. He became Speaker of the House and one of the most powerful players on Capitol Hill—constantly steering work, programs, and favors to Texas. His allegiances to the white landowners would remain uncompromising, as did some of his feelings on race:

> The Mexican race, as inferior and undesirable as U.S. citizens as
> they are, should not worry anyone, because they are genetically deter-
> mined with a homing pigeon instinct, of always returning to where
> they came from.[6]

Back in Austin, Edward House was doing the same things as Garner but in a more refined and overt manner. He continued to enjoy the highly segregated realms in Austin, and he put even more time into protecting and promoting the political and business interests of his family and friends. His true goal was to make sure like-minded members in his orbit were elected governor—and that the governor appointed his close allies. For House and the others emulating him, it was about maintaining a clear and certain order—especially when there were monumental changes in the forecast.

Predictions abounded that automobiles, flying machines, power lines, and telephones would soon be everywhere. And there were those rumblings for women's rights, greater freedoms for minorities, and safer and more prosperous working conditions. As unwanted as they might be in Texas, they were not going away. House watched it all unfold with his reserved but jaundiced eye: his own family fortune was tied to the original cotton and sugarcane heydays of slavery; he wasn't interested in pushing the men he had elected to consider progressive legislation. He wasn't raised that way:

> House and his companions often harassed recently freed Blacks, either verbally or otherwise. He recalled using slingshots, or a 'nigger shooter,' to pelt Black passersby with objects ranging from stones to shards of glass. House's diary entries throughout his teen years consistently reveal a deeply felt racism, a sense of Anglo-Saxon superiority and pride.[7]

Throughout his adult life, House enjoyed being saluted in Austin as "Colonel House," a title that an appreciative Governor Hogg bestowed on him. It carried no official military weight, but House liked it. It suggested he really did have authority and command. Today, high school football games in Austin are played at venerable House Park (aficionados know that a nearby shack called House Park Barbecue was one of the oldest barbecue pits in the city, dating to the 1940s). The land for the small stadium was donated by the earliest of the ultimate political insiders, a racist who wrote the rules for backroom influence in Texas.

A frail-looking, diminutive Republican senator from Indiana was gasping for air, his face turning red, as he felt a pair of strong hands closing around his throat. His tie and shirt had been ripped away, and his panicked eyes stared up at the enraged, oval-faced Democratic Texas senator trying to kill him. Joseph Weldon Bailey was pressing down on Albert Beveridge — and it looked like the looming, sputtering Bailey had simply lost his mind. Frantic shouts erupted as other senators and aides raced over, trying to grab hold of the bull-like Bailey.

It was June 10, 1902, and Bailey had started his assault by screaming for Beveridge to apologize for suggesting Bailey loathed another member of Congress. As the Texas Democrat charged at the Indiana Republican, Beveridge's desk thudded into a wall. "The Texas senator is a powerful man and it was with great difficulty that the two senators were able to drag him away," said one news account. "As he was removed a little distance he was heard to utter something that sounded like a threat about killing."[8]

If House was "Mr. Inside," then Bailey was "Mr. Outside"—an unfiltered and occasionally unhinged man who also did his part to cement a particular view of Texas and its politicians. Bailey was a lawyer, a native of Mississippi, and already infamous after being accused in the 1880s of inciting bloody violence and voter intimidation during local elections in the Deep South. Republicans on Capitol Hill opened a Senate investigation into whether Bailey and his Democratic allies were behind it. Then, not long after the accusations, Bailey decided that Texas would be a better, more tolerant place to pursue politics.

He opened a Gainesville law practice and worked hard to raise his profile by perfecting his public speaking skills. The segue to Texas political prominence proved far easier than he had imagined, and he was elected to Congress in 1890. He served as the minority leader from 1897 to 1899, and then as a senator from 1901 to 1911. In Washington, Bailey became a recognizable face of Texas—and a symbol of how the state could be home to pugnacious politicians, and remain a powerful outpost for the lingering sentiments of the Confederacy. Bailey was maybe even the last true public believer in the original spirit of slavery and segregation: "Master of the Democrat party of Texas, he became the most powerful voice of the Southern wing of the Democratic national party . . . in a certain rhetorical sense he was the final spokesman of the Confederacy."[9]

The hulking Bailey was a reliable, thundering messenger for the Texas protectionist measures that House, Garner, and the team of men from Austin, Houston, and Dallas had in mind. One thing most of them agreed on: Bailey was a hell of a speaker, someone who "excelled at public oratory and aroused the emotions of Texas voters as no other campaigner of his era could."[10]

Aside from knowing what House and the others in Texas really wanted—lower taxes and the holy grail of limited regulation—Bailey was also nimble enough to realize the way political campaigning was changing in the state. Voters had far more access to headlines and newsmakers. Politicans were more visible through an ability to travel more readily around the state for public appearances. Bailey became an early Texas political showman, a racist Foghorn Leghorn who could deliver flowery—or, if necessary, bellowing—opposition to women's suffrage, unions, and desegregation.

When Bailey returned to Washington from visits to Texas, he carried reassurances from dozens of citizens' councils, fraternal organizations, alumni associations, and Confederate reunion groups that routinely signed off on his reelection. On Capitol Hill, he patrolled the corridors and aisles for years with a growing sense of inviolability; he assumed he was the most bulletproof, hard-line Southern Democrat from Texas.

Maybe it was hubris that blinded him to early questions about his relationship with the Waters-Pierce Oil Company, which had been accused of violating antitrust laws. After the company's Texas business permits were revoked, Bailey had pushed state lawmakers to help the firm reorganize and get recertified, but his entanglement with Waters-Pierce—also under attack for being part of the massive Standard Oil monopoly—blew up. Critics accused him of turning his back on ordinary Texans, arguing that he was in bed with the oil giants and on their payroll. Another accusation emerged, that Bailey had accepted personal loans (of almost $400,000 in 2021 dollars) from the oilmen.

On top of it all, Bailey was blasted for remaining too close to high-paying clients from his days in private practice. Bailey was never convicted, but he was surely undone by recklessness: he had tried to strangle someone in the Senate, and then he was tied to megacorporations being investigated at a national level. Bailey had succeeded by knowing how to milk the modern political machine—getting his name in the newspapers—and now he was being drowned by the same tools he had used to get to Congress. Even more stories spread: that he was a hopeless, ham-fisted crook and tied to slick big-business interests from the Northeast, the kind that many Texans had escaped from, or rebelled against, or continued to loathe.

By the end of the 1900s, Bailey's reputation as a true Texas warrior in the lion's den—the very image that first endeared him to voters—was being swamped by the whispers. He confided to friends that he could hear more creeping populism inside the Democratic ranks; that his hatred of liberals, Republicans, and federal oversight was being blotted out by scandal—by the idea that Bailey, who said he was a man of the people, had proudly waded into a gilded swamp.

Bailey had always worked hard to deliberately perfect a bombastic approach to political races in Texas. He knew he gave a good speech, the kind that had farmers in East Texas and oilmen in Houston on the edge of their seats. But his barreling style—one that other elected officials would ape for decades—ultimately couldn't buffer him.

Bailey finally decided to step away from politics, guided by the realization that there was far more money to make as a Washington lawyer. Of course, he also thought that plenty of Texas voters had short memories, or that even if they remembered his scandals, they'd probably forgive him. He was Joseph Bailey, the man who wasn't afraid to tackle a spindly senator from Indiana and try to beat the hell out of him.

Bailey came back to Texas and ran for governor in 1920, but it really was over; he was defeated and he glumly opted to resume practicing law. Years passed, he made more money, and in April 1929, he was asked to come to a Sherman courtroom to present arguments in an interstate commerce case. For Bailey, it was as if he was remembering his feisty, early days as a barnstorming speechmaker offering up impassioned odes to the values of the Lost Cause, the dwindling memories of the old Confederacy.

Bailey stood before the Texas judge hearing the case in Sherman and began orating operatically about states' rights. It really was like the times when Bailey traveled around Texas, talked at the forums and rallies, or took to the floor of the Senate. Something also sounded familiar to the judge, who raised his hand and suddenly interrupted Bailey.

"Senator, your remarks have a familiar sound to those of us in Grayson County who recall that forty years ago you voiced those same views among us."

Bailey smiled and replied: "Yes, Your Honor. Those were my views then, and they are my views today."

Bailey sat down, and when he did, the papers he held in his hand slid to the floor. He collapsed, doctors were called, and Bailey was put on a courtroom table as the medical personnel tried to revive the sixty-six-year-old former senator from Texas. They were unsuccessful. Two days later, Bailey's body was put on a funeral train in Dallas, shipped to Gainesville, and buried in Fairview Cemetery.[11]

As the mourners watched the dirt being tossed onto his coffin, it was easy for them to wonder if it signaled the beginning of changes inside the inflexible bastions of old Southern Democrats in Texas—the parts of the party made up of men who not only refused to deny the Confederate heritage but wanted to promote it and preserve it in the most public ways possible.

Maybe, though, Bailey's death pointed to something more pragmatic. Maybe the subtle form of politics practiced by Edward House was a better way to go. Maybe drawing direct, unfettered attention to the sanctioned racism and segregation in Texas wasn't always in the best interests of the men who met in the backrooms where candidates were picked.

In 1901, state lawmakers trudged down the Austin lanes leading to the statehouse and gathered in small clusters to refine amendments to the constitution—ones that would reinforce poll taxes and support regulations ostensibly meant to fight irregularities in elections. Really, they were designed to keep out Black voters. The racist results were immediate and extremely effective. One *Texas Almanac* estimate had Black voter participation plummeting "from 100,000 in the 1890s to an estimated 5,000 in 1906."[12]

Meanwhile, money was pouring into Texas from myriad investors and more wheelers and dealers, more men fixed on extending railroad construction and searching for oil. Texas was destined for a singular, blazing economic revolution, and fortunes were going to be made that relied on the backbreaking work by armies of oilfield workers and subsistence-wage Mexican immigrants. With it, Texas-style monopolies were about to be born, many turning a blind eye to federal antitrust regulations.[13]

In 1901, the Spindletop gusher erupted and changed everything: one hundred thousand barrels of oil went soaring into the sky for nine straight days, and everyone from Joseph Bailey to John Nance Garner, from Edward House to Big Jim Hogg, began racing to grasp what it meant for the political calculus—and what it meant for their own fortunes, fiscally and politicaly. Power was still closely held among a few white men. Deals were still routinely brokered in the hallways of the statehouse. The receptive political system, lubricated by familiarity and personal favors, was in place. Texas was seemingly well prepared politically for the oil revolution, even if lawmakers had no real idea how much black gold was gurgling underneath them.

Lawmakers had worked overtime into the earliest days of the 1900s to add ports, roads, and railroad tracks that could be used to transport the oil; to provide an easily controlled workforce; to ward off distracting labor organizers; to limit taxes; to streamline political regulations; to keep some outside investors and Washington in check. It was as if Texas had been waiting for this moment. It would change everything political: how campaigns raised money, how they were run, who the candidates were. For the next 120 years, billions of dollars would flow from the oilfields into political races—not just in Texas, but around the nation. For the rest of the history of Texas, no one seeking high office could consider entering a race without carefully weighing their exact relationship with fossil fuels.

Waves of humidity and heat flutter and dance on a late-summer, gunmetal-gray day spent at Old City Cemetery in Brownsville. Weeds cover some markers, and as you stroll past several ever-alive plastic flowers, you are passing gunfighters, borderland rogues, and even victims of cholera epidemics. You will see soldiers who fought at the Battle of San Jacinto, in the Civil War, or alongside Teddy Roosevelt as one of his Rough Riders. You are looking for someone else, someone a bit lost to history. Measuring his sphere of influence, his legacy, is an imprecise art, but he is easily one of the most powerful figures in Texas political history: the Democratic Party boss James Babbage Wells.

Born on St. Joseph Island, a sliver of land north of Aransas Pass, Wells became a lawyer and a rancher, bouncing around South Texas cities before settling in Brownsville. In time, he became a "boss of bosses" in South Texas, and helped muscle the *patrón* system into existence. For those who devoted their time to understanding him, Wells was one of the true, broad-shouldered titans of Texas politics: "For four decades, Wells stood at the center of South Texas politics. At the height of his career, he managed the Cameron County Democratic machine, influenced the political evolution of three other counties, cooperated closely with the U.S. congressmen from his district, and distributed state and sometimes federal patronage for the Lower Rio Grande Valley," wrote one historian. "Beyond arranging patronage appointments and battling election reforms, the South Texas boss sought to influence the general policies of the state and national governments."[14]

Wells scooped up huge swaths of ranchland in South Texas and then committed himself to two things: first, to tamping down any unrest emanating from restless Mexico, anything that could threaten the economic and political holds he and other Valley families had created, and second, to coordinating the control of jobs, water, and the electoral system. When necessary, Wells and other ranchers and farmers would agree to convene. Oak timbers would be dragged to a ranch house or plantation, and mounds of meat would be smoked for a barbecue. Domestics would bring out drinks cooled by slabs of ice the railroads had brought in. The men would smoke cheroots from the Finck Cigar Company in San Antonio and marvel at how the miles of scrubland—the colonial places where the Spanish went treasure hunting—were now on their way to becoming an agricultural wonderland.

For almost two hundred years, the land was useful only to the vaqueros and cowboys who rode herd on cattle. But now, in a boom almost drowned out by the oil eruptions, clever and ambitious ranchers were importing machines that would steer water from the Rio Grande—and they needed thousands more malleable ditchdiggers, pipe layers, and farmworkers to help them do it. The *patrones* also talked about the way they were planting row after row of palm trees to serve as windbreaks alongside those new onion fields and grapefruit groves. They'd talk about the fifty new steam pump systems and the labyrinth of underground water pipes inside the miles of trenches scooped out, inch by inch, by Latinos and Tejanos. Sometimes John Nance Garner, their main man in Congress, would arrive by train to join the *patrones*, drink beer from buckets, eat the brisket—and talk about what he could do to help in Congress.

Garner knew full well that he had to come kiss the rings of the border Brahmins. Into the 1900s, with political unrest in Mexico rising, there was an even greater sense that power needed to be solidified, that things needed bracing in case Texas received an influx of fleeing Mexicans. Once Garner traveled south of San Antonio, south of Corpus Christi, he understood he was entering a world that had been hammered into a lucrative new order—but was also that much closer to a country seemingly spiraling out of control. The bosses told Garner they wanted as many low-wage workers as possible, but they were especially keen on quashing any hints of labor organizing—and any attendant calls for raising wages. Garner promised to do battle with unions back in Washington, something that would put him in direct conflict with Franklin Delano Roosevelt, the president he was supposed to serve.

Garner was well on his way to becoming the most influential politician from Texas. In the heat and dust of the Rio Grande Valley, some of the bosses studied the squatty fireplug of a man and wondered if he might actually become the first bought and sold dynamo from Texas to take the White House. If they could turn wasteland into a greenbelt, they could probably pull together the money to mount a national campaign.

For now, the bosses had more immediate matters on their minds. With millions of dollars at stake in the Valley, it was imperative to lock up the political apparatus. Wells and the others went to Austin to demand that the governor send armed Texas Rangers to patrol the valley and guard against union rabble-rousers and anybody else who might have been inspired by the growing political unrest in Mexico. Wells wanted to unsubtly remind the farmworkers and their families who was in charge. And he wanted Rangers to not only patrol the border but provide gun-carrying security for the farms and the irrigation pipes crisscrossing the region. Workers in the fields began seeing heavily armed men arriving by train and horse. And many of the farmhands learned to simply, quickly, avert their gaze. Going to vote, for some, seemed like a useless, even dangerous, exercise.

In the heat of the summer of 1905, several grim-faced Texas Rangers who had remained behind in Central Texas reined in their horses and formed circles around a mob of people lining the Brazos River outside of Waco. The Rangers and the crowd, corralling a small group of Black men, demanded to be told where a twenty-year-old named Sank Majors was hiding. He had been accused of attacking and stabbing a white woman.

The new Texas governor, Samuel Lanham, was obsessed with finding Majors and was traveling to Waco to offer a reward for his capture. Majors was finally cornered 120 miles away, near Lockhart and Plum Creek, where years earlier some Texas settlers had gotten into a running gun battle with Comanche. Majors was brought to the Waco jail, and then—in the middle of the night—he heard the hollow thundering of hammers smashing down the steel cell doors.

Attackers beat him, whipped him, and dragged him through the streets toward the Washington Avenue Bridge. Majors could hear the men arguing about whether to set him on fire or hang him. Finally, he was strung from a crossbeam, his body quivering until his head lolled to one side.

In that same awful ritual playing out too often in Texas, that despicable redundancy of public spectacle, onlookers gleefully yanked at his body for slivers of clothing—and even some of his chopped-off fingers. The Texas Rangers had arrived ostensibly to quell the violence. As they watched, another angry mob battered its way into the home of Jim Lawyer, a Black man who had tried to protest against the lynching. He was dragged outside, held down, and had a whip snap down on his back over and over again.

Ever since the 1870s, the state had been moving in perfectly predictable political patterns: wealthy white men, preferably those with an affection for the Confederacy and Southern credos, were assured of high office. Others of less modest means were elected through the graces of well-off supporters. The political bedfellows were not hard to find, and you could safely predict the long-range behavior of anyone going into office. But no one could have anticipated the barrel-chested, broad-faced Thomas Campbell.

He had grown up in rural Rusk County (where one of his childhood friends was the future governor Jim Hogg) and became a lawyer in Longview. He was a political geek, a keen student of civil statutes and the impact legislation had on the booming railroads. Late in the nineteenth century, state lawmakers in Austin came to Campbell and asked for his help sorting out the financial mess of the International–Great Northern Railroad—an operation that the arrogant business baron Jay Gould owned but had allowed to go into debt. Campbell stewarded the railroad for a number of years but was often in legal and bureaucratic battles with Gould and his lawyers. The fights alerted Campbell to all the Texas ranchers and farmers who were insisting they were in a life-and-death struggle with East Coast and Northern invaders, almost as if nothing had changed since the Civil War and Reconstruction.

Campbell's dive into the railroad melee was duly noted, and riding the belief that he was out to protect Texas, he was elected governor in 1907. But during his two terms, he began expanding central power in ways that only a few might have predicted. He broadened the scope of state government by creating the Bureau of Labor Statistics (now the Texas Department of Licensing and Regulation) and the Texas State Board of Health (now the Texas Department of Health). He pushed for building more public schools, regulating the insurance industry, and holding businesses accountable for food and drug safety. In 1907, the Robertson Insurance Law was passed, which "required companies to invest in Texas real estate and securities not less than 75 percent of their reserves devoted to insurance policies on the lives of Texans."[15]

Throughout his time in Austin, it was also abundantly clear that Campbell was never going to confront the embedded evils still slithering their way through his native East Texas—including the brutality and violence inside the convict leasing system. Campbell didn't call a special legislative session to address the leasing until 1910, the year before he left office.[16] He knew he wasn't a social justice crusader, by any stretch, but that his strong suit was as a buttoned-down executive who stuck rigidly to his sense of comportment and duty on behalf of the hard-working white Christian majority in the state. Campbell simply wore "the Anglo evangelical values of growing urban middle-class business and professional groups and labor organizations, as well as farmers, in North, Central, and East Texas, who collectively constituted a majority of the electorate."[17]

Each day he entered his office in Austin, Campbell knew there was a kind of political tide rising in early twentieth-century America, one that had more women seeking greater voices in politics, and one that saw working-class resistance to business empires. And as he hovered above the day-to-day legislative manuevers at the statehouse, Campbell grew increasingly attached to the notion that his best role was as a steward of civic order, someone who used state government, first and foremost, to keep the peace and enforce the laws. At his desk, he could sense that there was a bustle in the Texas heartland, that there were plenty of callused workers in the oil patches, farms, and fields developing cynical views of both big businessmen and career politicians. Campbell decided that what Texans wanted more than anything was consistency. If that meant a modicum of regulation, something that probably struck his enemies as creeping progressivism, then so be it. Campbell, in the end, wanted Texas to avoid becoming unmoored in uncertain times.

Campbell knew that in the larger cities and a handful of smaller towns, "women's clubs" were emerging—many committed to either charitable work or a moral battle against alcohol. In 1907, the Anti-Saloon League began in Texas.[18] In Houston, a trio of Finnigan sisters—Annette, Elizabeth, and Katherine—had created the Equal Suffrage League in 1903 and now were attempting to rally women around the state.[19] They organized another statewide group, the Texas Woman Suffrage Association, with Annette Finnigan as president. It staged a convention, and then the sisters traveled across Texas, urging women to open several other chapters.

In Austin in 1908, a women's suffrage club was organized.[20] The sisters assumed, hoped, they could galvanize supporters, but instead they found that many women were interested but "too timid to organize."[21] While they retreated to Houston to figure out how to battle the ingrained sexism, Granbury state representative Jess Baker tried to pass a constitutional amendment granting women voting power. He had pushed for a full two decades, but his measures kept being defeated.[22]

To the alarm of the white men dominating the statehouse, there were other troubling uprisings: thousands of workers were joining the Texas State Federation of Labor, which affiliated itself with the American Federation of Labor. The labor groups had long lists of goals, including ending convict leasing, raising wages, safeguarding factories, and stopping child labor. The Texas Farmers Union formed in 1902, and in five years grew to one hundred thousand members and became a taproot for the National Farmers Union. Around the state, other organizing fires were being lit: dockworkers in Galveston tried to coalesce, and in Houston, streetcar workers tried to do the same. And in a remote patch of North Texas, real trouble was brewing.

Seventy-five miles west of Fort Worth, Thurber was the center of a bustling coal-mining operation fueling the rambling expansion of the railroads. Thousands of dirt-poor Italian, Polish, and Mexican immigrants stepped off the trains after being lured by the siren song of good-paying jobs. Instead, "the miners were kept in peonage," while "anyone suspected of union sympathies was invariably beaten by company guards and certainly expelled. Miners worked 12.5 hours per day, six days a week."[23]

The miners and their families lived in stick-and-tar-paper shacks, scrambled for food and water, and were siloed into zones where they could speak their native tongues. Most had no understanding of alternate possibilities in Texas. As the mining operations expanded and more people were packed onto the prairie and inside the choking coal operations, union organizers from outside Texas set their sights on Thurber. Some began secretly infiltrating the mining camps afer cutting holes in fences meant to keep workers in and agitators out.

In 1903, a dead man was found close to an active mine. Word bounced around the encampments that he was a newly arrived labor organizer, perhaps of Mexican heritage, and that he had been brutally murdered— maybe by the white security guards, maybe by a Texas Ranger, maybe by a vigilante group. With the news spreading about the body in the ditch, several workers gathered to talk about their lives: children were sick, more men were on the job round the clock, and more families were barely able to bring food back to their tents and shacks. The handful of miners agreed to organize with help from United Mine Workers of America agents, some of whom were convinced they had never seen more abject, abysmal working conditions than those in Texas.[24]

The rebellion spread to the other disparate immigrant silos inside the mining camps, and "by 1907, every worker in town belonged to a union."[25] Thurber became the first "closed shop" in the nation, with any newly arrived miners required to join the union. In Austin, Dallas, and Houston, political and business leaders were unhinged—and they were hearing from angry Texas Rangers and local city officials about other people and movements making trouble around the state.

In San Antonio and then Fort Worth, C. W. Woodman was publishing pro-union newspapers and had become close friends with American Federation of Labor (AFL) leader Samuel Gompers (who died in San Antonio and had a statue erected in his honor in that city—a statue that became a long source of debate over both its artistic and civic merits). Woodman had raced to Thurber to help set up the union, and he celebrated the mining camp strikes in his Fort Worth paper, the *Union Banner*. Woodman hoped Thurber would become a national symbol, a kind of Alamo for ordinary workers who wanted to fight big business interests in America. Maybe the waves of blue-collar workers washing over Texas could collapse the conservative Democratic firmament.

Woodman wasn't alone in wondering if this was the time for a massive populist political revolution. As he roamed Texas, he could see the state bubbling with restless workers doing backbreaking work in factories and mines, on docks and oil rigs. He could also see that other people in the state were frightening the ensemble of Confederate sympathizers and anti-union conservatives huddling in Austin. A Harvard-educated attorney in Dallas, George Edwards, was taking an unusually aggressive interest in civil rights—especially after learning about the horrible housing conditions endured by cotton mill workers in South Dallas. He decided to spread the word through *The Laborer*, a publication that became the first official organ of the Texas State Federation of Labor. He didn't stop there. Edwards began accepting Black legal clients; he started free schools for the mill worker families; and he pushed state leaders to enact child labor laws (which weren't enforced until after the establishment of the Bureau of Labor Statistics in 1909).[26]

In the private clubs and fraternal organizations in the heart of Dallas, where wings of a revived and freshly emboldened Ku Klux Klan were taking shape, people began wondering what the hell was happening with men like Edwards, Woodman, and anyone else working with Blacks, unions, and God knows who else. In San Antonio, in the exclusive Travis Club, the private members were saying the same thing.

Edwards, for one, seemed unafraid. His willingness to represent Blacks was startling, as was his running for governor on the Socialist Party ticket in 1906. He and Woodman were among the earliest, boldest adherents of a Texas strain of iconoclastic political activism, one that would serve as an ongoing irritant to leaders from the two-party system. Like Norris Cuney and others, they served as lightning rods for future political movements, ones that moved sometimes gingerly and sometimes boldly outside the usual frameworks. Too, they served as cautionary lessons for how outsider political movements were dealt with in Texas—for demonstrating how Texas often doubled down on its resistance to equal access to the corridors of political power.

For a while, Woodman and Edwards dreamed that the staggering oil treasures at Spindletop and other places were going to lead unionizing drives in Humble, Sour Lake, Batson, and Saratoga to spread west across Texas.[27] They knew that back in Thurber, once the very heart of the promising uprising in Texas, the battle was ending. Coal began losing some of its currency, especially with industries turning to oil. The hardscrabble boomtown—and the union organizers—began fading.

Today, if you drive by the old coal fields, all you might see is someone with a metal detector looking for pieces of the past. Coal's greatest, lasting legacy in Texas is in Austin, where the miners in Thurber had inspired frantic meetings to talk about how to use state government to smash any labor rabble-rousers.

In 1901, a tenant farmer and cowboy named Gregorio Cortez, who lived on the Thulmeyer ranch west of Kenedy, heard the hoofbeats of mounted sheriffs and deputies thudding toward him. They were chasing down a horse thief, and they wanted to know what he knew. The tense questioning spiraled out of control, and Cortez wound up shooting one of the sheriffs dead. He fled, embarking on an almost eighty-mile journey in the general direction of Austin.

In another shootout in Gonzales County, another sheriff was killed, perhaps by Cortez. The desperate man kept moving, going another one hundred miles to the home of a friend who could loan him a horse and help him light out for Laredo, where maybe he could disappear inside the swirl and hum of the border.

As he traveled, Cortez's name was splayed across front pages around the nation. Texas editorials called for his capture and lynching, and in Austin, lawmakers were demanding that Governor Joseph D. Sayers—another ex-Confederate general—make Cortez an example of what happens when a Mexican man goes to war with the law. Cortez stayed on the run, a phantom, and then questions began to emerge about whether he had been set up as a pawn and falsely accused. The *patrones*, Texas Rangers, and state lawmakers were receiving reports that Cortez had become a folk hero: that Mexicans were shouting his name and taking to the streets in solidarity in dozens of small towns along the Rio Grande. Hundreds of armed men fanned out across Texas to hunt him. And in small town after small town, they heard reports that Cortez had just left, after being fed and clothed by families who had welcomed him into their homes. He traveled five hundred miles, sometimes on a borrowed horse, sometimes on foot. In Cotulla,

Gregorio Cortez, a tenant farmer and horseman suspected of shooting and killing two lawmen, eluded capture for ten days, becoming a folk hero to some Latino Texans. He was later convicted, then pardoned.

Bolton & Mitchell,   LAREDO, TEXAS.

he mingled with crowds and then disappeared again. More posses began to chase him, including one that had three hundred riders. Cortez walked along the Texas-Mexico border for almost 120 miles, constantly evading the Texas Rangers—and in villages and on sprawling farms, people composed ballads about his ability to escape the dreaded state police. There were other casualties of the hunt and the rising hate aimed at Latinos: at least nine people of Mexican descent were killed.

As news spread about how a thin Mexican cowboy had made a mockery of the biggest manhunt in Texas, a frustrated Governor Sayers announced a reward for Cortez's capture. After a full ten days as a fugitive, Cortez was finally cornered and captured after someone tipped off the Rangers. Sayers was relieved, especially after hearing reports that some political leaders in San Antonio were coalescing to support the fugitive— maybe in sympathy, maybe in a fit of enlightened self-interest because they didn't want pro-Cortez protests in the city. The big local papers had painted one portrait of Cortez as the cunning leader of a gang of thieves, but elswhere in San Antonio, and throughout South Texas and into northern Mexico, Cortez was already a folk hero—the man who had made fools of the mighty Texas Rangers.

Cortez was convicted of murder, but in San Antonio, two community leaders, Pablo Cruz and Francisco Chapa, both of whom helped run

Spanish-language newspapers, pushed for his exoneration and pardon. Chapa owned a pharmacy, served on the San Antonio board of education, and published *El Imparcial de Texas*. He was a Republican, but one who had denounced the Mexican Revolution and was trusted by many old-guard conservative Democrats, including Oscar Colquitt, the state senator, Texas railroad commissioner, and new governor. Chapa petitioned Colquitt to take a long look at Cortez's case—and to turn the eyes of lawmakers in Austin toward the growing revolutionary unrest spilling across the border. With urging from Chapa, and maybe to keep the peace in unpredictable parts of South Texas, Colquitt would eventually pardon the famous Cortez.

Five years after Cortez began his ramble, there were more troubles in South Texas. A Black officer with the 25th Infantry in Brownsville was accused of attacking a white woman. Throughout the Rio Grande Valley, all the way to Austin, stories percolated about shots ringing out, or armed white vigilantes attacking Black soldiers, or Black troops breaking ranks and running wild.[28] Orders came down from Washington for a federal investigation. Finally, 167 Black soldiers were dishonorably discharged by President Theodore Roosevelt.

Through it all, there were more national headlines and stories that read like postcards from another world—ones that reinforced, to people in Washington and elsewhere, the gnawing sense that Texas remained an unfathomable outpost. And as each new generation of Texas politicians scrambled to power, the lawmakers were going to be inheriting and facing that accumulated history—those images, those flashpoints, those defining moments like the hunt for Gregorio Cortez and the unhinged moments among dozens of federal troops in a Texas town upriver from the Gulf of Mexico.

For every major political leader in the state, there would always be that acutely personal decision: how exactly to respond to the struggles, the ambitions, the inequities, and the chaos that seemed to define the passionate nation of Texas.

CHAPTER 5

Legislative Rest: The 1910s

ON THE SECOND-TO-LAST DAY OF a bitterly cold February, people were going door-to-door near downtown Dallas, trying to find a lost little girl. It was 1910, and two-year-old Mary Buvens had been missing for most of the day. Rescuers fanned out across the city, and then the news came in: a search party announced that it had discovered the child in a barn loft off Ross Avenue—and that they had also found a Negro, sixty-five-year-old Allen Brooks, with her.

Brooks was well known to many people in and around the areas on the northern and eastern edges of the growing city. The burly man was someone you would summon when you needed outhouses cleaned or coal hauled for your stove. The horrified parents of the young girl asked a physician to examine her, and Dr. W. W. Brandau announced that there was "evidence of brutal treatment, though the perpetrator had not been entirely successful." After Brooks was taken into custody, Brandau also examined him. He said there was physical evidence that backed up his belief that the little girl had been attacked.

County sheriffs huddled to decide what to do. Dallas, more than many places in the nation, had enthusiastically embraced a very clear segregationist code even as it strove to present an image and a reputation as a reliable center of business, a crossroads of commerce that was amenable to investors and entrepreneurs. A decision was made to move Brooks out of town until he could be tried. Over the next few days, he was shipped to Fort Worth, Denton, Sherman, and McKinney—and finally brought back to Dallas in March and held on the second floor of the looming red sandstone county courthouse that had been built in 1892. A court-appointed attorney was ostensibly looking into witnesses who might help prove Brooks's innocence. The Dallas sheriff ordered guards to provide extra protection.

Early on Thursday morning, a crowd of 250 men punched and battled past the line of officers in the courthouse. The mob plowed upstairs, surrounded the terrified Brooks, and pushed him toward a tall, wood-framed window. Six men standing on the street tossed a rope up. With Brooks held tight, a noose was put around his neck. The men out on the street yanked hard on the rope, and Brooks was heaved out the window. He slammed two stories down, landing head first, and his blood seeped into the street. It was unclear if he was dead or unconscious.

The rope was still around his neck while several people with knives slashed at him. Then they dragged his body down Main Street toward the Elks Arch, a three-story-high white-and-blue steel structure that was crowned with lights, fake antlers, and a large statue of an elk. The lights on the sign spelled out a message in giant letters: "Welcome Visitors."

Brooks's pulpy corpse was strung up on one of the few Bell Telephone poles in the city. Hundreds of people pushed into the street for a better view. Within hours, five thousand gawkers had gathered, some captured by photographers as they milled about the torture scene. As often happened, the photographs would be sold as souvenirs. And, again, people would try to bring home a keepsake from the event, including pieces of the dead man's clothing. After a failed attempt to set fire to his body, the rope holding the old man was sliced, and his body came tumbling down. The crowd dispersed into the cold Dallas afternoon, no one was charged, and city officials said they couldn't identify any of the men who had abducted and killed the Negro.

Once again, no evidence exists that the most influential state lawmakers had boldly and publicly rallied to condemn what had happened on the main streets of one of the state's leading cities. There was a lynching in Texas every month for the next four months. On July 29, a fevered slaughter of perhaps as many as two hundred Black residents occurred in Anderson County, near the community of Slocum. Some said it was initially tied to a white farmer killing a Black man he claimed owed him money—and that white residents were afraid there would be some sort of a Negro uprising or revolt. It was nothing less than a full-on riot of hate, a cascading attack by white residents on Black families, and one that even shocked Sheriff William Black: "Men were going round killing Negroes as fast as they could find them and so far as I was able to ascertain without any real cause. These Negroes have done no wrong that I could discover. There was just a hot headed gang hunting them down and killing them."[1]

This time, some lawmakers demanded that the Texas Rangers do something. Skeptics could argue it was because Black citizens had decided to pick up scythes and defend themselves—and because the cornerstones of the local economy, the tenant farmer and sharecropper systems, were in jeopardy. Blacks weren't just attacking back; they also weren't working in the cotton fields. A troop of Texas Rangers was sent from Austin, and in time the nightmare in Slocum vanished from the news and perhaps even from posterity.

Elsewhere in Texas, the ghoulish season of murder and retribution marched on. In the late fall of 1910, another mob of whites went hunting, this time 175 miles west of Austin. A twenty-year-old cowboy named Antonio Rodríguez had been arrested in connection with the murder of a white woman at a Rocksprings ranch. When the crowd came for Rodríguez, they drenched him in oil and quickly set him on fire. The news about his being burned at the stake traveled to the Texas border towns and then all the way to Mexico City—where some people took to the streets demanding justice or some form of reparation.

In 1914, as the United States was nervously watching the revolutionary movement in Mexico, President Woodrow Wilson ordered US troops to invade Veracruz and occupy the city—ostensibly in response to anti-American sentiment and sailors being arrested when they wandered into restricted areas in Tampico. The lingering occupation of Veracruz by US forces was condemned in Mexico and in parts of Texas. One newspaper, *El Progreso* in Laredo, decided to publish a scathing editorial by the Mexican revolutionary Manuel García Vigil that attacked Wilson and the American soldiers who had taken over Veracruz. Quickly, lawmakers and Texas Rangers began planning their own invasion of the Laredo newspaper, suspecting it of being a mouthpiece for radicals wanting to import revolution across the border.

When a squad of armed Rangers arrived in Laredo and headed to the newspaper, it was ready to barrel inside and hammer away at the printing

Jovita Idár once stared down a contingent of Texas Rangers bent on shuttering a border newspaper. She ultimately settled in San Antonio, where she opened a free kindergarten, pushed for women's rights, and fought for social justice.

presses. But when the Rangers approached *El Progreso*, they were surprised to see a slender, short, stern-faced newswoman standing at the front door.

The twenty-nine-year-old reporter-editor Jovita Idár remained in the doorway and announced that the Rangers would have to go through her to get inside. The men conferred, whispered, looked back at her, and then retreated on their horses. The next day, when they knew Idár was going to be away, the Rangers returned. They broke in, smashed furniture, dismantled the presses, and began arresting journalists. The news about the invasion bounced around Laredo, across the border, and up and down the chain of cities along the Rio Grande. Jovita Idár's reputation began to spread along with the news.

She was one of eight children born to a civil rights leader and editor, Nicasio Idár, who had opened a Spanish-language newspaper, *La Crónica*, that promoted education and economic improvement along the border. Idár went to work in Webb County as a teacher in Los Ojuelos, another dusty, hidden community with no running water, stick shacks, and fewer than two hundred people. Outraged by the living conditions, she decided to join her father as a writer at *La Crónica*. She began reporting on the grinding lack of health care and living wages—and did it under several pen names, including A. V. Negra (*ave negra* is "black bird" in Spanish) and Astrea (the Greek goddess of justice).

Her paper chronicled political and cultural realities ignored by white-owned newspapers throughout the state, from segregation to lynchings and whippings. She even wrote stories and editorials accusing the Catholic Church of mistreating women—and she suggested that Latina women needed to assume their rightful place in the vanguard of social change.

In 1911, *La Crónica* also promoted the Orden Caballeros de Honor, an organization pushing for changes in South Texas. In turn, it led to the creation of the First Mexican Congress, which put journalist-activists like Idár in touch with other political leaders in the state. Idár began encouraging more women to attend their first political gatherings, and then she founded the Liga Femenil Mexicanista (League of Mexican Women) to unite working-class women in South Texas trying to open free public schools.

Idár's insistent, widening work kept lawmakers in Austin and Washington, DC, aware that there was a population along the Texas-Mexico border that was both growing and feeling political power. She had decided that the attack on her newspaper at the hands of the Texas Rangers was not an isolated incident—that they were often on a march through the borderlands, from El Paso to Brownsville, enforcing a white supremacist ethos under the banner of protecting the United States against the Mexican Revolution. And, by 1913, she was risking her life again—at the hands of Texas Rangers and Mexican soldiers—by crossing the border and volunteering to care for wounded revolutionaries. When her father died, Idár took over publication of *La Crónica* and also helped found *Evolución*, yet another newspaper that centered on improving living and working conditions for the poor, Tejanos, immigrants, and women.

By the summer of 1915, fears about an imminent invasion by Mexican revolutionaries were reaching a dizzying level. More lawmakers and Texas Rangers were talking about a document, the "Plan de San Diego," that had allegedly been composed months earlier by radicals in San Diego, Texas, and that said Tejanos, Native Americans, Mexicans, and Blacks would form a "liberating army" that would wage war, kill all adult white men, and form a new nation by taking back the Mexican territories stretching along the border from Texas to California.

As the spring rains ceased and the grinding heat came on in full force along the Rio Grande, a handful of small roving guerrilla bands were downing telegraph lines. Shots were fired at trains moving through the Valley. Local sheriffs told the Texas Rangers that they were overwhelmed, and the state police arrived again. Edgy *patrones*, anxious to protect the irrigation canals, created the Law and Order League, an armed vigilante group, to control the streets by any means necessary.

In September, Rangers patrolling Hidalgo County captured twelve men and decided to hang them—and then leave them on display. Three weeks later, the Rangers hanged four more men after an attack on a passenger train on the outskirts of Brownsville.[2] By early 1916, any rebellions inspired by the San Diego plan were over, but the paybacks seemed to multiply, encouraged by the specific and tacit endorsement of Austin lawmakers. Around the state, Mexican Americans and Tejanos sometimes disappeared, or their white supporters were threatened.

One South Texas attorney, an Anglo convinced that the Rangers were committing crimes, was pistol-whipped inside a courthouse.[3] The attacks spiked as the Mexican Revolution lingered, as the rebel leader Pancho Villa roamed across the border, and as the United States was sucked into World War I—with leaders in Texas and Washington wondering if Germany was in league with Mexico. The perfect storm pressed down on the hundreds of thousands of workers who had come to South Texas for work or to flee the uncertainties in their home country.

The Texas Rangers essentially had carte blanche to take action, but lawmakers also granted the governor the power to hire even more new officers, the so-called Loyalty Rangers. The aim was to have posses of Rangers roaming the length of the Rio Grande, where there still might be entrenched radicals sneaking into neighborhoods and organizing sporadic attacks on businesses, railroads, and the telegraph lines, and maybe hijacking the usual political processes. Outright hatred of Texas Rangers was already entrenched, but it had reached a new, stark level. In Laredo, in Roma, in Weslaco and McAllen, people gathered and accused the Rangers of driving Latino political participation to dramatically low levels—and turning their scare tactics on Latino officials.

Books, monuments, and even museums would be dedicated to the singular notion of the Rangers as heroes who traveled the land in a romantic cloud of dust: bringing killers like John Wesley Hardin or bank robbers like Sam Bass to heel; barreling into the kudzu-covered woods of East Texas to quash the utter lawlessness after the Civil War; roaming from El Paso to Brownsville to catch criminals and maybe keep Mexico on alert; and trying, often valiantly, to keep Texas from imploding from its excesses, greed, and land lust. Much good work was done to maintain law and political order, without question, and it was often well chronicled.

But the awful brutalities were also often ignored. The bloody lynchings and murders of Mexicans, Tejanos, and Mexican Americans are some of the most egregious instances of state-sanctioned violence in not just Texas history but US history. One observer put it in stark terms: "Between 1915 and 1919, hundreds—if not thousands—of Mexicans and Tejanos in South Texas were killed by the Rangers and other vigilantes."[4]

In 1917, Jovita Idár moved north from Laredo to San Antonio and quickly immersed herself in grassroots politics. She arrived knowing that the Democratic Party was still the dominant force but also that it was evolving in South Texas. A few populists, a few more progressives, and the random socialist were still inspired by the upheavals in Mexico, and thinking of entering the Democratic ranks. She believed that a kind of political melting pot was coalescing in the worlds south of San Antonio and Corpus Christi. And she was well aware that there were sparks of resistance to the jackboot Texas Rangers and even the old political bosses.

The local Democratic leaders anointed by the ranching barons and oil kings realized the expediency of allowing a handful of Latinos to participate in local politics. It was the political process that a Dallas writer would describe as "the accommodation."[5] Basically, it involved power brokers "allowing" people of color some semblance of control in their communities, but only on their side of the railroad tracks, and usually only in narrowly focused arenas like segregated school systems. And it involved identifying malleable, willing community leaders who would always ultimately swing votes to the *patrón*-approved candidates.

Idár could see the accommodation in action, the way some local leaders were being bought off with the hope that they'd be able to tamp down any political organizing or unrest in their neighborhoods. In San Antonio, she was determined to form new political vanguards, ones that wouldn't be compromised—and she continued to lay the groundwork for grassroots political movements by emphasizing economic independence and education as the precursors to political power. She opened a free kindergarten, worked as a Spanish-language interpreter at a county hospital, and served as editor of yet another newspaper, *El Heraldo Cristiano*. Given her city's large, ever-growing Latino population and its deep-rooted ties to Mexico, Idár nurtured a new political awareness—one that could take place only in polyglot San Antonio. Her spade work, her building a political awareness in San Antonio, would come to full fruition many years later when some Latino leaders from that city began shaking up the normal order in Texas.

In 1946, national newspapers and movie newsreels would note the passing of two famous, once-powerful people: twenty-year-old Ananda Mahidol, the king of Thailand, was discovered in his bedroom bleeding from what appeared to be a self-inflicted Colt .45 gunshot to his forehead. And Jack Johnson, the first Black man to become the world heavyweight boxing champion, died after the car he was driving from his native Texas to New York smashed into a light pole in a small North Carolina city.

At almost the exact same time in Texas, Jovita Idár also passed away—and though her death was hardly noted, mourners who gathered to see her buried in the old San Jose Burial Park in San Antonio knew that she was an extraordinary figure in the history of Texas. Her influence begins in those heated, grinding days of mayhem and murder—the unrelenting days of rage, lynching, political neglect, and suppression.

Oscar Branch Colquitt, the blustery and stout lobbyist, lawyer, East Texas newspaper publisher, and state senator, had become governor in the early winter of 1911. He was yet another tried-and-true son of the South and had been born in Georgia, where his father served in the Confederacy. His uncle Alfred Colquitt had also worn gray and risen to the rank of brigadier general. According to some accounts, the Colquitts came to Texas after they failed at conscripting freed slaves to do farmwork in Georgia, so the family decided to relocate to the more welcoming regions of East Texas.

Using his newspapers as a springboard, Colquitt was elected to the Texas Senate and then became a railroad commissioner. He ran for governor in 1910 under the slogan "political peace and legislative rest"—but from the outset he faced nagging debates about socially conservative issues. (For the next one hundred years, Texas lawmakers would find themselves in thorny disputes on how to handle matters of religion, gambling, and alcohol.) For Colquitt, Prohibition was an especially unsettling topic, and the pro-alcohol governor found himself confronting a majority of "dry" members in the Texas House and Senate. Perhaps it all led to his becoming a bellicose disrupter, someone with "stormy relations with the legislature," and who "quarreled with friends, feuded with other officials, and waged relentless war on his opponents within the [Democratic] party."[6] His lack of tact carried over into arguments about whether he was even really up to handling security along the Mexican border.

In his office in Austin, he had another glaring issue to address—what it meant for Texas as tens of thousands of newcomers pressed into the state in the wake of the railroad expansions and tales of black gold. Colquitt understood that the sheer size of Texas demanded at least a modicum of regulation, and he gingerly supported some centralized plans that wouldn't threaten many of his wealthy supporters: state hospitals, state schools for "delinquent" girls, workplace safety laws, and unification of the state prison system. Colquitt rallied other Southern governors to raise the prices on cotton. And in his second term, he pushed for schoolchildren in Texas to receive free textbooks. He urged the creation of state agencies to oversee the safety of children and animals, and he even backed a modest form of worker's compensation.

But, like his predecessors, Colquitt's ties to the core beliefs of the Lost Cause and the Restoration were steady and apparent. He never strayed from the very narrow view of equal rights held by his predecessors. After he left office in 1915, he tried unsuccessfully to run for the US Senate, then went to Dallas to run an oil company. Today, he is buried, along with several other governors, in Oakwood Cemetery, that first city resting place in Austin, surrounded by a few old homes, a university baseball field, and encroaching condominiums. His final lair looks like his tenure in office— careful, blunt, and deliberate.

If there were clues to how his administration would turn out, they were there in James Edward "Pa" Ferguson's childhood. Born into a farming family, the affable-looking Ferguson was booted out of his prairie school, Salado College, for being disruptive and unruly. Even though he lacked a formal legal education, he was able to get a law license with the cunning help of family friends—and Ferguson knew early on about the power of patronage and backroom wheeling and dealing.

All over the state, people were scrambling to scoop up pieces of property, and Ferguson wanted into the real estate game. Always angling to find symbiotic business plays, he helped form a bank in Temple. As he amassed money, name recognition, and a sphere of influence, he studied the way so many Texans were adamantly against big government taking away the right to drink alcohol. He threw his support behind lawmakers who were against Prohibition, including Gov. Colquitt. The more Ferguson leaned into the pro-wet forces, the more comfortable he became at a dais, stage, or podium.

In Austin, Democrats were squabbling over who would eventually replace Colquitt, and Ferguson saw his opening. By 1914, he knew how to deliver a speech in an assuring, folksy manner, and he enjoyed donning a good suit, shaking hands and telling people that he was their friend

"Farmer Jim." In real time, Ferguson was inventing a prototype that hundreds of future Texas politicians would insist on aping: the down-home and even self-anointed leader, a self-made man who was out to offer Texans his Lone Star version of noblesse oblige. Ferguson committed himself to being a political chameleon, the kind who could change stripes, and even his attire, in order to mingle with small-town farmers or Houston bankers. Texas, he had decided, was ready for his kind of campaign, one in which he'd insist he was a good pal to both the white working farmers and the white oilmen in the big cities—and, without having to aggressively repeat it, a staunch opponent to any uppity people of color diluting the political process.

As he bumped along the unpaved roads in Gonzales or the cobblestone streets of Dallas, Ferguson studied the distinct political groups anyone seeking state office would now have to court. Texas was hurtling into an urban age, it was coming faster and faster, and anyone who wanted to occupy the governor's office would have to have a carefully mapped-out plan to court people in Pampa as well as Houston.

On the strength of his soothing speechifying and his studied malleability, Ferguson easily won the governor's race. But almost instantly it became clear to the veteran lobbyists, lawyers, and aides in the statehouse that Ferguson might have been brilliant at campaigning but had no clue about how to handle the massive shifts in Texas demographics. At the time he was sworn in, almost half the farmers in Texas were leasing their land, and many were struggling to make their payments. It was easy to find families barely surviving day to day in falling-down cabins, with little access to education; dry goods; or city, county, or state services. Despite promises by lawmakers to provide safety checks for children, many minors were still working grueling hours on the land their parents rented—and plenty of freedmen and their descendants were still mired in a world that wasn't that dissimilar from the slave days of the Old South.

Moving into the governor's mansion and then strolling to the statehouse in January 1915, the straight-backed "Farmer Jim" was almost blind to the surges coming his way. Some brave state lawmakers were racing to pass laws regulating working conditions for miners and moving to limit a woman's workday to nine hours. When they visited Ferguson, he struck them as an amiable man who had unknowingly parachuted into a hectic battle zone with lawmakers pushing and pulling in different directions. As the months wore on, Austin veterans decided that Ferguson was more and more lost. Running for office was one thing, governing was another. Ferguson struggled to get only a single law passed, one that would establish limits on the rents large Texas landowners could charge farmers—but the bill was later overturned.

Around the city, talk mounted that Ferguson was in over his head and, worse, spending too much time figuring out ways to help old business friends. Ferguson heard the talk and began promoting himself as "Pa" Ferguson, the kindly leader of Texas. But in Austin, a growing cadre of jaded political operatives were saying he was really just a bored country club kid. Critics accused him of cooking deals and stacking several institutions with his allies. He booted out the head of Prairie View Normal and Industrial College—a man who had fought against his gubernatorial campaign. Meanwhile, for anyone hoping that Ferguson would be a man for all the people, not just some of the people, it was becoming clear that his racist philosophies were marked by the "contention that a Negro has no business whatever taking a part in the political affairs of the Democratic party, the white man's party."[7]

As he struggled to run Texas, a rebellion was uncorking just a few blocks away. At the University of Texas, administrators and professors had begun meeting and then publicly exposing the growing number of Ferguson's political favors. The governor wanted the school regents to fire the faculty members criticizing him. When they refused, Ferguson demanded that lawmakers slash the school's funding. A livid Ferguson told friends that the university was out of touch with ordinary people, and he promised "the biggest bear fight that has ever taken place in the history of the state of Texas."[8]

His obsession was teetering on the edge of a full-on meltdown, and even some of his allies said he was going too far—and that maybe he just needed to come clean about the real reasons he wanted to cut funding for the university. Ferguson dug in deeper and simply replied:

"I don't have to give reasons, I am the Governor of Texas."[9]

In May 1916, a Black seventeen-year-old man from Waco was arrested in connection with the killing of a fifty-three-year-old white woman. Jesse Washington confessed to murdering Lucy Fryer, though some in his community had their doubts about how his admission came about. The police decided to ship Washington to Dallas, telling people it was for his safety, while vigilantes gathered in Waco, talking about how to mete out justice. A week after the murder, Washington was shipped back to Waco. On May 15, 1916, a jury of twelve white men found him guilty, in four minutes.[10] In

Austin, Ferguson, the purported champion of the common man in Texas, had a full week to assess the bloody possibilities that could emerge in Waco. He really didn't have to think hard, or long. A self-proclaimed student of Texas history, he knew very well what could happen to a Black man accused of a crime against a white woman.

Waco officials walked Washington down the back stairs of the courthouse, and there he was turned over to a gang of white men, who wrapped a heavy chain around his neck. Washington was knocked to the ground, and several of the men began tugging him along the caked streets of Waco. His body scraping over the stones and mud, his head slamming into the ground, Washington no doubt heard the shouts and could see the white children—brought by their parents—bobbing and laughing. Washington's clothes were shredding, he was gasping for air, and when he was dropped in front of City Hall, his captors were also breathing hard.

Washington was pummeled and hacked with knives, and blood seeped into the City Hall grounds. Texas had seen this before—and Waco had seen it a decade earlier during the lynching of Sank Majors. Some men prepared a pile of dry-goods boxes. They poured coal oil on the mound. And then they drizzled the oil all over Washington's open wounds. By now, there were as many as ten thousand people watching. He was dragged to a tree, hung from a thick limb, and then lowered like a piece of dead hog up and down over the roaring fire. For two hours, his body was mutilated and scarred in the stoked flames. People came and went, cheering as a dry breeze spread the smell of burning flesh.

Eventually someone pulled out another knife and sliced the rope, and Washington's oozing remains were put in a bag and dragged six miles south to the small outpost of Robinson—where Fryer, the woman Washington was accused of killing, was from. The bag was ripped open, and the fractured, barely contained remnants of the Black teen were strung up again, this time on a power pole. Washington remained on display long enough for the message to sink in. Then he was cut down, and some locals buried him in a pauper's grave.

The latest horror in Waco boomeranged from Texas around the nation and then back to the statehouse. Even the most vengeful lawmakers knew that what had happened could linger nationally. The NAACP stepped up its anti-lynching efforts, urging Texans to consider passing new laws to crack down on the murders. It was as if Texas continued to march forward, but then would stall and even reflexively retreat into hideously dark habits from the past. Human nature is what it is, and deciding how to change it is an unending question. One step, many would say, was for a state's political leader to point the way, to boldly condemn and outlaw the heinous redundancies, to use the power of high office, as much as was legally possible, to make sure that the tortures and killings were ended—not to erase the memories of those crimes, but to simply stop the crimes from being endlessly repeated.

For decades, there were whipping or hanging trees all over Texas—on the outskirts of the smallest towns and even in the heart of the biggest city. In Houston, many Black residents would point to a looming tree immediately adjacent to the cemetery where the most influential white founders of the city were buried. Many simply knew it as "the hanging tree." You could also find the trees in the winding, hidden roads around the dark, cloudy waters of the Navasota River. In the heart of Seguin, there is still a weathered, somber-looking tree that older locals call the "whipping oak," directly across from the Guadalupe County Courthouse. Sometimes, brave people would cut these trees down, as if trying to eliminate at least one place where another murder could be committed. But often, the trees were left alone, because people feared what would happen to their families if they tried to take them down. They are still there, sprinkled around the state.

It was now as if there were two states of Texas: the lonely, hidden parts where nightmares were inflicted and endured, and the public face, the one that seemingly marched forward with unbridled optimism and pep, despite the violence in the woods outside Lufkin and down to Brownsville. And by 1917, the initial burst of enthusiasm for a Texas proselytizer like Ferguson was wearing thin. In just two years, he was living proof of the way things can go off the rails when the political grease is applied too brazenly.

A Travis County grand jury formally accused him of embezzlement and misusing state money. State lawmakers opened their own investigation, and Ferguson found himself facing twenty-one articles of impeachment, and a slew of accusations that would linger for years, including failing to enforce banking laws and accepting over $150,000 from German officials who, with World War I under way, wanted the governor of Texas to blast the idea of a military draft.

The Texas Senate convened a court of impeachment, and lawmakers voted 25–3 to convict Ferguson on ten charges of financial abuse. Ferguson huddled quickly with his aides and advisors and decided to quit before he was forced from office. He resigned on August 25, 1917. His many opponents in Texas, including proponents of a woman's right to vote, had thrown their support behind impeachment. So had all the people he had angered at the University of Texas and in the ranks of the Prohibitionists.

In Austin, political consultants and state senators and representatives held emergency meetings. Texas needed a steady hand, a diplomat, someone whose very presence sitting at the governor's desk would suggest that the state was back on track—and not veering into a whirlpool of corruption and vigilante mayhem. They decided they had at least one unflappable and unthreatening presence waiting in the wings: Lieutenant Governor William P. Hobby.

To the garrulous and chatty Ferguson, Hobby was always just a studious, rich dullard who would never be able to connect with the sweat-stained farmers of Texas—and probably another elitist like the ones who roamed the University of Texas campus. Ferguson told friends that Hobby was just a short, big-eared newspaper publisher, someone who had dutifully climbed the political ladders in Texas but had no spark or cleverness. Ferguson mocked him and said he was "a misfit whom God had failed to endow with the physical attributes that make up a man."[11]

Born in Moscow, Texas, the wavy-haired Hobby had risen through the newspaper ranks as a writer for the *Houston Post* and then co-owner of the *Beaumont Enterprise*. He began showing up at Democratic Party meetings in Houston, striking many in the city and then around the state as a sober, serious man committed to the party's conservative Southern platforms. Democratic leaders saw Hobby as a kind of calm adjunct to the ham-fisted Ferguson, and Hobby was elected lieutenant governor in 1914, then reelected in 1916. When Ferguson was impeached and ousted, and Hobby finally took over the governor's office, there was a sigh of relief around Austin. He was the youngest man, at thirty-nine, to serve as governor, and he seemed to bring a sense of calm or at least a modicum of honor to the office.

As Hobby prepared to move into the governor's office, the political cognoscenti in Texas were measuring Ferguson's legacy. In the pantheon of crooked Texas politicians, Ferguson clearly held a special place. He was a wily candidate and a corrupt leader—and when he was eventually buried in the Texas State Cemetery, his impressive monument would include these words: "He Loved His Fellow Man And Was Generous To A Fault."

Minnie Fisher Cunningham led the Texas Equal Suffrage Association, predecessor to the League of Women Voters of Texas. In 1944, Cunningham made a bold foray into politics; she placed second in the Democratic gubernatorial primary.

After Ferguson was ousted, lawmakers passed a bill, in 1918, allowing women to vote in primary elections and nominating conventions in Texas. It was the first step toward becoming the first Southern state to ratify the Nineteenth Amendment that finally awarded women full, equal voting rights. Moving things along in Texas was the Texas Equal Suffrage Association, led by the pioneering Minnie Fisher Cunningham. Her group would later become the persistently influential League of Women Voters of Texas. The women's organizations introduced kindergarten classes in public schools and laws requiring children between ages eight and fourteen to get an education. They told male lawmakers to consider creating more institutions designed just for girls and to provide pension plans for widows with children.

One of Cunningham's key allies was Annie Blanton, an English professor who had taught at what is now the University of North Texas. With Hobby in office and seemingly in support of a woman's right to vote, Blanton's supporters pushed her to run for state superintendent of public instruction. She endured a smear campaign from pro-Ferguson sources blasting her as an atheist—or a secret shill for politicians pushing Prohibition. But with women finally allowed to cast ballots in primaries, Blanton easily won her summertime 1918 primary race against entrenched incumbents and political professionals, and in the fall she became the first woman elected to statewide office in Texas.

She moved quickly to put her stamp on several issues, including raising wages for teachers and providing more free textbooks. She held office until 1922, then lost a bid to run for Congress, and finally went on to a long tenure as an education professor at the University of Texas, where a residence hall is named after her. Cunningham continued to champion women's rights and encouraged women to forge alliances through the creation of the Delta Kappa Gamma Society in Texas, with eighty chapters opening in thirty-five states.

On January 28, 1918, outside a small town in Presidio County, a posse of Texas Rangers, US Army soldiers, and cowboys coordinated their plans after reports about a series of thefts and shootings. The Rangers rode into the usually quiet village of Porvenir, south of Marfa, rousted people from their sleep, and then went to a nearby ranch and culled fifteen men and boys. In that remote region, a place where echoes can rebound in the night, they marched their captives toward a small hill overlooking the Rio Grande—and then shot each of them at point-blank range. Their names were Antonio Castañeda, Longino Flores, Pedro Herrera, Vivián Herrera, Severiano Herrera, Manuel Moralez, Eutimio González, Ambrosio Hernández, Alberto García, Tiburcio Jáques, Román Nieves, Serapio Jiménez, Pedro Jiménez, Juan Jiménez, and Macedonio Huertas.

For a while, news about the massacre spread only to parts of West Texas. Conflicting accounts emerged, and the affair seemed shrouded in mystery. Some said it was a racist plot designed to play on the lingering fears about the Mexican Revolution. Some said it was just a way of reminding anyone along the border that the Texas Rangers had even the most remote regions under their control. Some insisted that the villagers must have committed crimes—even though their relatives would insist, for years, that they were completely innocent.

Word finally reached Austin about one of the worst mass murders ever committed by state police in America. One lawmaker, José Canales, was beyond shocked. He was born into a well-off cattle ranching family that had inherited the sprawling Spanish land grant Espíritu Santo, which spread across most of Cameron County. He attended the University of Michigan, became a lawyer, and settled in Brownsville. And with the muscle of the South Texas political machine run by the Wells clan, Canales served in the Texas House from 1905 to 1910, representing Cameron, Starr, Hidalgo, and Zapata Counties.

The South Texas political cabal turned its back on him when he endorsed Prohibition, and Canales returned to Cameron County as a super-

José T. Canales, schooled to be a lawyer at the University of Michigan, won election several times to the Texas House from the Texas-Mexico borderlands. He spent years trying to bring the Texas Rangers to justice.

intendent of schools. But in 1917, he returned to Austin and to the Texas House, as the state's only Mexican American legislator.

Three days after the deadly massacre in Porvenir, Canales walked into the statehouse and filed nineteen charges against the Texas Rangers. He had a lot to think about from the minute that he had heard about Porvenir. As he wrote the drafts of his charges against the Rangers, he knew full well they had been given unchecked power by governors and other lawmakers—and were acting as judge, jury, and executioner. Canales made sure to arrive at the statehouse armed with firsthand accounts of the slaughter—ones he said proved the murdered men were unarmed and had been executed even though they hadn't resisted.

The Rangers had wrestled against the festering cauldron of lawlessness after the Civil War, they had raced to many rabid-dog moments in East Texas, and they had proved useful in interrupting any plans Germany may have had to aid Mexico in retaking lost territories north of the Rio Grande. But now, Canales was charging the heralded Texas Rangers with being rogue executioners with a special taste for targeting Latinos.

Canales mapped out a series of bold proposals: he called for the Loyalty Rangers, that adjunct to the Texas Rangers, to be disbanded. He demanded that the regular Texas Rangers be subjected to increased oversight and supervision. And with each proposal, Canales's friends bluntly told him he needed to be careful—that he would be the next person to disappear or be murdered. Canales began to wonder if they were right. He told his family and allies that the legendary Texas Ranger Frank Hamer, a crack shot who routinely roamed miles and miles of Texas, was stalking him—suddenly appearing near Canales in Austin, and even showing up unannounced in Canales's far South Texas congressional district.

What was clear was that Canales's criminal charges against the Rangers were never going anywhere, and in time, accounts of the Porvenir massacre dwindled in the newspapers. For decades, even the most well regarded writers in Texas would hem and haw about the wretched, murderous activities of the Rangers, sometimes politely acknowledging them as overly vigorous excesses. No one was ever convicted in connection with Porvenir, though some Rangers were fired and reassigned.[12]

In Austin, the very idea that a Mexican American man was threatening the Rangers was too much for some lawmakers. He was attacking the private emergency army at the beck and call of the governor. Canales, ostracized and still in personal danger, decided to leave the legislature in 1920 and never run for state office again.

The Rangers continued to loom as an ominous, ongoing presence for many people in Texas, including those still thinking about pushing harder for organized labor. Occasional work shutdowns were happening around the state, hinting to state leaders that a bigger movement was taking root even as World War I raged. For three months in 1917, almost ten thousand members of the Oil Field, Gas Well, and Refinery Workers went on strike. In 1918, streetcar workers set Waco on its heels: "A town of about 36,000 was shut down for four days, a rare act in American history, especially given its illegality during wartime."[13]

The Texas State Federation of Labor (TSFL) and other workers' groups were growing. The TSFL had an estimated fifty thousand members on its 1919 rosters. That same year, hundreds of Dallas construction workers staged a general strike. Local labor leaders in the city and elsewhere in Texas were inspired by a tragedy in San Antonio: a train engine had blown up and killed at least twenty-six men, and charges and countercharges arose over who was to blame. Lawmakers finally decided Texas needed some codified, consistent form of workman's compensation.

It's not that the status quo was being shaken to its core, but there were insistent signs that Texas was going to have to continue to adapt to its changing demographic, its urbanization, and its rapid industrialization.

Women were being allowed to vote, Latinos were raising complaints at the statehouse, more people were crossing the border from turmoil-haunted Mexico, plantation owners were fretting about the end of convict leasing, the unions were restless, more Catholics were opening churches, and new waves of poor European immigrants from New Orleans and Galveston were headed to Houston, Dallas, and San Antonio.

Segregation was still prospering, along with white-only primaries and poll taxes. But in direct reaction to all the things threatening the old social order, reenergized clandestine groups like the Ku Klux Klan began meeting more regularly. The decade had begun with the lynching of Allen Brooks under the bold archway near Main Street in Dallas, and the dark march had continued: at least thirty-two Blacks were lynched in 1915, but the true number in any year in Texas will never be known.

Now that he had control of the state, Hobby found himself facing several flashpoints, including what to do about the "alcohol issue." With World War I still flaring, Prohibitionists were arguing that the almost one hundred thousand soldiers in Texas—home to almost half of the US military posts and most of its air bases—needed saving from demon rum. In his first term, Hobby was forced to call a special session of the state legislature, and the Eighteenth Amendment to the US Constitution, banning the sale, manufacturing, and transportation of booze, was ratified. A bill to stop prostitution near army bases and another calling for statewide Prohibition were also passed. Of course, in a breakthrough of monumental proportions, lawmakers in that session also opted to finally give Texas women the right to vote in party primaries.

In the summer of 1918, with Canales keeping the memory of the murders in Porvenir alive, Hobby felt the pressure to respond. He asked for the resignation and reassignments of several Rangers and did away with the local Loyalty Ranger outfits. Ironically, in the coming months, he would have to turn his attention to another eruption, one that called for him to dispatch Rangers: reports were coming to Austin that Longview had gone completely unmoored in the wake of another accusation that a Black man was consorting with a white woman.

The situation was described as an out-of-control race riot, and Hobby was asked by local leaders to order martial law. He sent the Rangers and state militia troops, and then sat in the governor's mansion weighing the notion that entrenched local officials were still determined to sort out matters without state interference, all while a local sheriff might have intentionally turned a Black man over to a white mob. There was at least one murder, several burned buildings, and a wave of shootings before the spasm was subdued. Longview was occupied by hundreds of guardsmen and eight Texas Rangers. At least twenty Black men and maybe twenty-six white men were arrested. The Black prisoners were shipped to Austin to avoid being strung up or burned alive. In a few days, the troops and Rangers were recalled, martial law was suspended, locals were allowed to collect their confiscated weapons, and no one was ever put on trial.[14]

Hobby's response to the Longview Race Riot was emblematic of his tenure, and in keeping with those of so many of his predecessors. From his office, Hobby was a caretaker responding to events rather than remedying root causes—even though he was supporting women's suffrage, trying to find ways to help Texas farmers wilting under a lingering drought, and serving as an honest alternative to the bamboozling Ferguson.

When he stepped away from Austin in 1921, Hobby went back to his former career of running a newspaper in Houston. He settled into an English-manor-style, 6,300-square-foot home decorated inside with paintings by Picasso and Modigliani. The house was built for corporate entertaining: baked into the design was the idea that it would be used to host gatherings under its high ceilings where politicians would connect with businessmen. Hobby and his family took firm control of the *Houston Post*—promoting and chronicling the political ambitions of his many affluent friends. Hobby lived to be eighty-six, and an airport in Houston would eventually bear his name. One of his sons would try to follow him into state politics.

Hobby seemed to have a sense of self, or at least a sense of humor. He admitted that Farmer Jim Ferguson was right when he called Hobby homely—but he argued that it was better than being a con artist in Texas:

> I will admit that the Supreme Being failed to favor me with physical attributes pleasing to Governor Ferguson. But at least He gave me the intelligence to know the difference between my own money and that which belongs to the state.[15]

CHAPTER 6

The Second Coming: The 1920s

IN OCTOBER 1920, THE BRUTALLY high temperatures had only just bro-ken, and urgent telegrams were arriving at the governor's office about some unusual developments at a grand parade in Houston. The annual United Confederate Veterans reunion was under way, and former soldiers were marching through the business district. This year there was a new addition: the dusty Houston streets were echoing with the dull clamor of hooves, as several hooded and robed members of the Ku Klux Klan had come by horseback. They carried signs saying "We Were Here Yesterday, 1866," and "We Are Here Today, 1920," and "We Will Be Here Forever." Some rode alongside a platform that carried a masked Klansman sitting on what could have been a throne.[1]

The "second coming" of the Ku Klux Klan was building in Texas, with thousands of new members joining in almost every corner of the state. El Paso, not normally associated with the KKK, would witness a large num-ber of rallies and meetings. Dallas was going to become the Klan's national headquarters. For some residents of Texas, the KKK could seem like a haven, a unifying way to find a regional identity and a political fraternity— a place to bond with fellow travelers who believed Texas was a place where a white-supremacist social experiment could still work quite well.

In the early 1920s, "Texas led the nation with the most Klan rallies

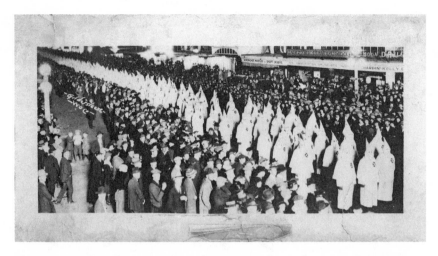

The racist Ku Klux Klan operated openly in Texas well into the twentieth century, including in this circa-1920s parade through Waco.

... 216 scattered throughout 112 cities. Of Texas cities, El Paso ranked third. Only Fort Worth and Dallas had more."[2] And with that explosion in growth—and all that it implied—state lawmakers would have to face some harsh political decisions.

In Galveston in 1920, a longshoreman's strike by sixteen hundred workers lingered for months. Labor leaders wanted higher wages, but more importantly, they wanted jobs closed to nonunion members. Lawmakers in Austin were hearing from steamship companies, cotton brokers, and businessmen in Houston about the bottom line being wrecked, and they demanded action. They knew that, as always, people on the ground were taking circumstances into their own hands and importing strikebreakers and scabs, including some from Mexico. Fueling the flames, racial tensions spiked after white scabs were hired to replace striking Black workers—and then Black scabs were hired to replace white strikers.

Cynics suspected local officials had a coordinated plan to turn up the burners on the animosity to the point that the unions would break, or Austin lawmakers would have to react. When shipping firms finally threatened to take business to other states, martial law was declared and Texas Rangers and guardsmen, including machine gunners and cavalry, were sent to the city.

The incident cemented the open-shop concept in Texas, and the long-term political ramifications were indelible: for years, lawmakers at the city, county, and state levels would rail about unions being thinly veiled socialist and even communist movements. Almost any politician had to take note of how powerful benefactors might see unions as anathema, a plague on profits, and how some voters might have been convinced that unions were something promoted by foreign agitators.

The Brotherhood of Timber Workers had already tried to organize loggers tied to the dangerous work of felling and processing the big trees in East Texas. But the union leaders were threatened and then denounced as new-era carpetbaggers. The mill operators knew they could rely on support from state leaders who would send Rangers or troops from Austin or look the other way if "security" teams beat the holy hell out of labor leaders — or arranged for them to be thrown in jail on trumped-up charges. An instant political message was promoted: unions were tied to socialism and communism, and they were all equal threats to the political order in Texas.

With that longshoreman's strike playing out in Galveston, and as the Confederates were marching into Houston, a handsome lawyer from Waco decided to enter the Democratic primary for governor. Pat Morris Neff had gone to Baylor University and had served two terms as a state representative, including a stint as Speaker. After he left the statehouse in 1905, he returned to McLennan County and developed a reputation as a no-nonsense prosecutor with an almost routine ability to win convictions in criminal cases.

Neff sensed that in uncertain times Texas voters would want even more solidity than Hobby had offered. He told his family that a clear window of opportunity was open. Hobby was leaving, and the default Democratic candidate for governor was the cantankerous ex–US senator Joseph Bailey. Neff knew that many Texans were tired of pro-alcohol ranters like Bailey. He also suspected that the state was filled with voters who felt disconnected from the insider political enclaves in Austin.

Neff warned his wife that he was going to be away a lot during his campaign, bumping over thousands of miles of pockmarked Texas roads to give speeches in county squares, in Baptist churches, and at rodeos. For months he coursed across Texas, embarking on the first big retail-politics, barnstorming campaign in state history. Neff rolled into three dozen counties that had never seen a gubernatorial candidate before. Though the race was suprisingly tight, he defeated Bailey in a runoff and took office in early 1921.

A few weeks after he was sworn in, Neff read the stories in the newspapers, including the one on the front page of the *Dallas Times Herald* of April 2: shocked guests at the city's grand Adolphus Hotel reported seeing a Black man staggering into the opulent lobby, half-naked and bleeding from the open wounds on his back. There was a horrific sight on his forehead—the skin was mottled with puckering bubbles of flesh. The man was an elevator operator at the city's finest hotel, and he had been accused of being unduly kind to a white woman. When the KKK heard about it, it was easy to round up a posse to come after him. Klansmen broke into his house on nearby Ross Avenue, in an area where freed slaves had been allowed to live. He was pummeled, shoved into a car, and taken over the murky Trinity River to the southern part of the city, where the roads ended and the dense, thorny woods began.

In coming years, prominent Texans would routinely gather at a nearby private enclave they decided to call the Koon Kreek Klub. Meanwhile, Black residents of Dallas had names for the many places where victims were taken by the Klansmen, by the police, and by vigilante groups: the Bottoms; the Whipping Grounds. And it was easy for children to point out those hanging trees that the Klan or the police liked to use, the ones they preferred to tie "colored people" to. By now, Black residents in Dallas and other parts of Texas were accustomed to the nightriders, or even the bolder Klansmen who would arrive in the daylight hours, and how people would just disappear and never be heard from again. Sometimes, after the Klan had beaten a man to death, the body was shoved down the slimy banks and into the capricious Trinity River. The murderers would watch as the bodies drifted downstream into the tangled, snake-infested curls and burrows hidden from most people.

(In the early 1980s, I met an elderly Black woman who lived near the river, close to the Elizabeth Chapel, one of the oldest Black churches in the state. The families in the old Dallas neighborhood founded by freed slaves had grown accustomed to calling on the woman—she was said to be in touch with the higher spirits—whenever another young Black man was dumped in the river. She had a reliable ritual: she would ask for an article of the dead man's clothing, and then she would ask to be rowed out into the Trinity. The old seer would stare for a while and then throw the clothing in the river. The cloth would flatten on the water's surface and then begin to meander here and there. The crowd that had gathered on the muddy riverbank would watch the cloth swirl and then come to a halt.

The old lady would tell people to dive right there—and that was where they would find the body.)

Back at the Adolphus Hotel, the elevator operator knew he could have been thrown in the Trinity but that the KKK wanted to use him to scare people, to make him a living, cautionary sign. They had pointed rifles and guns, held him down, twisted open a bottle of acid, and, drop by drop, poured it on his head. Now he was scarred for life with the letters "KKK" on his forehead. The incident made the front page in Dallas, probably as a way to send another message. State lawmakers raised no hue and cry, no one was prosecuted, and Governor Neff apparently never responded.

Neff announced he was going to end the Board of Pardon Advisors, a signal that he was not as easy to bribe as Ferguson, who had issued as many as three thousand pardons during his short time in office (with, of course, the suspicion that his allies were being rewarded, or that Ferguson was selling pardons). Neff's political ploy, his sales pitch, was that he was going to clean up Austin and address the rising suspicions that with all the growth, all the money, there had to be a consistently crooked bit of collusion. Neff was a Christian from Baylor, a law-and-order man, and he realized very early on that voters carried a degree of justified skepticism about the inner workings of the statehouse.

Growing up in the unspoiled Texas outdoors, he had spent his childhood running through groves and prairies where bobcats and wild turkey still roamed. He had watched the Brazos, Navasota, and Leon Rivers run strong, and his early affection for the outdoors contributed to a Teddy Roosevelt–inspired focus on the nation's wildlands. Neff backed the creation of the state's first public parks board, and his family donated 259 acres along the Leon in Coryell County, where he had been born, that would become Mother Neff State Park, the first state park in Texas.

Along with his falling in line with the "grandeur of American nature" movement percolating among national leaders, Neff realized that his unabashed sense of Texas superiority was political gold. He believed that the place had existed long enough and endured enough that its history should be commemorated or codified at a state level, and he pushed the creation of a state historical board or commission that would take a proactive role in identifying and preserving what he and other leaders—white men with fond nostalgia for the Confederacy—deemed worth remembering.

Neff remained a "dry" politician, and he further perfected another Texas political tradition, that of promoting policies through fearmongering: he said cunning smugglers were pushing liquor across the Mexico border, and that the oil boomtowns and woods of East Texas were harboring dangerous, illegal stills. Throughout the early 1920s, he sent Texas Rangers to tear down moonshining operations hidden in barns and field houses. Neff ordered airplanes to hunt down rumrunners who had set up shop along the Trinity River east of Dallas—it was the first time planes were used in criminal cases in Texas.[3] During a bruising roundup in 1921, over six hundred bootleggers were hunted down in Freestone County, hundreds of barrels were smashed, and thousands of gallons of booze were poured into the gumbo soil that some said yielded the best sweet potatoes in Texas.

Neff's thirst for order and not drink—and his reading of Texas as a place where old-timers were worried about change, while newcomers wanted to be reassured that they had done right by relocating to Texas or investing their fortunes there—extended to his own predictable impatience with organized labor. He saw how Hobby had once soothed wary voters as well as big business leaders by smashing the Galveston longshoremen's strike. Neff also marched troops and Rangers to Denison during a railroad strike, and then to booming Mexia to confront disturbances inside unruly camps crammed with oil workers. To make sure his political profile was clear, he gave a 1923 legislative message about crime being "the burning question" facing Texas—and he ominously added that, on average, three people were murdered every day in the state. Neff insisted that crime was his priority and that he would "revivify, rehabilitate and re-electrify" the state's criminal laws.[4]

Riding on the notion that he was the high sheriff, Neff was reelected in 1922. There were whispers in Austin that he might even become a presidential candidate. But if he had hopes of moving beyond Texas, he'd have to deal with a glaring problem: as he took office for his second term, more wings of the KKK were gathering on the main streets of the state.

The Dallas dentist Hiram Evans was named the Imperial Wizard at the organization's first national convention in November 1922—the same month Neff was reelected—and he had an aggressive, organized political strategy to fund state lawmakers, county and city officials, police and public school supervisors. Neff was learning that the KKK was an immutable political force, with as many as one hundred fifty thousand members in Texas—and that it was effectively controlling chunks of the state legislature.

In 1923, Texas lawmakers voted to ban Blacks from voting in Democratic primaries. And with relative ease, the Klan also got members and supporters elected or appointed around the state, including at hundreds of Texas schools. Millions of public school children would be required to learn Texas history, and they were going to hear lectures and read textbooks crafted as the state saw thousands of KKK members and sympathizers in city halls, in county courts, and on school boards.

In 1922, people picking up the San Antonio Spanish-language newspaper *La Prensa* read about a gang bursting into a Rio Grande Valley jail looking for Elías Villarreal Zárate. He had been arrested in Weslaco, just north of the border and across from the Mexican town of Nuevo Progreso, after scuffling with a white man. Ten people were allowed to remove Villarreal Zárate, and they hung him in front of that usual ensemble of curious and cheering onlookers. Given the complicated swirl in the Valley, and the reluctance and inability of white-owned publications to convey events, the news about his murder was especially absent for Anglo residents of Austin, Dallas, and Houston. The Mexican American population in Texas had soared from almost 70,000 in 1900 to almost 700,000 by the end of the 1920s, and now the social and political realities were even more defined by segregation, poverty, and those moments when a Black or a Latino was murdered in front of anyone who wanted to watch.

The same year as the lynching in Weslaco, Earle Mayfield, a lawyer from Overton, was elected to the US Senate, and Texas now had the distinction of sending what some said was the first Klansman in US history to national office. Mayfield didn't openly tout his Klan credentials, though he probably couldn't have gotten elected without them. He had served in the statehouse and then as a railroad commissioner before representing Texas in Washington, DC.

When he arrived, he carried all the rumors that the Klan had been bankrolling his campaigns and intimidating voters on his behalf. A Senate committee decided to investigate, and it eventually cleared Mayfield of being gusted into the office by Klan violence and cash. His exoneration didn't matter to many: political observers around the nation held to a lingering belief that in Texas, the Klan was a political powerhouse that could easily send people to City Hall or the US Senate.

In Dallas, Klan Chapter No. 66 was becoming the largest racist organization of its kind in the nation, with one out of every three grown white men in the city on its rosters. As many as thirteen thousand residents signed up, got their official membership cards, and were doing business with the many local businesses acknowledging their KKK allegiances: the All-American Cigar Company in Dallas touted its "Klansman" smokes in ads that showed a hooded man in white robes thundering along on a horse also shrouded in white cloth. The beautifully designed advertisements were like odes to a dashing, romanticized, vanished past—that Confederacy of noble men willing to take the law into their own hands to preserve treasured ideals and ways of life.

In many parts of the state, it was all just a revisited nightmare. Black families told their children to be indoors when the sun set. Windows were latched all night, and parents would wait, listening for masked Klansmen thundering in from the outskirts of the segregated zones.

In Austin, Neff appointed a record number of women to state agencies and posts. But in the end, he was yet one more Texas caretaker, someone trying to stabilize the state during its growth spurts. He didn't profess to speak for Black or Latino citizens, at least not in terms of expressing that Texas needed to make a priority of treating its residents with unfettered equality. And by winter of 1924, Neff was ready to leave Austin after two terms as governor and head back to McClennan County, where he could take stock of his legacy. In so many ways, things in and around Waco would be more predictable. He was a Christian, a Baptist, and he could be closer to his beloved Baylor, to the tight-knit collection of churches.

Before he left Austin, he asked aides for the state prison records of a particular Black man. It was someone he remembered meeting over the years when he had leaned into his tough-on-crime policies and toured squalid, suffocatingly hot prisons in Texas. Neff had especially liked taking trips to visit the Imperial State Prison Farm in Sugar Land, where the convict leasing program had once been in full operation.

When he arrived, he was hosted at the home of Warden R. J. Flanagan. Anxious to entertain Neff, the prison chief summoned a convict to play music while the governor ate supper. The inmate was Huddie Ledbetter, better known as "Leadbelly"—either a play on his last name or a nod to his constitutional fortitude. Leadbelly, who would emerge as an iconic figure in American music, had been imprisoned since 1918 on a thirty-five-year sentence for murdering a man during a fight over a woman.

Brought before the governor of Texas, Leadbelly screwed up his courage as he strummed and sang, "If I had the Governor Neff, like you got me, I'd wake up in the mornin', I would set you free." Neff was smiling; he had never heard anything like it before. On his next visit to Sugar Land, the warden made sure to order Leadbelly back for more serenading.

He sang the same song, and Neff knew exactly what it was—a petition for a pardon: "I beg you, governor, upon my soul, if you won't give me a pardon, won't you give me parole."

On the brisk January day before Neff finally left Austin, he announced that one of his last acts as governor was a rare pardon of a prisoner. During four years in office, Neff had pardoned ninety-one men. His predecessors—Colquitt, Ferguson, and Hobby—had been issuing almost five hundred a year.

Neff set Leadbelly free, then he packed up his belongings inside the governor's mansion and returned north to the part of Texas where he had grown up. Twenty years later, he was the president of Baylor University, accustomed to being heralded almost everywhere he went in Waco, and one day he had a moment of warm nostalgia.

He began thinking about the bold Negro he had freed, and he decided to write a letter to Leadbelly in California, reminding him that he was the reason he had been one of the lucky men set free in Texas: "Friend Ledbetter—Do you remember me vividly and distinctly?"

Neff would be buried in Waco's Oakwood Cemetery, and his striking memorial reads, "I have worked and wrought as best I could to make Texas a better place in which to live." On another portion of the memorial are the words: "He Was A Stately Oak In The Forest."

Leadbelly became internationally known as a patriarch of American song—including his classic "Midnight Special," a profound indictment of the cruelities of Texas and its prisons.

"Pa" Ferguson, friend of alcohol, still hadn't gone quietly into the Texas night. With Neff on the way out, Ferguson conferred with his wife and came up with a plan. She would run for governor—and she could win if she promoted herself as "Ma" Ferguson, tapping the same folksy, friend-of-the-ordinary-man tactics that had served him so well.

For all his grifter tendencies, Ferguson still had a special ability to read voters, to know what worked in Texas, and his wife successfully served it up like warm pecan pie: Miriam "Ma" Ferguson moved into the governor's chair in 1925 as the first female chief executive in Texas history and the second female governor in US history (two weeks earlier, Nellie Ross had been sworn in as Wyoming's governor).

Miriam "Ma" Ferguson, who won election as governor after serving as first lady, offered herself to voters much as her husband, James "Pa" Ferguson, did— as a "down-home" Texan.

Ferguson defeated the Klan-anointed candidate, Felix Robertson from Dallas, and political insiders marveled at both the resilience of the Ferguson family and the breakthrough that she had achieved in a state that had dragged its heels on so many social fronts, including granting women authority in government.

Depending on your point of view, her victory was either a callow example of style over substance or an authentic attempt to bridge the gap between well-connected political players and disconnected heartland voters who felt unheard and ignored. John Nance "Cactus Jack" Garner, the South Texas bantam rooster congressman who was constantly being reelected, was still chomping on cigars, donning his custom-made boots and Stetson hats, and passing himself off as a cussing, unpretentious Texan instead of the cunning, thirsty beneficiary of South Texas barons who sculpted what might have been the only congressional district Garner could win. The Fergusons and politicians like Garner were further cementing the fine political art of always appearing "more Texan" than the other candidate.

The Austin chess players knew Pa Ferguson was obviously the mastermind behind Ma Ferguson's campaign, and that her running for governor was just a thinly veiled attempt by her prideful husband to jam his hand again into the Texas political cookie jar. But, far beyond their own selfish motivations, it was also clear that her election was a game changer: several women's groups in Texas had formed the Joint Legislative Council (its leaders included Minnie Fisher Cunningham and Annie Webb Blanton) to argue for equal rights.[5] The council lobbied legislators and the governor to provide money for children's health care, day care, nurseries, orphanages, and adoption agencies. Their activism wasn't easily accepted: they were labeled communists by one member of the House and derided by others as the "Petticoat Lobby." But the council kept putting lawmakers on alert that women were not just nominally in office as governor, but were promoting issues, coalescing, organizing across the state. For the decade that the council existed, it was like a crash course in how the back rooms, underbelly, and public face of male-dominated Texas politics actually behaved.[6]

Through it all, Ma Ferguson continued to serve as a symbol for women interested in higher office. Born in Bell County, she attended Salado College and then Baylor Female College. During her campaign, she suggested that if she won, Texans would get the benefit of her husband's expertise, or "two governors for the price of one," as she put it.

As she entered office, the air in Texas was heavy with the sound of oil-field machinery, the ports were bustling with dockworkers unloading ships, more timberlands were being clear-cut, and more tiny outposts were becoming boomtowns. Word about the Texas "miracle" was zooming to Wall Street; investment money was raining down; and thousands more people were clambering off trains and looking for work as drillers, welders, pipe layers, and roustabouts. Texas was on its way to becoming the fifth most populated state. By the end of the decade, Houston was going to be the state's largest city, followed by Dallas, San Antonio, and Fort Worth.

With all the changes, the backbone of the rural economy was abruptly subject to a new invasion: a boll weevil epidemic had begun wiping out miles of cotton. The fragile industry would remain a constant source of concern for politicians as well as a small army of farm lobbyists making the rounds in Austin.[7] There was still clear optimism that Texas could eventually prosper beyond the plagues—that it was building its massive, constantly replenished oil economy that would allow the state to ride out any natural or human-made disasters.

Always baked into that hope was the notion that Texas, more than ever, needed to ease the brakes and allow the oilmen to operate even more untethered to state regulations, oversight, taxes, and whatever else could slow their momentum. It was hard to control God's vengeance in the form of a boll weevil or a drought, but Texans could keep the oil spigots turned wide open, flooding the state with enough money to keep it hurtling into the future.

Ma Ferguson surprised her skeptical critics by staying true to a campaign promise to enact an "anti-mask" law aimed specifically at Klansmen anxious to hide their identity. But the move was overturned—perhaps another hint of that constant, unyielding predeliction to anti-regulation, another tip of the hat to unfettered freedom Texas-style. Whatever it was, Ferguson was just like her previous peers in the statehouse; despite her moves against the Klan masks, she seemingly turned a blind eye to the virulent ritualized racism that dated back to the days when Stephen F. Austin, the "father of Texas," supported the system of human chattel and condemned freed slaves as "a nuisance and a menace."[8]

As she traveled Texas with her husband, promoting the Ferguson family as the kindly "parents" of the state, she could see blacksmiths, sculptors, and granite workers busy installing memorials, statues, and plaques in honor of the Confederacy. A beautiful building in Dallas, the Magnolia, was built in 1922 by a Klan leader. The largest public monuments in the heart of that city were dedicated to the Klan. A splendidly landscaped cemetery for Confederate veterans was carefully tended in South Dallas. Austin already had large Confederate monuments and streets, and schools everywhere around the state were being named after rebel leaders.

The list of cities with new public odes to the Confederacy was growing by the month: Baytown, Brownsville, San Angelo, Weatherford, Victoria, Vega, Texarkana, Sonora, Snyder, Sherman, Sanderson, San Antonio, Rankin, Perryton, Pecos, Paris, Pampa, Palestine, Odessa, Mount Pleasant, Marshall, Longview, Kermit, Kaufman, Jefferson, Hillsboro, Greenville, Granbury, Graham, Gonzales, Goldthwaite, Giddings, Georgetown, Galveston, Gainesville, Fort Davis, Farmersville, Denton, Crowell, Corsicana, Cleburne, Clarksville, Bonham, Belton, and Beaumont. (The list continued to grow into the 1960s, with more monuments and honors going up in Austin, Bastrop, and other places.)

The displays were so breathtaking and the marches and parades so public that a small handful of Dallas businessmen finally gathered to talk about the possible economic toll exacted by the Klan. Dallas didn't have Houston's proximity to shipping lanes or its growing industrial base. Dallas was increasingly dependent on lawyers, bankers, and insurers—many connected to firms outside the state—who wanted the city to be an even-keeled base of operations. They were especially averse to negative publicity, and they let George Bannerman Dealey, publisher of the *Dallas Morning News*, know it. He began ordering journalists to write anti-Klan stories and to note that the city and state should be recognized for other things. (One of the enduring hallmarks of Dallas has been its obsession with its public image and how it affects the economy. In the months *before* the assassination of President John F. Kennedy in Dallas in 1963, city leaders gathered to talk about how to tackle the fact that the city was increasingly seen as an outpost of violent intolerance. Their efforts, of course, were amplified after the president's murder in Dallas, when city leaders feared Dallas would be shunned forever.)

Dealey's anti-Klan stories were offset by the fact that his family was also an active endorser of the robust Confederate reunions and gatherings in Dallas; and that the dining facilities at Dealey's paper were segregated and would remain so past World War II; and that Dealey's son was prone to using racist descriptions of Black people in his correspondence with other editors in Texas. For Texas candidates for state or national office, it often didn't matter. They knew that they had to receive the blessing of the Dealey family.

Over just a few years in the 1920s, Odessa grew from several hundred residents to over five thousand. Breckenridge soared from fifteen hundred to thirty thousand. From Palestine to Mexia, from Kilgore to New London, there were surges. The idea that you could come to Texas and stab a gushing oil well in the ground—and do it fast—fueled the unbridled political code: if Texas was to capitalize on its trove of resources, lawmakers should be traffic cops waving entrepreneurs into the easiest lanes. With support from Austin, and from Congressman Cactus Jack Garner in Washington, by the end of the decade a small number of corporations controlled the majority of oil production in Texas, including ones that would endure in both famous and infamous ways: Gulf, Humble, and Shell.

As Texas tried to find a way to promote but also gingerly regulate the new bedrock of its economy, people clamored for more honest and influential women in politics. For some, the crusading activist Minnie Fisher Cunningham—who had spearheaded so many women's movements—was a logical antidote to the thin charade of the Fergusons. After some urging, Cunningham became the first Texas woman to run for the US Senate, thinking the state was ready to retire Senator Earle Mayfield, the KKK's chosen candidate. But in the primary Cunningham carried only one county, losing to the ebullient and windy East Texas congressman Tom Connally (who would spend a long and unremarkable thirty-four years in the Senate, highlighted by some early antimonopoly forays and, later, by several years on the Senate Foreign Relations Committee).

Through it all, Ma Ferguson kept channeling her husband and running a pardons monopoly. She issued more than four thousand pardons and heard the same accusation that her husband had endured: that she was being paid to release prisoners. At one point, Ferguson was issuing one hundred pardons a month, and the numbers were rising. Meanwhile, critics said she was also doling out state contracts and state funds to friends — ones who'd send cash back to the Ferguson clan. One allegation centered on paybacks for new roads in Texas, ones being rushed into existence to connect booming oil-field towns with the big refineries and ports on the coast.

Ferguson seemed either arrogant or oblivious, maybe overly secure in her own folksy "Mother of Texas" identity. But there was increasingly angry backroom talk by political strategists about how to block her reelection — or how to throw her out of office. She still had some support with apologists who said her constant pardons were a masterstroke of enlightened leadership, because they lightened the load in overcrowded, underfunded Texas prisons. But several people she pardoned had been busted on alcohol charges, which on the one hand suggested that she was still ardently anti-Prohibition, and on the other hand raised more questions about who exactly was lobbying her.

By 1926, the accusations were stomping all over her mom-and-apple-pie public image. Democratic operatives in Austin met in downtown cafés and decided that her husband was still running a con game, and that his wife and he had to go.

Dan Moody, a handsome, wavy-haired lawyer from Taylor and a graduate of the University of Texas, was catapulted into the ranks of Texas politicians as one of the youngest ever to become a county attorney, district attorney, and finally state attorney general. In the early 1920s, he had gone after the KKK in a way no one else had, filing charges against Austin-area Klansmen for pouring tar on a white man. Moody became the first prosecutor in America to get a conviction against the Klan (it should be noted that the prosecution involved a case of white-on-white violence).[9] For some, the energetic, polished Moody was a breath of fresh air, maybe someone who could lead Texas away from the tainted residue of the Fergusons.

To his many fans in Texas, the thirty-three-year-old Moody was not just the youngest governor in state history; he was also a dyed-in-the-wool conservative Democrat focused on restoring decorum and confidence. He loathed the way the Fergusons handed out favors like free candy, the way they had worked hand in glove with corrupt prison officials—and he promised to support women in a way that Ma Ferguson never did. Several women's groups threw their support behing him, hosted rallies and events for his campaign, and assumed he'd return the favor if he was elected.

When he took office in 1927, he quickly ramped up prison oversight and an overhaul of the way pardons were granted. And he appointed the suffrage movement activist Jane McCallum as secretary of state. Moody also pushed for an extensive overhaul of the state highway system, as well as a better accounting of where state money was coming from and how it was being spent, especially as the 1929 national economic collapse slammed into Texas. Moody knew that the true measure of the crash—and the coming Great Depression—was beyond unclear. Texas had oil, something that the world still needed, and he assumed the state could ride out the storm. Still, he created a state auditor's office to keep an eye on the budgets, and it inspired him to explore other ways to keep the state organized. Moody wanted to concentrate the entire state prison system in one location, perhaps a sprawling campus near Austin that would house all Texas prisoners. The attempt failed, as did proposals to give him more say in state appointments. People watching Moody's moves knew he was bucking a Texas constitution—and a mindset—that didn't grant the governor the same autonomy that his peers in other states enjoyed.

In early May of 1930, during his last full year in office, Moody was interrupted at his office by reports of a Black man being captured in Sherman, north of Dallas, after being accused of raping a white woman. Sherman, like other places, was a "sundown town" where Black residents were warned to stay indoors after dusk. Moody was told that hundreds, maybe thousands, of angry white men—farmers and businessmen—were gathering in the streets, trying to get at the man, George Hughes.

Moody ordered 430 National Guard troops and nine Texas Rangers, including the infamous Frank Hamer, to head to Sherman. The crowds grew, shots were fired, tear gas canisters were launched—and the troops began to retreat. People were barreling inside city offices. Someone was rallying the mob by waving an enormous American flag. At the courthouse, Hughes pled guilty as rocks and bricks thudded against the win-

Some of the infamously violent cowboy-hatted Texas Rangers who patrolled the vast Texas-Mexico border region included Captain Frank Hamer (second from left, bottom row), a crack shot who later tracked Clyde Barrow and Bonnie Parker to their deaths in Louisiana.

dows and doors. Secretaries and courthouse workers pushed toward side windows and scrambled down ladders instead of going out the front door and into the melee.

Hamer and the squad of Texas Rangers told people that Moody had ordered them not to shoot anyone. They steered Hughes into the district court vault and locked him inside. The crowd invaded the courthouse and some of the attackers set fire to the building. For hours the flames licked away at the building, until only some walls and the vault remained. Up until midnight, the Rangers watched as the crowd used blowtorches and even dynamite to crack open the vault.

Hughes was dead, probably from the blast, and his carcass was tied to a car, pulled through Sherman, and then hung from a tree in front of a pharmacy that served the Black community. Chairs and desks were pulled from other stores in the neighborhood, and a bonfire was lit underneath

Hughes's corpse. The skin melted on his body until only ash-coated bones remained, and his body remained in view for hours until the crowd dispersed and soldiers cut him down. Other members of the mob set fire to any storefront—including medical and dental offices. The Black funeral homes in town had been destroyed, and no one seemed to know what to do, until the remains of the dead man were carted to a white funeral operator, who quickly had someone take them to a field outside of town.

Fourteen white men were indicted for rioting or arson. No one was charged with the lynching. Two men were sentenced to two-year terms. It was the most challenging bit of violence during Moody's time in office, and like those other problematic moments for Texas leaders, it would be more or less muted or scrubbed from some histories. Moody left office months later, went back to his law practice, and then served for a while in the US attorney general's office in President Franklin Delano Roosevelt's administration. He is buried in the Texas State Cemetery, under an elegant, arched monument with his family name at the top. On his individual marker is a quote chosen from Shakespeare: "This above all: to thine own self be true, And it must follow, as the night the day, Thou canst not then be false to any man."

The way to enforce white supremacy in the Texas political system was still quite linear: deny Blacks and Latinos the right to vote by making them pay poll taxes and enforce laws that blocked them from participating in primaries, particularly ones held by the ruling Democrats. It was political segregation, exclusion, and voter suppression. The primaries were especially key to creating a "legacy" pattern of politics, with leaders handpicked and guided into office. In Dallas, that regimen was enforced by the Dallas Citizen's Council, which would emerge as the dominant political force in the city.

It was a group of well-acquainted, well-connected white businessmen who ran the local newspapers, banks, and other important corporations. Dubbed the "Dallas White Citizen's Council" by some minority residents and political reporters, its methods were remarkably similar to those of the South Texas boss system. At convivial breakfasts and power lunches in private dining rooms on the upper floors of the downtown Dallas buildings, the men would choose one another—or a likely ally—to be the candidate for City Hall, the statehouse, Congress, or Senate. In "petroleum clubs" around the state, the same pattern was occurring. The carefully con-

The physician Lawrence A. Nixon moved from East Texas to El Paso, where he became a civil rights pioneer, forming the city's first chapter of the National Association for the Advancement of Colored People (NAACP) and waging a court fight against the Democratic Party for keeping Black citizens from voting in its primaries.

structed political systems ensured that power would be handed down in a predictable fashion, and, if necessary, with influential clergy and fraternal organizations called on to help.[10]

Lawrence Nixon, a Black doctor born in Marshall, was well aware of the way political power was doled out—and he was more than attuned to the brutalities still unfolding in East Texas. He had moved to El Paso, but he could never shake what he had once seen.

On a Monday afternoon in November 1907, a Black man in Cameron, Texas, Alex Johnson, was attacked by a mob that had rushed into the local jail where he had been held for allegedly trying to attack a young girl. As many as five hundred people hounded Johnson into the streets, which led to a painful, predictable sorrow: Johnson was hung from a sturdy oak tree.

Nixon was the only local doctor willing to treat Blacks, and when he first heard the rattle and hum in the streets, he went to a safe place and watched as "chairs were placed on the balcony of the two-story building to accommodate the crowds gathered to witness the lynching." He retreated back inside his medical practice, locked the doors, and counted the minutes while "listening to the cries of the dying man."[11]

He decided to flee to El Paso, thinking the edge of the West would be a safer place for a Black man to practice medicine and maybe even participate in the political process. In El Paso, Nixon formed the city's first

National Association for the Advancement of Colored People (NAACP) chapter. And then he made the difficult decision to fight the 1923 Texas statute barring Blacks from the Democratic primaries.

In the summer of 1924, Nixon became the frontline soldier in a coordinated NAACP plan to attack the rigged voting system: he volunteered to be a plaintiff in a lawsuit against the poll tax–white primary trap in Texas. He knew he had a long, established record as a poll-tax-paying Democrat in Texas. He also knew that if he suffered any blowback, it wouldn't hurt his income, since his patients were Black or Latino. He had nothing to lose, in one sense, but he was still putting himself at enormous peril in a city that had a vigorous KKK presence.

That summer, Nixon paid his tax and took the receipt to his precinct voting station. He insisted on obtaining a ballot, but election officers refused to hand him one. With NAACP-supported lawyers, he took his case to the US Supreme Court, and it ruled unanimously in 1927 that Texas was violating the federal constitution. The ruling, spearheaded by Justice Oliver Wendell Holmes, had little bearing in Texas—Democrats continued to simply refuse Black participation in primaries until near the end of World War II.

Back in El Paso, while he waited, Nixon put himself at greater personal and professional risk by pushing for the desegregation of public pools and the creation of quality public hospitals and clinics for minorities, and also by filing another suit against Texas officials still refusing to let him vote in the primaries.[12]

Five years after the initial Supreme Court decision declaring the Texas Democratic primary system unconstitutional, Justice Benjamin Cardozo ruled for Nixon again: "The petitioner, a Negro, has brought this action against judges of election in Texas to recover damages for their refusal by reason of his race or color to permit him to cast his vote at a primary election. This is not the first time that he has found it necessary to invoke the jurisdiction of the federal courts in vindication of privileges secured to him by the Federal Constitution.... Barred from voting at a primary the petitioner has been, and this for the sole reason that his color is not white."[13]

Cardozo, in his ruling, suggested that Texas was practicing state-sponsored racism, and that the Democratic Party in Texas had tried to wiggle around the federal rulings by describing itself as a private association or club that could pick and choose its members. In Texas, the ready answer was at hand: the Democrats were going to ban Black voters from the party's political conventions, the ones where candidates would be nominated—and the exclusion, the segregation, would roll on.

Nixon kept battling, filing more suits, and remaining on the front lines of breaking the Democratic Party's racist stranglehold. Years later, on July 22, 1944, he and his wife went back, yet again, to an El Paso voting booth and were finally able to cast a ballot in a Democratic primary. It was a monumental personal breakthrough, one he had been striving toward for almost forty years—ever since he watched in horror as a Black man was hung outside his medical office.

Nixon's persistence, his ability to crack the Democratic wall, would change many patterns. By introducing more Black voters into the ranks, into the primaries, it would aid in the long, slow evolution of the Democratic platforms in Texas. In time, as unlikely as it might have once seemed, the Democratic Party in Texas would become the home and wellspring for many groundbreaking minority politicians.

In 1955, Nixon was admitted to the once-all-white Texas Medical Association. He died on March 6, 1966, following a car crash—almost exactly a year after the landmark federal Voting Rights Act was passed, flatly outlawing racial discrimination in the US electoral process. Today, a small street in El Paso is named in his honor, as is an elementary school. "When you look at the trajectory of the civil rights movement, Nixon's role was phenomenal. He was a man who had local, state and national importance—a crusader for justice, a visionary and remarkable humanist," said Maceo Dailey, director of the African American Studies program at the University of Texas at El Paso.[14]

Archer "Archie" Parr, born on Matagorda Island, had bare-knuckled his way into the high-dollar ranching and farming worlds of South Texas. In the process, he developed a keen appreciation for voter intimidation and outright chicanery in taking advantage of the growing Mexican American and immigrant population. Parr worked overtime to exert maximum control of the local election systems spreading out from his power base—and the state senator became known as the "Duke of Duval" and even the "Boss of the Valley" (maybe an unsubtle nod to Boss Tweed and other political machine potentates from the North). With thousands of Mexican laborers in indentured servitude on freshly irrigated farms, Parr was able to control if and when Latinos would vote. The intimidating presence of Texas Rangers or the quick summoning of vigilante groups that could issue behavior modification—at best a whipping, at worst a lynching on the parched edges of town—served as clarifying political messengers.

Parr knew enough to sell himself as a gatekeeper to the Texas dream. He could speak Spanish and used it often, and it could make him seem like a paternal, sympathetic godfather. Parr, more than many in Austin, understood the complex history along the Rio Grande, what drove people across the river, and how families were in a state of almost constant unease—it had been that way in uncertain South Texas since the Spanish, the Mexicans, the white settlers, and anyone else had arrived. And he was active at a time when national anti-immigrant measures—the Emergency Quota Act (1921) and the Immigration Act (1924)—were inspired by a xenophobic backlash against "undesirables" like the "swarthy" Italians filling up New York, New Orleans, Boston, and Chicago.[15]

The *Austin Statesman* featured a March 25, 1923, story: "Hordes of Aliens Smuggled into Texas: European 'Scum' and Multitudes of Asiatics Slip Over the Border." The story goes on to say that "Immigration Authorities Regard the Situation as Alarming; Airplanes Being Used in Illicit Traffic by Powerful Smuggling Ring."[16] The hysteria about immigrants was set to multiply during the Depression, with fears mounting that precious jobs would be lost to the "aliens."[17]

Close to Christmas in 1929, a deportee named Carlos Espinosa recrossed the border into Texas from Mexico and willfully surrendered to patrol officers at the side of a road near Laredo. The belief was that he preferred incarceration in Texas to the uncertainities in his native country. The story garnered some small publicity in South Texas newspapers, and it was a precursor to how politicians would have to always wrestle with the insistent implications and true meanings of the words "immigration" and "undocumented" well into the twenty-first century. The matter of who could move across the river would be forever linked to the political futures of countless Texans—including those who aspired to the White House.[18]

The political *patrones* like Parr had an almost perfectly corrupt routine in place: they would promise jobs for the immigrants as irrigation diggers, cowboys, citrus pickers, and onion harvesters, and then pay them barely enough to shop in stores or live in homes owned by the *patrones* and their friends. It created a cycle of poverty that easily and naturally extended to politics. Parr served in various local offices, including as county commissioner, which allowed him to control the voting ranks and direct public money. Heavily armed police would guard local polling stations and the poll tax offices. If they didn't like you or your political inclinations, you'd never vote. It was a passport to impunity, and Parr pushed the deception to another level—handing out already-filled-out election ballots to voters who might have no idea what they were signing off on. If you wanted to run for office, let alone vote, the rules were manifestly clear, and the fear was very palpable.

Residents of Duval County still talked about how the courthouse burned to the ground in 1914—at the same time that an investigation was brewing into corruption and missing money. Somewhere in the ashes and embers was the paper trail that many suspected could connect crimes straight to Parr's kingdom. He was indicted on various charges of corruption while serving as a Texas state senator, but nothing stuck, and he remained in office until 1935, a two-decade run in which he buttressed a system rigorously enforced to control and block Latino participation—as the Latino population was rapidly growing. Though tainted by myriad accusations—bribery, stealing votes, and evading taxes—Parr was never convicted. It could be that sprawling South Texas seemed so inscrutable, in constant flux, that Parr and the others in the Valley were left to their own devices. Whatever it was, a giant swath of the state was mired in corruption reinforced by careful control of the ballot box—at times with the real or implied threat of Texas Rangers being sent to the border.

Parr certainly was not alone in his version of South Texas supremacy—many others, including John Nance Garner, endorsed it or profited from it. What they had in common was a calculated, pragmatic system of countering the growing Mexican American population. It was a way of doing politics that seeped into the soil and would linger for many years. National, state, and local candidates knew that they had to pay their respects to the families that inherited the land and the power from men like Parr. It was a two-way street—Parr and the citizen kings of South Texas knew that if they wanted favors from Austin or Washington, DC, they would be well served to keep things well oiled, humming, and all-powerful.

After Parr died in Corpus Christi, he was buried in Benavides Cemetery, named after Confederate soldier Plácido Benavides, at the corner of Palacios and Depot Streets in Duval County. Some observers appreciated the irony of Parr being buried in a place named after a Latino Confederate general. Given his legacy as Valley royalty, his marker is surprisingly understated. It merely lists his name, the day he was born, and the day he died—October 18, 1942.

CHAPTER 7

Black Blizzards: The 1930s

THE DAUGHTER OF A WHITE-SILK-SUITED oil tycoon once invited me to dinner at the Houston Yacht Club in La Porte and then said we should walk toward the beach to see "the White House." As lightning flashed over the murky waters in Galveston Bay, we clambered over some fences, and there it was: former Governor Ross Sterling's extraordinary "Texas White House" rising up on land facing the Houston Ship Channel. It was near where the channel opened up to Galveston Bay, at a place old-timers still called Morgan's Point in honor of James Morgan, the slave-owning plantation owner. Morgan is credited with cracking open key parts of the Texas coast for early white settlers, and one of Morgan's mixed-race servants was the famous "Yellow Rose of Texas"—Emily West, often called Emily Morgan. A minor debate has welled up over the years about her exact role in the Texas fight for independence, with those in favor of a romantic version arguing that the servant artfully distracted the Mexican general Santa Anna during the Battle of San Jacinto in 1836 that secured nationhood for Texas.

Staring up at the decaying, ominous building that had once been the biggest home in Texas, I found it easy to feel the profound history—not of the old slave trader Morgan, or the servant Emily, or the birth of the

Ross Sterling, who rose to governor after defeating Miriam "Ma" Ferguson in the Democratic primary, helped found Humble and Exxon and built his own replica of the White House on the Texas coast.

Republic of Texas, but of a master of the universe like Ross Sterling. He had cofounded Humble Oil, which would become the outpost of Standard Oil and morph into Exxon. He owned banks and published the newspaper that would become the *Houston Post*. A legend, apparently untrue, emerged that after he sold a slice of his oil empire for a sizable fortune, he told an architect to turn over a $20 bill and build him a home on Galveston Bay that looked exactly like the building on the back.[1]

The legendary Texas gossip columnist Maxine Mesinger (she said of herself that she "snooped to conquer") often used the word "swankienda" to describe the most lavish homes of the Texas oil elite—and Sterling's place was the sine qua non of swankiendas: it had thirty-five rooms, nine bedrooms, fifteen bathrooms, a ballroom, a rotunda, a grand salon, and foot-thick Texas limestone walls that could bear the brunt of hurricanes howling in from the Gulf of Mexico. Besides a bowling alley and an indoor shooting range, Sterling told his architect to put in a few other flourishes: a replica of the South Portico of the nation's White House and a rooftop lair where he could have an easy view of his giant Humble Oil plant across the bay. This stretch of the coastline was the governor's playground—and watching the Humble operations meant he could wake up every day and see the source of his power.

Ross Sterling was the son of Benjamin Franklin Sterling, a native of Anahuac, and when he defeated a still-hopeful but perhaps delusional Ma Ferguson in the 1930 Democratic primary, it marked the fully realized emergence of oil's primacy at the highest reaches of state politics. Sterling had drilled hundreds of wells and worked hard, during his earlier position on the Texas Highway Commission, to make sure there were enough big roads to transport oil, gas, and minerals around the nation. He was more interested than any governor before him in making sure that oil was afforded the help it needed from state lawmakers, and he spelled it out in his inaugural address in January.

> I think the most important function of this government is to build Texas. Build it industrially, economically, physically, mentally, socially and spiritually. If we cease building, we suffer and die; if we continue, we have prosperity, and prosperity means business. Happiness is the ultimate goal of all and the only true happiness lies in development—progress.[2]

Sterling also talked about the "gushers of liquid gold" and how to capitalize on the millions of dollars in sulphur and other mineral resources, as well as the importance of industrializing along the state's rivers and coastlines. He reaffirmed the idea that Texas lawmakers had to be willing to keep as light a rein as possible: "In order to further encourage industry here, we must not so restrict its operations as to repel newcomers . . . in some respects there is too much government in business, too much regulation and restriction for the state's own good."[3]

Later that same January, he spoke to state lawmakers at a legislative session, noting that he wasn't really worried about the Great Depression that was engulfing other chunks of the country. Texas, he said, was an "empire" destined for greatness: "Texas has fared better than other parts of the nation; and as far as Texas is concerned, we know the depression is merely temporary. This State has yet a destiny of empire to fulfill."[4]

Finally, Sterling added that the lawmakers should put their political will to some specifics: beefing up the ability of law enforcement officials from around the state to coordinate their work; easing the overcrowding in state hospitals; improving schools in rural regions; building even more highways; and keeping an eye on public utility companies that were growing by leaps and bounds but remained mostly unregulated. "Texas has no adequate utility regulation," Sterling suggested.[5]

Even if he wanted a modicum of control over electric companies, Sterling's short time in office was defined by a literal open-door policy toward the captains of industry in Texas and from around the nation—he welcomed them to his office, to lunch, to dinner, and was attuned to their ideas that Texas needed to widen waterways and carve out bigger coastal ports. Sterling felt that he was in the engine room of a barreling freight train loaded with natural resources and with a malleable coastline that could be sculpted and molded to make processing, refining, and shipping that much easier.

With his own deep history in the oil game, Sterling knew that black-gold speculators were searching hard for the pure, tangible commodity that would tide them over during rough economies. Just like tiny Thurber had become a boomtown during its coal mining heyday, new places in Texas were still bulging with dreamers stampeding after a piece of the oil prize. With them came a higher likelihood of swindles, frauds, claim jumpers, and tax schemes. Sterling and other politicos worried that things could get too out of hand, and the governor nudged the Texas Railroad Commission for a plan to put a few more parameters on oil development, but the idea was tossed out in court. Wildcatting, that perfectly Texas commitment to unfettered and often unregulated oil exploration, simply increased over the years.

Sometimes it began with a sudden darkening of the sky. Then there would be an eerie silence and stillness until flocks of birds zoomed away. A cold wind might begin to rattle the dresses drying on the clotheslines. Parents would sprint out of shacks, scooping up their children and retreating inside. They'd shutter windows and doors—and then they'd sit and wait for another grinding "sand blow" or terrifying "black blizzard" to pass over them: choking waves of dust, dirt, and sand roaring across naked, vulnerable pieces of the Texas heartland.

For years before the boll weevil plague, there had been a "cotton rush," with miles of trees cut down and hundreds of farms planted to take advantage of rising prices. In the 1920s, the state population had grown by almost 25 percent, and thousands of farmers were arriving or expanding their operations. New, heavier machines ripped up earth and took out the stabilizing root systems through the widespread tilling that led to erosion. When the rains were sparse, the land became caked and blistered, and sometimes those dark blizzards would hover for days.[6] When the storms blacked out the sky, some thought it was an event straight out of the Bible—rapidly moving columns of dirt-laden mist soaring as high as eight thousand feet inside bone-shaking electrical storms.[7]

But then, as cotton prices plummeted and as the Depression spread, farmers began trooping into banks to beg for survival loans, or selling their equipment, or weighing whether to join the diaspora to the golden promises of California. Churches and benevolent aid organizations set up programs for destitute farmers and field workers, nurturing the sense that local officials could sometimes move more quickly than officials in either Austin or Washington, DC, and that there should be even more community groups, chambers of commerce, and fraternal organizations to oversee politics.

As the Depression crept into Texas, a nagging fear grew that the destitution could also lead to an invasion of homeless and "unwanted itinerants"—ragtag armies of farmworkers and migrants who would gravitate to towns and sap city, county, and state services. True or not, it reminded state lawmakers that they had starkly different constituencies to contend with. Finding a balance, at least for Sterling, would prove tricky. Voters began to blame him for the woes lapping at Texas, including some Texans who harbored nostalgia for the manufactured populism Ma and Pa Ferguson had been peddling.

Their legacy was still resonating in regions that were wary of "foreigners"—the areas where anti-Sterling forces believed the expansionist governor helped usher in unwelcome high-rollers and modern-day carpetbaggers from New York and other distant planets. Sterling decided to call an emergency legislative session in September 1931, pleading with lawmakers to do something to rescue the swooning Texas cotton industry. Sterling's plan to keep prices afloat by reducing the amount of acreage devoted to cotton farming was controversial, but he put a hard sell on it: "The voice of the people is resounding through the South in a clamor of distress, seeking relief from their gravest agricultural crisis of modern years."[8]

The Sterling plan was approved, then thrown out in court, then reintroduced, and the back-and-forth suggested to skeptics that Sterling was too busy accommodating his partners in the oil business to really understand how to nurse parched parts of rural Texas back to health. In

1932, sensing that Sterling was wounded and that he'd stumble in a bid for reelection, Ma Ferguson decided to try a modern-day political miracle by running for governor again, with her husband still presumed to be pulling the strings. She beat Sterling in the Democratic primary and became living proof that second and third acts are possible in Texas politics, and that the state had a special capacity for forgiving candidates who got their hands dirty.

Defeated, Sterling simply went back to adding to his immense personal fortune. He returned to the oil exploration and refining game, dabbling in various investments, and when he died, in 1949, he was laid to rest in a subdued, shaded family lot in Houston's Glenwood Cemetery. His Texas White House was used by various people and organizations over the years, but it fell into immense disrepair and for a while was like a huge, silent, decaying beast that surprised the hell out of people like me who stumbled across it. There were rumors that a mysterious millionaire from France had purchased the place—and then, in early 2017, it was sold to a different private investor for $2.8 million after having been listed for $6 million.

During the last Ferguson administration, some Texas voters were officially worried about broader issues long haunting other states, including the growing divide between the extraordinarily affluent and the millions of people mired in abject poverty. Ma Ferguson, bowing to the hard realities that she and Sterling had hoped Texas could avoid, issued an executive order to create the Texas Relief Commission in 1933, which would steer federal funds into public works projects centered on agencies such as the Civilian Conservation Corps (CCC). In coming years, especially with the Works Progress Administration (WPA), thousands would go to work creating camps, parks, art, and public buildings in Texas. Even with some lawmakers in Austin and in Congress resisting what they saw as the "welfare" or "socialist" underpinnings of the recovery programs, projects like the WPA would provide much-needed work, and as many as 120,000 people were hired by early 1936.[9]

Ferguson and state lawmakers watched the economic devastation in rural areas driving more people into the cities, just as Houston and Dallas were becoming even more politically potent outposts—the places to find the barrels of money to run for statewide or national offices. The political power balance was neatly shifting from the older, historic centers like Galveston and San Antonio, and working-class whites, Blacks, and Latinos were headed to Houston—hitching rides, taking buses, and hopping on trucks headed from the played-out logging camps, cotton farms, and the oppressive borderlands in South and Southwest Texas. The demographic shift would lead to complex political moves, and strategists began to wonder how to court middle-class white voters who were watching their cities change before their eyes.

When they arrived in the big cities, the new families would find that the political dividing lines were usually codified by legislated mandate. In Austin, Black residents were quarantined under a master plan that would cluster them on the east side of the city, where, in turn, local and state agencies would open up wastewater treatment plants, halfway houses, and power plants. In the mid-1800s, Austin had issued a blanket order that Latinos had to leave the city unless they had strict permission from white residents to be there. Into the 1930s, a more contemporary sociopolitical maneuver was under way in Texas, with Black and Latino residents, newly arrived or there since the formation of cities, sequestered near railroad tracks, cement plants, refineries, chemical plants, and other heavy industries.

In Dallas, there was a mosquito- and cholera-prone area west of downtown and the usually sluggish Trinity River that was devoted to cement production. For decades, the low-income neighborhood of small shacks was called Cement City. Local church leaders, neighborhood organizers, and civil rights groups petitioned city and county politicians for better services and more pollution protections, and demanded that politicians make good on campaign promises to pave streets, provide better schools, and stop the spread of cholera and other diseases. Leaders at the local, county, and state levels argued that overregulating areas like Cement City would harm workers in the long run by leading to layoffs and lower wages.

One thing was clear: the new political-business partnerships in the 1930s were no different from the ones that existed when wealthier entrepreneurs first began sculpting political districts through patronage, poll taxes, redlining, voter control, or gerrymandering. Minority residents were often siloed in the dangerous, toxic areas along the waterfront in Port Arthur or the ship channels leading into Houston. In Texas City, Black residents were pushed close to the growing labyrinth of heavy industry on the waterfront and near a growing collection of refineries and chemical plants spewing fumes and dumping by-products into the marshlands.

After Blacks and Latinos had built houses of worship, opened stores, and buried their dead in segregated cemeteries, those same neighborhoods could be appropriated, bulldozed, or paved to make way for warehouses, more railroad lines, and highways that could move big trucks across Texas. In time, with that constant manipulation in Black or Latino neighborhoods around the state—in the east and west sides of San Antonio, in the *segundo barrio* of Houston, in South Dallas—some residents were also beginning to talk about common ground and how to use politics to reverse the racist patterns, how to register more people to vote, and how to send more minorities to office.

Many Black Texans descended from slave families hoped that the bigger cities would serve as safer havens—cities where, during Reconstruction, they could seek help from Freedmen's Bureau agents; cities where they could escape the evils that had consumed doomed souls all the way to the Sabine River. But then, after they had walked all the way to Dallas, San Antonio, Fort Worth, Houston, Corpus Christi, and El Paso, they'd find themselves ordered to harshly segregated corners of town. One of Texas's greatest musicians—Aaron Thibeaux "T-Bone" Walker—had fled his part of East Texas, near Linden, and arrived in Dallas. He wished the city would give him sanctuary, some sense of protection against the shadows headed toward Louisiana and Arkansas.

In Dallas, Walker immersed himself in his craft and studied with the primogenitor blues genius Blind Lemon Jefferson (whose silhouette would later be used on Texas license plates). And he learned quickly that Blacks in Dallas were going to live in the Bottoms, those moist, snake-infested areas along the flooding banks of the Trinity River. In 1929, Walker's first record was called "Trinity River Blues," recorded under the name "Oak Cliff T-Bone," a nod to the once-vibrant city that Dallas had annexed. His song was an eloquent, aching ode to how tenuous life was for the men, women, and children mired in the many places where Blacks or Latinos "had to live."

Segregation was enforced by police under direct orders from lawmakers— and it was enforced by vigilantes whom lawmakers chose not to control. At the same time, crusading minority newspapers, church leaders, and teachers continued to remind residents to access the political process. Membership in city, state, and national groups dedicated to political rights— including the NAACP and fraternal organizations—began to grow. The rising awareness led a number of white women to respond to the lynchings, including a carefully thought-out political response led by the Association of Southern Women for the Prevention of Lynching, founded by the Texas-born suffragette Jessie Daniel Ames.

Her idea was to convince lawmakers that lynchings were too often justified as a de facto response to perceived attacks on "Southern womanhood." Ames and other women interested in politics in Texas, including Minnie Fisher Cunningham, hoped that confronting the lynchings would become part of a broader dialogue about social calamities, and open up discussions about equal rights for women in the workplace, in higher education, and in marriage. Ames was also the legislative chairman of the League of Women Voters in Texas, and she wanted women to unite into a voting bloc: "Gradually it came over me that someone with enough background to do it was going to have to get out and tell white Texans—and women especially—that until we were ready to stand up and say in public that we would include Negroes in social benefits we might as well quit."[10]

In Austin, weary insiders were shaking their heads and saying the same thing: Texas seemed addicted to style over substance, and Ma Ferguson was proof. She was almost too predictable, and once again haunted by issuing too many pardons, and by the complaint that she and her husband still enjoyed shady connections with contractors doing state work, especially ones hired to lay down the tar for Texas highways.

In 1935, the fiery and young-looking Texas attorney general, James Allred, ran a gubernatorial campaign promising to once again cure the worst inclinations of the Fergusons. He said he would clean house, tame lobbyists, and make electricity and other utilities more affordable. In a direct blast leveled against the doomed Fergusons, a clan he had observed up close and personal during their tidal wave of criminal pardons, he added that he also wanted to empower a state board to oversee pardons and paroles.

Allred was a staunch Democrat, in constant contact with Cactus Jack Garner in Washington, and also a strong supporter of the Roosevelt administration. Texas was going to be receiving $350 million in New Deal money from FDR's New Deal programs, in large part because Cactus Jack Garner was steering the money to the state. Allred also had the public relations good fortune to be in office during the greatest moment of self-celebration in Texas history: the 1936 Texas Centennial Exposition at Fair

Park in Dallas was created to honor the one-hundredth anniversary of the Republic of Texas and was meant to be a Depression-era diversion of the highest order.

The initial eighty acres for the fairgrounds were donated by William Gaston, a diehard Confederate captain who had seen extensive action in the Civil War and then willed great portions of Dallas into existence. He was the richest man in the city, and he created the earliest iterations of the city's most important financial institutions—First National Bank and Republic Bank. The Centennial planned for the old Confederate soldier's land was meant to be the brashest, boldest proclamation of Texas exceptionalism.

The Dallas architect George Dahl designed the Art Deco buildings, lagoon, and esplanade to his exact wishes and described the pervasive style as "Texanic." Dahl wanted a brawny look: "Strong and bold, a quality possessed to an unusual degree by the majority of the residents of Texas."[11] Fifty new buildings were erected in less than a year, along with giant sculptures and intricate, flowing murals devoted to chapters of Texas history—minus the lynchings, the ethnic cleansings, the mighty influence of the KKK, and the iron-willed way the Texas Rangers had enforced matters in Old Mexico.

With President Roosevelt relying on advice from his so-called Black Cabinet advisors, centennial organizers were pressured to make room for a federally funded Hall of Negro Life. The one-story building was filled with books, exhibits, and dozens of works of art, including murals by the Harlem Renaissance painter Aaron Douglas. The images showed the first known Black slaves to arrive in Texas, with a poignant portrait of families in chains as they watched the ship that had delivered them to Texas sailing away.

When the Centennial opened, in early June 1936, thousands of curious visitors toured the Hall of Negro Life, and many were startled to learn it had integrated bathrooms. A. Maceo Smith and other Black leaders in Dallas hoped the Hall would play a lingering, pivotal role in reshaping the way Texans viewed minorities. Smith was emblematic of the minority activists who were using neighborhood resources and grassroots canvassing to organize voters and push for change. A native of Texarkana, he had a graduate degree in business from New York University and had also studied at Columbia University before running his own advertising agency in New York. When he moved to Dallas in the early 1930s, he ran the *Dallas Express*—required reading for anyone who wanted to know the realities of life in Black Dallas and, frankly, Black America. Smith helped oversee and run the Hall of Negro Life, and hoped it would lead state lawmakers to view the Black voter in an entirely different way. That hope was mitigated by another spectacular unveiling in Dallas just days after the Centennial opened. President Roosevelt was in the city to attend the Texas celebration, but he also made time to travel to a small area near Turtle Creek for the dedication of a towering sculpture of Confederate General Robert E. Lee. The fourteen-foot-tall sculpture depicted a defiant Lee charging ahead on horseback with a faithful, unnamed soldier following him on another steed—installed on a massive granite base and flanked by a viewing bench. Plans were under way to add to the memorial site by building a replica of Lee's Virginia mansion.

Roosevelt offered some remarks at the dedication: "All over the United States, we regard him as a great leader of men and a great general," and "one of the greatest American Christians and one of our greatest American gentlemen."[12]

Against that backdrop, the Hall of Negro Life was simply an aberration for many in Texas—a regrettable concession to liberal Republicans and weak-willed Democrats, and to all the ill-informed leaders still wanting to impose something unwanted on Texas. Dallas had been the national headquarters of the KKK, and its members were still in place throughout the city administration. The Negro Hall was built on land provided by a Confederate general. A year after it opened, Dallas leaders voted to have the Hall of Negro Life torn down and demolished—it was, at the time, the only Texas Centennial building to be razed.

At the urging of the media mogul William Randolph Hearst, John Nance Garner had flirted with his own run for the presidency in the early 1930s before deciding to accept the vice presidential slot under FDR. Hearst had loved the idea of selling a Texas stereotype like Garner to the American people: he wanted to promote "Cactus Jack" from Blossom Prairie as the crusty but benign friend of the common man, a true rootin'-tootin' son of the romanticized West, a tough-talking, buck-stops-here Texan. But Garner and Hearst couldn't summon the right traction, so when FDR's political machine outflanked them, Garner very reluctantly agreed to serve as FDR's vice presidential candidate.

Garner told his powerful friends from Starr and Duval Counties that the vice presidency wasn't worth a "bucket of warm piss" (some of those friends said he used the word "spit" instead of "piss"). But still he managed to bargain for the power to patrol the hallways of Congress, to be the president's backroom muscle—cajoling, urging, and shoving congressional leaders into doing FDR's bidding. Garner loved plying Washington power players with bourbon in backroom meetings until he landed the legislation he wanted—including federal funding, in the middle of the Great Depression, for the world's tallest masonry column: the San Jacinto Monument, on the Houston Ship Channel, that is topped with a 220-ton star commemorating the Battle of San Jacinto, which led to the birth of the Texas republic.

With FDR anxious to push his New Deal, he wanted Garner to keep going below deck, into those drinking sessions, and into the hallways to work his magic. Garner took on the social lubrication, thinking it would position him for another run for the Oval Office. Meanwhile, he kept playing the Texas caricature in public—the blunt, pug-bodied man with cigars and short-brim cowboy hats (Stetsons and then Resistols, the Texas-made hats that claimed to "resist" sweat). His wife was his secretary and chief of staff, and cooked pots of beans for him in his office.

If there were doubts about his influence as vice president, they disappeared when he convinced the president to name the Houston magnate Jesse Jones as the czar lording over the intricate financial and regulatory maneuverings that could prop up banks stumbling through the darkest days of the Depression. Jones was an enormously wealthy banker, developer, and media mogul from Houston, and FDR agreed to appoint him to lead the mighty Reconstruction Finance Corporation, overseeing billions of dollars in funding and government loans that might help cities, states, and businesses rebound from the Great Depression. The political calculus involved in FDR appointing the most powerful man in Houston to oversee a national financial empire is beyond measure. Lyndon Baines Johnson summarized it best when he referred to Jones as "Jesus H. Jones."

Having Jones in charge of a huge domestic program was only one of Garner's gifts to Texas. From the outset of the war on the Great Depression, he was resolute, moving from agency to agency in Washington, from one politician's office to the next, offering deals if he could be assured of support for FDR's proposals—and maybe support for airports, military bases, ports, canals, and highways in Texas.

His Lone Star swashbuckling wasn't lost on many, especially those still prone to marginalize his home state as both a strange beast and a legislatively ineffective outpost—a place so incestuous, corrupt, and inelegant that it could hardly be the kind of prominent political flagship that would house useful, electable national officials. Garner kept dancing on the head of a pin by playing to the Cactus Jack image that Hearst and his supporters loved, but also by trying to reassure Northerners that Texas could produce men who could translate to the rest of the country.

Perhaps it was hubris, a kind of Texas pride from a man who had been accustomed to getting reelected for several decades, but Garner eventually turned so hard against the latter stages of the New Deal that he attempted a palace coup. Even though he was vice president, Garner wanted to replace FDR, and he conferred with conservative Southern Democrats to see if he could actually do it. But the takeover was never going to work, especially with a nation solidifying amid the perils of World War II, and Garner lost out in his scramble to run against his own boss.

For a while he was the most powerful Texan in the nation—or at least the most influential politician from Texas. He was a congressman, Speaker of the House, and vice president, and he had mentored generations of climbing Texas politicians, including several who wanted to be president. Garner would eventually board a train bound from Washington to Texas, vowing never to cross the Potomac again. He "retired" to Uvalde after a half century of active politics and became a cagey shadow advisor to dozens of the most important politicians to emerge from Texas—from Speaker of the House Sam Rayburn to Lyndon B. Johnson. National figures, from presidents Truman to Kennedy, always knew to call on him long after he had gone home to Texas.

Under the eyes of loyal caretakers, Garner would spend his final years in Uvalde working in real estate—and overseeing the destruction of many of his personal papers. For reasons that remain unclear, his wife set fire to many of his documents, and history lost key clues to the man who paved the way for Texans to move to the Oval Office.[13] He had raised the profile of politicians from the state and demonstrated that people born in a Texas log cabin could battle at dizzying levels, especially when they had access to spigots of wealth. Garner's great gift to future generations was to blunt the view of Texas as a barely cohesive political backwater. And his crafty, brutal efficiency led others to see the state as a place they could move to for political opportunities—and maybe use as a cushy, monied launching pad for universes well beyond Texas.

Eighty-four miles east of Uvalde, a young girl named Emma Tenayuca was clutching the hands of her grandfather as they left their west San Antonio home and traveled to the Plaza del Zacate near Santa Rosa Hospital.

When she was as young as sixteen, Emma Tenayuca of San Antonio walked picket lines on behalf of workers—most famously, pecan shellers—who were being denied fair wages and benefits. Her activism corresponded with a deepening understanding that women were particularly subjugated in both the workplace and the political arena.

Her grandfather, a carpenter, was beginning her political education. He wanted her to hear speeches from organizers, activists, and old revolutionaries who had gathered in the plaza, often talking excitedly in Spanish about their various struggles in Texas and Mexico.

Her family had Native American blood in its heritage and could trace its roots to the very beginning of San Antonio and Texas, and her grandfather believed that the children needed to know their history, especially the way the indigenous people, Tejanos, Mexicans, and Latinos had not just lost their land but been subjected to racism and political exclusion, all while providing the hard labor that went into running the farming operations and vast ranches stretching across South Texas.

Sitting on the plaza grass in San Antonio, the teenaged Tenayuca was mesmerized by the eloquent soapbox speakers. They stood, one by one, to talk about the news of the day, to quote from the Bible, to read from the pages of Spanish-language newspapers, and to convey what they knew about the still-shifting political climate south of the Rio Grande. As she grew up, she began connecting the dots between the unsettled conditions in Mexico and the way families were heading north for jobs and more security. San Antonio especially was attracting more Mexican immigrants, many desperate for any kind of work, even if it involved being paid next to nothing inside sweltering factories or on dangerous assembly lines.

A heavy influx of those immigrants to Texas occurred in the late 1920s—almost three hundred thousand had arrived from 1925 to 1929— and Tenayuca felt that people were being "segregated into colonies" and that "disease, low wage[s], discrimination and lack of educational facilities" were typical.[14] Often the only jobs—paying $2 or $3 a week—were for garment workers, migrant workers, maids, pecan shellers, and tobacco rollers. Because they lacked proof of citizenship, immigrants were routinely barred from New Deal employment efforts like the WPA. Cotton pickers in Texas were earning as little as thirty-five cents for every hundred-pound bale. And when Tenayuca tried to determine how many Latinos were registered to vote in San Antonio, she learned that almost half the city, about 125,000 residents, had Mexican heritage but just 8,000 had the right to vote.

By the 1930s, lawmakers in Texas and around the nation were sending more and more immigrants—and native-born Americans—back to Mexico. The 1917 Immigration Act had moved into high gear in the 1920s after the creation of the federal border patrol agency, and now many people were trapped inside a system that had once been wide open, with thousands of new arrivals migrating into the country and often unaware of how to seek any official documentation. After 1929, when it became a federal crime to cross the border without the right papers, the Depression-era anti-immigrant fervor led nativist white politicians, including President Herbert Hoover, to argue for aggressive deportation.

Orders were issued to round up residents, and into the mid-1930s hundreds of thousands of people, perhaps close to two million, were "repatriated." It was another staggering round of aggressive ethnic and racial cleansing, a shattering assault tied to all the others that had preceded it. From the eradication of the Native Americans, to the seizure of lands from the earliest Tejanos, to the wicked ways segregation was whipped forward, there was a cold efficiency in the laws and the politicians entrusted to enforce them.[15]

Some Texas leaders, including Garner and his young protégé, Congressman Martin Dies from southeast Texas, were convinced that Mexicans were either an inferior addition to the human race or destined to be a nagging, unemployed burden. They were joined in the racism by labor leaders clamoring about saving jobs for white workers. No one knows the exact final number of people forced to leave Texas and other states during the Depression, but the upheaval, the uprooting, fed the bitterness—and groomed grassroots political efforts centered on better schools and bilingual education, issues that would remain at the hot center of Texas politics for decades.

In San Antonio, Tenayuca continued to visit the plaza, known to many as Milam Park: "It was there that I learned," she remembered later. "There was always some talk of politics. I had become very, very interested in the labor movement."[16]

The League of United Latin American Citizens, LULAC, had formed in Corpus Christi in 1929 and was filled with small business owners. Tenayuca knew her grandfather had traversed San Antonio to summon Latino resistance to the KKK, even rallying support for Ma Ferguson in the 1920s when she was running against a Klan-endorsed candidate. Tenayuca studied newspapers and flyers, reading about the American Federation of Labor (AFL) and the Congress of Industrial Organizations (CIO). She also knew her family—and so many others—had lost their life savings when the banks had collapsed in the stock market crash. And in the wake of the Mexican Revolution, after the 1910 uprising, San Antonio and other cities had seen the great arrival of what she called "peasants"—farmworkers who spent winters in city plants and then, in the spring and summer, moved to the Rio Grande Valley, Colorado, Michigan, and so many other places to pick beets, onions, spinach, and other crops. Money was brought back or delivered to San Antonio, and "they would buy a little piece of land and then start building little shacks."[17]

She also dwelled on the fact that women were often the ones going to work in dismal factories, including one run by the historic Finck Cigar Company in San Antonio. And when she heard that four hundred female cigar rollers and tobacco strippers were going on strike, the sixteen-year-old Tenayuca joined the picket line downtown. City and state lawmakers were staggered to see Mexicans, mostly women, protesting, and the police were ordered to round people up. It was not the last time Tenayuca would be arrested, and her activism corresponded with a deeper understanding that women were particularly subjugated in both the workplace and the political arena.

She had heroes, women she admired: Babe Didrikson Zaharias, perhaps the greatest athlete ever from Texas. In the 1932 Olympics, Zaharias set four world records and became the only athlete, of any gender, to win individual Olympic medals in running, throwing, and jumping contests. Tenayuca also revered the mercurial aviator Amelia Earhart, who dominated national headlines. And she admired Eleanor Roosevelt, who was carving out a legacy in Washington during her husband's administration.

Tenayuca weighed how women were excluded from the upper ranks of LULAC. She quit an auxiliary branch of the organization in 1933 and, barely out of high school, helped form an offshoot of the International Ladies' Garment Workers' Union in San Antonio. Tenayuca organized seamstresses and dressmakers who were being paid pennies per article of clothing. She was also developing a reputation as a reliable counselor to freshly arrived Spanish-speaking immigrants, and to many longer term residents who didn't know where to turn after being injured on the job, or who had seen their work hours or wages trimmed, or who were afraid of being picked up and shipped back to Mexico—even if they were legal citizens.

Then, in 1937, she and many others in Texas—and around the world—were reminded of how poorly the state was regulated, and how some political leaders had put more emphasis on industrialization than on the welfare of working people.

In New London, Texas, workers and their families had been crowding into the once sparsely populated area, racing toward the jobs in the new oil patches. Drillers had hit the "big elephant field," the mother lode of oil in Rusk County—and the world changed almost overnight. Money was pouring into local coffers, and city leaders spent an almost unheard-of $1 million on the modern, sprawling London School. Hundreds of students of all ages and grades attended, and some reports suggested that the unlikely New London had one of the richest educational districts in the nation.

On Thursday, March 18, 1937, the school building began to rock, buckle, and heave, and then there was a deafening roar as the entire place exploded. Children were hurtled into the sky, metal lockers were rocketed into the air, and the rumbling could be felt for miles. Close to three hundred people were killed, including dozens of students who were obliterated by the blast. Their bodies were mangled, some virtually unrecognizable and others simply never found. It was, together with the 1900 hurricane in Galveston, the deadliest disaster in state history, even eclipsing the number of people killed in the racially charged Slocum Massacre.

A young reporter named Walter Cronkite was on the scene, covering one of his first assignments. German chancellor Adolf Hitler sent a telegram to the survivors expressing his condolences. In the wake of the unspeakable horror, scientists began adding a strong smell to the normally odorless natural gas. And for political activists, there was blood on the hands of the governor and state officials: Texas hadn't done enough to regulate and safeguard the oil and gas industry, the boomtowns, and the legions of unsuspecting workers and families who had seen the still-gurgling oil industry as an economic safety net. But, like many other subsequent human-made tragedies at industrial plants around the state, often deep inside petrochemical plants along the mechanized Texas coast, the New London disaster would shock political leaders into making robust denouncements and promises for change. And then the tragedies would fade into memory, plants would be built in the same places where they had claimed lives, and jaded observers of industrial Texas would count the days until another explosion occurred.

After the nightmare in New London, Tenayuca knew changes had to be made, and that any strike that was going to succeed in Texas had to be centered on a particular trade. In San Antonio, she had met several women working in the city's pecan-shelling plants. San Antonio had become the epicenter of the state's robust pecan industry, with growers shipping produce from orchards in the Texas Hill Country. Four hundred shelling plants operated in the greater San Antonio and South Central Texas region, processing close to half the nation's supply. As many as twelve thousand pecan shellers—sometimes children, often women—sat in unventilated warehouses and breathed in suffocating clouds of dust and dirt. Sometimes a worker would stand up and stagger to a doorway as she coughed up blood. Doctors began diagnosing record numbers of cases of tuberculosis among the shellers: the city had 148 tuberculosis deaths for every one hundred thousand people. (Nationally, the average was 54 for every one hundred thousand people.)

Women of all ages—some lied about how old they were just to get a job—worked twelve hours a day sardined alongside one another and hunched over wooden tables. They picked the pecans apart by hand and put the nut meats in old motor oil or soup cans. There were flickering, dim lights overhead, and a sooty cumulus of dust coated faces, hair, and clothing. Expensive modern shelling machines were available, but it was usually cheaper to use the women to pinch, crack, and excavate every pecan by hand. Workers were only given a few breaks during the day—and when they were able to get one, they had to resort to using fetid wooden outhouses on a patch of dirt behind the plants. At dusk, people in San Antonio grew accustomed to seeing the lines of women leaving the plants and beginning their miles-long walks back to their tiny homes on the west side of the city: El West Side was dotted with one-hundred-square-foot lean-tos that families were renting for less than a dollar a week.

Tenayuca decided to test the will of lawmakers.[18] She was sure the city's progressive congressman, Maury Maverick, often accused by foes of being a socialist bordering on communist, wouldn't stand in the way. On the last day of January 1938, after some shelling companies had cut wages in half—from six cents per pound to three cents per pound—Tenayuca convinced hundreds of workers to walk off the job.

News of the shutdown and its implications raced immediately to Austin. The number of strikers was growing, well into the thousands. The work stoppage in San Antonio was unnerving and not just because of the scale: it was led by a Latina, and it involved waves of workers once presumed to be docile. Worse, it could serve as a model at other plants, fields, refineries, and waterfronts around Texas. Given the broader dangers, state lawmakers and local police decided to clamp down hard, and they ignored Maverick's tacit endorsement of the walkouts.

Hundreds of workers—including many American-born shellers—were arrested, gassed, or brought to immigration authorities and threatened with deportation. The chief of police oversaw at least seven hundred arrests, declared the strike to be a "red plot" by communists, and sent so many people into county jails that the imprisoned workers complained they were stacked on top of one another.

Tenayuca urged the women to stay united, to share what food and money they had. She was amazed at the solidarity, and it suggested to her that there was a deep, festering rage at inequities—not just in the pecan plants, but also in the schools, in the neighborhoods, in the fields. She kept rallying workers, and the standoff lingered for thirty-seven days. In the end, the shellers agreed to arbitration and saw their wages raised to as high as eight cents per pound.

Political leaders—especially those aligned with Rep. Martin Dies, someone developing a reputation as one of the nation's fiercest "communist hunters"—learned that Tenayuca had married a member of the Communist Party. That fact was broadcast around the state by newspapers friendly to Dies, Garner, and hardcore conservative Democrats. After the strike, Tenayuca found herself routinely stopped by the police or brought to a station for questioning. Friends told her to be careful and to watch her back, and that there were probably more people than she knew who wanted her dead.

In the deepest part of the summer of 1939, in late August, she got word that Maury Maverick—whose grandfather had signed the Texas Declaration of Independence, and whose last name gave "maverick" to the English language—was going to allow her to use the elegant Municipal Auditorium in San Antonio. She was planning a big rally to fight for the end of segregation.

Maverick was a courageous figure in the history of Texas politics (as was his son, Maury Maverick Jr., who would serve as a crusading state representative and staunch ally to many progressive and minority political figures in Texas). A former county tax collector, he campaigned in the poorer Latino neighborhoods of the city and was sent to Congress in 1934, where he'd serve until being elected mayor in 1939. Maverick was derided by his worst opponents as a closet Marxist, a pro-labor radical who was too enamored with most of FDR's New Deal. In Washington, he had endured the scorn of the domineering Garner, someone who had risen to power, and stayed in power, with the direct support of the feudal political systems that subjugated poor Latinos in South Texas—a system that drove many to escape to Maverick's San Antonio. (During his 1934 campaign for Congress, Maverick had relied on help from a young political newcomer named Lyndon Johnson.)

Maverick's pro-labor inclinations made it easy for him to sign off on letting Tenayuca hold her rally in the main city auditorium, but his decision was quickly condemned by business leaders. Local newspapers stirred up hysteria, suggesting that the rally was going to be a radical hive. (When I worked as an arts editor in San Antonio in the 1970s, the *Express-News* was nationally infamous for its lurid political headlines, anti-gay editorial cartoons, and sensationalized stories.)

On the day of the rally, just as she tried to give her speech, Tenayuca could hear a commotion echoing outside. Thousands of people had circled the building, and it was unlike anything in the city's history. KKK members were chanting, hurling bricks, and demanding that Tenayuca be strung up. Tenayuca, only twenty-two years old, was quickly ushered into a hidden tunnel and out a back door before she could be killed.

Even after Tenayuca fled, the death threats against her lingered. She was blacklisted from jobs until she finally decided to relocate to Houston—and to use a different name to land work. In time, she left Texas altogether and enrolled in college in San Francisco. She eventually came back to Texas to work as an educator and continue her activism and organizing. She taught hundreds of children to read, including many whose parents were pecan shellers. She died at the age of eighty-three and was buried in San Antonio's Mission Burial Park grounds, where several other Texans, native and adopted, are laid to rest: Elizabeth Toepperwein, considered by some (including Annie Oakley) to be the greatest female marksman in history—she could shoot while standing on her head; baseball Hall of Famer Rube Waddell; the so-called Prophet of Spindletop, Portillo Higgins, a one-armed explorer who was there when the wells blew and hundreds of thousands of gallons of oil rocketed into the air; and the constable and Texas Ranger Johnny Klevenhagen, who had investigated "The Alligator Man"—a murderer who fed his victims to five alligators in a pond he had installed behind the Sociable Inn. Three Texas congressmen—Lewis Featherstone, Thomas Paschal, and James Slayden—are also buried in Mission Burial Park.

And, finally, there is Emma Tenayuca's very simple grave. She is not far from the old Mission Road and a gentle curve in the San Antonio River. Her resting place is noted by a rectangular marker lying on a lush patch of grass. The marker is decorated with garlands of flowers.

It has four words on it: "Thy Will Be Done."

CHAPTER 8

Beautiful Texas: The 1940s

AT THE BURRUS FLOUR MILL IN Fort Worth, a stout and beaming Wilbert
Lee O'Daniel had a brainstorm: he was going to convince his bosses to
spend money on the latest way to reach the most customers possible, the
radio airwaves. When they finally agreed, he assembled a band of cracker-
jack musicians called the Light Crust Doughboys, who had been busy inventing ways to merge blues, jazz, and country into a catchy style called
Texas swing or Western swing. The group featured Bob Wills and Milton
Brown, two of the state's greatest artists.

O'Daniel felt good, like he was on the verge of something that was
going to be so big, so huge, that it would change his life forever. Born
in Ohio and raised in Kansas, he had grown up living hand to mouth in
a tenant-farming family before going to work in flour mills around the
country. At every stop, he seemed to make friends instantly, telling jokes
and even breaking into song. Each mill that he worked at recognized him
as a natural-born marketer—someone who was gifted at selling flour,
especially at a time when more and more women were keeping struggling
households fed by making their own bread.

O'Daniel left Burrus in the mid-1930s and formed his own firm—
Hillbilly Flour—where he started another band called the Hillbilly Boys.
O'Daniel penned ditties about the joys of flour, raising families, whole-

some living, and the romantic legacy of cowboys and their steeds. Five days a week, close to noon, Texas families would gather around the radio and listen to the soothing patter from "Pappy" O'Daniel: *How do you do, ladies and gentlemen, and hello there, boys and girls. This is W. Lee O'Daniel speaking.*

It was conversational, like having a country uncle or grandfather sitting with you on the front porch swing and sipping iced tea. In a state with thousands of newcomers and even many longtimers in search of both community and continuity, O'Daniel dished dollops of Jesus and Texas hosannas, reminding listeners they weren't alone, that they were bonded by being part of a blessed oasis and that the decision to come to Texas was divine providence. O'Daniel was building a political constituency through mass media, crafted folksiness, and religion. Simultaneously, he was selling himself, Texas, his business products, and Christianity. He was also reaching, on a daily basis, a neglected group of possible political supporters.

O'Daniel preached directly to countless women running households across sanctified Texas: *Hello there, mother, you little sweetheart. How in the world are you, anyway, you little bundle of sweetness?* It was corny and it was effective. He sold tons of flour as your friend Pappy, an understanding and caring soul, a person predisposed to write poems and odes to women. The kind of person *you* might be predisposed to vote for.

On Palm Sunday in early April 1938, those women and others who had made his show the most popular in Texas listened as O'Daniel confided that he had come across a special letter inside the massive stacks of mail he regularly received. He said it was a plea—allegedly from a blind man—that Pappy save the citizens of Texas from the un-Christian cesspool run by the oily professionals in Austin. O'Daniel humbly asked his audience if a son of Jesus like himself should run for higher office—maybe for governor. A month after he had teased his audience, he was on the air again, announcing that the listeners and God wanted him to run for governor. He added that his campaign platform was simple: the Ten Commandments.

A few weeks before the Democratic primary, O'Daniel led a musical caravan with a bright-red circus wagon and his Hillbilly Boys to Waco. The city had only about ten thousand residents, but people flooded in from surrounding cities and towns, and O'Daniel spoke from a stage to more than twenty thousand supporters. The same thing happened over and over again. In Houston, twenty-six thousand were waiting for him, many of them shouting his campaign slogan—"Pass the Biscuits, Pappy"—and waving flyers that read "Flour, Not Pork."

He kept traveling, hawking himself as the upbeat, blessed antidote to the somber, crooked devils running the statehouse—someone who would take a broom to the stables and clean out the political Pharisees. He had other slogans: "Less Johnson grass and politicians, more smokestacks and businessmen." As Texas tried to shake the Depression dregs, O'Daniel was a sunshine optimist promising to restore faith in all senses of the word to the state. He offered a palliative to voters tired of being wary of outsiders, immigrants, aliens, invaders, communists, and carpetbaggers. The Depression had sapped spirits, and news headlines were pointing toward mounting tensions in Europe—and with the state so spread out, so large, so often disconnected, O'Daniel had found a brilliant way to form his own Texas congregation. His rallies would often kick off with a rendition of a song he had written called "Beautiful Texas," which would become a country standard over the years, performed by everyone from Hank Thompson to Willie Nelson:

> Beautiful, beautiful Texas
> Where the beautiful bluebonnets grow
> We're proud of our forefathers
> Who fought at the Alamo.
>
> You can live on the plains or the mountains
> Or down where the sea breezes blow
> And you're still in beautiful Texas
> The most beautiful place that I know.

He never stopped selling his flour, he shouted lines from the New Testament, he steered his catchy band through the sunny tunes, and he issued outrageous political promises, including guaranteeing every older Texan a pension. His impossible enticements were early warning signs that O'Daniel was massively underqualified to swim with the seasoned sharks in Austin, Dallas, and Houston—in all the places where the Texas political hierarchy had taken root.

Years later, the officially appointed biographer of Ronald Reagan shocked the president's family by writing that Reagan possessed an "encyclopedic ignorance," including his lack of understanding about the very way governments worked. That harsh assessment wouldn't be an unfair one applied to O'Daniel, but it didn't seem to matter to the Texans who voted for him. He wasn't a soaring visionary, nor was he someone who had his nose in a book or tried to emulate the great men of history. He understood that many voters in the state wanted to relate to their political leaders more than they wanted to be impressed by their leaders' academic pretensions.

(It was a political plan followed by future generations of Texans: a friend of mine at the *New York Times* would write a wonderful book about Texas governor George W. Bush's campaign for the presidency—one in which Bush's media strategist in Austin, Mark McKinnon, worked overtime to market Bush as the unpretentious friend of the common man, an anti-intellectual guy from the heartland, someone who could understand the hopes and ambitions of farmers along the Red River, ranchers in San Benito, and factory workers in Pasadena, as opposed to being a multimillionaire Ivy Leaguer from New Haven, Connecticut, with a drinking problem. My friend's book was titled *Ambling into History*, suggesting that a politician could succeed in Texas and beyond even if they were fundamentally unclear on history's details or short on a true grasp of the legislative gears. You could be highly electable to some voters uninterested in intellectuals or master parliamentarians and looking instead for candidates who mixed a bit of Jesus with a splash of Will Rogers.)

O'Daniel won his first primary, then the general election, and began giving hungry Texans even more of what he believed they really wanted— a colorful sideshow away from the grinding realities of the Depression, the oil patches, the cotton fields, and the areas where whites recoiled at the way Blacks and Latinos increasingly questioned why life was still the way it was in Texas. When he was sworn in for his first term, he said the state capitol steps were too small and had his ceremony moved to Memorial Stadium at the University of Texas, where sixty thousand followers could watch him put his hand on the Bible. As many as one hundred thousand of his loyalists descended on Austin. He wanted parades on Congress Avenue, dozens of marching bands, and streets cordoned off for dancing.

After O'Daniel waltzed into Austin, he wanted the good times to keep rolling. His plan to fork over state pensions to every Texan over the age of sixty-five fell on its face when he was unable to figure out how to fund it. He tried and failed to rewrite the state constitution so it would allow a permanent cap on taxes. Meanwhile, he kept airing his radio show, his odes to flour and Texas, but this time from his desk inside the governor's mansion. And the deeper into his tenure he went, the more whispers circulated that he was no different from Ma and Pa Ferguson in terms of lining his pockets and doling out jobs, appointments, and patronage to friends (one of the musicians in the Hillbilly Boys was installed in the Texas National Guard as an officer). A researcher would later find some correspondence from the governor's office with a little message at the bottom: "Buy Hill-billy Flour."

The Fergusons might have had enough experience inside the political system to at least lurch occasionally toward a modicum of effectiveness. Even if their legacy wasn't defined by crusading work, they knew their way around Austin better than the flour salesman from Kansas. The writer Robert Caro, who spent decades trying to fathom Lyndon Baines John-son, considered O'Daniel—a man who would figure prominently in LBJ's political fortunes—a complete mess. "Totally ignorant of the mechanics of government ... unwilling to make even a pretense of learning," said Caro. "He offered few significant programs in any area, preferring to submit legislation that he knew could not possibly pass and then blame the legis-lature for not passing it."[1]

In 1940, O'Daniel conscripted a photographer from the Texas Depart-ment of Public Safety to join him on a madcap swing across the state. O'Daniel told aides he was going on the road to reach out to voters, to his people. It was unprecedented and beyond ambitious. His master plan was to visit the towns and even the homes of every single state senator and rep-resentative, and then pose for pictures with locals, shake hands, and get his name in front-page newspaper stories announcing his triumphant ar-rival. O'Daniel would barrel in with his entourage and jump out to make a speech; sing a song; curl an arm around the mayor, librarian, and school principal—and then sleep in his car before hitting the road again. He'd pack in as many towns as he could in a single day, making sure to know the names of anyone important that he'd be meeting.

When Europe erupted in war, Texans, like everyone, wondered what the future held. The nervousness was palpable, and O'Daniel sensed that voters feared they had placed their futures in the hands of political and business "insiders" who could profit from war but who would no doubt never have to serve in a war. Adept at reading the Zeitgeist and taking the tempera-ture of the electorate, O'Daniel touched on the fears and used them. Gear-ing up for reelection in 1940, he adopted an "angry populist" persona, tell-ing voters that his first term as governor had opened his eyes to the very problems real Texans always suspected were going on in Austin: infighting, more corruption, and cabals of small-minded political hacks acting in their own interests instead of fighting the socialists, union organizers, and communists threatening jobs, schools, and neighborhoods.

Veteran politicians were still worried that his lack of interest in the nuances of governing was setting Texas back years. O'Daniel doubled down. At a time when Texans were being warned about so many issues, organizations, and people—from spies to war—O'Daniel said that dark forces were afoot: that a rich, closely held group of men were conspiring to run the state and were dedicated to ousting him from the governor's mansion. As a testament to the loyalty he enjoyed on the airwaves, to how fearmongering can work, and finally to how many Texas voters craved continuity, he won his second term.

After his election night victory, he promptly traveled to a ranch in the Texas Hill Country. He wanted to be photographed hovering over a penned buffalo that he was going to shoot from a few feet away and that would be served up at a record-making, swearing-in barbecue party back in Austin.

Drivers cruising by the governor's mansion in early 1941 must have screeched to a halt and stared at the men and women toiling at the Greek Revival building with its half dozen twenty-nine-foot-high columns and stately veranda. Workers were setting up almost two hundred tables in the nearby streets, and thousands of people were lining up for free food. Men were digging out deep pits, dropping logs inside, and lighting the barbecue wood, and then an army of Black servants was carrying in forty thousand pounds of beef and mutton. And they had something else: small batches of buffalo that "Pappy" had killed at point-blank range.

When O'Daniel first put his name down as a candidate, veteran Austin political consultants had scoffed at him as a buffoon, a supremely unqualified freak who was lucky to blow away all the somber political protocols passed along by the sons of the South, the law-and-order candidates, and the oilmen. Later, the kingmakers had to retreat to their offices along Congress Avenue and consider the possibility that O'Daniel had rewritten some of the rules of campaigning in Texas. Despite his obvious flaws as a statesman, he had found a new way of pursuing office.

There was one particularly hungry politician watching and learning from Pappy's triumphs and his abject ineffectiveness. The young US Congressman Lyndon Baines Johnson understood that Texas had never seen a candidate like O'Daniel, so capable of buttering up voters. O'Daniel had taken the Ferguson and Garner "Texas flavor" and pushed it into another orbit, but then he simply fell into a drowning pool by thinking his sheer popularity and public relations expertise would help him survive the politicking required inside the statehouse. Johnson was studying very closely, borrowing and subtracting exactly what he needed from the O'Daniel political playbook.

In 1941, the sixty-five-year-old US senator Morris Sheppard, the Texarkana man who had held his seat since 1913 and was often most memorable for his passionate stance against alcohol, had a brain hemorrhage and died, on April 9. Immediately, several Democrats began circling to take his seat, including O'Daniel, Rep. Martin Dies, and the thirty-two-year-old Johnson, the pro–New Dealer and supporter of FDR who had been elected to Congress four years earlier.

O'Daniel, sick of his growing number of critics at the statehouse, told friends he had a genius idea for how to connive his way into the Senate: he appointed eighty-six-year-old Gen. Andrew Jackson Houston, the last surviving son of Sam Houston, to temporarily fill the seat, banking on the fact that Houston was frail and, if not at death's door, standing on the walkway leading up to it. Houston passed away three weeks after O'Daniel appointed him, clearing the path for a special election, and O'Daniel was convinced he could easily win.

Johnson, meanwhile, was roaming Texas, pressing the flesh and suggesting that even though he was young, he could take the place of Sheppard—who had spent almost as much time in the Senate as Johnson had been alive. Building toward the June special election, Johnson made sure to hand out photos of himself posing with FDR—something he knew would make John Nance Garner's blood boil but that might show skeptical voters he had big connections. Political analysts began huddling about Johnson's improving chances, how his crowds were growing, and that he had O'Daniel's common man touch, but with a sober congressional record.

Johnson's campaign was being managed by John Connally, a handsome graduate of the University of Texas at Austin law school and a newly minted attorney who was only in his early twenties. Eager to hear the final tallies, he asked election officials to release vote totals early. When they did, O'Daniel's aides in East Texas promptly and mysteriously found several more late returns that handed O'Daniel a victory by just 1,311 votes. Johnson licked his wounds, pondered the defeat, and realized that O'Daniel had bamboozled him in one of the most suspect elections in state history.

John Connally served as the bridge between the old Democratic dominions and the modern Republican empire in Texas. He helped boost LBJ to power, defined the state for outsiders, and unabashedly abandoned party loyalties.

He and Connally decided that next time they'd work the system to their advantage.

O'Daniel took office in the Senate in August, more or less floundered for the next several months, and then ran in the regular election in 1942. This time, insiders in Austin had enlisted former governors Dan Moody and James Allred to try to run against him. Even though he won, O'Daniel seemed even more stridently concerned about communists, unions, and the way desegregation might chip away at the superior white race. In Washington, he was treated like a leper: he was ignored by other lawmakers, he seemed fixated on his anti-communist rants, and the Associated Press simply labeled him "the Senator who walks alone."

He had already isolated himself by abandoning any support of the president and by voting against a military draft. Into the 1940s, his approval ratings plummeted until he finally opted to leave Washington. He stepped away from the Senate without passing a single bill, and said he would never run again. In 1948, he moved to Fort Worth and dabbled in insurance, real estate, banking, and ranching. He responded to the political siren call two times in the 1950s, trying to win the Democratic nomination for governor, but he was soundly defeated.

He died in 1969 and is interred in a tree-shaded and green-lawned part of Sparkman-Hillcrest Memorial Park in Dallas—a place where baseball star Mickey Mantle, Sen. John Tower, football coach Tom Landry, and other luminaries are laid to rest. His granite memorial, made from stones quarried in the Texas Hill Country, has slight hints of blue in it, giving it a sort of twinkling look if the sunshine hits it at just the right angle. A Texas Historical Commission marker at his site notes that he was a "flour mill executive" who "pioneered in radio advertising and country music." Almost as an afterthought, the marker adds that "in his first try for public office he won a primary over 12 opponents and became governor of Texas." In 2000, a movie made by the Coen brothers, titled *O Brother, Where Art Thou?*, featured a flamboyant, music-playing politician named Governor Pappy O'Daniel.

The newsreels playing at the local movie theaters were turning to the heated situations in Europe. Sears catalogs were still hawking Lionel toy trains, plastic dolls, and electric vacuum cleaners as splendid Christmas gifts. Walt Disney's *Snow White and the Seven Dwarfs* was thrilling viewers. Optimists said that Texas—surfing the oil waves and already enjoying the pork barrels sent down by Garner—was poised for yet another impressive industrial jolt. In Austin, some lawmakers wondered if the city might become a breeding ground for socialist, communist, union organizers.

Emma Tenayuca's activism had alerted Texas leaders to the possible political power of organized labor. The CIO tried to establish a Texas beachhead, hoping to sign up oil workers and dispatch lobbyists to court people in the statehouse who might be intrigued by a union voting bloc. But most Texas lawmakers continued to scowl at the mention of unions. Sensationalist editorial writers, frowning chamber of commerce heads, and conservative powerhouses like Cactus Jack Garner and Martin Dies railed against organized labor and bodies like the Texas State Industrial Council. In public, the Democrats bemoaned unions as threats to the American way of life, and in closed-door campaign strategy sessions, they fretted about voting movements, the kind that would throw support to pro-regulation Republicans.[2]

As the politicians plotted and fretted, chemists were conferring with Monsanto and other companies about ways to turn Houston, Texas City, and other towns on the coast into a connected petrochemical epicenter, working with a kaleidoscope of minerals, alloys, and compounds that would usher America into a twentieth-century Age of Alchemy. Nickel, tin, plastics of every type, natural gas, engine oil, diesel fuel, and myriad other marvels were being processed, refined, and shipped around the clock. A maze of miles of pipes, a metallic Oz of roaring tanks, flares, hoses, storage tanks, and train tracks, was growing on the shallow bays and marshes that a few decades earlier had been mostly devoid of human presence, except for the crab collectors and oyster men pushing their flat-bottomed boats past the great blue herons.

With Hitler threatening Europe, some Texans, including Jesse Jones, had urged President Roosevelt to think about the preparatory possibilities and to build what would become the biggest tin smelter in the Western Hemisphere, on land donated by the Texas City Railway Company, which had been busy transporting oil and chemicals destined for points around the world. In Austin, as the politicos gathered for sandwiches at the newly opened House Park Barbecue, they agreed on a few matters—especially that even with the massive uncertainties defining the 1940s, there was a damned good chance that Texas could continue to profit. There were military bases all over the state; bombs were being made in the Panhandle; the tin smelter was opening; and Texas was going to provide fuel for jeeps, tanks, bombers, and fighter planes.

Anyone who has ever driven Interstate 35 in Texas—or the highways from Houston to Galveston—has heard the complaint that those major arteries have been under construction for decades. Some newspaper wags in Dallas dubbed the highway from Laredo to Dallas and beyond "the highway of death," because it was forever cluttered with car wrecks, overturned eighteen-wheelers, and impossibly narrow lanes jammed with big vehicles hauling goods from Mexico, from the ports, from one end of the nation to the other. In Houston, some locals talked about how you could decorate your home and fix your car by driving up and down the Gulf Freeway—because there would be engines, refrigerators, beds, and televisions that had spilled off pickup trucks and onto the roads and shoulders.

As the automobile and tire industries in the United States conspired to turn the nation into a car-addicted country, a slow but insistent move arose to mute the possibliites of mass transportation in Texas—effectively ending a robust and healthy system of interurban rail lines, all replaced by plans for fresh new highways beginning in the 1940s. City and state lawmakers began to greenlight plans that allowed new roads to be built immediately after the destruction of "freedmen's towns," where Black residents had been allowed to live once slaves were released from bondage. Homes were condemned, some were seized by banks, others were appropriated through eminent domain—with political leaders emphasizing that road construction on a large scale was going to be for the greater good.

Developers, sometimes funded or assisted by local leaders, began the persistent process of scooping up land in and around the freedmen's towns, knowing that the real estate values would skyrocket once the roads were installed. Office buildings, hotels, or apartments could be marketed as having easy access to highways. In Dallas, the highly coordinated effort would eventually lead to the erasure of the historic State Thomas zone, once a thriving, culturally rich area filled with churches and burial grounds.

Central Expressway and then Woodall Rogers Expressway in Dallas would cut the city's most vibrant freedmen's area in half by separating homes from churches and Booker T. Washington High School, which had served as a community center for the city's Black population. (Political leaders ultimately expedited events to a regrettable degree. During one later renovation of Central Expressway, construction workers were horrified to find that the graves of freed slaves and their descendants had been simply paved over by Texas highway crews.)

The road-building and the political patterns in the 1940s and 1950s were really just bits of latter-day Manifest Destiny, with land and whole neighborhoods annexed, acquired, and, some would say, conquered for the sake of economic expansion. In Houston, Interstate 45 and other major roads were going to be ramrodded through the heart of historic Black neighborhoods, and residents were also going to be cut off from their old churches, schools, and businesses that had formed the lifeblood of the Fourth and Fifth Wards. In Austin, Latinos and Blacks saw Interstate 35 and Highway One, often called MoPac in honor of the Missouri-Pacific rail line that it paralleled, erode once vibrant neighborhoods, including Clarksville, where groups of stonemasons from Italy had also once settled. The rush to build Texas highways and to widen shipping lanes along the coast was celebrated on the front pages of newspapers and with hearty congratulations at the statehouse. In time, enormous political power and breathtaking budgets would be given to the Department of Transportation in Texas—a state agency that obviously bridged farflung portions of the state, but that also worked hand in glove with the big economic forces that kept politicians in office.

Coke Stevenson was bumping his car down the narrow roads leading out of rural Kimble County. When he was by himself, Stevenson liked to puff on his pipe and make mental notes about attending the next meeting of the Masons at Lodge 548, which had first formed in 1881. Stevenson stared at the endless rows of angora goats marching in formation from

Coke Stevenson, raised in the Central Texas Hill Country, could not convert his popularity as governor into a winning US Senate bid against Lyndon B. Johnson, who slipped past Stevenson thanks to votes miraculously uncovered in a rural South Texas county.

one end of every pasture to the other. It was only a 150-mile trip from his ranch to Austin, but it was like going from Kabul to London—disparate worlds, languages, and customs.

Broad-shouldered and sturdy, Stevenson had fished in his closet for one of the double-breasted suits that he preferred—the ones with lapels that looked like sharp arrows rising up over his chest. He had made this trip so many times—enough to feel that he was able to move from one side of Texas to the other like a bilingual, bicultural traveler with two passports and two homes. He had long promoted himself as a "real Texan," and he had the bona fides to back up that claim.

Stevenson was born at the family cabin, in the spring of 1888, at the northwestern edge of the Texas Hill Country, near the tiny farming and ranching communities of Fredonia and Pontotoc. He learned to rope and ride all over Mason County before he was a teenager, growing up in the Junction area, where the north and south forks of the sometimes capricious Llano River merge. When he was in his teens, he worked to promote and run a freight line that sent his family's dry goods, including mohair, from Junction to Brady. Enormously ambitious, Stevenson crawled his way up through the ranks in local business circles, going from being a janitor at one Junction bank to forming and becoming president of another. He helped run a car dealership, a movie theater, the Fritz Hotel, and the *Junction Eagle* newspaper. Eventually he became a lawyer, invested in more companies, and began scooping up ranchland. At one point, Stevenson owned fifteen thousand acres, and he became a modern cowboy businessman, the rancher who knew how to handle horses as well as work the corporate boardrooms in Fort Worth, Dallas, and Houston.

Stevenson began his foray into local politics by becoming a county attorney, then a county judge, and then serving as a state representative from 1929 to 1939, including a stint as Speaker of the House from 1933 to 1937. He seemed like a perfect candidate, a confident Texan who could talk to farmers and cut deals in the high-rises, and no one really stood in his way when he was elected lieutenant governor. Once Pappy O'Daniel raced to the Senate, Stevenson stepped in and then won a full term as governor in 1942.

Robert Caro, the man who spent a lifetime studying LBJ, once found himself in the unique position of defending Stevenson—by suggesting that he was one of the least understood governors in Texas history. Stevenson, he said, garnered "a higher percentage of the vote in the crucial Democratic primary than any gubernatorial candidate before him in the history of Texas, and once carried every one of the state's 254 counties, the only gubernatorial candidate in the state's history who had ever done so in a contested Democratic primary." Caro added that Stevenson was in fact a "folk hero" and "one of the most beloved public figures in Texas history."[3]

In San Antonio or in San Angelo, Stevenson gripped your hand with a confident resolve, and you had the sense that he was incapable of the fizzy flimflam that O'Daniel would serve up like a sugary Dr Pepper on a mid-August afternoon. Hearing Stevenson was like being sent to the calm but uncompromising principal's office at high school. He was from the taciturn, hard-working world of ranchers and German settlers in the areas blossoming out from Llano, Castell, and Mason—where he and other older residents still talked about the Lipan Apache and Comanche that had roamed the area, and how a ten-year-old named Herman Lehmann had been abducted by the Native Americans and raised as one of their own.

Stevenson had learned how to make sure that mohair and pecans from his father's general store were easily shipped to Brady. He grew up committed to the idea that big modern roadways were part of the Texas future, and one of his hallmark moves as governor was to promote and expand the state highway department and put in motion the dissolution of mass transit, all while ramping up that regrettable destruction of fragile minority enclaves in almost every major urban center. His fiscal conservatism certainly didn't apply to highway and road expansion, which he thought was key to the lifeblood of the state, especially as World War II erupted and the Texas economy began to benefit from the nation's need to feed the war effort. Whether or not he really was a folk hero is left for others to decide, but he was once enormously popular: Stevenson was the first person in Texas history to serve as governor, lieutenant governor, and Speaker of the House.

Pearl Harbor was attacked a few months after Stevenson first took office, and the urgent call went out for oil, bombs, gas, chemicals, and hundreds of other items that Texas could provide. It was an awful irony, but Stevenson profited politically in that he was in office when the state sought cohesiveness amid the vagaries of war—and when Texas stood to be tapped for its endless resources. America was going into battle with boatloads of fuel, metal, and weapons from Texas.

War was also figuring into the way other politicians were jockeying for power in the state: Sam Rayburn had granted his blessing to Lyndon Johnson, and he was there to both protect and promote him during Johnson's eleven years in the House—and to console Johnson after LBJ lost his Senate race to Pappy O'Daniel. LBJ was commissioned as a lieutenant commander in the US Naval Reserve in 1940, and he reported for active duty three days after Pearl Harbor. As a congressman in the military, he was sent on fact-finding missions to the Pacific. Johnson served for little more than six months, until FDR decided it would be better for congressmen to be back in Washington and not overseas. Johnson left the navy with a Silver Star, returned to Washington, and began plotting his next moves from Texas.

He, Rayburn, and others were suggesting to power players in Washington that the state was uniquely set up to be in the vanguard of the domestic war effort. In Beaumont, Port Arthur, Houston, Galveston, and Corpus Christi, the waterways were ready with workers and expanded ports. The petrochemical industry was ramped into overdrive. In the Sabine River, Big Thicket, and Piney Woods areas, logging operations were also poised to crank out paper, wood pallets, and construction lumber. Ammonium nitrate, an almost magical compound, was being used to fertilize Texas farms, and, because of its unique chemical nature, it was also being used to build bombs in the Texas Panhandle ready for shipment to air bases around the nation and world.

Texan Lyndon B. Johnson kisses the head of his mentor and trusted political ally, US House Majority Leader Sam Rayburn of Texas.

Farmers and ranchers were capitalizing on rising prices, with crops and beef being shipped by rail to other states or to booming Texas ports for export overseas. Heavy industry expanded, including massive plants that would build airplanes and military equipment in Fort Worth, Grand Prairie, and other cities. For years, Garner had done his job steering pork barrel and government projects to Texas, and now the state could promote its 175 military installations as the home for hundreds of thousands of soldiers. That enormous tin smelter that Jesse Jones had envisioned, the largest one in the Western Hemisphere, had opened outside Texas City, not far from the crowded, bustling docks with rows of oceangoing freighters. Steel factories were humming in Houston and nearby Daingerfield. One estimate had manufacturing zooming in Texas from $453 million in 1939 to almost $2 billion by 1944.[4]

On the coast, job seekers who washed ashore in Texas were reeling from the overpowering tang and smoke wafting from the plants—and smiling when they were told it was the "smell of money."

In October 1941, a mob of two hundred men from the town of Pittsburg came for a forty-three-year-old Black janitor from Dallas named Willie McNeeley. The married father of small children had been visiting relatives and then found himself accused of that oft-alleged crime of being overly friendly with a white woman. He was held down and castrated. He wasn't lynched or set on fire, perhaps because his attackers wanted him to serve as a living symbol of how justice was still served in certain parts of Texas. The incident passed without coverage in any of the major newspapers, though it received front-page coverage on October 25, 1941, in the *Dallas Express*, the often-heroic outlet serving the Black community in North Texas; the paper's editors even asked McNeeley to write a first-person account of his ordeal.[5]

Several months after that hidden bit of hell, readers around the country did see a piece in the *New York Times* with the headline "Texas Whites Lynch Negro."[6] A twenty-five-year-old Black man named Willie Vinson was accused of attempting to attack the twenty-two-year-old white wife of a war plant worker inside a Texarkana cabin trailer. Vinson was cornered in a café, shot in the stomach and shoved into the basement rooms reserved for Negro patients in a local hospital. He was pulled from his cot shortly after midnight and tied to the back of a car. The speeding vehicle dragged him through the streets of Texarkana to a cotton gin on the city outskirts, where he was hung from a twenty-foot-high winch. In the early morning hours, curious onlookers drifted to the scene and stared up at the swaying body that was illuminated faintly by streetlights.

It was a Sunday, July 12, 1942. And it was the last known hanging of a Black man in Texas, lost amid so many other matters that week: German armies were still on the march in Europe; US ships were attacking Japanese targets; a new Orson Welles movie, *The Magnificent Ambersons*, was released; and the British-born actor Cary Grant had just been given American citizenship, and had promptly married the fabulously wealthy socialite Barbara Hutton.

The extraordinarily popular governor, the sturdy-looking and stoic-sounding Stevenson, had followed the murder of Vinson from his office in Austin. To him, it was a form of righteous retribution. Stevenson simply said, "Even a white man would have been lynched for this crime."[7]

If his words reached Black residents in East Texas, where year after year people were attacked, they wouldn't have seemed shocking at all. In Paris, Jefferson, Marshall, and a thousand other cities, towns, and neighborhoods, there was an expected political order. For many in Texas, Stevenson was the human face of an enduring Lone Star monolith: an immutable, hard force that channeled slavery's deepest memories. As Robert Caro said, "Certainly Stevenson expressed himself on more than one occasion in decidedly racist terms."[8]

Beaumont had beome a wartime boomtown, with thousands of new people moving in during the 1940s. With strangers arriving seemingly every day, tensions began to rise. People squabbled over available housing and jobs that might pay a little more. Lines formed at grocery stores, and some-times the shelves were bare. The unthinkable was also happening—Blacks and whites were being shoehorned into closer proximity in crowded quar-ters of the city.

Just as Black residents were preparing for the annual June 19th June-teenth celebration honoring Emancipation, some Texas Klan leaders were inviting members from around the state to a big convention, a gather-ing that they hoped would engulf the city, maybe bringing in as many as twenty thousand Klansmen. While the planning for the two events was under way, a Black man was accused of raping an eighteen-year-old white woman. Police officers shot a suspect, and he died of his wounds. But then, just four days before the Juneteenth parades and celebrations, rumors moved around the city that another white woman had been raped.

That night, as many as four thousand white men—several with guns and bats—began roaming the streets of Beaumont. The windows and doors of Black-owned stores were smashed. Buildings were torched. Steelworkers from the Pennsylvania Shipyards, which had been bustling to build US Navy transport ships, joined the mob as it moved into Black neighborhoods near downtown and the northside. Black families coming home from work or headed out to eat were surrounded and beaten. Bands of attackers clobbered the front doors of homes, trooped inside, and looted the houses. Long after it was too late, two thousand soldiers and police de-scended on Beaumont, a curfew was declared, liquor stores were told to close, checkpoints were set up—and the Juneteenth celebration to mark the anniversary of the end of slavery was ordered canceled. At least three people died, hundreds were injured, and somehow over two hundred were finally arrested.[9]

The nightmare on the coast was one of the last large-scale bouts of public racism in Texas, and it was another incident destined to be exiled from permanent accounts in history books and classrooms. Each hour of the riot, and long after, some Texans waited for a wholesale condemnation from Stevenson and anyone else in Austin, along with a plan for repara-tions to get the obliterated businesses and neighborhoods back on their feet. Stevenson was handed a petition from Texas chapters of the NAACP, also signed by several residents of Beaumont, but he declined to act. He hadn't investigated Vinson's murder in Texarkana; he wasn't predisposed to accommodate the NAACP in Beaumont.

But the bloody erasure of a good part of the city didn't go unnoticed nationally. The poet Langston Hughes reflected on the tragedy by drawing a poetic connection between the behavior of the fascist Italian dictator Benito Mussolini and the inhumanity on the streets of Beaumont. Hughes wrote that Mussolini had an "evil heart," the kind that could be traced all the way to a town called Beaumont, Texas. Hughes added that even if Mussolini had never been there, that town was where "he had his start."[10]

Back in Austin, Stevenson was placing a premium on very careful, measured fiscal policies—trimming expenses and avoiding spending state dollars on what he felt were unnecessary social services or progressive measures. Into the early 1940s, members of the University of Texas board of regents were growing restless with syllabi, curricula, and professors they deemed sympathetic to unions and the "socialist" tendencies of FDR's lingering New Deal programs. Stevenson was ready to step in, especially after university president Homer Rainey pushed back against the regents who wanted professors fired, tenure abolished, and books—particularly the *USA* trilogy by John Dos Passos—banned. In November 1944, Rainey was told he was being fired, and out of the front door of the stately governor's mansion in Austin Stevenson saw thousands of students, faculty, and supporters lined up to protest. Stevenson felt he had long done enough for the university, steering funding for new buildings and increasing faculty salaries, but he wanted Rainey gone.

It can be hard to pinpoint how a single incident can turn into a long, lingering political sensibility, but the Rainey affair galvanized many people in Austin who were tied to the university. It became a kind of North Star for liberals and academics, a watershed moment at a time when progressives were trying to bond in conservative Texas. Austin's reputation as a liberal outpost in a conservative nation is linked to that singular moment when Coke Stevenson and other leaders decided they needed to tame the big university.

One day, the combative Texas congressman Martin Dies was in his office in Washington, fielding congratulations from supporters and old friends for his work as the first chair of the House Un-American Activities Committee (HUAC). Dies stared down at one of the several telegrams he had received: "Every true American, and that includes every Klansman, is behind you and your committee in its effort to turn the country back to the honest, freedom-loving, God-fearing American to whom it belongs."[11]

Dies was born in 1900, in Colorado City, west of Abilene. He graduated from the University of Texas and became a lawyer in Marshall before working for his father's law firm in Orange. With strong support from the KKK, Dies was elected to Congress in 1931, becoming the youngest man in the body. Like Garner, he was an early proponent of FDR's New Deal, especially programs that seemed to bail out Texas. But, also like Garner, he had grown disenchanted with Roosevelt's views on organized labor, and especially with the way the New Deal seemed to give free license to liberals — people who might be hinting at more radical ways to address social inequities. It was almost natural, then, that he became the first chair of the House Un-American Activities Committee — the so-called "communist hunting" body.

Dies was brusque, a large man, and physically intimidating, and he took quick, hard aim at Hollywood as a bastion of communism. He scoffed at artists who said they were anti-Nazis or anti-fascists and accused them of being closet communists. Dies was quickly reviled by filmmakers and musicians: "May I express my whole-hearted desire to cooperate to the utmost of my ability with the Hollywood anti-Nazi League. If this be Communism, count me in," said the director John Ford.[12]

Dies wrote a book in 1940 that he hoped would help him move to the Senate: *The Trojan Horse in America*. In it, he argued that several New Deal programs were putting the entire country in danger of a Stalinist takeover. He called the Works Project Administration "the greatest financial boon which ever came to the Communists in the United States. Stalin could not have done better by his American friends and agents."[13] Dies would later insist that Roosevelt had told him, in the 1940s, that he wasn't concerned about communists and that Stalin was in fact a useful leader who had done right by the Soviet people.

Under the command of Dies, the HUAC had a mandate to look at a wide range of subversive groups, but Dies and other HUAC members steered clear of the KKK. Dies tried to convince other congressmen about socialist-communist conspiracies, and told people he was being constantly thwarted by weak-willed colleagues from Texas — especially House Speaker Sam Rayburn. An angry Dies was certain Rayburn "never ceased to maneuver behind the scenes to destroy the Committee, and to hamper it in every conceivable way. He was too clever a politician to oppose it publicly but without showing his hand he made our task extremely difficult."[14]

Dies failed miserably in the 1941 Senate primary against Pappy O'Daniel, and three years later, he announced that he was going to retire from Congress — just as labor unions were coming to Texas to organize voter drives specifically targeting him. He would take various stabs at office again, and then reappear in Congress in the mid-1950s, perhaps empowered by the way the communist hunter Senator Joseph McCarthy had become a hero in ultraconservative quarters. During his final days in Washington, Dies was known for his support of the "Southern Manifesto" composed by hardcore opponents to the Supreme Court–ordered desegregation of American public schools.

Frustrated by the achingly slow inclusion of women in the political hierarchy—and by the way lawmakers in Texas were resisting some New Deal programs—Minnie Fisher Cunningham decided to run for governor in 1944. A committed coalition of liberals had failed to draft the writer J. Frank Dobie as a candidate, and she thought she could fill that vacuum and gauge exactly how receptive Texas was to an independent woman finally running for the highest office in the state. She was friends with Eleanor Roosevelt, and her campaign was one of the first truly bold forays into politics by an independent woman in Texas. Unlike Ma Ferguson, she was running on her own merits. But Stevenson blasted her in a landslide, even though she did manage to finish second in the primary.[15]

Stevenson went on to carry all 254 counties in Texas and win 91 percent of the vote. When he had first started as governor, the state treasury was in arrears; by 1947, the state budget was enjoying a surplus. He had remained confident of his popularity and enjoyed visiting the places where he had grown up or first done business, talking to farmers and ranchers in their language and putting on his favorite boots and cowboy hat. He was convinced that his record as a fiscal conservative guiding Texas's booming economy, and as a standard-bearer of the "old Texas traditions"—including segregation and a distrust of overregulation from Washington—would translate into a new phase for him: being elected the next US senator from Texas.

As he looked forward to that almost rightful ascension, he wanted to make sure that he was leaving the statehouse the way he wanted. Stevenson liked orderly political progression, and he was concerned that Homer Rainey, the university president he helped fire, was going to run for governor. Stevenson threw his name behind Beauford Jester, a Texas railroad commissioner, during the Democratic primary—and he assumed that most voters would associate Rainey with socialist-leaning inclinations like higher taxes, unions, desegregation, and, of course, permissive policies for liberal, tenured professors.

Rainey was squashed in the primary, but his contribution to new political realities came in the form of the unique liberal and progressive coalition that had supported him—one that brought together formerly disparate bedfellows who had focused, often with tunnel vision, on their respective interests: forming unions, workers' rights, Latino issues, Black issues, academic freedom issues. Rainey's campaign, and the coalition that supported it, was filled with political outliers who were beginning to realize they needed to find common ground.

Stevenson was pushing toward sixty and firmly convinced that his unflappable manner, the way he could mingle with both the goatherds in San Angelo and the oilmen in Port Arthur, and his adherence to Southern and Texas racial customs would carry him past his main opponent, the almost ferally ambitious Lyndon Baines Johnson. Stevenson couldn't have anticipated that this was going to be the one rancorous, bitter race that would reveal so much about how Texas politics had once been practiced and how it would roll into the future.

Stevenson had made his stance on race fairly easy to ascertain, and it also wasn't difficult to find out where Johnson stood. Johnson knew that Texans resisted federally regulated desegregation and perhaps the way the White House wanted to codify the attempts to stop lynchings. It had only been five years since the Beaumont riot and only six years since yet another Black man had been executed by a mob in Texarkana. LBJ had a steady record in the House of Representatives siding against civil rights measures or federal attempts to beat down the poll tax. He had denounced President Harry Truman's civil rights initiatives as a "farce and a sham— an effort to set up a police state."[16]

The 1948 Democratic primary was tight, a runoff was called, and Stevenson was convinced he had won by 112 votes out of almost one million cast. Even with a few more final tallies coming in days after voting had ended, he remained sure that it was a lock. But then, 202 returns from a "Box 13" in Jim Wells County suddenly appeared. Two hundred of those votes went to Johnson. The late-breaking news gave LBJ an 87-vote victory.

Stevenson tried to fathom the only loss in his political career, and he instantly argued that something was crooked—that the election was rigged. He raced to South Texas to launch an investigation, along with the seemingly omnipresent Texas Ranger Frank Hamer, who had cemented his legend by chasing down the West Dallas outlaws Bonnie and Clyde. Stevenson argued his case to the US Supreme Court, but the justices

Lyndon B. Johnson poses with supporter Mayroe W. Cowan in front of Johnson's US Senate campaign helicopter; rumors swirled that LBJ stole the election.

said there was nothing they could do about the machinations in Texas—especially after the voting lists from Box 13 went missing and other South Texas returns went on fire.[17]

That box became the most infamous election receptacle in Texas history, one containing the magic tickets that would lead to Johnson's eventual ascendancy to the White House. The story goes that voters' names on the tally sheet inside Box 13 were all written in what appeared to be the same handwriting and with the same color of ink, and that the tally sheet was missing when the ballot box was opened in court. Rumors swirled that the old, deep, powerful South Texas political forces—this time in the hands of George Parr, a convicted felon and the son of Archie Parr, the boss of political bosses—had pulled together just enough bogus votes to make Johnson the winner.

In Austin, it was all anyone could talk about. Conversation drifted to how some people had always thought the cantankerous Cactus Jack Garner would have become the first Texan elected president. Some said that perhaps a panderer like O'Daniel might have fooled or scared enough Americans to get there first. Or, maybe the steady, unflappable Rayburn would have succeeded as a safe choice. Or, well, maybe it would have been Coke Stevenson; perhaps the Oval Office should have been Stevenson's destiny in the lion-in-winter portion of his political life. But now, maybe it was LBJ destined for the Oval Office.

One of the remarkable looks back at the Stevenson-Johnson race comes from the dogged historian Caro—in part because he moves beyond the notion that there surely had to have been profound human-made mysteries involved in those votes coming from Jim Wells and Duval Counties in Texas. The idea that human malfeasance occurred is now almost a given among countless attempts to parse the race. But Caro wanted to touch on something truly eternal, at least as it applies to political warfare: Johnson and his allies partially accepted that there might not be shining policy differences between the two candidates, so they began plotting how to attack Stevenson in ways that hadn't been done as brazenly before. The scheme was to deconstruct Stevenson's popularity by promoting disinformation, what some might call lies, suggesting he was a zealous isolationist, or maybe too comfortable with socialist-leaning labor leaders. "In sum, there was really only one issue in the campaign," muses Caro, "Coke Stevenson's reputation—the basis of that reputation, the strength of that reputation, the destruction of that reputation."[18]

It was well-financed and highly organized dirty politics in Texas. And it wasn't about just securing "lost" votes in one isolated county. It was a watershed moment, maybe a signal that election battles would never be the same in the state: "Lyndon Johnson's 1948 campaign for junior United States Senator was, in that sense, the first mature flowering of the new politics in Texas."[19]

Stevenson was from deep in Mason County; from the very place where

After World War II, Héctor García, a physician from Corpus Christi, helped found the American GI Forum out of concern that Hispanic veterans were not being treated equitably upon returning stateside.

German immigrants, cowboys, and ranchers had come to wrestle away Native American lands; from where families carved out a hard life near Honey Creek, the James River, and Comanche Creek. Stevenson's rise from the heart of Texas and then to enormous political power seemed almost perfectly scripted. But maybe Johnson's work was coldly efficient. Maybe Stevenson, as Caro contends, was once a folk hero, but it would be very hard in twenty-first-century Texas to find many folks, apart from academics, historians, and political junkies, who could easily cite his legacy.

He died in San Angelo's Shannon Memorial Hospital at the age of eighty-seven. He was buried in 1975 at the Stevenson Family Ranch Cemetery in Telegraph, Texas. Much like his careful life, one that tended to shy away from the operatic dramas that O'Daniel and LBJ resorted to, Coke Stevenson's resting place is hidden from public view.

In South Texas, in a town carved out of the old, prickly-pear-studded Capsilloa Ranch, an earnest high school student listened as his Anglo teacher told him, "No Mexican will ever get an 'A' in my class." Héctor García, who spent his summers picking cotton, filed the admonition away. When he walked to school, it was still easy to find signs around Mercedes, Texas, that warned "No Dogs, Negroes or Mexicans." He had been born 270 miles away in Llena, Mexico, and his family moved to Mercedes in the wake of the Mexican Revolution. His father was a professor and his mother a schoolteacher, but they resorted to opening up a small food and supply store that also became a kind of community center where people could gather to debate news and politics.[20]

The acceptance of Blacks and Latinos in the Texas political system was still sporadic into the 1940s. But as some military veterans began returning home from World War II, they arrived with a sense of frustration and even outrage at the ongoing segregation and exclusion. In South Texas, the hotly debated outcome of the LBJ-Stevenson Senate race only underscored the belief that the state's sprawling political system was hopelessly rigged, that white power brokers could tug important races in any direction they wanted.

At home, at his family business, and at school, García began wondering if there was any way for the ironclad political process to be breached. His part of Texas seemed cemented in decades-old patterns, ones that had been passed from generation to generation, ones that simply didn't allow for minority political clout. García turned out to be a very good student: he became the valedictorian at his segregated high school, studied zoology at the University of Texas, graduated near the top of his class, and then attended medical school in Galveston.

When war broke out, he joined the army, served in North Africa and Italy, and earned a Bronze Star. García married a woman he met during his time in Italy, and they returned to Corpus Christi. As he worked to set up a medical practice, his wife was stunned by her new world: "In Italy and in many European countries that I have visited, the word America is always associated with liberty, equality, and the freedom of opportunity.... I was dumbfounded at the attitudes displayed toward Mexican people."[21]

After he saw his last patient for the day, García attended meetings held by local leaders with the League of United Latin American Citizens (LULAC), founded in Corpus Christi almost twenty years earlier. And then he decided there might be room for another organization specifically catering to military veterans. On March 26, 1948, inside the auditorium at the Mirabeau B. Lamar Elementary School in Corpus Christi, García outlined his plans for the American GI Forum. Almost seven hundred veterans were on hand, and García and the others knew that they posed a tricky political dilemma for segregationists in the state capitol: as many as five hundred thousand Latinos from America had fought in the war. Didn't they deserve equal rights?

As García rallied the veterans in South Texas, he began to focus hard on an incident that he thought might shock lawmakers in the statehouse and even around the nation: a soldier named Felix Longoria from Three

Rivers, Texas, had lost his life in the Philippines. His body was only discovered in 1948, and arrangements were made to bury Longoria in the Three Rivers cemetery—the only one in town, and one where barbed wire separated the white section from the Latino area. But a local funeral home director refused to allow the family use of the cemetery chapel because "whites would not like it." The Longoria family had gone to see García, and he agreed to negotiate with the funeral home. When he and his wife and children visited Three Rivers, they were denied service at a restaurant. Then, at the funeral home, García was told there would never be memorials for Mexicans.

Back at his medical office in Corpus Christi, García pondered the long line of mothers and sick children whose voices were echoing in the waiting area. He decided to mount a public campaign to let Texans know what was happening in Three Rivers. He organized community meetings, made phone calls to the other members of the GI Forum, and tried to get word to local newspapers. LBJ read the news accounts, and, motivated by either empathy or political pragmatism, he said he would help arrange for Longoria to be laid to rest in 1949 in Arlington National Cemetery.

Forcing lawmakers to think about a Latino soldier from Texas served as a signal for other political possibilities. García's GI Forum, LULAC, and other organizations weren't just highlighting inequities, they were putting power brokers—even LBJ—on notice that there was a constituency that might be willing to unite in ways the Democratic and Republican machineries had never seen. García's ability to extract big-time action from a US senator wasn't lost on some around the nation. Edna Ferber, who wrote the book *Giant*—which would become a movie that defined Texas, for good or bad—said she admired García. Amid his political battles, García had continued to treat almost anyone who needed medical attention, and she decided to model one of her characters, Dr. Guerra, after him.[22]

García turned quickly to more political moves. The GI Forum gave cash to poor voters so they could pay their poll taxes. García and the Forum began taking public stands against the Bracero Program, the sweeping arrangement, started by executive order in 1942, that allowed several million Mexican "guest workers" into the country to fill low-wage jobs, at a time when big farmers and ranchers were worried about a shortage of cheap labor. Workers were being paid less than promised, wages were being held back under the guise of federal deductions, and families were warehoused in filthy camps and compounds that shocked federal inspectors who came to see them in Texas. The Department of Labor official who headed the bracero initiative characterized it as "legalized slavery."[23]

As his political mobilization expanded, García began receiving both veiled and direct threats. Johnson watched and accepted the idea that García, his group, and other Latino organizations really could be portals to chronically underrepresented parts of Texas. New voters, new constituencies, new Democrats. García would come in contact with several presidents—Kennedy, Johnson, Carter, Reagan, and Clinton—and his hand in the sociopolitical awakening of Texas would last virtually until the day he died, on July 26, 1996, at the age of eighty-two. He is buried at Seaside Memorial Park in Corpus Christi, in the city he had returned to after World War II, and where he had decided that if you had served your nation, you were owed something for your service.

On July 11, 1949, a Black porter moved through a midnight sleeper train headed to Houston from Austin. He was approaching an elegant, three-bedroom compartment discreetly confined at the back of the train. It was a fancy lair, one reserved for a special passenger: Governor Beauford Jester.

Some said that Jester occasionally enjoyed bringing his mistress on the train rides. And that maybe she was with him on this particular night—and maybe she had watched in horror as the Democratic governor of Texas suddenly stopped breathing. Maybe she had been discreetly escorted off the train in College Station. What was clear was that the train with the dead Jester rumbled through the night, across the gently sloping plains of East Texas. It kept aiming for Houston, where the news about his death was released.[24]

Jester was a native of Corsicana, an ambitious and studious young man who had gone on to serve as a captain in World War I. Handsome, well dressed, and prone to sporting double-breasted suits with sharp lapels, he attended Harvard Law School but came back to his home state to finish his studies at the University of Texas. As a plugged-in, well-heeled attorney, he began moving up the preordained social and political ranks, and was named a University of Texas regent. Jester was sociable, was easy to talk to, and wore his privilege in an easy, affable manner. In a prescient bit of fate and poetry, he eventually became a state railroad commissioner. Then he served as president of the Texas state bar and developed a reputation as a very reliable conservative—and, since he had served on the board of regents, someone perfectly suited to run in the Democratic gubernatorial primary against Homer Rainey, the deposed president of UT.

People in Austin said that Jester was just another Southern Democrat like Coke Stevenson—someone who had grown up in segregated Texas while keeping a wary eye on liberals, socialists, and unions. And for many in Texas, his clear victory over Rainey was like a a comfortable passing of the torch. It also helped keep an enduring wariness alive at the state's biggest, most influential university. There was always going to be that sense that the school would be at war with state leaders clucking about it being a breakaway hothouse.

Jester was suave and enjoyed going to social events in the city, but he did not exhibit the excesses of Pa Ferguson or Pappy O'Daniel—except, perhaps, for his rumored predilection for illicit romance in railroad cars. Overseeing a state budget that topped the billion-dollar mark for the first time, Jester steered funding for prisons, new roads, and state parks, and set up a blueprint for regular funding of the state educational system. In Austin, if anyone knew about his having a mistress, they usually kept it secret. Maybe it was a dangerous indulgence, the kind that his political foes could use to their advantage. Maybe it was, for some, something Jester was allowed to get away with because he was a faithful torchbearer for all the things that Coke Stevenson had endorsed.

The true story of Jester's final train ride is to be determined, but one thing was certain: he became the only Texas governor to die in office, and he was laid to rest in Houston's Oakwood Cemetery under a blocky hunk of marble. Some suggest that the memorial, with a giant "Jester" at the base, has a certain phallic quality. One Texas writer would say that Jester was the "last happy man to govern Texas."

When Sam Rayburn was five, his family moved from Tennessee to the small town of Windom, Texas, and he was almost instantly sent out into the fields. One of eleven children, he grew up working on the family's forty-acre cotton farm. He became an earnest small-town schoolteacher, then got his law degree from the University of Texas, after which he immediately began exploring ways to enter politcs. When he was twenty-four, he won a tight race for state representative and used it as a springboard to win the Congressional District 4 seat in 1912. At that point, he knew enough to seek out the advice of the godfather of Texas politics, Congressman Cactus Jack Garner.

Garner relished serving as a mentor to new lawmakers from Texas. He'd explain how Washington worked, cajole them into voting for whatever he wanted, and then extract favors from them as needed. The round-faced, eager Rayburn was invited to Garner's "board of education" meetings in a quiet room on Capitol Hill, where he joined all the other lawmakers sipping caramel-colored bourbon and toking on Travis Club cigars from Texas. Rayburn would lower his balding, dome-shaped head and listen hard as Garner told him to make sure to keep his boots on the ground in Texas, to get back as often as he could, and to mingle with the farmers, ranchers, goatherds, and county preachers.

Following this wisdom, Rayburn regularly returned to Texas to make the rounds with local allies, and then, just like Garner, routinely got re-elected. He followed Garner's lead, making sure to wear his Western clothes rather than his tailored suits when going to the county fairs and festivals to see voters. On those trips back to Texas, Rayburn had plenty of time to weigh how Garner had become a political survivor—with one foot in the old *patrón* system and another in the gilded orbit of moguls like William Randolph Hearst. He must have viewed Garner as a kind of consummate political performer, someone who could play both the tough-as-cedar old man from Texas and the smooth, cunning negotiator for the president of the United States.

When he arrived back in Washington, Rayburn grew even closer to Garner, who had ascended to Speaker of the House. He agreed to orchestrate Garner's campaign for the White House in 1932 after Hearst had identified Cactus Jack as the perfectly colorful "prickly pear" presidential candidate.

But when Garner and Rayburn began to realize that they'd never defeat FDR's political machine, Rayburn said he would find out whether Garner might play a role in FDR's administration. He learned that Roosevelt really wanted Garner to be his vice president—he could use a powerful ex–Speaker of the House, a skilled Southerner, to ramrod his New Deal plans through the House and Senate. It was a savvy play by FDR, and a fortuitous move for Rayburn: giving Garner the license to barrel through Congress would keep him occupied and maybe less inclined to undermine FDR. But it would also ensure that Rayburn could inherit Garner's throne as House Speaker. Rayburn, seemingly quiet and unassuming, had studied under the master, and he was playing political chess just the way Garner had done for decades.

Rayburn took over the chairmanship of the powerful Interstate and Foreign Commerce Committee, instrumental in creating the Securities and Exchange Commission as well as the Federal Communications Commission. He became Speaker of the House in 1940 and enjoyed enormous

Vice President John Nance Garner (left) with House Majority Leader Sam Rayburn (right)—Texans with national clout—plot strategy with House Speaker William B. Bankhead.

loyalty in Washington when the nation was marching toward the great war in Europe and Asia. For years, he was reelected again and again, and his closest friends in Texas wondered exactly where Rayburn's ambitions could take him—and if he could ever cash in on the goodwill he had accumulated with FDR by supporting chunks of the New Deal in Congress.

Maybe FDR would want another Texan to be his vice president after Garner decided to step away from Washington. But Roosevelt chose Harry Truman from Missouri instead, and Rayburn, forever disciplined, decided to be a good diplomat—and to make sure that Truman was invited to Rayburn's own backroom poker and booze sessions on Capitol Hill: the same kinds of political lubricating sessions that Garner had once invited him to attend.

One day Truman walked into one of Rayburn's off-the-cuff "board of education" meetings, but was abruptly pulled aside by an aide. Truman was steered to an emergency phone call. Truman listened, hung up, and muttered: "Jesus Christ and General Jackson." With Rayburn and the backroom wheelers and dealers watching, Truman raced grim-faced to the White House. The world was still gripped by war, but FDR had just passed away—and now Truman was president.[25]

As Rayburn watched Truman rush away, he might have wondered if that could have been him inheriting the White House.

Though he had carried bundles of FDR's New Deal legislation, Rayburn was careful to push back against any hints in Texas that he was becoming a liberal, or worse, a closeted socialist. When he visited Bonham and the other towns in his district, Rayburn would work the handshake line at the Baptist church or the Future Farmers of America livestock show, and he made sure, more than ever, to ditch his pressed pants and wing-tip shoes for jeans, boots, and a beaver-pelt Stetson.

Rayburn knew that plenty of people in Bonham and elsewhere in Texas were listening hard to Congressman Martin Dies and his thundering anti-communist rants. After moving through the food line to put brisket and beans on his plate, he would reassure the farmers and ranchers that he was certainly anti-communist too, but that he was also a calm man in the cockpit. "A jackass can kick a barn down, but it takes a carpenter to build one," he announced.[26]

Later, as he drove with aides through the little Northeast Texas towns bordering the Red River, it was like seeing and even feeling the history of Texas excesses—the lynchings, the rollercoaster rides of Pappy O'Daniel, the swindled elections, Dies's hunt for communists, the legions of diamond-studded oilmen, and the outlines of the old slave plantations. Staring out the window, Rayburn knew he was a bridge, just like Garner, to that entire Texas heritage. And he was well aware that each time he left Fannin County, or Bowie County, or Delta County, he was going to go back to Washington circles that still viewed Texas as some sort of independent beast.

Being circumspect, beyond measured, might have been in his nature anyway, but Rayburn had to know that his smooth, workmanlike demeanor on Capitol Hill would go a long way toward offsetting the wary views of Texas: the views still being informed by a lonely actor like O'Daniel or a domineering xenophobe like Dies. Rayburn vowed to, at least, be as clean as they come, so no one could question his character. Word began circulating that he was turning down all-expenses-paid travel junkets, fancy gifts from donors, and honorariums offered by industry executives and their shills. Some people on the Hill couldn't believe it: Rayburn decided to pay for his own airfare, for his own hotels and motels, and for his own food on a fact-finding mission to the Panama Canal.[27]

On a late Monday afternoon in mid-October 1961, President John F. Kennedy was striding down the hallway of Baylor Medical Center, aiming for Room 729. He had landed in Dallas just before 4:00 p.m. and had zoomed right to the hospital.

Rayburn was in bed, his chemotherapy failing as he succumbed to cancer. Nurses had helped prop him up so he could watch a flickering TV and the final game of the World Series between the New York Yankees and the Cincinnati Reds—Mickey Mantle had to sit out the game with a hip injury, but the Yankees already had an eight-run lead by the fourth inning. Kennedy talked to the doctors, and they told him Rayburn's case was hopeless. In Rayburn's room, aides were asked to leave, and Kennedy and the congressman whispered for twenty minutes—about the old days, about how Rayburn helped the Democrats win so many elections. Kennedy was on his way out of Dallas just after 5:00 p.m.[28]

Rayburn slipped into a coma two days later and passed away on November 16. At his funeral, 105 members of Congress pressed into First Baptist Church in Bonham. Some thirty thousand people lined up to listen outside. When he was laid to rest in the sloping blacklands of Willow Wild Cemetery, along Powder Creek, presidents Kennedy, Truman, and Dwight Eisenhower where there, along with LBJ.

After he died, some details about his estate emerged, including one report that said the man known as "Mr. Speaker" had just over $25,000 in cash, a family home and land, a Cadillac, two pickup trucks, and a tractor. Some people were shocked at the small size of his estate, especially considering how enormously influential Rayburn had been and the admirals of industry and commerce who had sought him out.[29]

If he had accumulated one thing more than any other, it was a polished equanimity at a time when the political plates were shifting internationally and nationally. There was a Cold War, and at home there were giant social movements. The Northern and Southern wings of the Democratic Party were battling. And there was Rayburn, on center stage and often playing two roles: the down-home Texan in his San Antonio–made Lucchese boots and the Washington insider with his foulard ties and double-breasted jackets. The centrist and the conservative. He walked easily in different political hallways and brokered dialogue at a time when desegregation, a war in Korea, voting rights, and the threat of nuclear nightmares were being debated on Capitol Hill and in churches, on campuses, in cafeterias, and in living rooms around the nation.

The historical marker at his gravesite is matter of fact: "His long and successful political career began with his election to the Texas legislature in 1906. It continued through 25 consecutive terms in the U.S. House of Representatives, where Rayburn served with 8 presidents and held the Speakership for 17 years."

CHAPTER 9

I Have a Plaintiff: The 1950s

DOCKWORKERS IN TEXAS CITY, SOUTH of Houston, had been busy since daybreak loading oceangoing freighters with seemingly endless bags of fertilizer that had arrived earlier by train. It was a pleasant mid-April morning, one that began with a soothing sunrise but would end with a tragedy that would linger through the 1950s and beyond.

The cargo of fertilizer was going to be shipped to war-ravaged farms in Europe as part of the Marshall Plan, the enlightened self-interest mission to reseed damaged nations, to restore economies, and to keep parts of that continent out of the grip of the Soviets. That morning in 1947, a dockworker mindlessly flipped a cigarette in the air, and it sailed into one of the lower holds of a rusting ship crammed with tons of the ammonium nitrate–based fertilizer. It was made from a compound that thrilled and also terrified scientists around the world. They had discovered that ammonium nitrate was chemically coded in a unique and deadly way: in addition to making a brilliant, life-saving fertilizer that could make crops grow like never before, ammonium nitrate could be used to make powerful bombs. Throughout World War II, bombs made in Texas, ones packed with ammonium nitrate, had helped demolish armies, buildings, villages, and German strongholds all over Europe. After the war, countless bags of ammonium nitrate, none marked with warning signs, were being put to another use—they were being sent to France and other nations to bring war-torn farms back to life.

In Texas City, the lit cigarette tumbled onto one of the bags. A little, colorful flame popped up. Then the dancing flame seemed to jump from one bag to another. There was a gathering of heat and smoke, and then the giant cargo ship began to quiver and rattle. As the plumes rose from the lower holds of the ship, children began riding their bikes to the waterfront. They clapped and watched the purple and orange flames filling the sky.

Small fires sometimes erupted on the docks, and they passed as amusement for a few of the families in Texas City. The city was a kind of boomtown, a petrochemical wonderland hiring thousands of veterans and other Americans to work inside oil refineries, gas plants, and the big Monsanto factory. A small industrial fire wasn't really that unusual. There was so much industry, so many rail lines, so many storage tanks. The hardworking fire department, with fewer than thirty men, was always able to tamp down the flames—while people gathered to cheer and watch them at work.

But this time, something was clearly wrong. The ship, a well-worn freighter called the *Grandcamp*, began to heave, swell, and then buck. Then there was a deafening boom, and the earth felt as though it was going to crack in half. Burning, melting hunks of metal soared into the sky. Balls of fire licked at the nearest chemical plants and oil tanks. Other freighters were picked up off the water and tossed inland. A ten-foot-high tidal wave of chemicals rushed inland and over homes. Planes were sucked out of the sky, and scientists in Colorado and Louisiana were detecting what seemed to be seismic shifts, rumbles, maybe the force of an atomic bomb, coming from Texas City.

A young man, his eardrums bursting, staggered to the door of his house and saw black waves of energy moving across the horizon and bodies flying, cartwheeling through the air. Downtown, a decapitated woman was moving down the street and trying to grasp the hand of a child. Almost every member of the fire department vanished in the blink of an eye. The detonations, the thunderclaps, kept occurring, one after another, followed by screams, sirens, and eerie moments of utter silence. Some people fell to their knees, convinced it was Judgment Day. Others assumed the nation was under attack by terrorists or a foreign power. Black residents were coated white with asbestos from the plants and fracturing buildings. White residents were coated black from oil and even molasses from an enormous wounded molasses plant. Rescue workers and medical personnel were confused about who was white, who was Black, and whether the wounded should be taken to the "colored wing" or the "white wing" at area hospitals

Within hours, thousands of volunteers began descending on the city, but it took weeks for the smoke and fires to die down, and for some form of order to be restored. The Monsanto chemical plant was destroyed, railroad lines were ripped apart, and people were finding huge chunks of metal that had been shot a mile from the dock and into their yards. The president sent in troops, investigations were ordered, and families made their ways through morgues set up in the local gymnasiums, trying to identify the remains of their loved ones by the tags attached to the toes of corpses. Dozens of victims were never found, and dozens of bodies remained beyond indentification. An area cemetery refused to bury some of the unidentified remains, worried that they might belong to Black people.

Tons of chemicals seeped into the soil or gushed into the bay, and then crews began spraying DDT to ward off contagious diseases. No one knew the real toll—maybe 584 dead and 5,000 injured. There was speculation that many more people had died: Texas City had been filling rapidly with newcomers anxious for work, and maybe they hadn't all been accounted for. Some were convinced Black and Latino residents were never accurately counted. Emergency fund-raisers were arranged, including one that brought Frank Sinatra to Texas. For a very long time, a numbing procession of burials took place.[1]

In Austin, Texas leaders were being blistered by accusations that they hadn't done enough to warn people about the horrendous demons inside paper bags of ammonium nitrate. It was the largest industrial disaster in US history, and Texas had another "negative superlative" to weigh— alongside the London School explosion and the 1900 hurricane in Galveston. Was Texas so anti-regulatory that it was horribly negligent? Why couldn't the state adopt a modicum of oversight, some program or checklist that could have saved Texas City? Couldn't Texas do something to regulate a fertilizer that had been used on farms all over the state? (In 1993, terrorists would use ammonium nitrate in an attempt to take down the World Trade Center in New York; in 1995, Timothy McVeigh used ammonium nitrate to destroy a federal building in Oklahoma and kill 168 people; in 2013, an ammonium nitrate explosion in the city of West, Texas, claimed fifteen lives.)

Texas moved on in brisk fashion, or at least without a lingering sense that lawmakers needed to accept more federal oversight. It was too late to change the state's impulses. Texas had a firm political system so wedded to big business that accepting federal oversight, or even ramping up state monitoring, was anathema: something that might make the economy pause and keep people from work, from money circulating, from the state growing. In Austin and elsewhere, more than a few people were saying, quietly, that there were hard prices to be paid for growth in Texas. There always had been, and there always would be. Texas was occupied, settled, conquered, and carved out in hard, sometimes brutal ways. But Texas would rebound, rebuild, move on. Into the 1950s, Texas City was slowly pieced back together, and the refineries, docks, and petrochemical plants were reopened and even expanded. Texas continued to take its place as a leader in the Age of Chemistry, that postwar era when multinational companies said they were on the cutting edge of wondrous discoveries that would make life easier for all humankind.[2]

In Midland, Odessa, and other smaller cities and towns across the state, people were leaving their windows open, hoping for a breeze, anything that might offset the fact that Texas was in the smothering grip of another drought. After a sweaty, fitful sleep, parents would check on their slumbering children and find that there had been a dry wind in the night, and it had blown in dirt and sand and formed an outline around the children, just like the chalk outlines around a dead body. The Texas drought would linger from the early 1950s until 1957, with rainfall dropping dramatically below the averages and temperatures soaring. In homes all over the parched parts of the state, families huddled around kitchen tables and started to talk about doing the unthinkable—packing up and leaving, moving from their homes and heading into the cities.

By the beginning of the decade, there were nearly eight million people in Texas—an increase of 20 percent from 1940—and more were living in urban areas than in the country. The drought was a lingering, suffocating jackboot, and ultimately almost one hundred thousand family ranches and farms went out of business, despite such desperate measures as feeding cows and goats prickly pears to keep them alive. Only 10 of 254 counties escaped being declared "federal drought disaster" zones. In Austin, lawmakers scrambled to address the parched nightmare. There were angry political debates about water—how to get it, who deserved it, how to control it, and how best to use it. (LBJ had once helped ramrod through the creation of a chain of lakes west of Austin by damming up the Colorado River and bringing "the electric" to areas that had never had it. When I moved to one of those areas, a member of the local electrical power cooperative came to my land and stared out over the two-hundred-year-old live oaks dotting the property. He said: "You know, there was a time when people here were damn glad to get the electric.")

Water, more than ever, was a political commodity, and lawmakers were worrying about how to placate big backers who needed guarantees that they'd be able to draw water from rivers around the state. Texas was going to build more reservoirs, and legislators were racing to figure out where they would be, who would administer them, and what parts of the state would get them first. For many in Austin, it was a sobering, abject lesson: Texas had yielded cotton, oil, livestock, and citrus. Water was diverted out of the Rio Grande to soak the farms; the timber forests in East Texas had been chopped down; and all along the coast oil was being bent, shaped, and mixed to make plastics and solvents and a thousand other products.

Texas had an industrial bedrock unlike any other, but it hadn't counted on a lingering act of God—a drought of seemingly biblical proportions. There wasn't, in the end, much to do but wait it out and begin thinking about more ways to haul and store water. Years later, the biggest political power brokers in the state, notably oil billionaire T. Boone Pickens, would talk about how to make money selling water to thirsty parts of the state.[3]

Lulu Belle Madison White enjoyed spending hours in the library at Terrell Colored High School in Fort Worth with her favorite works by W. E. B. Dubois and Booker T. Washington. She read the histories and thought about her sharecropping parents and the world she had inherited. She was born in 1907 in a tiny outpost called Frog, near Elmo, east of Dallas, and alongside the railroad tracks that cut through a remote, tree-shrouded world where people still made their own moonshine from muscadine grapes and used folk remedies made from persimmons to treat the sick. Her father had been a slave, and she knew he was always in awe of the way Texas was trying to change, and of how his daughter could read and write so well.

She enrolled in Prairie View College, one of the cornerstones of the Black university network in Texas, earned a degree in English, and then moved to the bungalow-laden Heights neighborhood in Houston to take a job in a segregated school. The city was still filling with Black residents moving from rural areas of East Texas. A culturally rich ecosystem was

Lulu Belle Madison White of Houston, whose father had been a slave, initially focused on attaining voting rights for Black residents. White traveled the state as an NAACP leader. Later, she spearheaded the lawsuit opening the University of Texas to Black Texans.

taking shape, with influential educators, artists, business leaders, and clergy gathering to address the lingering menace of the Klan, complaints about a racist police force, and the way poorer minorities were mired in swampy, snake-infested areas near Buffalo Bayou. Around the city, musicians were adding to Houston's influential cultural scene, including masters like Sam "Lightnin'" Hopkins, the songwriter who chronicled the vagaries of life as a Black man in Texas in his painfully accurate and poignant ways.

White began gravitating to the Houston branch of the NAACP and volunteering to help open up Democratic primaries to Black voters. She attended more meetings and by 1939 was elected president of the state's most important chapter—and the largest one in the South. She traveled Texas, organizing fund-raisers, growing the membership, and advising local leaders on how to register voters and work around the poll taxes. With her influence, the Supreme Court ruled in 1944 to ban whites-only primaries.

In mid-October of 1945, White wrote a note to NAACP attorney Thurgood Marshall and dropped a bombshell: "I think I have a plaintiff for the educational case."[4] She had convinced her NAACP allies that they needed to finally roll forward with a plan to desegregate the University of Texas—and that they could do it by using a bookish, balding thirty-three-year-old mailman from Houston's Third Ward named Heman Marion Sweatt. He would try to enroll at the university, and when he was denied, he would file a lawsuit. White told people that Sweatt was the perfect human face of the cause. She knew the family: Sweatt's father had organized Black mail clerks, first in Houston and then around the nation, and was one of the earliest members of the city's NAACP chapter.[5]

Sweatt applied to the University of Texas law school in 1946 and was promptly denied admission on the basis of race. School officials argued that he could study elsewhere—maybe at a university reserved for Blacks, or maybe on his own with a few textbooks. Sweatt was also told he could apply for admission to a just-formed School of Law of the Texas State University for Negroes, which state officials had rushed to open inside a handful of office basement rooms near the state capitol. The governor, Coke Stevenson, said all Sweatt needed was "one good lawyer, one set of encyclopedias and one set of 'Texas Statutes.'"[6]

Thurgood Marshall became Sweatt's lawyer (and would later be named the first African American to sit on the US Supreme Court), and he successfully argued the case to the highest court in the land. For the first time in state history, a Black man was allowed into an all-white school under a court order. Sweatt was finally enrolled in 1951, easing the way for more students and further desegregation efforts, including the groundbreaking *Brown v. Board of Education* ruling in 1954 that would forever change the nation's educational apparatus.

But even with that national victory, there was a lingering price: the Texas attorney general's office sent police to seize NAACP files in 1956 and accused White and her branch of not paying taxes and of ginning up lawsuits. White told people she knew exactly what it was: a plan to drive the NAACP out of Texas. For weeks and then months, White received threats, and the word coming from Austin was that state legislators were cooking up specific bills to crush the NAACP.

Back in Houston, White met with aides and mulled over ways to survive. There was talk of aligning with the handful of prominent white liberals in Texas, including the writer and historian J. Frank Dobie. And there was a plan to seek out Progressive Party candidates, or to simply ask for help from around the nation.[7] White wondered if people outside Texas knew what she knew about how Texas was evolving.

By the mid-1950s, one out of every five citizens in Houston, Dallas, Fort Worth, Beaumont, and Waco was Black. Because of the migration from farms to cities—and the federally mandated desegregation—Texas was changing like never before. In South Dallas, there was still the nurtured cemetery for Confederate veterans not far from Forest Avenue (that street that some said was named in honor of KKK founder Gen. Nathaniel

Bedford Forrest). But South Dallas, like many zones around the state, was headed into an uneasy limbo and then outright violence as Black residents began moving into the older wooden bungalows near Fair Park, where the grand Texas Centennial celebration had taken place in 1936. Their arrival was met with bombings, beatings, and cross burnings.[8]

Thousands of white residents began relocating to suburban zones outside the cities, places where a new kind of political class was taking shape: disenchanted middle-class or affluent white voters, ones who had decided to self-segregate, ones who would perhaps support ardently conservative white candidates. The mounting anxiety about desegregation—and what would happen to property values, jobs, and elections—ramped up all over Texas.

White was in touch with one local Black leader in South Dallas, a widow named Juanita Craft who was working overtime to sign up young people with the NAACP and formulate plans to integrate schools, restaurants, theaters, and even the annual Texas State Fair. In 1944, she became the first Black woman in Dallas County to cast a vote. She was enduring bomb threats, volunteering to serve as a Democratic precinct chairman, and regularly contacting White about ways to keep the NAACP functioning in Texas—among, them, by expanding the youth movement and registering even more Black residents to vote.[9]

Craft told White about how she had ridden a train across Texas and had decided to sit in the section reserved for whites. A conductor had ordered her to move, she had refused, and he had hinted at something dark—maybe a lynching. Craft and White both knew that public lynchings had all but ended but that there were new miseries inside the cities, some perpetrated by vigilantes, some by the KKK, and others by the police. Finding news about the new breed of calamities was really a matter of choice, as savvy readers knew there were two universes in Texas: the one depicted by the *Houston Chronicle*, *San Antonio Light*, and *Dallas Morning News*, and the one depicted by the *Dallas Express*, *Houston Defender*, *San Antonio Register*, and the other newspapers serving Black and Latino communities.

In 1956, several of those minority publications began tracking a major political push led by White and the NAACP to get Texas lawmakers to follow through on federal orders to desegregate one small school district in Mansfield, near Fort Worth. Word spread that sixty Black students would be enrolling alongside the seven hundred white students, and a mob surrounded the high school, boxed in automobiles, and hung Black mannequins in effigy. In Austin, the new governor, Allan Shivers, ordered Texas Rangers to head to Mansfield—not to break up the mob, but to make sure that the school remained segregated.

A year after the Mansfield incident, White died in Houston at the age of fifty-six. She had kept the NAACP in Texas alive and remained state director until her death. In her position she had worked side by side with Roy Wilkins and America's most important civil rights leaders. At her crowded memorial service, attendees listened as Marshall, the general counsel for the NAACP, read a long list of testimonials from around the nation. Her obituary said she had written "her name in the hearts of men. She served humanity."[10]

After the services at the Antioch Baptist Church in downtown Houston, White was buried at Paradise North Cemetery toward the northwest side of the city. Her marker bears just her name and her birth and death dates.

Latino leaders were watching what had happened to White and the NAACP. The rules for segregation in Texas restrooms, airports, diners, parks, and buses were being struck down by federal court orders, but in a crystal-clear nod to "states' rights," the pace varied from city to city, from neighborhood to neighborhood. Dallas simply refused to integrate its schools for another decade. And seemingly every issue of the minority newspapers described another confrontation, another moment of rage and menace. The violence in Mansfield wasn't an isolated incident. The governor of Texas had dispatched the Texas Rangers to enforce "local customs"—just as they had done for almost a century.

In South Texas, where people still feared the Rangers, the American GI Forum raised eyebrows by releasing a study called *What Price Wetbacks?*[11] Latino lawyers were filing lawsuits to make it it illegal for school boards to put Mexican American children in separate buildings. In 1954, the Supreme Court ruled, in *Hernández v. the State of Texas*, that Latinos should be allowed on juries, after hearing arguments by San Antonio attorneys Gus García and Carlos Cadena, the first Mexican Americans to present a case before the nation's highest court. In 1957, *Hernández v. Driscoll CISD* ruled that public schools could not hold back Mexican American children longer than whites—it had been a blatant, unsubtle way to keep segregation enforced.[12]

More Latino leaders were emerging, particularly in San Antonio. The city had a deep heritage of political discourse and even support from white writers, artists, and politicians like the Maverick family. On the West Side, more and more people were talking about one promising figure: Henry Barbosa González, said by friends to be poised to succeed in public life—and who as a small child had stood in front of a mirror and recited quotes from the great philosophers, especially Descartes.

González's family's roots were in northern Mexico, in Mapimi, near where his ancestors had labored in silver mines. Like many others, his parents raced away from the revolution in Mexico and came to San Antonio. His father was a voracious reader, a writer, and an editor at the newspaper *La Prensa*. González would come home from Jefferson High School and find activists, teachers, and organizers eating and debating at the family dinner table. He attended the University of Texas, then St. Mary's Law School, and joined the US Navy during the war.

When he came home, he worked in various city positions, including a stint with the housing authority. As part of his job, he roamed the city's West Side with its ever-growing Mexican American community. Residents grew accustomed to seeing the long-faced man with the deep-set eyes and gravelly voice; he was omnipresent, and spent hours patiently trying to answer questions about rents, housing, and jobs. In 1947, he became executive assistant for the Pan American Progressive Association (PAPA), a local business fraternity, and it seemed like it could serve as a political springboard.

To many people, González, as he made his rounds, was the man downtown who served as a connection to the white powers-that-be. He seemed like an artful negotiator, someone who could nimbly urge change. "Given that the power to influence decisions that affect our lives is concentrated in the established systems of our government, I felt that I could contribute by participating in that process," González told people. "There is a place for those who remain outside these processes, but I felt that I could contribute by influencing policy from the inside."[13]

With the support of several San Antonio liberals, union sympathizers, and the families he had met on the West Side, González tried to secure a seat in the Texas Senate in 1950. He lost but rebounded three years later by winning a slot on the city council—the first Latino ever elected to the post. He used his seat, and a stint as interim mayor, to address that slow pace of desegregation in schools, restaurants, jobs, and city swimming pools—where he had once been ordered out of the water because of his brown skin.

Other men and women were stepping forward in San Antonio. Another navy veteran, Albert Peña, was a member of his father's law firm, where he handled civil rights cases, including one aimed at integrating schools in Hondo. He became a Bexar County commissioner in the 1950s and helped organize both PASSO (the Political Assocation of Spanish-Speaking Organizations) and MALDEF (the Mexican American Legal Defense and Educational Fund). Peña served as a county commissioner and a municipal court judge, and solidified a political operation aimed at electing or appointing Mexican Americans to local offices—from city council to justices of the peace. Like Lulu White and Thurgood Marshall, he filed anti-segregation lawsuits and traveled Texas to meet other civil rights leaders. The organizational efforts led by Peña were guided by an innate political sense that he could find common ground with other minority leaders around Texas.[14] He recognized the practical impact of linking with Black activists, and he would join arms with members of the extraordinarily important Sutton family of San Antonio.

Samuel Johnson Sutton and his wife, Lillian Viola Smith, were among the first Black educators in Bexar County, where they encouraged civic participation and an awareness of history. Word spread in certain political and civil rights circles that any visit to Texas should include a conference with the Suttons. One of their children, G. J. Sutton, became the first Black elected state representative from San Antonio. Another child, Percy Sutton, was a lawyer who represented Malcolm X, ran the iconic Apollo Theater in Harlem, and served as Manhattan Borough president.

From his offices in New York City, Sutton helped spread truths about his home state and served as a reminder that there were political triumphs to be achieved, even if some were well beyond the state borders. He talked frequently about his upbringing in Texas, how San Antonio had neatly segregated almost its entire Black population on the East Side—and how a rich cultural and political network had taken shape, a place with common reference points in the neighborhood, from the famous Cameo Theater to the Carver Community Cultural Center, from the barber shops on Commerce Street to the mom-and-pop businesses near the railroad tracks separating Black San Antonio from white San Antonio. In Harlem and then around the nation, Sutton explained why Texas was the way it was—and why he felt he had to leave. In his lifetime and after his death, he was lauded by politicians of all ranks, including President Barack Obama, for his contributions to civil rights. (I once spent the day with him, and he talked about how he had found so many similarities between San Antonio and Harlem. His theory was that the Black neighborhoods in San Antonio had developed cohesive political, religious, and economic systems much like Harlem had. As we walked down 125th Street, the main artery in Harlem, Percy Sutton from the East Side of San Antonio was stopped on every block and saluted: "It's the mayor of Harlem!")[15]

Back on the West Side of San Antonio, González was meeting with more supporters, and he won a 1956 race for the Texas Senate. González met quickly with Laredo state senator Abraham Kazen, and they decided to filibuster a slew of bills, ten of them, designed to push back against federal desegregation orders. The duo wound up filibustering for thirty-six hours, until weary lawmakers conceded defeat and dropped eight of the bills.

Right away, González began enduring whispers and then outright condemnation from white lawmakers in the statehouse, and they only intensified when he decided to run for governor just two years after arriving in Austin. In towns across the state, people could see a cloud of dust on the outskirts as González and campaign aides caravanned in, trying their own version of Pappy O'Daniel's rolling political tours. González weathered the stares from folks unaccustomed to seeing a Latino man approaching in a suit, his hand extended, and asking them to vote him into the governor's office. It was to no avail; he lost his bid for history. Maybe it was because he was woefully underfunded, or Texas wasn't ready for a Latino leader.

In mid-April 1950, the handsome, well-dressed, six-foot-two Allan Shivers was outside the Municipal Auditorium in San Antonio, somberly clutching a wreath. As the sun lowered and the shadows covered the clusters of stunning red and purple bougainvillea, he began walking to the Alamo. He strode the wide blocks near the curling river, passing the Paris Hatters store, with its impressive array of custom cowboy hats. Twenty-five thousand people packed the route all the way to Commerce Street and Broadway. At the Alamo, Governor Shivers stepped to a microphone and let his voice bounce off the weathered walls of the mission: "You and I cannot be too humble as we stand before this great shrine."[16]

Shivers was born in Lufkin and grew up working at an East Texas logging mill and then at a refinery in Port Arthur. He studied as an undergraduate and law school student at the University of Texas, and then moved back to Port Arthur and began attending Democratic Party gatherings. He came back to Austin to serve as the assistant sergeant-at-arms of the Texas House, and then in 1934 became the youngest person elected to the state senate, with some saying it was only a result of the twenty-seven-year-old's good looks.

He married into the Shary family empire, which once included thirty-six thousand acres in the lower Rio Grande Valley, one of the largest citrus-farming operations in the nation. With his ties to loggers in East Texas, to oil operators on the coast, and to the *patrones* on the Mexican border, Shivers had all the support he needed for bigger political ambitions. After serving in World War II, Shivers came back to Texas, ostensibly to manage his family's sprawling business, but he quickly turned to politics. In 1946, he was elected lieutenant governor, and plenty of insiders in Austin were assuming he saw the post as a way station before running for governor or Congress. Shivers used his time as lieutenant governor to urge lawmakers to continue easing business regulations, and to fund separate universities for Blacks, including the school that would become Texas Southern University in Houston. In office, he studied Texas history.

He perfected the art of picking state committee heads who could bull-rush through the state legislature any issues that the governor might not have had the constitutional authority to enforce. And when Governor Jester took his fateful train ride in the summer of 1949, almost all the kingmakers in Austin agreed that an Alamo-loving, well-connected climber like Allan Shivers would be a capable replacement.

For a minute, but maybe not for the last time, some inattentive lawmakers in the statehouse had no idea what the new governor was talking about. Shivers had summoned them to a special legislative session, and now he was shouting: "First in raising goats—last in caring for state wards!"[17]

Shivers knew he had lucked into the governor's office, but that he had also taken over at a time when oil revenues were down and the state was struggling to fund needed health care and other social programs. He weighed the political stakes and took the long view that he needed to shame the legislature into raising taxes and hope that voters would forget he was behind the hikes. His carefully crafted speech was designed to keep the state solvent, to put the tax burden on consumers and not businesses, and to burnish his legacy as someone who kept agencies funded and Texas afloat. Texas did indeed rank first in the nation in terms of raising goats, and around the statehouse, plenty of observers marveled at how the forty-one-year-old governor had appealed to Texas pride by saying that if the state could win the goat race, then it could afford a little money to pay for public hospitals.

Shivers had other plans: to spend the state's money on its precious roads and highways, to bump up salaries at public schools, and to redraw some legislative districts to make them more friendly to the hardcore, old-school conservative Southern Democrats. For any liberals and progressives wondering how Shivers would address racial divides, the answer was neatly spelled out by his opposition to the *Brown v. Board of Education* decision—and by his ordering Texas Rangers to head to Mansfield and make sure that Blacks never entered white schools.

Shivers liked being driven to Houston to confer with city leaders and the growing number of oil executives who were gathering at the new clubhouse at the River Oaks Country Club. After some golf, they would tell Shivers that maybe there was something to that "red menace" that Congressman Martin Dies had been yelling about. Shivers listened, even if he didn't need convincing that there might be forces dedicated to undermining the businesses he and his family ran or profited from—from the forests near the Sabine River, to the citrus fields hugging the Rio Grande, to the oil and gas plants in Port Arthur. The men at the country club said that the fears were real, that voters were wondering if the Democrats had the stomach to take on the communists, that some voters were forming local groups to ferret out subversives in schools and city councils. Shivers heard them say that even more white voters in the cities were beginning a bitter relocation to the suburbs. And that maybe they were talking about new political paths, maybe even converting the Texas Republican Party into a conservative army.

Each time he returned to Houston, Shivers heard it again: more people in the city were operating under the assumption that the federal government was crawling with socialists, communists, and spies—and that the long arm of a corrupted Washington, DC, was reaching into local schools. At community meetings, they shouted down attempts by federal inspectors to provide free lunches to poor students, or by federal regulators to check the quality of school lunch meat—even after word leaked out that a supplier was selling school districts horse sausage instead of beef. The Minute Women organization was growing, with several hundred ardent members gathering at homes to talk about how they could take on the red menace. The John Birch Society and other groups were opening branches in Texas, many of them convinced that a cabal of liberal elites was controlling the media, museums, universities, and libraries.[18]

In Houston, the deputy school superintendent was fired. Texans voted against compulsory attendance in integrated schools, and state lawmakers pushed bills giving school districts the ability to reject federal mandates. In Dallas, the archconservative Republican Bruce Alger was elected to Congress—the perfect harbinger of how once-strict party allegiances in Texas were changing.

GOP leaders in the state were watching those angry, displaced white voters who had moved out of the inner city. They could see that newcomers were still barreling into Texas, especially in Dallas and Houston. Many were settling in without the usual kneejerk devotion to the Southern Democratic Party. It was becoming more and more accepted in some circles to be a Republican, as long as you could prove your conservative credentials. The tall and angular-faced Alger became the first Republican congressman from Dallas since Reconstruction, and, in 1958, he was also the only member of Congress to vote against giving free milk and food to poor students as part of a federal school lunch program. He condemned it as "socialized milk." Alger was the most conservative legislator on Capitol Hill, a committed segregationist, and he took to the floor of Congress to offer an ode to General Robert E. Lee. It was something the paper from his home district celebrated: "The birthday of Robert E. Lee would have gone unnoticed in Congress this week except for Dallas Congressman Bruce Alger, lone Republican member from Texas," said the *Dallas Morning News* in an editorial. "It was fitting, though ironical, that a Republican ... was the only congressman to get on his feet and salute Gen. Robert E. Lee on his birthday. Fitting, because Lee fought for the rights of the states. By resisting big government in Washington, so is Alger. Where were the Democrats—so called party of the South? Courting the support of Eleanor Roosevelt and the NAACP?"[19]

When he returned to Austin, Shivers learned that federal regulators were trying to acquire the rights to the huge amounts of offshore oil waiting to be drained from 2.5 million acres in the Gulf of Mexico. In what was quickly dubbed the Tidelands Controversy, Shivers argued that Texas had a historic right to crack open what might be the next motherlode of black gold. Billions of dollars were at stake, and in the penthouse petroleum clubs in Houston, Midland, and Dallas, the oilmen were downing drinks and frantically complaining that Texas was in danger of surrendering a massive treasure: the Elephant Field of all Elephant Fields. No one knew how much oil was under the water, but the pencil pushers and the petroleum geologists suggested that it could be endless.

Shivers sat in his office and remembered the time he had gone to speak at the Alamo. People outside the state, especially the Northern Democrats, had no clue how Texas had saved the world during World War II. *And now they were suggesting that Texas was being greedy?* In West Texas, in Midland, one family was watching closely.

George Herbert Walker Bush had been sent by his father to invest money in the oil game, and he had made so many millions of dollars he had decided to stay in Texas. He was reporting back to his parents, especially the Republican US senator from Connecticut, Prescott Bush, that Texas was not just wide open for adding to the family's enormous fortune, but also now wide open for political possiblities. The father and son conferred, and the younger Bush said he was sure that Shivers would do the right thing.

True to form, Shivers ordered state attorneys to line up against federal agencies, President Truman, and anyone else in Washington trying to seize the Texas tidelands. Shivers even threw party allegiances out the window and said he was going to support a Republican, Dwight D. Eisenhower, in the presidential race. Adlai E. Stevenson, the Democratic candidate, was refusing to help Texas, and to hell with him.

More than a few Democrats in Texas shuddered over the Shivers power play, wondering what his breaking ranks really meant. He decided to reassure them by backing a bill that would send members of the Communist Party to death row in Texas. The death penalty bill failed; another, threatening communists with twenty years in prison, passed.

The lawyer, judge, and former assistant state attorney general Ralph Yarborough had made several enemies chasing down corruption inside the Texas oil industry. Urged to run for governor by labor leaders and civil rights activists, Yarborough, from Chandler, Texas, tried to beat Shivers in the 1952 Democratic primary. It was a lost cause. Shivers appeared on the November ballot as both the GOP and the Democratic nominee and essentially won every vote.

Yarborough tried again in 1954, traveling to little towns across the state and painting Shivers as a silk-pajama oligarch out of touch with the hopes and dreams of ordinary people in Wichita Falls, Colorado City, and Eden, Texas. He told people that Shivers had allies in the Texas Land Office who were hip-deep in defrauding war veterans and minorities. The Texas land commissioner was slapped with a six-year prison sentence, and Yarborough leaned into his campaign pitch that Shivers was guilty by association and just a slick downtown con artist who couldn't care less about working Texans.

Shivers had his own battle plan, which was to call Yarborough a cunning servant of the liberals from the North, just the kind of dupe who would let the communists and socialists creep into the Houston school districts or electrical cooperatives in the Hill Country. Shivers won the nomination and then relection, but Yarborough's attacks lingered with some voters. And they seemed to sap something from the proud, angry Shivers.

He knew he had been tainted by the notion that someone inside his inner circle was defrauding military heros, and doing it after a war fought by thousands of Texans. In Austin, aides said that Shivers seemed weary, and they wondered if he had had enough. Maybe he could see the long-range prognosis, maybe he possessed some innate fear that changes were coming in Texas that would overhaul the normal Old South social order he had tried to keep in place.

For now, Shivers was stunned at how the two most powerful Texans in Washington—Rayburn and Johnson—were sometimes leaning toward liberal wings. Johnson, especially, seemed to be turning his back on his early, solid record of voting against civil rights legislation. Things were building to a confrontation.

Heading into the 1956 Democratic National Convention, Shivers had formed a coalition of supporters called the "Shivercrats"—politicians devoted to time-honored Southern Democratic principles but also willing to bolt from the national party if it didn't protect business interests in Texas. At the convention, it was clear that Rayburn and Johnson supporters were going to outflank Shivers and that his Shivercrats would lose control of the Texas delegation. It was a breaking point, and Shivers decided he wanted out. He told people he was stepping away from politics in January 1957, and that after he left the governor's mansion he would go back to overseeing the giant farming interests he had inherited in South Texas. He also helped run banks and pipelines, and became president of the United States Chamber of Commerce. Shivers was given a six-year slot on the University of Texas board of regents. He became board chairman at a tumultuous time on campus, with student unrest and faculty demands.

For most of his life, Shivers was as addicted as anyone to the mythology of Texas, and from the minute he was elevated to the governor's office—after what might have been Beauford Jester's salacious last moments in a railroad car headed to Houston—he was determined to be the standard-bearer for matters he believed were deeply held in the state's heart. He loathed Northern Democrats, whom he knew to be blind to the brilliant economic miracles of Texas. The state fed the nation—and kept it fueled. The last thing Texas needed was more direction from leaders who were probably weak on communism, still bowing to unions, and still fixated on ending racist Southern customs that had served Texas since it was founded.

On January 14, 1985, the seventy-seven-year-old Shivers sat in his chairman's office at InterFirst Bank Austin and felt his chest tightening. He was rushed to Seton Medical Center, where, just as the sun began to set, he died from a heart attack. He was buried under an impressive sculpture created by Charles Umlauf in the Republic Hill section of the Texas State Cemetery. His granite tomb is topped by a "Spirit of Flight" bronze statue—cast at Vignali and Tommasi Fonderia d'Arte in Pietrasanta, Italy—that depicts a winged, mostly nude, muscled man standing on his toes and facing the sky. The towering resting place has the words "Fame is vapor" and "Riches take wings."

The cigar-smoking, hard-drinking newspaper people who had known Marion Price Daniel from his days as a reporter for the *Fort Worth Star-Telegram* and the *Waco News Tribune* would say that he had moved on up—and married on up. Daniel, a native of Dayton, Texas, had left the newspaper game, gotten his undergraduate and law degrees from Baylor, and then married the great-great-granddaughter of Sam Houston. In the courtroom, he developed a reputation as a nimble, skilled orator, famous for springing murder defendants, and able to easily pluck famous quotes and bits of history from memory and insert them into his closing arguments.

Daniel was elected to the Texas House in 1939 and quickly raised his profile by fighting sales taxes and then making a brash play to be House Speaker. After serving as a wartime army captain, the thirty-five-year-old was elected the youngest state attorney general in the nation. He made national news for his work arguing that the law school at the University of Texas was free to ban Black students—including Heman Sweatt, the mailman from Houston who would make history by finally breaking down the campus barriers against minorities.

Daniel also made more headlines when he led the legal fight against Northerners who wanted federal control over the big oil fields in the coastal tidelands. All of Daniel's high-profile cases—fighting hard for segregation at the state university, protecting the oceans of Texas oil—gave him a path to victory in the US Senate race in 1952. One of his first acts was to draft the papers signed by President Eisenhower that awarded the state of Texas power over the tidelands and opened them to unfettered drilling.

In Washington, Lyndon Johnson was keeping an eye on his new colleague from Texas. He decided to let some of Daniel's aides work and learn the ropes inside his office. Johnson was the Senate minority leader, and maybe he also wanted to keep an eye on a possible political usurper. After little more than a year, Daniel was clearly moving his own way. He and nineteen other senators signed the segregationist Southern Manifesto that rebuked the Supreme Court's stunning *Brown v. Board of Education* decision in 1954—but Johnson refused to add his name.

For Daniel, clambering up from his junior senator base would be difficult as long as Rayburn and Johnson were at the top of the Texas ladder. When he learned that Shivers had had enough and was leaving the governor's seat, Daniel announced that he wanted to come back home—and that he'd "rather be governor of Texas than President of the United States."[20]

Ralph Yarborough, square-jawed and with piercing eyes, had always seemed to run his own way. He loved Texas history, especially learning about the issues and moments that weren't in the usual books and papers. His part of North Texas, around Chandler and in the areas between Dallas and Tyler, had been witness to dozens of racist debacles. He had seen dirt-poor farmers of all colors fending for themselves in the rudderless days of the Great Depression. The older he got, the more he seemed to question Texas mythologies. What appeared to be a personal existential rebellion manifested itself when he decided to drop out of the US Military Academy at West Point and become a teacher. He went on to law school in Austin and began his foray into Texas politics in the 1930s.

Yarborough had bounced around several races, never winning, but he decided to try one last time in the 1957 special election to fill Daniel's Senate seat. One of his opponents was Martin Dies, the congressional scourge of communists. Yarborough won with an almost unlikely blend of unions, liberals, and minorities, and with the support of the small, muckraking *Texas Observer*.

His victory suggested there was an untapped army of populists and progressives who just needed someone to rally around, and that maybe

Liberal Democrat Ralph Yarborough (right), talking to a man at a campaign stop, ran many times for statewide office before voters elevated him to the US Senate. Yarborough, who fell to conservative Democratic challenger Lloyd Bentsen in 1970, once offered as his slogan "Let's put the jam on the lower shelf so the little people can reach it."

there were more people in Texas willing to follow federal orders to integrate the state. There were other signs: in 1957, an accountant and military veteran named Raymond Telles Jr., in El Paso, was elected the state's first Mexican American mayor—and the first Mexican American mayor of any large American city. Now, maybe Yarborough's election signaled that Texas could be more amenable to other things that had once seemed utterly impossible—letting workers organize, scrutinizing oil monopolies, and even hiking corporate taxes to pay for more schools, hospitals, and social services.

In Dallas and Houston, where the most affluent political kingmakers had settled, Yarborough's campaign slogan—"Let's put the jam on the lower shelf so the little people can reach it"—seemed cute and even benign. But for some, his rise to power was more than scary. Was he talking about a dreaded "redistribution" of wealth?

The fears multiplied when Yarborough began attaching his name to civil rights measures that would have had the long line of early Texas Confederates in the statehouse bewildered. Through 1970, Yarborough remained the only Southern Democrat to support every bit of civil rights legislation that appeared in the Senate. He not only rejected the Southern Manifesto but also supported environmental measures, public health initiatives, and funding that would make public education more accessible for people of all races and ethnicities.

The year after his special election, Yarborough faced a primary showdown with Daniel's handpicked candidate, the conservative Dallas millionaire William Blakley. Yarborough beat him and then trounced the GOP's Roy Whittenburg, an Amarillo oilman and newspaper publisher who had said he would support a plan to allow citizens to vote for Supreme Court justices. In Austin and the other big cities, there were more and more glum meetings being held to decide what to do about Yarborough.

When LBJ squeaked into the Senate with a handful of magical, maybe illegal, votes, skeptics dubbed him "Landslide Lyndon." He never looked back and simply moved on to profile-raising paths that could position him for even bigger possibilities. As the Senate minority leader, and then majority leader beginning in 1955 (the same year he suffered a heart attack), Johnson was being watched by national Democratic strategists mapping out ways to take back the White House. At forty-four, he was the youngest majority leader ever in the Senate. There had already been some rumblings of support for him during the 1956 presidential race, and he garnered a handful of mostly symbolic votes at the Democratic convention. And during the early jockeying for the 1960 presidential race, Johnson's name kept coming up as someone who might be able to bring in the Southern vote while proving palatable to Northern Democrats.

Johnson had seen how Garner, and then Rayburn, more or less got their way in Washington—moving right or left when necessary, or walking across the aisle to back-slap with Republicans. Johnson also learned to seduce journalists and the other unelected people who greased the political process. He was intentionally unfiltered when he needed to disarm an operative and get them to promote legislation or a committee appointment. But as he pondered his national chances, he also wanted to build what he thought might be more of a statesmanlike image, especially at a time when parts of the nation were impatient with the pace and depth of the mandated civil rights moves ordered by Washington.

Johnson and his family were increasingly worried about his health, so he cut out the two to three packs of cigarettes he was smoking each day. Then he decided to risk his political future by steering the watered-down Civil Rights Act of 1957. It was the first civil rights bill since Reconstruction, and though it was diluted through compromise, it put him at odds with Southern Democrats and more than a few members of his base back home. A year later, President Eisenhower helped raise Johnson's national profile by asking him to promote space exploration at a time when the Cold War was looming and a nervous world was watching the competition and tensions soaring with the Soviet Union.

Through it all, Johnson was searching for that fine line between his conservative roots and the way he saw Democratic politics shifting outside Texas. He knew, without question, that he had to keep moving beyond the inherited stereotypes and realities in Texas—all those racist ciphers, signs, and symbols he had carried from the Fergusons, O'Daniel, Shivers, and Stevenson.

His closest friends were studying him and sometimes wondering if he was too feral, too consumed by unquenched ambition. His longtime ally John Connally told people that LBJ was "cruel and kind, generous and greedy, sensitive and insensitive, crafty and naive, ruthless and thoughtful ... he knew how to use people in politics in the way nobody else could that I know of."[21]

Connally understood that Johnson's heart attack—just two days before the Fourth of July in 1955—had changed him a bit. Maybe it had reoriented him to his modest upbringing in the pecan and peach regions of Johnson City and Stonewall, near Pedernales Falls, Jones Spring, and Miller Creek. Johnson spent time recuperating in the Hill Country, and it put him in touch with the heartland, with his deep base, perhaps in ways that might prove useful later on.

Back in Washington, political reporters were meeting after work and comparing notes about the presidential horse race, and Johnson's name was still in the air. He had courted many of them at his palatial office, nicknamed the "Taj Mahal" because of its marble fireplace, murals, and chandeliers. They knew that even when he was ill, he was single-handedly running bills, moves, and other political campaigns.

It was only a matter of time, they said, before Lyndon Johnson would want to vault beyond the Senate.

CHAPTER 10

The Mink Coat Mob: The 1960s

JOHN F. KENNEDY AND HIS BROTHER Bobby, his campaign manager, were summoning LBJ to emergency meetings. The 1960 presidential race against Richard Nixon was now the tightest in US history, and Democratic insiders were wondering why the hell Johnson was even on the ticket. In exchange for being the vice presidential candidate, he was supposed to serve up the South, handing over "his people" in the states that didn't like Kennedy's Catholic religion, Northeastern accent, and Ivy League education. But there were early warning signs that the Kennedy-Johnson ticket was in danger, maybe even in Texas. Kennedy had been especially hearing it over and over again from Bobby, who disliked Johnson more than ever.

For his part, Johnson was measuring his time in Washington against the Kennedy clan and whether they had the same savvy congressional skills he had acquired—or if they could ever dream of matching the draw Johnson assumed he had in the rural outposts and growing Southern cities like Houston. Johnson knew Kennedy had outhustled him on the way to the presidential race, but he also knew Kennedy desperately needed some of the South. LBJ, like so many others, had studied at the feet of Cactus Jack Garner, or at least had learned to emulate him from a distance. He knew Garner had been the ballsiest vice president in US history. Maybe there was room for another.

On his trips back to Texas, riding in his Lincoln along paths near the Pedernales River, LBJ wrestled with his fears: Garner had sometimes muttered, with his face darkening, about how he should have been president. About how he decided to bide his time as the vice president, to go below deck on Capitol Hill, to call in favors owed him after spending decades in Congress—and wait for the right time to take the White House. Of course, it never happened. Maybe Garner had only succeeded in reinventing the office of the vice president, by making the rounds during the early rollout of the New Deal, by serving as the demanding enforcer for White House mandates. *But what did it get him in the end?* Garner was maybe destined to be an afterthought, a footnote. And Johnson wondered what it would mean to be the next Texan to be second-in-command behind another slick Northeasterner.

He had his self-doubts, and Bobby Kennedy certainly had his own doubts about whether Johnson could be trusted. At various times, he tried talking Johnson out of the race, but LBJ almost begged to stay on board. The animus and unease had to be tied to some of those long-lasting impressions of Texas as a snake pit filled with conniving politicians who might appear to bend and sway but who remained at the beck and call of a hard-core group of anti-Washington, anti-labor, anti-regulatory tycoons who ran whole cities and counties. The Kennedy brothers were products of an incestuous political system of their own, one in which the rules and regulations were passed down from ward boss to ward boss. They knew Johnson was also a product of a patronage system, but one that the Kennedy clan, so culturally disconnected from Texas, had no way of controlling.

It wasn't just an idle notion inside the Kennedy inner circle: *Who really knew what was going on in Texas? Was it filled with hillbilly populists and billionaire oilmen who saw socialists and communists behind every federal regulation? Was everyone there like the madcap Pappy O'Daniel, or the unforgiving Martin Dies, or the reactionary Dallas congressman Bruce Alger?* It wasn't a far leap for anti-Johnson forces to assume he was really a Christian archconservative with racist tendencies in his closet—and the fake air of a moderate who was really just a trained emissary for the oil monopolists.

As the questions and suspicions swirled, Texas lawmakers voted to allow Johnson to run for Senate reelection at the same time he ran for the vice presidency. Some said it was a sure sign Johnson was hedging his bets. Johnson campaigned hard with Kennedy, but at one quick stop in Ama-

rillo, they were stunned when they tried to give speeches at the city airport. They were drowned out by feisty pilots gunning their plane engines.
JFK and his brother left Texas more than concerned, and the doubts only
mounted into the fall.

The numbers were too close: Nixon was running neck and neck with
Kennedy, and JFK said that Johnson needed to make an emergency campaign visit to Dallas. Word was coming from Dallas Democrats that the
city's most powerful Baptist preacher, Rev. W. A. Criswell, had been warning his thousands of loyal followers that Kennedy was a papist prone to
doing the bidding of the Vatican. The powerful publisher of the *Dallas
Morning News*, Ted Dealey, was ordering up anti-Kennedy editorials and
calling Kennedy another Northern integrationist too worried about the
rights of Negroes. The world's richest man, the eccentric Dallas oilman
H. L. Hunt, was pumping millions of dollars into anti-Kennedy leaflets,
newsletters, and radio programs.[1]

Johnson, who had his pajamas monogrammed at the elegant Nieman
Marcus emporium in downtown Dallas, made hasty arrangements for the
last-minute swing into Texas. He landed in Dallas four days before the
November 1960 election, more concerned than ever about what would
happen if Nixon stole the state. The political forces that Shivers had unleashed—that rush by Democrats to register as conservative Republicans—were blowing up the old political order.

LBJ had been in touch with his suave and erudite friend Stanley Marcus, who ran Neiman Marcus and had been providing reconnaissance on
almost every powerful white preacher, politician, and businessman in Dallas who was working against the Democratic ticket. Marcus promised he'd
be in the city, with supporters, to welcome Johnson and his wife, Lady
Bird.

As LBJ's motorcade approached the historic Adolphus Hotel—the
swanky Beaux-Arts building built by the founders of Anheuser-Busch—
Johnson could see a crowd waiting. Johnson stared out the window of
his limousine and past the motorcycle escort. Dozens of well-dressed
women—some in fur coats—were pacing back and forth on the wide sidewalks lining Commerce Street. Many of them had carefully painted signs:
TEXAS TRAITOR, JUDAS JOHNSON: TURNCOAT TEXAN, LET'S
BEAT JUDAS.

As the limousine pulled to the curb, a jumble of angry, contorted faces
began pressing close to the car. As the Johnsons stepped into the windy
downtown canyon, they were suddenly swarmed by a screaming horde.

People spat at them, taunted them, ripped at Lady Bird's gloves and threw them in the gutter. LBJ put his arms around his wife and tried to guide her through the melee.[2]

The Johnsons retreated to their hotel room, peeked out the windows, and then slumped in chairs, trying to digest what had just happened. The police arrived, saying the scene was getting worse. A shaking, nervous Stanley Marcus came to the suite and tried to explain why LBJ and his wife had just been ambushed. He said it was a carefully coordinated Republican plot, led by the tall, forceful Dallas congressman Bruce Alger, and it had obviously gotten way out of hand.

There was quick discussion on what to do next. LBJ insisted he was going to go on and give his scheduled campaign speech. Surrounded by police and guards, he and his wife rode the elevator to the lobby. Stepping out, they could see dozens of people slashing the air with their signs. As they walked through the hotel, there were jeers, screams, and insults. Alger was on the scene, bellowing against LBJ and urging the crowd on. News cameras were rolling. Some women began stabbing the air and bystanders with hat pins.

Millions of readers and television viewers around the nation heard about the melee in downtown Dallas by a well-dressed army of anti-LBJ protesters. It was quickly dubbed a "mink coat mob" riot, and plenty of people were left wondering what the hell had just happened in Texas. The mob—filled with the newest members of the Republican Party, those conservative, wealthier Texans fed up with the compromises inside the once-faithful Democratic Party—had lost its mind.

By an almost two-to-one margin, Nixon carried Dallas. It was his biggest margin of victory in any American city. Kennedy and Johnson won Texas and, of course, the national race. It was closer than any previous presidential race.

As Kennedy and Johnson took office in Washington, political scientists began to search for the clues to the Democratic victory. Some of them kept circling back to Dallas, back to the riot on Commerce Street. Some said the wild Republican rally in Dallas had moved fence-sitting voters around the nation to throw sympathy and support to the Kennedy-Johnson ticket.

Nixon also tended to think he had lost the state, and maybe the national election, because of the dizzy day when modern-day Texas Republicans attacked a son of the old Democratic machine: "We lost Texas ... because of that asshole congressman," said Nixon.[3]

John Connally had steadfastly clung to his own political dreams, even as he worked as LBJ's apologist, strategist, secretary, and legislative aide. Like his boss, Connally had been a navy man during the war, and he was discharged as a lieutenant commander after seeing action in the Pacific. He dove right back into LBJ's campaigns and got his hands dirty during that infamous race against Coke Stevenson and the mysterious emergence of a handful of votes in Jim Wells County—that county named after one of the most powerful of the South Texas Democratic *patrones*.

JFK and LBJ rewarded Connally by making him secretary of the navy. The appointment raised his profile and suggested he could be trusted at a delicate time when the nation wondered if the United States and the Soviet Union were going to destroy each other, and maybe the planet, with atomic bombs. Connally had never run for office but decided he would test out a run for governor.

In strategy sessions in Austin, his aides debated whether voters were suffering from "Daniel fatigue"—Price Daniel had been reelected in 1958 and again in 1960. He had been laboriously efficient in the statehouse, successfully pushing dozens of proposals: expanding even more Texas highways, opening up mental health agencies and institutions, reexamining the growing prison system, and looking for ways to raise the pay at public schools.

But Daniel also hadn't resisted the state's first sales tax—and maybe Texans wouldn't want a four-term governor. With his obvious connections to the White House, Connally was invited to meet more of the deep-pocketed oilmen in Texas, as well as the new breed of businessmen relocating to Dallas, Houston, and other cities to take advantage of cheap land, inexpensive construction costs, minimal regulations, and the steady labor supply.

Connally's hunch was right. He beat Daniel in the primary, won the governor's seat, and spent a good deal of time crafting an image that he knew would play well in many parts of Texas. He wore well-shined boots, and he liked to enter a room flanked by swaggering Texas Rangers—all of whom had to be at least two inches shorter than Connally. From the minute he took office, he continued to provide political reports to LBJ—and he also agreed to ride in President Kennedy's motorcade when it came to Dallas in November 1963.

On November 22, Cactus Jack Garner, the powerful and profane old man of Lone Star politics, was at his comfortable home in Uvalde on the southern edge of the state's rolling Hill Country. The previous day had been his ninety-fifth birthday, and this morning he was waiting for his loyal caretaker to inform him when there was a phone call from Fort Worth.

Kennedy was 350 miles to the north, inside his suite at the Hotel Texas. He was preparing to head to Dallas, where he was scheduled to travel by that open motorcade through the city's downtown streets, past Dealey Plaza, named for the father of Ted Dealey, the influential publisher of the *Dallas Morning News* and the most virulently anti-Kennedy member of the American media. Too, it would pass by something called the Texas School Book Depository.

The president had decided that as he made a political swing through Texas he at least ought to pay homage to Garner. Maybe place a call to Uvalde. It wouldn't be right if he ignored Cactus Jack (who once led an unsuccessful attempt to have the prickly pear blossom declared the state flower instead of the bluebonnet). Kennedy knew that Garner and LBJ had somehow survived decades of infighting, conspiracies, and roiling antagonisms in Texas that were as intense as anything he had seen in the Irish wards of Boston. Kennedy also knew that Garner was LBJ's spirit guide as well as a living symbol of where Texas had come from: Garner was born just after the Civil War ended, he was raised in the horse-and-buggy era, and then he had endured into the space age.

Garner was witness to the last shadows of legalized slavery; the dominance of racist Southern Democrats; the emergence of conservative Southern Republicans. Garner had seen Texas shift from a rural outpost—where white settlers were offered money if they'd seize Indian territory—to a place with a coastline run riot with miles of industry; with dams on the big rivers and entire bays carved out to accommodate giant freighters; with oil sheiks building mansions in a desert where they had found underground oceans of fossil fuels.

As he had watched the changes, Garner was well aware that there would be everlasting political codes at work: things settled so deeply into the Texas marrow; things ceaselessly carried forward by the nostalgic inclinations of mythologists; things that could buffer some strong-willed Texans against outside definition, control, and political interference. Garner had always loved the way reporters marketed the trope of a Lone Star Nation whose citizens refused to be herded. He wasn't alone. The political beasts had always been emboldened by imagined versions of Texas. Garner rode those versions to high office; he made them his calling card. And he loved the way Texas was often rendered by its chroniclers. So did LBJ. He liked to think of political journalists as "servants."[4]

Even into the fall of 1963, Garner still served as a template for how to climb the mountain in Texas—and how to stay at the summit. He was the quintessential political personality: brutally effective even if he wasn't always right; someone who professed to be a man of the people while being sponsored by a handful of gilded patrons; ruthless, ambitious, spontaneous, colorful, and often generous. He was a politician who loved Texas to such a degree that one might wonder whether he loved it more than the United States. And he was a politician who hated the overbearing ways of Washington but who saw the need for centralization and federal handouts when events got dire. He had one foot in the Angora goat lands of Texas and one foot in the upper reaches of oil-rich Houston. When he had said that being vice president of the United States wasn't "worth a bucket of warm piss," some people took it as a sign that he thought being a Texas politician was a hell of a lot more satisfying.

Kennedy might also have known that when Garner was a congressman, he had arranged to have two statues put on display in the nation's capital—one for Stephen F. Austin and one for Sam Houston.

Back at his home in Uvalde, Garner was still waiting to hear from President Kennedy. Finally, his faithful caretaker came to his side and whispered that the president was on the phone from Fort Worth.

Kennedy was on a tight schedule and ready to head to Love Field in Dallas, but he had told his staff that he had to squeeze in the salute to the elder statesman of Texas politics. Without Garner, there would be no LBJ. Without LBJ, there might not be a Kennedy in the White House.

Garner's caretaker, Ray Scott, a wiry young man with a wide, smiling face, tried to listen in on the conversation between the president of the United States and the former vice president of the United States. All he could pick up was a raspy-sounding Garner whispering: "You are my president. And I love you."[5]

Before Kennedy boarded the presidential plane for the short flight from Fort Worth to Dallas, he turned to First Lady Jacqueline Kennedy. To him, Johnson, Garner, and so many others from Texas were inscrutable men from a foreign land.

Kennedy muttered to his wife: "We're headed into nut country today."[6]

In Dallas, of course, shots rang out, Kennedy was assassinated, and Lyndon Baines Johnson from Stonewall, Texas, was sworn in as the next president of the United States.

Cactus Jack Garner died four years after the assassination, and a few days short of his ninety-ninth birthday. Garner was laid to rest in the family plot in Uvalde on a late fall day in 1967. He had made Sam Rayburn and Lyndon Baines Johnson—and a wave of other Texans—viable figures on the American stage. Without him, the New Deal might not have succeeded. Without Garner's guidance, Johnson might never have been president. A million things in America might have been different. Garner's mercurial cantankerousness changed the nation, the world, in so many ways. It was a long way from Blossom Prairie.

His marker in the Uvalde cemetery, flanked by towering Lone Star and American flags, displays his political credo: "There are just two things to this government as I see it—the first is to safeguard the lives and properties of our people—the second is to insure that each of us has a chance to work out his destiny according to his talents."

But, even as he was buried, another slogan of Garner's was being remembered. It was one that applied in so many ways to all manner of politics and politicians in Texas, no matter what side of the aisle you were on.

According to Garner, when it came to playing the political game there was one simple rule: "You've got to bloody your knuckles."[7]

After he was wounded in the attack on the presidential motorcade in Dallas, Governor John Connally became a national figure, someone strengthened politically by his brush with death. That scarring, surreal, and tragic day was the worst of blights on the state image. Countless stories appeared about Dallas being "a city of hate"—and Texas being a zone where retribution or justice was carried out by anyone willing to pull a trigger. (Years later, in the 1990s, I was reporting in Russia on behalf of the *Dallas Morning News*, and when I told someone what city I was from in Texas, they raised their fingers in the shape of a pistol, whispered the name Kennedy, and pretended to shoot me.)

Determining the exact impact of the assassination on the political future of Texas would take miles of volumes. The immense international focus, the objectification of the state, caused leaders to wonder how to keep investors coming to Texas. How to keep Washington from pressing down. How to soothe anyone who thought the state was still breeding the lawlessness that had engulfed it in the 1870s and 1880s, when gunfire routinely rang out all over its hollows and hideouts. It was the most infamous murder in the state's history, one that changed the world, one that brought LBJ to the White House, along with dozens of aides and allies from the very state where the president had been gunned down.

The agony and unease only persisted as the true circumstances of how and why Lee Harvey Oswald had acted—and how and why Jack Ruby was able to kill him—were debated for decades. There was going to be a never-ending sense of a conspiracy, of dark manueverings, in Texas—that things were never what they seemed. The accusations took on a life of their own, with countless books and overheated theories, including some suggesting the assassination was a carefully designed plot by Texas politicians ... including Lyndon Baines Johnson.

If it was possible to salvage Texas's reputation, then maybe it could be done by making it even more friendly for corporations—the ones that were still thinking of flocking to the state to avoid big taxes, messy regulatory bodies, and organized labor. Connally's sales pitch to corporate leaders was simple: come to Texas and you'll find the best damn pro-business climate in the world. As businesses began exploring relocating to Houston and Dallas, promises were made of bigger, better airports; the best shipping routes and highways; easy connections between the coastal ports and the urban areas. There were miles of land on the outskirts of the big cities, perfect for huge subdivisions, new homes, places for factories and plants. As the distrust of Texas began to ebb, the money and the influencers flowed in. And many of the newer, well-funded business executives happened to be conservative Republicans.

Connally and other Texans weaned on Democratic politics began burrowing closer to the Republican apparatus.

It's one thing to parse the bills and policies coursing through the statehouse in Austin, but sometimes, when it comes to men like Connally, it's especially worthy to linger with his personal baptism in Republicanism. Connally simply began a spectacular reversal: growing closer to Richard Nixon, finally switching to the GOP, and then holding a high office in a Republican presidential administration. His conversion inspired countless candidates trying to solicit oil money and votes in Texas, including the members of the Bush dynasty. Without Connally, the march of George H. W. Bush and George W. Bush from Texas to the White House would have been far more complicated, certainly less streamlined—and maybe eternally delayed.

In the grinding, hot summer of 1966, Connally had a vexing annoyance on his mind: organizers with an early version of the United Farm Workers were introducing themselves to men and women stooping in the melon fields near Rio Grande City. They handed out literature, gave speeches, and urged the field hands to demand living wages from the half-dozen major growers. Some workers were earning 40 cents an hour, at a time when the federal minimum wage was $1.25.

Picket lines were formed, four hundred people went on strike, and quickly, the police and Texas Rangers arrived to take the the workers to jail. Labor leaders gathered and made a fateful decision to launch a new mission on the Fourth of July—another strike and a 490-mile-long march by hundreds of people that would take them from Rio Grande City to Kingsville, to Corpus Christi, to San Antonio, and then to the granite steps of Gov. Connally's statehouse in Austin.

The march was almost impossible for Connally to comprehend and then to ignore. The story was making news across Texas and the nation. In meeting with his aides, he said he wanted to do something bold—he would intercept the marchers once they arrived in New Braunfels. Maybe he could scare them away from their symbolic assault on the capital. As they inched across Texas, the marchers were given shelter by churches and parishioners. Strangers handed them cups of water. Cowboys on the iconic King Ranch offered tacos. Some Texans heard that the field hands were walking dozens of miles a day, and when they passed by, they were given new shoes.

In August, Connally made arrangements to go dove hunting in South Texas, but he told his driver to stop his limousine in New Braunfels, where the marchers were resting before their final leg to Austin. Connally stepped out of his car and glowered at the farmworkers. His security detail fanned out. Connally began dressing the protesters down, scolding them, and then said he wasn't going to be in Austin when they arrived. He'd still be hunting. They should all go back to the Valley.[8]

The marchers watched as Connally climbed back in his car and his limousine sped away. The organizers debated and opted to press on. When they finally made it to Austin on Labor Day, they were joined by the increasingly famous leader of the farmworkers, Cesar Chavez, and as many as fifteen thousand supporters.

The standoff with the farm hands lingered for weeks and then months, and Connally finally ordered Texas Rangers to break the strike. Several workers were beaten or threatened. One suffered a concussion and spinal damage—and others were taken to railroad tracks and pressed, facedown, near roaring freight cars. The so-called Starr County Strike was in part a political awakening, a political confrontation, and it put state lawmakers on notice that there could be direct action from constituencies who had endured a long, heated walk across Texas and seemed resolutely determined to keep marching for as long as necessary.

John Tower was the son of a Methodist minister from Houston, and he studied political science at Southwestern University before joining the US Navy in the summer of 1943. After serving on an amphibious gunboat in the Pacific, Tower returned to Southwestern to finish his bachelor's degree. He received a graduate degree in political science at Southern Methodist University in Dallas, and then studied at the London School of Economics. Back in Texas, he took a position as an assistant professor at Midwestern University in Wichita Falls.

Throughout his academic career, he remained in the Naval Reserve and also tried his hand at sales, investing, and even radio broadcasting. Into the early 1950s, the diminutive Tower kept his eyes on the way mid-twentieth-century Texas was becoming a more urban world, one that could provide safe haven for hawkish Republicans, including ones supporting the presidential aspirations of Arizona senator Barry Goldwater. Tower was seeing more fiscal conservatives, men who saw the financial gain in taking strong stands against communism and societal shifts that they assumed would threaten the easy flow of commerce; men committed to a strong military, who saw it as a natural link to a strong economy.

Between classes at Midwestern University, Tower began to explore Republican possibilities, and he ran for state representative in 1954. He lost, but two years later he served as a delegate to the national GOP convention at the Cow Palace in San Francisco. By 1960, the hard-charging Tower was the GOP senatorial candidate in Texas. He tried to paint Johnson (who was running for both the Senate and the vice presidency) as a liberal traitor and an office-chasing political opportunist, someone who cared more about working with Kennedy in Washington. Tower was outspent and facing the powerful LBJ brand. He was defeated but ready to try again once LBJ left his Senate seat to become vice president.

Until a special election was held in 1961, the megamillionaire William "Dollar Bill" Blakley was named interim senator. Blakley was a conservative Democrat from Dallas, the largest shareholder in Braniff Airlines, and one of the richest men in the state. Worth almost $300 million, he had amassed a fortune through hotels, ranches, shopping centers, investing, and insurance. In the May 1961 runoff for Johnson's open Senate seat, the thirty-five-year-old Tower beat the sixty-two-year-old Blakley by just over ten thousand votes, and Tower became the first Texas Republican senator since Reconstruction in 1870.

His friends and aides knew that Tower was never lacking in swagger. Behind his back, some people said he had a Napoleonic complex, that he tried too hard to be tough. If he was stunned that he had made history in Texas, he didn't let many people know, and he simply moved briskly to establish himself as a key player in the GOP evolution in the South.

Tower went to Washington and told national Republican leaders that he would put his shoulder to the wheel on behalf of Barry Goldwater and then Richard Nixon. Tower proved his white conservative bonafides by resisting both the Civil Rights Act of 1964, which sought to outlaw segregated public facilities, as well as the Voting Rights Act of 1965, designed to extend election protections to minorities. Even his foes said he was extraordinarily resolute, almost zealous, about wanting the GOP to control Texas and the nation. Though he had cut his teeth as a teacher in Wichita Falls, Tower viewed himself as a kind of impeccably tailored diplomat—the epitome of that sophisticated, new-breed Texas Republican who was attuned to national and international matters at the highest levels. On Capitol Hill, he was predisposed to weigh in on global matters, and he served as a role model for more emerging GOP power brokers, including the Houston attorney James Baker (who would serve as President Ronald Reagan's chief of staff and secretary of the treasury—and then as President George H. W. Bush's chief of staff and secretary of state).

When George H. W. Bush became president, he wanted to give Tower a plum, perhaps as payback for all Tower had done to make the GOP a viable option in Texas. The Bush family liked to call its confidantes and allies "good men." To the new president, Tower was a good man, and without him, Bush might not have been in the Oval Office. Bush told Tower he wanted him to be his secretary of defense—but, almost immediately, Tower was consumed by allegations that he was a sloppy, incorrigible drinker and had played fast and loose outside his marriage.

One day, Tower stared impatiently at a journalist from the *New York Times* and said: "Have I ever drunk to excess? Yes. Am I alcohol-dependent? No. Have I always been a good boy? Of course not. But I've never done anything disqualifying. That's the point."[9]

Tower and his daughter were killed in 1991 when their plane, Atlantic

Southeast Airlines Flight 2311, crashed as it tried to land in Brunswick, Georgia.

In Houston, Felix Tijerina was still fussing over his patrons and leaning in for another photograph. He ran what might have been the most recognizable Mexican restaurant in the state's biggest city and he was an omnipresent figure, dashing from table to table, greeting loyal customers — and ignoring the whispers from Latinos who were saying he was serving watered-down Mexican food for the rich gringos.

He had grown up working in the humid cane fields near Sugar Land, where his family had settled in the wake of the Mexican Revolution. When he turned seventeen, he went to work as a busboy at a downtown Houston restaurant. He learned the business, saved money, and opened his Felix Mexican Restaurant in 1937, beginning the long process of becoming a kind of staid political touchstone for white candidates savvy enough to recognize there were votes to be had inside the city's minority community.

For years, he met with Houston and state leaders who presumed he had a read on what Latino voters might want. "He was widely viewed as the most esteemed and influential Mexican American resident of Houston, Texas," wrote one biographer.[10] And unlike the members of more activist organizations, Tijerina was always more interested in assimilation than outright confrontation.[11]

Some of his impatient critics said that his food served as a metaphor for his careful political approach: his sauces and cheeses were groomed for the white customers. His increasingly popular inner-city eatery was a place where many Texans had their first Mexican food — or first dined side by side with Mexican Americans. His restaurant's success led to local political opportunities, and he was named the first Mexican American on the Houston Housing Authority board. He was eventually selected to be the national head of LULAC, and he worked on community education drives that would form the basis for the federal Head Start program.

In San Antonio, Henry González's friends heard him tell the story about a stint he and his brother once shared as young men at the University of Texas: "The González brothers spent a cold and hungry winter at the University. They could not afford a heater and, consequently, learned of the warmth of newspaper blankets.... Austin was not an easy town for Latin Americans.... They were often called 'greasers' or 'spics.'"[12] González also talked about the time he and a Black friend in San Antonio had visited a normally segregated drugstore on Commerce Street and González somehow convinced the owner that the Black man was not a "real Negro" but a visiting Ethiopian prince. The owner, impressed by royalty, allowed the men to sit at the counter.[13]

He had always felt that he had paid his dues in the city, and that included leading a "Viva Kennedy" voting drive. In 1961 he decided to run in a special election to fill a congressional vacancy after the San Antonio lawyer Paul Kilday resigned after serving two decades in Washington. The enormously popular Mexican movie star Cantinflas arrived in San Antonio to work the crowds. LBJ took time out from his duties as vice president of the United States to show up at local shopping centers and urge people to support "Henry B."

González won, and his name bounced around Washington as someone who was loyal to President Kennedy and more than useful to Democrats. Kennedy, for one, wanted to see him if he ever visited Texas—maybe González could even be included in a presidential motorcade in Dallas.

As he inched toward national prominence, González was sometimes very self-aware: "Some would never vote for the Irish Kennedy or the Mexican González; and some would only vote for us because he was Irish and I am Mexican; but most would decide the issues on the merits, and us on our ability."[14]

He was reelected seventeen times—and often ran unopposed. González would last in Washington for thirty-seven years, setting a record for longevity. He was a key member of the House Committee on Banking and Currency. He pushed for the final dissolution of poll taxes, and for limiting the funding for the House Un-American Activities Committee. González argued for an end to the Bracero Program. He was one of the only men from Texas to back the Civil Rights Act of 1964.

One representative from West Texas, Ed Foreman, labeled him a communist "pinko." González told Foreman he'd see him outside the House chamber—and when the two stood face-to-face, González shoved him hard enough for his hands to sink into Foreman's chest: "It was a shove. But my hand went into him three inches—he's so soft."[15]

González kept a sign on his office door that said "This Office Belongs to the People of Bexar County," and he was instrumental in bringing federal urban renewal funding to HemisFair '68, the world's fair that drew jobs and international attention to San Antonio and his district. But not everyone back home loved him.

One day in a venerable San Antonio eatery, a man wobbled up to González and called him a communist. Amid elderly patrons trying to concentrate on their chicken-fried steaks and tall glasses of sweet iced tea, González measured the man for a second, leaned back, and then punched him in the face.

At the age of seventy, González had just assaulted someone in a restaurant on Broadway in San Antonio. Maybe it was a sign of his popularity, maybe the man knew he'd never win in a trial, but the charges were dropped and González went back to Congress—where he'd make news, again, by demanding that Ronald Reagan be impeached for his role in trying to secretly overthrow Nicaragua.

In 1963 in Crystal City, five Mexican American candidates ran against incumbent city and school officials. Latino organizers and activists had told voters their poll taxes would be paid and anyone who needed a ride to the election booths would get it. Some workers from the Del Monte cannery were told they'd be fired for wearing campaign buttons; the Texas Rangers were sent to the city to monitor events; and the cannery announced that it needed employees working longer shifts, ones the organizers knew would keep them from the voting booths. The intimidation tactics failed. The five Mexican American candidates were elected, forming the first all-minority city council in Texas.

By now, leaders in Austin had begrudgingly accepted the presence of pioneering groups such as the American GI Forum—while still trying to buy off or accommodate minority leaders by appointing them to do-nothing civic boards. Frustration with the "old ways" was palpable among younger activists, including some college students who were forming the Mexican American Youth Organization (MAYO).

"All of us were the products of the traditional Mexican American organizations. All of us were products of the changing mood in the community," said MAYO co-founder José Ángel Gutiérrez.[16] He added:

> We were Chicanos who were starved for any kind of meaningful
> participation in decision making, policy making and leadership
> positions. For a long time we have not been satisfied with the type
> of leadership that has been picked for us. And this is what a politi-
> cal party does, particularly the ones we have here. I shouldn't use
> the plural because we only have one, and that's the gringo party. It

doesn't matter what name it goes by. It can be Kelloggs, All-Bran or Shredded Wheat, but it's still the same crap.[17]

Gutiérrez, particularly, emerged as a powerful—and more threatening—organizer. His La Raza Unida political party wanted to pursue more targeted attempts to put minority candidates on statewide ballots. His father was a doctor in Crystal City, and Gutiérrez had grown up a bit buffered against the virulent forms of racism that other, poorer Mexican Americans had known. When he was twelve, his father died and life changed: "I had grown up with a strong dose of self-esteem, with the support of my parents. I was bilingually fluent, confident, poised, the whole thing. Now I was being told, 'You've got to keep your place.' 'Place' being kid, Mexican, wrong side of the tracks, all those things. I wasn't used to being treated like that. I began to connect the dots. I discovered it meant something to be Mexican."[18]

His political metamorphosis zoomed forward with the heady Crystal City revolution of 1963. He had been out of high school for only a year when he helped transform his hometown's entire political system. He went to college in Kingsville, and when he graduated, he returned home and tried to get a job as a teacher. He was turned down repeatedly, and

José Ángel Gutiérrez, who grew up in Crystal City, Texas, helped found the Raza Unida Party. The party achieved local successes before offering candidates for eleven statewide offices in 1972.

Gutiérrez began devoting even more time to political causes, and organizing and planning campaigns to put Mexican Americans in office around
Texas. He wanted an edgier organization, and his La Raza Unida was in
the vanguard of other unblinking national movements devoted to civil
rights, from the Students for a Democratic Society to the Black Panthers.
Gutiérrez and La Raza colleagues began calling for a new look at Texas
history, and for more strikes, sit-ins, marches, and protests. He developed
a particular view of the Texas Rangers and their role in state politics. They
were, he said, "the governor's private army."[19]

George H. W. Bush had come to Texas after World War II, armed with
wads of investment money from his family in the Northeast. The Bushes
had made millions on Wall Street, and had served on the governing boards
of major corporations and even Yale University. The well-financed Bush
almost instantly made another family fortune with a series of lucrative
wells in the Permian Basin oilfields.

By the end of the 1950s, he told family members in New York and
throughout the Northeast (his father was the US Senator from Connecticut) that the next big play in Texas oil was out in the Gulf of Mexico. He
told them to reallocate their resources to Houston, that he was moving
there, and he was going to get in on seemingly endless reservoirs of underwater oil, stretching across hundreds of miles from Texas to Louisiana.

By 1963, his father had decided to step down from the Senate—and his
always-half-grinning oilman son announced his own candidacy to keep
a Bush on Capitol Hill. Bush told his father that the time was right, that
white voters were going to be fleeing the Southern Democratic Party that
John Nance Garner had once solidified. Bush saw how Richard Nixon and
Barry Goldwater had enormously faithful supporters in Texas. He became
Harris County chair of the Republican Party in 1963 and used his position
as a springboard to win the GOP primary for the Senate seat. Then, Bush
rambled to parts of the state he had never seen, trying to convince rural
voters that he wasn't just a "Connecticut Yankee" or a "limousine Republican" but someone who could understand the realities of the heartland, the
working-class voters, and all those people buying homes in the Houston
and Dallas suburbs.

Even though he said he was a states' rights man opposed to civil rights
legislation coming from Washington, Bush was easily defeated in November 1964 by the Democratic incumbent Ralph Yarborough. He lowered his

George H. W. Bush (right), alongside the state's first Republican governor since Reconstruction, the pugnacious Bill Clements. Together, they plotted the Republican takeover of Texas.

sights and two years later ran for Congress in Houston, defeating Harris County district attorney Frank Briscoe. Bush became the first Republican to represent the Seventh Congressional District in Texas. He threw his support behind Nixon and Goldwater, and he quickly aligned himself even more with right-leaning leaders opposed to the Civil Rights Act. In Houston, he had far bigger designs in mind—and he was convinced, more than ever, that Texas would be the perfect launching pad for a Lone Star Republican to one day take the White House. A decade or two earlier it would have seemed unlikely, even laughable. But he was living proof that Texas had permanently, irrevocably, changed its political soul.

The progressive liberal attorney Don Yarborough, no relation to Ralph Yarborough, tried to unseat John Connally in the 1962 Democratic gubernatorial primary, and he surprised some observers by getting 49 percent of the vote and then barely losing in a runoff. The race was "a nationally noted near-upset in a state long dominated by the conservative faction of the Democratic Party," and "although Yarborough never became governor, his campaigns contributed strongly to the reform of the Texas Democratic Party, uniting ... New Deal loyalists, organized labor, African Americans, Mexican Americans, and reform-seeking liberals."[20]

Yarborough's quixotic campaigns—he'd try to run for governor two more times—led to other political coalitions that served as seemingly safe havens for liberals and populists who wanted to remain Democrats and who might have also wanted to reestablish a connection to the Reconstruction-era Republican echoes of Edmund Davis. Up-and-coming Democrats like Ann Richards and Robert Eckhardt would inherit some of the political base Yarborough had laid down in Texas. "In political life he supported civil rights, economic justice, environmental protection, and women's equality, and he challenged the business establishment that had long dominated Texas politics," one writer observed.[21]

Ralph Yarborough would represent Texas in the Senate until the end of the decade, and given the extraordinary might of oil barons in Texas, it remained a wonder that he had succeeded and stayed in political power at all: he had first caught the public eye decades earlier when, as a prosecutor in the attorney general's office, he had tried to regulate oil firms and steer profits into the state education system. And by the time he took office in the Senate, in 1957, Yarborough was firmly committed to social welfare and social justice policies that ran completely counter to many of the ones espoused by his more hidebound Southern Democrat colleagues. His ability to frighten some people in Texas stemmed from one of his core beliefs: "Texas is a happy hunting ground of predatory wealth."[22]

Yarborough might have felt moderately emboldened with LBJ in the White House—and by Johnson's ability to paint Barry Goldwater in the 1964 presidential race as a lunatic and right-wing alarmist. Surfing Johnson's wave, Yarborough turned his attention to trying to prop up many of LBJ's plans for the "Great Society." Yarborough was one of only three Southern senators to push for the Voting Rights Act of 1965, and he was the only Southern senator to vote for the Civil Rights Act of 1964.

Through his time in Washington, Yarborough seemed to channel the indefatigable campaigning stamina of Pappy O'Daniel. He "lived on the road nearly every day, traveling from one small town to another, making speeches on courthouse lawns, giving radio and newspaper interviews, and constantly telephoning friends and supporters ... he frequently gave as many as twenty speeches per day and delivered countless remarks to individuals and small groups at roadside cafes, gas stations, feed stores, and street corners."[23]

Yarborough also ran away from the anti-regulatory ethos that stretched back to the days of the Texas Republic, the Civil War, and Reconstruction. "He was a proponent of federal involvement in schools, integration, environmentalism, affirmative action, and social security," said a writer for the *Texas Observer*, the publication that supported and revered Yarborough perhaps more than any other high-echelon elected official in modern state history.[24]

He voted for Medicare, bilingual education, and anti-poverty programs, and steered federal efforts to protect Padre Island, the Guadalupe Mountains, and the forests of East Texas.[25] He also opposed the war in Vietnam, and maybe it was one more thing that would lead to his political downfall in a state that could only bear so much liberalism.

Lloyd Bentsen Jr. — whose father had created an enormous Rio Grande Valley oil, ranching, and agriculture empire — upset Yarborough in the 1970 primary. Two years later, Yarborough tried to win back a Senate seat but failed. He decided to settle in Austin to work as a lawyer, where he knew he would be regaled by hundreds of admirers predisposed to his kind of politics. He died at the age of ninety-two, in the winter of 1996, and was buried in the Texas State Cemetery. His mocha-colored granite marker has his name inscribed as a cursive signature, the same one he affixed to various bills and measures and proclamations.

The marker notes: "Every major legislation on civil rights, education, the environment and health care written between 1957 and 1971 carries his name."

CHAPTER 11

Bitten by the Political Bug: The 1970s

AT THE FULL FLOWERING OF Barbara Jordan's enormous political influence, a white writer for *Texas Monthly* magazine once tried to explain her
wellspring. He suggested that her roots were in a part of Black Houston
where there was a "surging stream of sex and energy that could easily ex-
plode into violence."[1]

Jordan would have quibbled with the triple alliterative version of the
neighborhood she was raised in and that she always dearly loved. For
her, the streets of Houston echoed with the rich history of the African
American experience—the things that Langston Hughes and Maya Ange-
lou would say were the triumphant, tragic, deeply poignant hallmarks of
storied Black communities around the nation. To Jordan, her political
birth began in a place defined by boundless creativity and a great sense of
family and community—things often ignored by chroniclers parachuting
in like wary anthropologists and returning home with broad brushstrokes.
(To his credit, the writer went on to summarize Jordan's career by saying
she was "the Jackie Robinson of Texas politics.")

Jordan was born in Houston in 1936, and her father was the charismatic pastor of Good Hope Missionary Baptist Church. Her mother was
also known to be extraordinarily comfortable and confident talking to

Barbara Jordan, the breakthrough state senator from Houston who would go on to national prominence in the US House, served as "Governor for a Day" in 1972.

large groups. Their daughter grew up as a studious and voracious reader, someone encouraged to think about competing for roles not normally granted to women and people of color. Knowing she wouldn't be admitted to the segregated University of Texas at Austin, Jordan enrolled at Texas Southern University, and then went on to receive a law degree from Boston University in 1959. Back home in Houston, she opened a law practice in the family home but also turned her attention to the Kennedy-Johnson presidential campaign.

Around the city, day and night, people grew accustomed to seeing the resolute Jordan and fellow volunteers walking, block by block, canvassing neighborhoods and urging people to vote. She was convinced of the cause-and-effect of her efforts when Kennedy and Johnson squeaked by Nixon in the fall of 1960: "By the time the Kennedy-Johnson campaign ended successfully, I had really been bitten by the political bug," she would later write.[2]

Two years after that narrow victory, she ran for state representative but lost. She tried again in 1964, but also lost. But during her campaigns, she was refining her oratory skills and a particular form of sobering, even commanding elocution. It would become one of her hallmarks, something that vaulted her to office and then to the national stage. In 1965, when there were new court-ordered mandates that led to political redistricting around the state, she decided to run for the state senate in the just-designed Eleventh Senatorial District—which included the city's Fifth

Ward, the welcoming home where so many important cultural figures would gather, including the jazz pioneers Arnett Cobb, Illinois Jacquet, and Milt Larkin.[3]

In 1966, she became the first Black woman elected to the statehouse and the first Black state senator in the nation since 1883. That same year, two Black men—Joe Lockridge from Dallas and Curtis Graves from Houston—were elected to the Texas House. In Austin, she took her place among the thirty white men serving as senators. Right away, she wanted the lawmakers to know she was not a sideshow: "As it turned out, the Capitol stayed on its foundations and the star didn't fall off the top," she said about her arrival in Austin.[4] From Washington, LBJ was watching the history being made, and he invited her to the White House. Some national newspapers began describing her as one of America's "civil rights leaders."[5]

She was reelected in 1968, cementing a reputation as a committed, forceful parliamentarian and negotiator. She pushed for better minimum wages and equity for minority contractors, and then, after a downtown Houston congressional district was redrawn—based on new census figures showing a majority of possible voters as Black or Latino—Jordan decided to aim for Congress. Her opponent in the primary accused her of being too cooperative with conservative white leaders in the statehouse. Jordan responded, "I'm not going to Washington and turn things upside down in a day.... I'll only be one of 435. But the 434 will know I'm there."[6]

Well before the November 1972 congressional election, Jordan was named "Governor for a Day" as part of her responsibilities as Texas Senate president pro tempore. It was a ceremonial, symbolic moment on June 10, but it allowed her to become the first Black governor in the nation, if only for a day. The moment was noted in Texas and around the country as a sign of things that might be. Outside the statehouse, visitors could see the towering memorials and monuments to the Confederacy and its legacy of slavery. Inside, Jordan issued a statement to her "dear friends" in the Texas Senate that had given her the day as governor:

> "Governor for a Day" celebrations are traditional and old. This day is open and new for me. It is a time to focus on the past and renew my search for meaning in the future.
>
> The past holds as its prisoner indifferent inter-personal relationships, pain and poverty, fears and frustrations. The past reminds us

of dreams deferred and killed; of growth stunted as we struggled to touch and feel a man's humanity.

What about the future? What are its offerings? The future can mean a Bold New Venture for Texas. It can mean an end to poverty and human suffering. The future can signal the beginning of a New Commitment by the Government of the State of Texas to the people of the State of Texas. This must be a commitment which recognizes that the quality of a man's life is measured by his job, health, home, school, environment, spirit and opportunity for personal growth and development. My faith in this State and its people makes me optimistic that this commitment will be made and fulfilled.[7]

The next day, her father, her role model in many ways, passed away in Houston. The thirty-six-year-old Jordan tried to focus on her congressional campaign and won eight out of every ten votes in the primary—and then won by the same margin in the general election. On the third day of January 1973, her mother, in Washington after taking a long bus ride from Houston, watched as Jordan was sworn in as the first Black woman from the South elected to Congress.

Her unprecedented arrival had been nurtured over the years by support from LBJ, and he passed away a little less than three weeks after she went to Washington. In Congress, Jordan sought to carve out an identity, and her sonorous, booming voice quickly stood out as a new, profound sound from Texas. It would resonate in even bigger ways in 1974, when accusations of high crimes and misdemeanors ensnared the Nixon White House in the wake of the Watergate affair.

In May, she delivered an impassioned commencement address at Howard University, cautioning that there could be an erosion of civil liberties and that "it is possible for this country to stand on the edge of repression and tyranny and never know it."[8]

Then, in July, she gave a stirring, fifteen-minute televised speech to her colleagues on the House Judiciary Committee as they and the nation weighed the possible impeachment of President Nixon:

Earlier today, we heard the beginning of the Preamble to the Constitution of the United States: "We, the people." It's a very eloquent beginning. But when that document was completed on the seventeenth of September in 1787, I was not included in that "We, the people." I felt somehow for many years that George Washington and Alexander Hamilton just left me out by mistake. But through the process of amendment, interpretation, and court decision, I have finally been included in "We, the people."

Today I am an inquisitor. And hyperbole would not be fictional and would not overstate the solemnness that I feel right now. My faith in the Constitution is whole; it is complete; it is total. And I am not going to sit here and be an idle spectator to the diminution, the subversion, the destruction, of the Constitution . . .[9]

Jordan's forceful eloquence moved her onto center stage in American politics; it is impossible to truly measure what her presence in Washington did to alter the national view of Texas and its elected leaders. After decades of hearing from white patricians, plutocrats, supremacists, populists, xenophobes, milquetoasts, fence-riding compromisers, larger-than-life characters like Garner and LBJ, and the occasional stray progressives and liberals, Jordan was unlike any other to come from Texas. Part of her political aura was defined by her dignified carriage, that pastor's eloquence, but also her command of the Constitution—Jordan could thunder home a coherent understanding of history and context unlike almost any other Texas politician.

She was a product of inner-city Houston, she had tasted racism and segregation firsthand, and she had emerged in a state with a well-planned program of excluding people from the political process—with lynchings, poll taxes, and the intimidation of the Texas Rangers. Somehow, Jordan had arrived in Washington as a triumphant survivor of all the calamities in Texas. For party officials, it was an easy choice to have her appear as a keynote speaker at the Democratic National Convention in 1976—when the nation was still grappling with the fallout from the crooked, contentious unraveling at the highest levels of government.

Nixon had not gone gently, someone from the Charles Manson Family cult had tried to assassinate President Gerald Ford in Sacramento, and there had been another assassination attempt on Ford in San Francisco. The nation seemed on edge, maybe unclear about how far Nixon's treachery had gone and what really needed to be done to keep the country focused. The Democrats were pinning their hopes on Georgia governor Jimmy Carter when Jordan delivered her convention address on July 12 in New York:

There is something special about tonight. What is different? What is special?

I, Barbara Jordan, am a keynote speaker.

A lot of years passed since 1832, and during that time it would have been most unusual for any national political party to ask a Barbara Jordan to deliver a keynote address. But tonight, here I am. And I feel—I feel that, notwithstanding the past, that my presence here is one additional bit of evidence that the American Dream need not forever be deferred ...

Now, I began this speech by commenting to you on the uniqueness of a Barbara Jordan making a keynote address. Well I am going to close my speech by quoting a Republican President, and I ask you that as you listen to these words of Abraham Lincoln, relate them to the concept of a national community in which every last one of us participates:

"As I would not be a slave, so I would not be a master. This expresses my idea of Democracy. Whatever differs from this, to the extent of the difference, is no Democracy."[10]

In the early 1970s, Frances "Sissy" Farenthold picked up the phone and called her liberal Democrat ally Ralph Yarborough. She was hoping to ask him about a bill he had once sponsored in Washington. They talked for a while, and then Yarborough told her, "You know, it is much more difficult today to defeat ... the political establishment or whatever you want to call it ... it's much more difficult today than it was in the '50s."

She listened and then replied: "Yes, I think that is probably true."[11]

After she hung up, she no doubt thought about the conversation with the last truly liberal senator from Texas—and how, by the 1970s, the entire nature of political campaigning in Texas and the nation had moved so far from what it was when she and others were first getting started. She thought about the modern accoutrements of the New Political Age: Lear Jets and computers and focus groups—and how messages and campaigns in Texas were crafted in ways that were now enormously expensive and more calculating.[12]

Farenthold had a blueblood pedigree and was born in 1926 into a stalwart Democratic household in Corpus Christi. Her father was a prosecutor, and her grandfather had been the chief justice on the Texas Court of Civil Appeals and also a state representative. She was sent to the exclusive all-women's Hockaday boarding school in Dallas, where the world's wealthiest magnate, H. L. Hunt, had sent his own daughter. She attended Vassar and in 1946, at the age of nineteen, she graduated alongside Martha Firestone Ford, whose grandfather had founded the Firestone tire company and whose husband was the grandson of Henry Ford. At college, Farenthold studied state and local politics, as well as the Constitution, and she decided to follow the family path into the legal profession. When she enrolled in law school at the University of Texas at Austin, she was one of three female students.

After graduating, in 1949, she moved back to Corpus Christi to practice in her father's firm. The next year, she married a divorcee, the local oilman George Farenthold. He was a native of Belgium who had moved to the United States fourteen years earlier, and then served in the Air Force during World War II. She put her law career on hold as their family grew— she had five children (and served as a stepmother to another child from her husband's earlier marriage). Corpus Christi wasn't immune to segregation and Jim Crow laws, and she became interested in civil rights cases and anti-poverty programs in the city.

After serving on the city's Human Relations Commission in the early 1960s, she became the director of the Nueces County Legal Aid Program from 1965 to 1967, and it opened her to realities far beyond Hockaday and Vassar. It was a solid two years of exposure to grinding realities for many Mexican Americans in Texas, including plenty who had labored in the *patrón* and bracero systems, or who had very specific stories to tell her about being hounded by the Texas Rangers or being denied the right to vote. The more she listened, the more she perceived that there were issues that needed addressing in Austin—and that there might be an untapped coalition of voters. She told her family that she was going to run for state representative in 1968. "Growing up, my family was always interested in politics. But when I ran, I actually thought it would be another 10 years before a woman could run and win down here in South Texas. This was during the War on Poverty, and I was working with the poorest of the poor in Nueces County . . . and I saw what poverty was really like firsthand and how the indifference of state government plays such a part in that."[13]

Without knowing it, some local attorneys and political leaders were already trying to put up roadblocks through a divide-and-conquer strategy. They urged her to enter the race, assuming she would not win and would just peel off votes from other unwanted candidates. Farenthold was facing two men in the primary, including one whose slogan was "Send a Man to

Do a Man's Job." She aimed her campaign at women and minorities and tried to be creative by placing campaign posters on coffin lids affixed to cars.[14] "I had such naiveté when I ran in '68, I took the hardest race on in our district. But I simply took it on because that office was held by a Republican and at that time, I thought that there was a difference between Democrats and Republicans."[15]

In a stunning upset, she ousted the incumbent, Charles Scoggins, and then learned that some voters had no idea that Frances Farenthold was actually a woman: "The day after I won, I was at an event shaking hands and a man said to me, 'I voted for your husband' and I said, 'That was I' and he said, 'Well, if I had known that, I wouldn't have voted for you!'"[16]

Headed to Austin, but this time as the "only woman in the statehouse," Farenthold knew that many of her male colleagues had no idea what to make of her. Maybe as a jest, maybe in some nod to a notion of Southern chivalry, some of her fellow lawmakers asked the Texas poet laureate to read a Valentine's Day poem to her. Farenthold sensed that people were only being nice because they were afraid of what she might unleash in the late 1960s, when tensions were escalating around the nation: "There was all this talk about being a team player. It fell on deaf ears in my case."[17]

For affluent liberals in Texas, Farenthold had gone to Austin at the right time, especially with the state hip deep in the ongoing Republican makeover. Molly Ivins, who would become the most famous and perhaps the most influential political journalist in Texas, was studying the patterns and Farenthold.

Ivins grew up in the affluent River Oaks section of Houston, and she was the daughter of the president of the Tenneco oil empire. She attended exclusive private schools as well as Smith College. And Ivins could relate to Farenthold as a well-off white woman who had experienced a political apotheosis, a Saul-to-Damascus awakening that made her realize there were millions of Texans mired in poverty-stricken and segregated worlds. Ivins and Farenthold were both political rebels, bonded by being the only women allowed in certain circles in Austin—but not the private clubs where lobbying and real power were exchanged. Those were still reserved for men.

In the 1970s, Ivins and a colleague, Kaye Northcott, were given the reins of the *Texas Observer*. They made sure to chronicle the presence of the one woman in the Texas House—Farenthold—and, of course, the one woman in the Texas Senate—Barbara Jordan.

When the 61st Texas Legislature convened in early 1969, Farenthold learned how much sexism she'd be enduring: she tried to attend the males-only clubs downtown where state politics were hammered out, but was told she couldn't come in. State police assigned to guard the capitol grounds and parking lots routinely demanded that she fork over her ID. Farenthold must have known that pushing for liberal reforms, civil rights, and environmental protections was going to be a Sisyphean struggle. Ivins detected a sense of early exasperation and called her a "melancholy rebel."[18]

When she pushed open the towering doors to the statehouse, Farenthold was not only entering a male lair; she was headed into a place fraught with the corrupt consequences of a long-running good-old-boy network. She quickly condemned a state land commissioner for allegedly profiting from a private firm's venture to salvage treasure off the coast. It was hardly easy, absorbing the stares from lawmakers who were gathered in small groups in the hallways and watching her as she walked to her office. In Corpus Christi she had a ready, steady network of supporters built up over her years doing work in the community. Austin was a different orbit altogether, and she confided that she was enduring painful lessons: "I learned what it means to be alone on an issue."[19]

That fact, those boundaries, were laid bare when she became the only House member refusing to support a measure to praise LBJ for his commitment to the war in Vietnam. Farenthold, like Yarborough, was moving into isolated waters. Yarborough had been doing it in Washington, while she was on the front lines in the heart of a state dotted with military bases and defense contractors. She reflected on how politics in Texas was defined by its violent, frontier history: "I can recall being stunned when I first went to the legislature ... I think that the frontier theme has had a lot to do with the treatment and the attitude towards Mexican Americans."[20]

Her time in the House reminded her how inflexible large parts of the state could be. How it was easy to suggest that minority voters were ready to organize and enter the political systems, but that the reality was far more difficult. Old traditions, in the statehouse in Austin and in the woods of East Texas, were as alive as ever: "I went out into rural Nueces County ... and into Kleberg County. And it was like fifty years behind even Corpus Christi. That's the way it is in West Texas. And in East Texas, in every campaign, you talk to some Blacks and they say, 'We are going to organize and we are going to register some voters.' And it just doesn't happen. So, that part of Texas is very old Confederacy."[21]

In 1971, Farenthold joined Houston lawmaker Don Braun in an effort to pass a state Equal Rights Amendment (ERA), and Barbara Jordan pushed the bill in the Texas Senate. It was a bold attempt that would pit Farenthold against Phyllis Schlafly and other conservatives fighting federal versions of the amendment.

But while that was being debated in Texas, more and more attention was centering on a festering scandal that was threatening to reach into every pinnacle of political power in the state. When it was over, the contretemps would push forward the final transformation of the old Democratic order in Texas.

On January 12, 1971, Farenthold listened as Speaker of the House Gus Mutscher called lawmakers together for a new legislative session that would run until the last day in May. Mutscher, from Brenham, had worked as a marketer for the Borden Dairy company and was famous among male peers for having married a former Miss America. Mutscher had a neatly groomed look and demeanor, and had been in the House for a decade. Reasonably steady at making the trains move on time, he became the Speaker in 1969, and, now, as he gaveled the new legislative session into order, it seemed like business as usual.

There were, of course, a few nagging matters to keep an eye on: the women in the statehouse—Farenthold and Jordan; the anti-war rumblings on campuses; the annoying federal inquiries into desegregation; the restless Latino farmworkers. But Mutscher knew that Texas had shaken off hiccups over the years, and there would always be that calm predictability under the statehouse dome.

Meanwhile, a team of federal attorneys was gathering two hundred miles north, in Dallas. They were about to file a set of sweeping charges accusing Democratic Party leaders, past and present, of stock fraud—and maybe of receiving sweetheart loans, or pushing rigged bills that would line the pockets of Texas bankers. The allegations were stunning, as were the people the federal investigators were looking at: House Speaker Mutscher, Governor Preston Smith, and state Democratic leaders.

At the soul of the accusations was the wealthy Houston real estate developer, insurance executive, and banker Frank Sharp. Born on an East Texas farm, he had only a high school education, but had gone on to build sprawling subdivisions around greater Houston. By the end of the legislative session in May, more rumors emerged about Sharp and his connections to the most powerful Democrats in Texas. Dozens of people in high office in Texas were tainted, fairly or not, by innuendo and whispers. The scandal dominated headlines, and many questions were raised about prominent officials, including the handsome and affable lieutenant governor Ben Barnes—someone once presumed to be destined for greater things in Texas or even national politics.

With the rumors swirling, Farenthold seized the moment as a way to take on the old-guard Democratic machinery. Thirty state lawmakers coalesced into a group dubbed the Dirty Thirty, with Farenthold front and center and ramping up calls for Mutscher and others to be prosecuted. In the fall, Mutscher was indicted, and a trial in Abilene was set for him, an aide, and a Fort Worth lawmaker named Tommy Shannon. During the trial, Governor Smith was named an unindicted co-conspirator. In 1972, Mutscher and the others were given five years of probation after being found guilty of taking bribes.

The stunning news that the governor of Texas was named but never charged became an open door. Farenthold and others could position themselves moving freely outside the entrenched Democratic establishment. The primaries were coming in the next few months, and liberals and progressives began jockeying to sell themselves as pure-hearted reformers. Two dozen current and former Texas officials were facing charges—and Farenthold announced her candidacy for governor. She was going directly against several men who had been groomed or promoted for politics in Texas: Smith, Barnes (who had the support of LBJ), and the conservative state lawmaker Dolph Briscoe, who ran a ranching and investing empire from his hometown of Uvalde.

Farenthold's admirers wondered if she was an audacious Don Quixote, taking on a battle that she would never win.

Preston Earnest Smith sometimes liked to rummage through his collection of neckties, looking for something that would make a statement. Maybe it was a nod to the fact that he had run movie theaters back in Lubbock before he clambered onto the usual ladder that seemed to guide some to the top of Texas politics. Another deeply conservative businessman, he went to the Texas House during the waning days of World War II, then went to the Texas Senate a decade later, before becoming John Connally's lieutenant governor. When Connally decided to move on, Smith began sporting colorful polka dot ties and creating ads that asked Texans, "Don't you think it is about time one of us was governor?"

Smith was the first governor to come out of deep West Texas, and some hard-core insiders wondered if he would ever really master the wily, cut-throat maneuverings in Austin. Early on, he struck lawmakers as being almost blissfully out of touch with some of the edgier issues unfolding around him. In 1970, he traveled to give a speech at the University of Houston and was greeted by protesters who had arrived to support Lee Otis, a former Texas Southern University student activist. Otis had been sentenced to thirty years in prison for offering a marijuana joint to an undercover cop. Otis was linked to the national Student Nonviolent Co-ordinating Committee (SNCC), and plenty of people believed that the powers-that-be in Texas and Harris County had set him up and simply wanted him put away. As Smith began his speech in Houston, chants of "Free Lee Otis! Free Lee Otis!" sprang up. Smith had no clue what was going on. Bewildered, he told people that he was flummoxed by why Black people were chanting "Frijoles! Frijoles!" over and over again.[22]

Though Smith was "only" an unindicted co-conspirator in the Sharps-town debacle, his political career was essentially over once the investigations began. Both Farenthold and Dolph Briscoe crushed Smith in the primaries, and a runoff was declared. Farenthold thought she knew a lot about the state, but the campaign taught her a few lessons, including ones tied to the state's deep Baptist roots and even the anti-alcohol or anti-wet sentiments: "I remember being in Wichita Falls in one of the '72 campaigns and a man said, 'You just can't mention the fact that you are a Catholic, that you are a woman, or that you are a wet.' I mean, I was just shut out," she would later say.[23]

The sheer act of running for governor in Texas had not gone unnoticed. Farenthold began receiving calls from national Democratic leaders who were also watching how she had been shepherding the state version of the ERA—Texans were going to vote on it in November. Maybe Farenthold had tapped into something in the usually intractable South. Maybe she might succeed Ralph Yarborough in the US Senate. She was white, liberal, and articulate, and she seemed to have support from both deep-pocketed progressives and coalitions of Blacks and Latinos. With America still un-raveling over the Vietnam War—and a spree of riots, assassinations, and bombings—maybe Farenthold might be a reform-minded alternative. Maybe she could even be vice president or president.

Dolph Briscoe was channeling the same stoic Texas rancher aura that Coke Stevenson had routinely ridden to victory, and he beat Farenthold in the runoff. Perhaps Texas wasn't ready for its second female governor (after

Ma Ferguson). And her allies wondered if Farenthold had miscalculated in thinking that many Texans harbored a deep commitment to populist politics. Or that she had made a mistake in thinking that the Southern Democratic firmament was so wounded it would lead to a chorus of new voices: women, Blacks, and Latinos taking their rightful places in the party hierarchy.

Weeks after her bitter defeat, she was invited to Miami Beach, to the Democratic National Convention, where several women's organizations were nominating her for the vice presidential slot. She finished second behind Senator Thomas Eagleton from Missouri, but she had achieved another first: no woman had gone that far, come that close, to being a presidential running mate.

Back in Austin, the political sharks reviewed the way massive amounts of money were being injected into politics from wealthy Republicans in Houston and Dallas, like the pugnacious oilman Bill Clements, who was heading Nixon reelection efforts in Texas. Nixon had named the former Democratic governor John Connally as his treasury secretary—a position he had taken in 1971, and one that spurred a "Democrats for Nixon" movement in the state and elsewhere. The state clearly loved Nixon, and he won just over 66 percent of the vote in 1972. Nixon locked up all but 8 of the state's 254 counties. He took a bigger slice of the Texas vote than LBJ had received in the 1964 presidential election. Into the twenty-first century, no GOP presidential candidate would get a higher percentage of the Texas popular vote.

Meanwhile, Farenthold went on to become the National Women's Political Caucus chairwoman and tried to unseat Briscoe as governor in 1974 but lost to him again. In her short, mercurial time as an elected official (she only served two terms in the statehouse), she had rocketed to national stature on the heels of a major political scandal. She remained insistent on the politics of Ralph Yarborough and other lonely liberals, supporting striking farmworkers, desegregation, and school busing; raising corporate taxes; and making someone's first possession of marijuana a misdemeanor. She cut to the heart of Texas history by saying she wanted to disband the Texas Rangers, or at least block them from ever entering parts of South Texas where Mexican Americans feared them.[24]

As she weighed the possibility that she was never going to be elected to anything again, she reflected on her career as a self-described insurgent: "I have never gone into a race without fighting my life out to win. And I have always been grossly offended, beginning with my first race, when people would assume, maybe because I was a woman, maybe because I was a long shot, that it was just some kind of exercise."[25]

She knew that at least there would be a kind of cleaning of the stable after the scandals in Texas: the state attorney general was losing his job; close to half of the House of Representatives was going to be replaced. But she had to wonder if deep, true change would really occur. As long as big money dominated the increasingly high-wattage campaigns, there would always be political patronage—the kind that had existed for so many decades: "I think one of the most significant powers of the governor is, because of that spread-out kind of authority that we have, is in the appointments. . . . By and large, Texas has been governed by campaign contributors." And, she added, the governor would continue picking friends to oversee schools, oilfields, railroads, beaches, and banks. She boiled it down to one thing: "Appointments. Straight-out appointments."[26]

No one in Austin had a clear forecast about what would happen to Farenthold in the rest of the decade. She had a searing moment in political history, and Molly Ivins and others had chronicled her as a latter-day political Joan of Arc. But now, an almost weary-sounding Farenthold tried to summarize her political ambitions in Texas: "I am working for the time when unqualified Blacks, browns and women join the unqualified men in running our government."[27]

New conservatives began arriving at the statehouse: the Houston newspaper publisher William P. Hobby Jr. became lieutenant governor; the Houston lawyer John Hill became attorney general; the son of former governor Price Daniel, Marion Price Daniel Jr., was the House Speaker. Dozens of different faces appeared in the chambers, including one liberal Black Houston state representative named Mickey Leland. A native of Lubbock, he had been raised, like Jordan, in inner-city Houston. He was shaped by student activism at Texas Southern University and would serve for six years in the statehouse, with a focus on affordable health care and prison reform.

Governor Smith had pushed Texas officials toward measures to make campaign financing and government business more transparent: he wanted a Texas Open Records Act that would allow citizens a peek at government records. And for the next few decades, there would be greater scrutiny by activist groups, journalists, and "opposition researchers" hired to dig for dirt during political campaigns. The beams of ethical sunlight might not have been as comprehensive as some reformers would have liked, but one thing was evident: the Sharpstown affair had derailed the normal order of political progression. Many of the heirs to the political thrones in Texas were forced to settle into different nonelected roles in Austin—they might have left public office, or been denied reentry, but they slid into a growing world of high-dollar lobbying and consulting that would sometimes involve billion-dollar decisions or even bids for the presidency. In the dizzying way politics can work in Texas, many ostracized politicos began making more money than they ever had, by opening up offices in Austin and selling their consulting wisdom to businesses or candidates.

The former lieutenant governor Ben Barnes was never convicted in the Sharpstown scandal, but he lost his job anyway—and though he was ostensibly sent to the political sidelines, he became a highly sought-after backroom barterer in Austin. For years, he continued to exert unofficial power, all while publicly trying to salvage his reputation. He sounded bitter about how his star had fallen: "There were several things that pushed the Sharpstown affair beyond the bounds of a straight-up investigation and into the realm of a political witch hunt."[28]

But, on a bigger, cosmic level, he would come to view Sharpstown as the event that "decimated Texas Democrats" to the point that "the legacy of Sam Rayburn, Lyndon Johnson, and John Connally gave way to the twenty-first-century governance of George W. Bush, Tom DeLay, and Rick Perry."[29]

In Austin, there was almost an audible sigh of relief that the enormously wealthy and influential Dolph Briscoe had settled into the governor's office. More than a few of the unsettled Democratic power brokers hoped he could calm the party, restore some sort of order, and serve as a living link to the reactionary politics sculpted by his Uvalde mentor, John Nance Garner.

Briscoe's great-great-grandfather had signed the Texas Declaration of Independence from Mexico in 1836, and then the family spent decades acquiring hundreds of thousands of acres and controlling banks in Uvalde, Crystal City, and Pearsall, where cowboys, wildcatters, and Mexican immigrants parked their money or sought loans. Briscoe's family became the largest overseers of ranch and farming land in Texas, owning or leasing as much as 1.3 million acres. His father co-owned property with former governor Ross Sterling, the man who helped found Humble and Exxon and then built his replica of the White House on the Texas coast. Briscoe, like other heirs to immense fortunes in Texas, didn't necessarily believe that he was part of a gilded political-economic dynasty but rather that he was someone who had worked as hard as his predecessors to extract every possiblity out of it.

Briscoe had fond memories of Sterling, especially the time he let the young Briscoe sleep in his hero Sam Houston's bed in the governor's mansion. There wouldn't be much in his political platform that Sterling would disagree with—limiting taxes, slowing the growth of big government, and spending more money on schools and teachers. When he became a member of the Texas House in the late 1940s, Briscoe carried legislation to pave roads all over the state, creating the farm-to-market road system. And as governor, he empowered state highway officials and contractors to plow across Texas, building superhighways and making the roads wide open for commerce. It was enlightened self-interest. He owned so much land in remote locations that turning the state highway department into one of the most powerful in the nation was an easy decision.

Briscoe said he was going to "pull ranchers and farmers out of the mud" and put them on smooth, paved roads. If they were the ranchers and farmers who lived on his property, or were in service to his family's mammoth holdings, all the better.

Briscoe sold himself as a consummate businessman, someone who understood the twin towers of Texas industry: the ranching-farming heritage and the fossil fuel empires. He suggested that he was focused on keeping Texas economically free of seesaw rides. Briscoe tended to see the Texas economy through the prism of global affairs: "The necessity of fiscal responsibility in all levels of government is second only to world peace in our survival."[30] In part because Texas voters were grateful to not be hearing about any new scandals in Austin, and in part because Briscoe was seen as an unbelievably well-funded political powerhouse, it was a given that he'd be easily reelected.

In the 1974 election, he won all but 7 of 254 counties and 61 percent of the popular vote. With a change in the state constitution, he was going to serve the first four-year term since Edmund Davis in the 1870s. During the race, Briscoe noticed the arrival of a candidate from the Raza Unida Party. Briscoe suggested that its members were communists, and he even explored ways to keep the party off ballots. He wasn't successful, but his moves made plenty of political insiders wonder if Briscoe was either paranoid or presciently pragmatic. Maybe he was seeing political rustlings that other Democrats hadn't taken seriously.

José Ángel Gutiérrez and other Raza Unida members were elected to the Crystal City school board in 1970, and immediately plans were made for bilingual education and culturally sensitive curriculums. By the spring, Raza Unida organizers were lining up other candidates for city and school board elections in several small South Texas cities. That year, fifteen Raza Unida–supported politicians were elected, and by 1971, several party leaders wanted to push their efforts around the state. Eleven people were picked to run for state offices, including the Baylor-educated lawyer and gubernatorial candidate Ramsey Muñiz. Alma Canales, a migrant worker and journalist who had grown up in Edinburg, was the first Mexican American candidate for lieutenant governor.

In the 1972 election, Muñiz picked up 6.3 percent of the tally, or almost 215,000 votes—and Briscoe was furious. Muñiz had almost opened a window for a Republican. Wags dubbed Briscoe the first "minority" governor in twentieth-century Texas because he had only squeaked by his Republican opponent by 47.8 percent to 45 percent. Muñiz ran for governor again in 1974, along with several other Raza Unida candidates aiming for the statehouse from San Antonio, Houston, and other cities. Muñiz suggested he wasn't just a "minority candidate" but had clear positions on education, transportation, and crime. He only won just over 93,000 votes, and all of the Raza Unida candidates for state office were defeated. In Austin, Briscoe was soothed that things had returned to a more predictable political order. He and other Democrats were comfortable with La Raza Unida settling into what they expected would be a semipermanent state of low-level contrariness. Outsider political movements never lasted in Texas, and to Briscoe, the Latino rebellion was no exception.

Still, during its startling arrival on statewide ballots, La Raza Unida positioned several Mexican American women in leadership positions, including the formation of a party caucus called Mujeres Por La Raza. Olivia "Evey" Chapa, a native of Alice, Texas, and the daughter of a police officer, helped organize, run, and promote the party's main branch in the state. Meanwhile, Virginia Múzquiz served as the national head of the party from 1972 to 1974. Raised in a migrant worker family from La Pryor, she was the first Mexican American woman to run for the House in Texas, the

Ramsey Muñiz speaks at the University of Texas. He ran twice for governor representing the Raza Unida Party.

first Mexican American woman to run for city council in Crystal City, and the first Mexican American woman to run for and win the county clerk position in Zavala County in 1974.[31]

Even if she and other activists had put Briscoe and the entrenched Democrats on notice, Muñiz's second bruising defeat slowed the Raza Unida momentum. Party members began to leave, some looking for ways to join the Democratic machine, some working with the Mexican American Democrats, founded in 1975. Some activists focused on simply urging more people to register to vote.

In San Antonio, William "Willie" Velasquez started the Southwest Voter Registration Education Project in 1974. He had grown up in the city, graduated from St. Mary's University, and become an omnipresent labor organizer and political activist from the mid-1960s on. He had cofounded MAYO and had worked with the United Farm Workers, and was also immersed in the Starr County strike—the historic slowdown that had made Governor John Connally so angry he had confronted farmworkers as they walked all the way from the Rio Grande Valley to Austin.

Into the 1970s, Velasquez began concentrating his efforts on studying voting rosters, demographics, precinct boundaries, and even voting patterns. His granular, fastidious approach to examining the most remote Texas cities and counties led to his door-to-door voter registration project and his promotion of the slogan "Su voto es su voz" (Your vote is your voice). Velasquez was convinced that grassroots victories were more easily attainable and might serve as the prelude to changes at the state and national levels. The consequences of his work are immense; in Texas in 1973, 565 Mexican Americans were elected to public office, and fifteen years later three times that number were sworn in.

Velasquez had seen minorities voting for Democrats, from Roosevelt to Kennedy, at the national level, but that still hadn't changed life in profound ways on the streets of Brownsville or McAllen or the West Side of San Antonio. His theory was that with each local race—at the school board, city hall, or county court—minorities would be building a longer-lasting political apparatus. Bringing tangible economic remedies right to neighborhoods—getting streets paved, garbage picked up, bus routes put in—would be daily reminders of the power of the vote. "We have to be different," he once said. "We must show intelligence, compassion, and innovation as part of our leadership. It is not enough to be like the people we replace, using patronage for personal ambition. We must be better."[32]

In 1972, San Antonio native and Trinity University graduate Joe Bernal became the first Mexican American picked for the Democratic National Committee. Bernal had served in the Texas House and Senate from 1965 to 1972 and had pushed for Texas's first bilingual education bill and for the University of Texas system to open a branch in San Antonio. And by 1976, Bernal and others affiliated with the Mexican American Democrats were holding more state meetings to explore new ways to bring more Latinos into the political process.

That same year, the former Raza Unida candidate for governor, Ramsey Muñiz, was charged with trying to move 6,500 pounds of pot across the border from Mexico. Muñiz was given a fifteen-year sentence, and the Raza Unida Party lost its most visible face. La Raza Unida put one of its cofounders, Mario Compean, on the ballot in 1978, but he won only one-half of 1 percent of the ballots—a little more than 14,000 votes. After the election, La Raza Unida's leaders and members moved on, and the party disappeared as an on-the-ballot, registered political entity. But its legacy would remain apparent, as dozens of Texas cities and communities were going to send minority candidates to office. The MAYO and La Raza Unida explosions were the necessary igniters that moved Latino political participation from its earlier, tentative lanes. In so many ways, La Raza Unida had to burn fiercely and aggressively in order to kickstart political participation.

As he settled into his second term in Austin, Briscoe was increasingly perceived as a caretaker of the old status quo, even if he wasn't the ass-kicking Texas conservative some would like. He struck his liberal critics as another willing, buttoned-down standard-bearer for Big Oil. He struck critics on the Right as so middling, so stuck in neutral, so often absent from Austin and at his massive Uvalde ranch, that he could never be a firebrand for the fading Southern Democratic heritage.

On either side of the political aisle, some lawmakers were beginning to wonder if Briscoe was just incompetent: as he marched through a flurry of handpicked appointments to state agencies, he inadvertently named a dead man to the State Health Advisory Commission. Rumors were flying in Austin that he suffered from deep psychological problems, had undergone shock therapy at a hospital in Galveston, and maybe was on a steady diet of heavy tranquilizers and other drugs, including Lithium. A writer for *Texas Monthly* tried to analyze his body language and a "recurring remoteness during serious conversations," and interviewed lawmakers who said, anonymously, that Briscoe was acting "like a robot." At one point, Briscoe decided he had to summon the state press corps to a news conference—where he somberly told reporters that, in fact, he wasn't mentally ill.[33]

Maybe Briscoe was too rich to care or too confident to worry. Or maybe he was ignorant of some modern political realities. Lawmakers and lobbyists were complaining that he wasn't in his office when they needed to see him, not coming to the phone, and not even playing the game with the media—he was noticeably absent from Sunday morning political TV shows.

In the 1978 Democratic primary, Attorney General John Hill blew Briscoe away with 52.4 percent to 42.4 percent of the vote. That fall, an even more stunning change was coming.

Bill Clements was born in Dallas in the waning days of World War I, and after he turned down a football scholarship at the University of Chicago, he did what thousands of young Texans were doing—he headed into the oil fields. He worked as a roughneck in South Texas, came back to Dallas to attend Southern Methodist University, and, when he was thirty, ambitiously launched his own business.

Funded by loans, Southeastern Drilling, or SEDCO, started with two used oil drills and then grew into a billion-dollar firm operating around the world. In mega-oil circles, Clements quickly earned a reputation as a ballsy negotiator with little patience for government restrictions. State GOP leaders knew Clements was a hard-core archconservative, and obviously deep pocketed, and some of them asked Clements to consider running for the US Senate in 1964. Clements declined but persuaded another big proponent of offshore drilling—George H. W. Bush—to run instead. Clements served as the campaign finance manager. Ralph Yarborough wound up trouncing Bush, and Clements was left to wonder if he could have done better.

He immersed himself deeper in GOP politics and devoted his efforts to Nixon's 1972 reelection bid. Nixon, pleased with his extraordinary, record-making win in almost every corner of Texas, rewarded Clements with an appointment as deputy defense secretary. For the next few years, Clements nimbly rode the Washington roller coaster, past Nixon's departure and through President Gerald Ford's tenure. After Jimmy Carter won the 1976 race, Clements left the defense department in 1977 to run as a Republican for the governor's seat—even after Carter had carried Texas.

During the 1978 campaign, Clements and John Hill, his gubernatorial rival, were appearing at a chamber of commerce banquet in Amarillo. Clements wanted to steamroll Hill, and he decided that he would accuse him of being a lame, neutered Democratic flunky for the sissy president Jimmy Carter. Clements studied the audience and then barked that Carter was a "dead chicken" hanging around Hill's neck. Suddenly, Clements reached into a bag and pulled out a floppy rubber chicken. He raised it in the air and aimed it at Hill's head. Instead, the fowl wobbled across the room and thudded into the food plate and lap of the mayor of Amarillo's startled wife.

The bad aim was overshadowed by the fact that Clements had correctly envisioned how unpopular Carter was in certain parts of Texas—too liberal, too regulatory, too out of touch with big ranchers and oilmen. Clements wanted to show that Hill was just like a Texas coon dog being punished with a dead chicken around its neck.

Clements put three times more cash than Hill into the 1978 campaign—$7.2 million of his own fortune. It was a staggering personal investment, and it led the aging Ralph Yarborough to say there is "still only one party in Texas. The party of money."[34] As he barnstormed Texas, Clements remained immutable and theatric; he promised to cut state spending by $1 billion and fire as many useless state employees as he could find.

It worked: the Democrats lost the governor's office for the first time since Reconstruction. A Republican oilman from Dallas won with 1,183,828 votes to Hill's 1,166,919 votes. Clements was the first Republican governor of Texas in 105 years. And once in office, he remained unapologetically unfiltered: after he learned that physicians advised pregnant women to avoid deep-sea diving because it could do irreversible damage to a fetus, he decided to make a joke: "They're always looking for birth control. We might say, 'Go deep-water diving and exercise birth control.'" During a radio broadcast, he insulted the governor of the Mexican border state of Tamaulipas as being from "Tamale-puss," and he said that one of Mexico's prominent scholars was "just another Mexican with an opinion."[35]

After serving in Washington, Clements liked to view the Texas governor's office as a position of potent national and international authority. If Texas leaders were guided by that inherited history of an independent republic, then Clements was guided by the knowledge that his oil drilling company had been doing business in twenty nations across the planet (he had put his oil business shares into a blind trust and then had his son named head of the company). Clements took power in Austin believing he had global influence, and he visited Mexico on several occasions to talk about oil, immigration, and even drug issues. He also traveled to the Soviet Union, and one national newspaper said, "It is hard to tell whether William Perry Clements Jr. is just the 40th governor of Texas or the sixth president of the Republic of Texas."[36]

In the late 1970s, if you checked into small motels near Corpus Christi, you would find a plastic bottle on the bathroom counter, one lined up next to the shampoo and hair conditioner bottles. It had two words on it: "Tar Removal." Out on the sandy beaches, thousands of softball-sized blobs of oil marred the oceanfront. People were stomping on them by accident or driving their cars over the hunks of goo. They seemed like black, oozing, otherworldly meteorites dotting the coastline. They were part of the world's largest oil spill.

And Bill Clements knew all about the environmental disaster. News stations around the state were broadcasting harrowing images and saying the disaster had been caused by a blown offshore well his billion-dollar drilling company owned and had leased out in the Gulf of Mexico.

Clements responded, "There's no use in crying over spilled milk. Let's don't get all excited about this thing."[37]

CHAPTER 12

The Sands Have Shifted: The 1980s

JUST AFTER DAWN ON JUNE 24 in 1980, one hundred farmworkers began gathering on a dusty road not far from Highway 60 and the Santa Fe railroad lines in Deaf Smith County. It was the six-week summer onion harvest season, with temperatures soaring above one hundred degrees. The workers were worried about many things, including the fact that the onions they picked by hand were earning them 45 cents a bag. It could take hours to make $5 to $10. There were no toilets near the fields. Drinking water was sometimes scarce. And when some labor organizers arrived, only a handful of workers were brave enough to join them.

Sheriff Travis McPherson told people that he was dealing with terrorists: "These people are outsiders and they have no business in our area and I'm not going to cater to them. I think I've made that clear to them time and time again, but however, they still come back. We're going to treat this just as they do in a terrorist situation. They're operating in the same manner. They're using the same techniques and all and we're going to use counter-intelligence, we're going to use dogs. . . . Now, you know, these people are involved in communism."[1]

Cesar Chavez and the United Farm Workers union had opened the eyes of America to the plight of field hands. Chavez was becoming a household name, and the farmworker movement had spread to Texas, but with twists and turns that led to offshoot organizations, including the Texas Farm Workers Union. Eight out of every ten migrant farmworkers earned incomes below the poverty line; thousands of people lived in impromptu camps without running water; there were outbreaks of cholera; infants were dying at higher rates than in most places in the nation.

Officials with the Santa Fe Railroad arrived in the onion fields and told the protesters they were trespassing. The organizers said there were no signs posted, but the officials pointed to ones that had just been staked into the ground. They also pointed to the Texas Rangers who were taking pictures of the farmworkers.

The field hands decided to head into nearby Hereford, a small High Plains town of fifteen thousand. The local Catholic bishop had announced his support for the farmworkers. One local grower drove a truck down the road and tried spraying the protesters with ammonia; another grower began exposing himself to some of the female farmworkers.

Many of the field-hand families had been living in old World War II–era barracks that had housed thousands of captured Italian and German prisoners. Among the Italians were artists who were conscripted to paint portraits of people in the area; other prisoners were sent to a nearby Catholic church to design murals and iconography. During the war, it was the second-largest POW camp in Texas, and local ranchers and farm owners also began to realize that it could provide a steady source of forced labor—a latter-day form of the postslavery convict leasing program that had once been prevalent in parts of Texas.

Now, thirty-five years later, union organizers were demanding that Latino farmworkers in Deaf Smith County be given a fifteen-cent raise for each chest-high, fifty-three-pound bag of onions they picked.[2] There were sometimes as many as sixty thousand farmworkers on the High Plains, especially after the expansion of lush, irrigated fields. Many of them were living crammed into "a hodgepodge of hovels, plaster and dirt" with "no city water, city sewage, city electricity." It was, said one visitor, like seeing people exiled into a "1980 concentration camp."[3]

When some of the onion pickers walked off the job, farm owners brought in strikebreakers to work the fields. Some filed a lawsuit against the Texas Farm Workers Union. The union then filed a civil rights suit against the growers and asked for $150,000 in damages. The case dragged on until labor leader Jesus Moya received $500 in damages. Moya and others would continue to fan out across Texas, trying to organize and summon attention. Into the 1980s, he came back to the Hereford onion fields:

"Moya's confrontations with those in power in this county bring to light the slow but steady reform over the years, but they also demonstrate how much further there is to go."[4]

Moya once tried to explain what he and others were aiming for: "When we're talking about the farmworker movement, we are not just talking about an economic movement of the workers for better wages and better working conditions. We're talking about fighting the discrimination of the Mexican people in this state, particularly in West Texas. We're talking about getting better housing for them. We're talking about getting better education for our children. We're talking about bilingual education. And we're talking about entering the political arena to remove certain politicians."[5]

The confrontations on the plains were a reminder of how permutations of the *patrón* system still existed—they had been there during World War II, with prisoners of war, and were there with Latino migrants living in the same barracks that had once housed "aliens" from other nations.

If there was still a sense among progressives that the 1960s–1970s Frances Farenthold–Ralph Yarborough movement could prosper in 1980s Texas, it was slammed hard by the fact that Ronald Reagan was elected president, beating Jimmy Carter in the state by 55 percent to 41 percent. Unforeseen issues were emerging, including the AIDS crisis beginning to move through Houston and Dallas, a sobering plummet in oil prices, and even high-profile threats by white supremacists to unleash a new, modern-day wave of bloody violence. One hatemonger had very specific ideas about how to proceed.

Louis Beam was a short, lean man with piercing eyes who had been raised in Lufkin, served in Vietnam, and then came back to Texas to revive the Ku Klux Klan, form paramilitary groups, and reach out to neo-Nazis. He began to place special focus and anger on Vietnamese immigrants operating small shrimp boats along the Texas coast. Beam and his followers were drawing national attention to Texas, for all the wrong reasons, all while he was racing to spread his messages through databases, computers, and other high-tech means.

News crews came to Texas, along with the FBI, to see what Beam was planning. Beam had several scary catchphrases that suggested that not all was well in Texas, that the state could still be a violent backwater not far removed from the lynchings and even the assassination of an American president: "Where ballots fail, bullets will prevail" and "The time is past for talk … We must begin the preparations necessary to retrieve our country from the hands of the enemy which now controls it. It should be plain to everyone what is needed: knives, guns and courage."[6]

Anyone who wanted to trace lines through Texas history could look at Beam's preferred use of the pseudonym Nathan Bedford Forrest—the Confederate general credited with forming and leading the original Klan, and who had a street in Dallas named in his honor.

As Bill Clements planned his reelection bid, it was becoming clear that his bluster might not be enough to save him. He promoted himself as a can-do candidate who had pushed through dozens of bills, including ones giving the police expanded use of wiretaps. He also had the support of some wayward Democrats in the statehouse—but the oil spill fiasco had sullied his image. Young voters, liberal voters, and minority voters were coalescing—and Clements lost the 1982 election to Attorney General Mark White by 46 percent to 53 percent.

The well-dressed White was raised in Houston and attended Baylor as an undergraduate and law school student. He settled into a career as a Houston attorney, worked on Dolph Briscoe's gubernatorial campaign, and was rewarded with an appointment as secretary of state—Briscoe said he picked White because he was "loyal."

Meanwhile, Lt. Gov. Bill Hobby Jr.—whose father had been governor and whose mother had been picked by President Eisenhower as the first secretary of health, education, and welfare—was sent back to the seat he had held for the last decade. Another Democrat, the patrician Lloyd Bentsen Jr., a lawyer, insurance executive, and heir to a Rio Grande Valley farming fortune, was reelected to the US Senate. Bentsen was a centrist in the mold of his mentor Sam Rayburn, and was one more profoundly wealthy heir to Texas political power. One critic simply said, "I bet he sleeps in a tuxedo."[7]

Other Democrats were elected that year: Travis County commissioner Ann Richards became state treasurer, the first woman in a half century elected to a statewide office, and Jim Hightower became agriculture commissioner. Both specialized in cornpone politicking, offering calculated dollops of down-home-isms tracing straight to Pappy O'Daniel and Ma and Pa Ferguson. (I was once on a national television show with Hightower when he began describing George W. Bush as "a gopher on Astro Turf—he can't find a hole to dig into").

Another Democrat, barrel-chested Jim Mattox, was elected attorney general; he was a former prosecutor for Dallas district attorney Henry Wade, who had developed a reputation for ruthlessly running the most aggressive, scary office of its kind in Texas, with perhaps dozens of people unfairly imprisoned. Mattox had served in the state legislature and as a congressman from Dallas with a surprising, growing reputation as a defender of the common man—and he sold himself as a cantankerous "people's lawyer." One more Democrat, Garry Mauro, became Texas land commissioner. Like Hightower, he once worked in Ralph Yarborough's office, and then at the age of thirty had become the executive director of the Democratic Party in Texas. A Texas publication called Hightower, Richards, Mauro, and Mattox "the golden kids" of progressive politics.[8]

Gov. White, normally never prone to public emotional extremes, sounded almost exultant as he stomped on Clements in interviews immediately after the election: he talked about his foe's "arrogance, indifference, insensitivity ... and meanness." And he added that Clements was rejected by voters for specific reasons: "He abused people. And he abused me. A lot of people stood in the rain for the opportunity to say, 'Quit that.'"[9]

As Republicans sifted through the defeat, they learned that Democrats had patched together support from far-flung elements—minorities in the big cities, frustrated rural residents who felt that the Republicans and Clements were too focused on their high-dollar oil supporters, and moderate voters who just wanted better schools.

In the 1960s, Jim Hightower had been Ralph Yarborough's legislative aide, and in the 1970s, he worked as editor of the *Texas Observer*. Funded by the Waco insurance executive Bernard Rapoport—some jokingly called him the only real socialist in Central Texas—the *Observer* never enjoyed the level of readership that the mainstream dailies in Dallas, Houston, Austin, or San Antonio did. But it had an influence in its willingness (on a shoestring budget) to do in-depth stories on the often arcane maneuvers in the bowels of the statehouse. It would become the longest-running political magazine in the state, a kind of insider's Bible. The *Observer* took a persistently skeptical view of the sticky connection between business and politics, and since its creation in the 1950s had been instrumental in understanding the ways in which state history often drives policies in Texas.

The *Observer*'s old editor was now the new agriculture commissioner, and Hightower began pushing for changes that had been unheard of before. He argued that Texas needed to explore organic produce. And that it needed to shore up minority farmers and meatpackers instead of companies like Hormel and Del Monte. And then, seemingly out of nowhere, he began supporting the Reverend Jesse Jackson's bid for the presidency.

Reporters began flying to Texas to profile him, well aware that Hightower was always going to deliver a spicy quote ("Ronald Reagan promised us a seven-course dinner, but all we got was a six pack and a possum"). Ann Richards was watching him, and it inspired her to think about how she could move to a bigger stage, too. In Austin, even GOP strategists were marveling at Hightower. He wore a droopy moustache, cowboy hats, worn denim shirts, and crinkled boots, and managed to talk about organic grapefruits in earnest, almost infectious tones.

Very early in his political career, Hightower learned to toy with the symbolism, the public profile, of certain state offices—and he knew how to play with political images. Too, his time working with Yarborough in the Senate had convinced him that lower-rung state offices in Texas might give him more political freedom: "Whether you're fighting a toxic dump going on a farm in your county, or supermarket price-fixing in San Antonio, or looking into how the railroads are screwing over the farmers by manipulating the grain-car supply at harvest time. Stuff like that's gonna be highly visible," Hightower confided one day. "And then the office is a beauty in terms of the bully pulpit, giving me a way to go into the cities. See I'm coming in, politically, the best way you can do in Texas, which is out of the rural areas into the cities. You've gotta remember the rural areas are the vote, still. I mean you're talking about 40% of the vote coming out of the rural areas. They vote; they don't vote in the cities. There's more numbers in the cities so 60% of the vote is coming out of the cities, but you can't win in Texas without the rural vote."[10]

He and Richards began to see their often-overlooked offices—state treasurer and agriculture commissioner—as perfect means to a political end: "To run for the higher office, for our movement, we have two things going for us. I mean me and Ann [Richards] and other people who are going to be at this mid-level. First of all, an office that can be highly visible that has the tools that can actually do something—it's not like being in Congress or the legislature where you can't do anything. . . . I began to understand that these offices are wonderful because you do something, and particularly agriculture commissioner because it's done so little, particularly that urban people understand. So I can make quick progress, a good bit of it symbolic."[11]

The national fascination with the drawling Hightower seemed to multiply, and writers gushed: "Since his election, Hightower has rewritten the Democratic Party's national farm policies, attacked the Reagan Administration's handling of the farm crisis in a give-'em-hell speech to the party's National Convention in San Francisco and now he's flying around the country, giving speeches in Chicago, Des Moines and in Washington to the National Press Club. . . . Seldom has such a low-profile office produced such a high-profile politician."[12]

Kathy Whitmire knew what she was getting into.

"So, people were regularly talking to me about running for mayor . . . a lot of people from the women's movement [were] very excited about the possibility of electing a woman mayor[,] which seemed, you know, almost impossible," she said. "I felt somebody was going to do it and why not me?"[13]

In 1982, the accountant nicknamed "Tootsie" became the first woman elected mayor of Houston, the largest city in the state and the fourth largest in the nation. She had already broken ground by being the first woman elected to city office, serving for four years as the Houston controller. As with the elections of Hightower, Richards, Mauro, and Mattox, national political writers turned their attention to the fact that she seemed so unlikely in Texas—and had beaten the tough-talking former sheriff of Harris County in the mayoral race. She hadn't just won against an established, sixty-three-year-old white man, she had crushed him by 62.5 percent to 37.5 percent: "The developers and bankers and oil millionaires who used to handpick candidates can no longer be said to dominate the political scene," said one political writer.[14]

Her emergence had analysts scrambling to figure out what was changing, evolving, in Texas. The political makeup had been altered by waves of Americans and immigrants relocating to Texas in the 1970s, chasing the oil boom, the absence of state income taxes, the cheaper housing, and that forever-protected sense of deregulation. The consensus was that Whitmire was at the right place at the right time, in a New South city that had thousands of newcomers willing to look at a woman as their leader.

"Kathryn Jean Whitmire is no revolutionary. But she is a deeply committed feminist. She learned to speak in public by stumping against the repeal of Texas' ratification of the proposed equal rights amendment. As early as 1973, she was an active member of the National Women's Political Caucus," wrote the *New York Times*. "She has taken strong stands in favor of nondiscriminatory hiring policies in city agencies, including the hiring of homosexuals as police officers if they apply and are qualified. In matters of human rights and equal opportunity, she would be called a liberal elsewhere. She shies away from the term, however, because it is anathema in Texas politics; she prefers to call herself a 'progressive.'"[15]

The national paper also duly noted that she was a fiscal conservative and someone who had found a way to straddle political lines in a state where hard-and-fast boundaries had long existed. Whitmire, more than many politicians in Texas, had carefully studied the way larger urban areas were changing, and she found a base of support in the growing Black, Latino, and gay populations in Houston.

She named the first Black man to be city police chief, and she also turned attention to a community that had long been ignored by politicians and the mainstream media: Houston's gay community had become one of the largest in the nation. Whitmire pushed for equal rights for gays seeking city jobs, and she drew attention to issues and communities almost utterly ignored and neglected by previous high-profile politicians in Texas. Houston's flourishing gay population, and Whitmire's election, ignited a sense not only of pride but also of political possibilities. Whitmire was clearly being watched by political observers around the country, and *Newsweek* ran a story called "Gay Power in Macho Houston."[16]

In Austin, Governor White was hearing from national Democratic leaders who were asking what the hell two minority Texas congressmen, Henry González and Houston's Mickey Leland, were doing filing impeachment papers against Ronald Reagan for ordering the 1983 invasion of Grenada without the approval of Congress and without allowing the media to cover the "war."

White had appointed Elma Salinas Ender as the first Hispanic woman to serve as a district court judge in Texas. But liberals said he hadn't done enough: "He is not out to balance the power between the big business sector and the people," wrote the *Texas Observer*.[17] Meanwhile, conservatives thought he wasn't doing enough to prop up the economy in the wake of stalling oil prices. White believed that Texas needed to wean itself from its über-dependence on fossil fuels, and he had begun to see the possibilities for a high-tech empire in Texas through his close friendship with the Dallas magnate Ross Perot (who had just seen General Electric buy controlling interest in Perot's Electronic Data Systems corporation for $2.4 billion). Perot's influence on state and eventually national politics marked a reassertion of the Texas citizen king—the kind that exercised enormous clout without any elected portfolio, and did it in unabashed, some would say presumptive, fashion. Perot would propose bold funding plans for Texas and eventually launch his own independent bid for the presidency. He had an abiding interest in how Texas would pay for public education, and he watched closely as White pushed for higher teacher salaries and "no-pass, no-play" rules that would bar student athletes from playing if they hadn't received at least a grade of 70 in every course.

As Perot and White huddled about how to lure high-tech investment to Texas, and how to improve Texas schools, alarm bells began to sound around the state. Some small banks and savings and loan institutions were beginning to wobble under the weight of faulty and maybe crooked loans. Large-scale construction projects were stalling. Office towers in down-town Austin and other cities were going vacant, and federal investigators were wondering if Texas financial institutions had been too invested in oil. At the beginning of the decade, the oil industry accounted for almost 30 percent of state revenues, and now it had dropped to half that figure. The economic realities had hard-core ramifications: Texas would be look-ing at ways to diversify its economy, and political leaders would talk about subsidies, corporate tax breaks, and even more devotion to deregulation.

Through the sea changes, political insiders said White lacked a Lone Star verve, the kind of brio that might appeal to voters officially worried about their personal financial fortunes. White rarely seemed passion-ate about issues other than education and making sure Texas prisoners on death row were executed. Early on, as governor-elect in 1982, White heartily endorsed the first execution of a prisoner in Texas since 1964—a Black man named Charles Brooks Jr., who was put to death by lethal in-jection. White ran political ads that said, "Only a governor can make exe-cutions happen. I did and I will." The courts had shown "great courage" in denying "frivolous" appeals, White once said.[18] During his time in office, nineteen convicts would be put to death (though later in life, White be-came an outspoken opponent of the death penalty).[19]

One frustrated Texas publication finally just said that aside from his unswerving devotion to death row and Texas schools, White was never cut out for the wheeling and dealing, the bartering, the seduction of the press, that many of his predecessors—from Garner to LBJ—had mastered: "The picture that emerges is of a well-meaning political dilettante. White is a child in a grown-up's world," said *Texas Monthly*. "He could have been the greatest governor in Texas in the twentieth century ... but he didn't know how to lead."[20]

With oil prices plummeting, White was forced to call a special legislative session and beg for tax increases. He addressed the lawmakers, some of whom no doubt saw him as a dead man walking, and tried to explain how desperate he was when it came to asking for the Texas hikes: "I'll defend it. I'll explain it. And to those who try to blame you for what we do here, tell them we had to do it. Blame me."[21]

A few months later, Bill Clements defeated White in the governor's race—Clements with 53 percent, White with 46 percent. It was a divisive and costly battle, with over $25 million spent by the two men. Big-name GOP leaders—John Tower, George H. W. Bush, Ronald Reagan, and newly elected US Senator Phil Gramm—had weighed in with full-throated support for Clements.

Gramm was particular proof that the Republicans were now cemented in Texas, and likely to never let Democrats sweep statewide elections again. When he won in 1984, he was the first Texan to ever receive over 3 million votes in a Senate race, only a year after he had switched from the Democratic Party to the GOP. He had been to Congress, representing Fort Worth and a long stretch of Central Texas, as one of the staunchest arch-conservative Democrats in Washington. The bespectacled economics professor at Texas A&M would remain an iron-willed conservative until he left the Senate, in 2002, and over the years, he further helped galvanize voting bases that would ease the rise of more Republican senators, including Ted Cruz and John Cornyn.

Some cynics said that the religion of football in Texas had doomed White. He was indelibly linked to his no-pass, no-play rule, and some wondered if he was being blamed for overregulating the sacred tradition of Friday night football. Other wags ascribed his defeat to his dispassionate public personality, that nagging sense that he had almost fallen into a job that he was never enthused about: "People were ready to follow him. But he didn't know how to lead."[22]

He might not have ruled with electric force, but he did possess a certain amount of self-awareness. Before he left office, a wistful White gave one more speech to state legislators.

"I asked for a tax increase and said, 'Blame me,' and you did."[23]

President Ronald Reagan won Texas again in 1984, while ten Texas GOP members were going to Congress. Sixty-one GOP lawmakers were being sent to the statehouse—six in the Texas Senate and fifty-five in the Texas

House. The GOP had 278 city and county elected officials in 1980—and almost 500 six years later.

But, almost immediately, Bill Clements began sucking oxygen from the Republican momentum. Investigative reporters at the two daily newspapers in Dallas raced to beat each other to unravel exactly how the governor was tied to the football powerhouse program at Southern Methodist University. Allegations emerged that higher-ups in SMU's governing board, including Clements, were hip-deep in hefty payments to student athletes—stud players who had made the small school a national force.

While the investigation was turning into an embarassing albatross, Clements was also forced to look at harsh economic realities in Texas and then resort, like White, to exploring a dreaded increase in taxes. Under his watch, lawmakers unleashed a $5.7 billion state tax hike, the largest for any state in the history of the nation.

First it had been an oil spill, then a college football scandal, and then accusations that Clements was taxing Texans to hell and beyond. The ingredients were in place for what many in the state and nation would consider the unlikeliest of power grabs.

Ann Richards had been watching, along with the legions of political consultants and forecasters in Austin, as Clements seemed to self-destruct. She met with friends, including Hightower and the increasingly influential columnist Molly Ivins, who had left the *Texas Observer* to work for the *New York Times* before retreating back to Texas to work for newspapers in Dallas and Fort Worth.

Richards was born outside of Waco, in Lacy-Lakeview, as Dorothy Ann Willis, daughter of Cecil and Ona Willis. Her parents had grown up in the hidden rural Texas burgs of Hogjaw and Bug Tussle. Her grandparents were poor farmers, and her father did deliveries for a drug company. Hoping she'd profit from a bigger high school, the family moved to Waco, where she joined the speech-and-debate team. Richards attended Baylor and married a fellow student who happened to be her high school sweetheart. He became a lawyer, they had four children, and she settled into being a full-time mother and homemaker, but one with a growing interest in volunteering for local Democratic politics. She helped run election campaigns for two state lawmakers, and after the family moved to Austin, Richards ran for Travis County commissioner and became the first woman to hold the position.

For parts of her life, she struggled with a drinking problem that even-

Democrat Ann Richards of Austin proclaims a "New Texas" after being sworn in as Texas's forty-fifth governor on the south steps of the Texas Capitol. Richards survived a bruising 1990 campaign against Republican oilman Clayton Williams before losing four years later to George W. Bush.

tually led her to seek treatment at a hospital in Minnesota. She endured a divorce and kept leaning into her Texas twang, ladling her stories and speeches with dollops of cornpone regionalism. Unlike many well-heeled politicos (and Ivins, who vigorously tried to ape Richards's colloquial arts—even though Ivins was educated at the Sorbonne, spoke fluent French, and loved sailing at the Houston Yacht Club), Richards could go drawl-for-drawl with anyone. She memorized a barrel of country humor one-liners, and audiences were applauding. Too, Democratic operatives in Washington were monitoring her magical abilities.

Richards had already earned some national stripes. She had delivered a nominating speech for Walter Mondale at the Democratic Convention in 1984 and then went into deep Texas to campaign for him and his running mate, Geraldine Ferraro. Now, the Democrats in Washington asked if she'd appear at the 1988 national gathering—and please lay into George H. W. Bush. That summer, people around America watched as a woman with mile-high hair and a bold grin took the stage at the Democratic National Convention in Atlanta:

> I'm delighted to be here with you this evening, because after listening
> to George Bush all these years, I figured you needed to know what a
> real Texas accent sounds like.... Poor George, he can't help it. He was
> born with a silver foot in his mouth.[24]

She added a few other stinging lines: "When we pay billions for planes that won't fly, billions for tanks that won't fire, and billions for systems that won't work, that old dog won't hunt. And you don't have to be from Waco to know that when the Pentagon makes crooks rich and doesn't make America strong, that it's a bum deal."[25]

It was a national performance that went straight into the pantheon of political punditry. And it wasn't just memorable and oft quoted, it was a signal to her that she was destined for bigger political possibilities than state treasurer—ones that would lead her into a fateful Texas showdown with the namesake son of "poor George."

When she returned to Texas from Georgia, she and her aides pored over the glowing articles and opinion pieces. Political destinies are sometimes shaped by a sense of inevitability, and more than a few of her aides said it was only a matter of time before she could translate her win in Texas to a national stage. Maybe as proof that she had more on her agenda than a career as state treasurer, Richards wrote the requisite autobiography—hers was called *Straight from the Heart: My Life in Politics and Other Places*—that candidates produce when they know they're going to launch a big campaign.

In Dallas, voters had put a Black woman, Eddie Bernice Johnson, back in the statehouse, this time in the Texas Senate. Almost fifteen years earlier she was the surprising landslide winner of a Texas House seat and the first Black woman elected to state office from Dallas. Increasingly, Dallas and Houston were in the vanguard of bigger political opportunities for Black Texans.

Though Mickey Leland was born in Lubbock, his roots were in the culturally rich but often neglected Fifth Ward of Houston. After six years in the statehouse, Leland won a seat in Congress in 1978 and held it through the 1980s. He was one of seven congressmen to try to impeach Ronald Reagan; he chaired the Congressional Black Caucus; he created a select congressional committee to study hunger in America and around the world; he pushed for federal programs to provide healthy food to needy people, and for studies on homelessness and the root causes of infant mortality.

His interests led him to call for large-scale relief efforts in famine-stricken areas of Africa. Leland, who would sometimes dress in dashikis, traveled the world to meet with foreign leaders, including Fidel Castro. On a fact-finding trip to Ethiopia in the summer of 1989, his plane crashed, and he perished along with fourteen other passengers.

In San Antonio, the tall, lanky Henry Cisneros was elected mayor in 1982—and instantly, reporters around the nation wondered if he'd eventually become the first Latino president. Cisneros, who had been teaching public affairs at the University of Texas branch in San Antonio, had won handily—supported by minority voters, the kinds of newcomers who carried Whitmire in Houston, and some business owners who saw the self-described "neoconservative" policy wonk as a lightning rod for economic growth that could energize a city economy mainly tied to tourism and its military bases.

He was handsome, engaging, and safe enough to draw white voters and the bigger political bankrollers. And his election was trumpeted in print profiles and TV reports, with an emphasis on his rise from the less affluent West Side of San Antonio to attain a master's degree in public affairs at Harvard. One story summarized him this way:

> In 1975, at the age of 27, he was the youngest San Antonio City Council member ever. In 1981, he was mayor. In 1984, there was talk with Walter Mondale about being vice president of the United States. In 1985, a book was published about him. In 1986, he had a cologne, "Henry C.," named after him. In 1987, the man from the poor side of San Antonio had been tabbed by some as a front-runner for Texas governor — or for whatever else he wanted. But in 1988, he abruptly abandoned his impending coronation. The nation's "First Hispanic" — as *Esquire* had anointed him — said his son's fragile health was more important to him than even the highest higher office. The "Aztec god" — as *Life* magazine had called him — said he would leave the mayor's office at the end of his term. Suddenly, that same year, an affair with a campaign aide screeched across the front pages of the nation's newspapers.[26]

The marital scandal, and the ongoing commitment from a president who would suffer his own lifestyle accusations, dented Cisneros's once promising political career. Plenty of admirers and observers in Texas had assumed he really would become the state's first Latino governor or US senator. As he faded from political view, some progressives didn't necessarily weep and wail at his demise, but a few remained exceedingly wistful about how the man from El West Side could have broken through the ultimate glass ceilings and allowed others to follow him.

For over a century, the Bushes were there at almost every industrial and economic milestone in US history — the expansion of the railroads into the Midwest, the creation of the modern investment banking system on Wall Street, the sprawling plantations in the Deep South. Bushes sat on the boards of the biggest corporations. Prescott Bush, the senator from Connecticut, served on the board of trustees at Yale University, where he had gone to school and where his son and grandson would be admitted. Bush family members were there, metaphorically, in the background of photographs when the baronial clans from America's gilded age gathered — the Rockefellers, Astors, and Vanderbilts. They did business around the world — and then gathered in family compounds, mansions, and enclaves in Florida, Maine, and other places.

Prescott's son, George H. W. Bush, was sent to private schools in the Northeast, and then to Yale. He joined a fraternity and was admitted to the selective Skull & Bones private club. He was a big man on campus, a good student, and a star of the baseball team—one day he posed for a picture with a visiting Babe Ruth. He married a descendant of President Franklin Pierce and spent winters at the extended family's South Carolina property—with "toasty fires" lit by the Black servants. When the attack on Pearl Harbor sucked the nation into World War II, he signed up for the military and became a flight crew member on dangerous military missions. Somehow he survived being shot out of the sky in the war against Japan.

When he finally made it back home, his father told him he wanted him to go to Texas as soon as possible, using millions of family dollars to chase down new finds in the Permian Basin oil patches. Bush knew nothing about petroleum geology. When he arrived in the Midland-Odessa area, family friends sized him up and said that maybe he could start as the smiling, affable "land man" knocking on the doors of shacks owned by dirt-poor farmers and making offers for their seemingly useless desert property. Homesteads in arid West Texas were sometimes available for pennies on the dollar. Several people took Bush's lowball offers and fled the unforgiving area. Then, with the help of skilled petroleum explorers and engineers flying in from around the nation, Bush's bargain-bin purchases began to pay off one by one. Drillers were hitting what they liked to call "elephant fields" of fossil fuels.

On the weekends, for socializing, Bush invited the other Yankees from the Ivy League who had joined him in the oil hunt. He was famous for wearing loafers and Bermuda shorts at his backyard martini parties—he wasn't wearing overalls and downing whiskey like the locals. His idea of eating barbecue was putting some hot dogs or burgers on a little grill, not tending and smoking hunks of brisket and sausage for hours. Once in a while he'd excuse himself because he had to get to the airport to meet his father, the US senator from Connecticut, who was coming to check on his son and the family investments.

For a decade, Bush worked his way to the top tiers of the game in West Texas, alongside a growing gang of other Ivy Leaguers arriving from the Northeast. It was an invasion, another black gold rush. Old-timers in Odessa said it was really just more post–Civil War carpetbagging—or just like the British arriving in India.

By the late 1950s, Bush had made millions, and his petroleum geologists were telling him that the next big play was in another part of Texas.

Bush called his wife and children together and told them they were moving to Houston. He said he needed to be close to high-stakes investors and oil corporations in the big city—and closer to the next "elephant field."

Federal regulators wanted to control the once pristine parts of the Gulf of Mexico, but Bush and his business partners were pushing to be allowed to dot the waters with rows of offshore oil rigs. He told friends it was a billion-dollar affair, something that would irrevocably alter national and global affairs. If his geologists were right, the Gulf of Mexico could be as important as the Permian Basin, and there would be hundreds of miles of underwater areas to carve out—and the Gulf of Mexico would never be the same. (Decades ago, some older residents of Galveston told me about wading into shallow waters near their homes to harvest constantly replenished oyster beds—a hard-to-imagine scene when considering that by the 1990s, oil exploration had led some marine biologists to call large portions of the Gulf of Mexico ecological "dead zones.")

In Austin, lawmakers from both parties fought like holy hell to make sure Texas was going to be able to do what it wanted with the tidelands and beyond. It was a crucible moment, and it simply opened up another flood of profits and investments for Texas. What had already been the world's most sophisticated refining and petrochemical belt was expanded across hundreds of miles of shoreline and deep water. Shrimp boat captains, divers headed to coral reefs, and families on vacation at the beach would return each season to see more and more towering oil rigs set against the horizon and rising out of the water.

Bush's grand slams in Midland and off the coast convinced the family that they could summon the big money to open political doors in Texas. Getting the cash to run a Republican campaign would be easy. The hard part would be tamping down attention to the fact that dating to the 1800s, the Bushes were far from Lone Star natives. Selling the family name was always going to be an ongoing battle—in Texas and beyond.

Bush moved into the growing Republican circles in Houston, attending meetings and talking about the right way to portray a GOP candidate. He was the county chair for the party and he vocally backed Barry Goldwater's reactionary national movement. People were coming to him and saying that now was the time—that Houston was filled with oilmen and newly arrived Republican investors hoping to cash in on the Texas economic miracles. Bush listened and decided he'd run for the US Senate against the longtime liberal Democrat Ralph Yarborough—and do it by leaning into his own hard brand of conservative politics.

Bush began assailing Yarborough for supporting the 1964 Civil Rights Act, which would attempt to finally outlaw most forms of public and even private discrimination. Bush argued that it was just another attack on states' rights, another heavy-handed order shoved on Texas from Washington. There were whispers that he was a racist, and Bush was trounced in the election. He decided to lower his sights and run two years later for a seat representing Houston in Congress.

This time, he had even more help from his oil partners in the city, and this time he won. Instantly, Bush began trying to organize the spread of local GOP leaders in far-flung parts of the state. He did fieldwork for Richard Nixon's winning presidential campaign, and then he tried to run for the Senate one more time. He lost again, but Nixon was watching, and he rewarded Bush by naming him ambassador to the United Nations. When Bush took the job, he and his wife, Barbara, moved into the Waldorf Astoria and talked about what it would take for him to one day be president.

There were twists and turns coming: Bush became national chairman of the GOP and then head of the CIA, and as he continued to plan his climb, he seemed like the perfect vice presidential companion for Ronald Reagan in 1980. Maybe Bush would deliver white suburban voters like the ones filling up the subdivisions in Southwest Houston and north and west of Dallas. And, of course, maybe he could tap his family's century-old financial connections.

When the Reagan-Bush ticket won the White House, strategists from both parties said the differences between the two men were more evident than ever. Reagan, far more than Bush, had mastered some sort of political theater. When Reagan was filmed or photographed riding a speckled horse and wearing a white ten-gallon hat, he seemed perfectly at ease. He had been an actor, he knew the value of an image, and he hardly broke a sweat as he channeled the American West. It was a performance that Cactus Jack Garner would have appreciated. Maybe even Pappy O'Daniel.

Bush appreciated it, too, but he remained envious that it came so naturally to a Coca-Cola cowboy like Reagan. Bush tried to recast himself as well. Though some didn't believe him, he said he was now a big fan of fiddles and banjos and was developing an interest in the music of the Oak Ridge Boys. And that now he liked squeezing into pinch-toed western boots. And that he finally had the hang of the barbecue thing. But it hardly ever seemed . . . easy. Not Ronald Reagan easy. In a state whose most famous residents were Willie Nelson and Ann Richards, there were still people who viewed him as a Connecticut Yankee in the court of the Country Kings.

Bush was painfully aware of his political limitations. He knew, based on his failed Senate races, that plenty of people in the Texas heartland still viewed him as an anemic Yalie, in an ascot and a yachting cap, who loved riding motorboats along the gold coast of Maine and then playing croquet at his manicured summer mansion.

Sometimes, in awkward moments, Bush mused about Reagan having the touch, that ability to appear to be something that he really wasn't. I once listened to Bush giving a speech in the Texas statehouse. For reasons unclear to me, he was allowed inside the House chambers to talk about a book he had coauthored. Bush began to drift into what seemed to be a wistful bit of melancholy. I think he said that Ronald Reagan had some sort of "fuel" or "jet fuel" in his political marrow. And maybe Bush was really suggesting that Reagan could so easily look like that tall-in-the-saddle Texas Ranger riding into town, ready to enforce Manifest Destiny. It seemed to me that Bush was thinking hard about how he would one day be remembered.

Anxious oilmen in Houston and West Texas were also wondering if Bush had what it takes—if he could run for president after Reagan stepped down. Into the mid-1980s, they were calling him more and more in Washington, or huddling with him at the River Oaks Country Club, and telling him they would bankroll his campaign. Maybe he could just surf Reagan's wake all the way to the White House.

In 1986, Bush hired a manic, foul-mouthed, and hard-drinking master of smashmouth politics to run his campaign. Lee Atwater had worked miracles delivering parts of the South to Reagan and the GOP. His "Southern strategy" was to cleverly refashion the blatantly racist themes that ran through the old Dixie Democratic circles—to, well, update them so they were less obvious. Atwater wanted his candidates to be far more subtle than the hard-core Confederate-flag-waving politicos from the 1950s and 1960s. He told them to dress up; stay away from the KKK; and perfect some speeches denouncing forced busing, gun control, and abortion.

Atwater was a brutal, often intimidating character, someone the Bushes had never seen in the world of limousine Republicans from the Northeast.

But they figured he was their best guide to places they couldn't fathom but really needed. Atwater was from Georgia, he had grown up in the South, and he knew that the Confederacy's legacy had seeped into a dedicated fight for socially conservative issues. And that it was still a tie that brought together thousands of voters who felt perpetually ignored or abused by Washington.

As he drove along the leafy, winding roads leading to the Bush compound in Maine, Atwater had plenty of time to reflect on how it was like entering a gated world—one far removed from what he had seen at the country picnics and county fairs in Alabama, Missisippi, and Louisiana, places with peanut farms, paper mills, and cotton gins. When he arrived at the estate, Atwater talked about ways to attract what he called "the movement," what he said was a mass of Holy Roller voters hiding in plain sight: maybe millions of evangelical Christians, born-again, Jesus-loving voters who felt disenfranchised and were waiting for someone to take them seriously. The idea was simple: as Democrats tried to cater to minorities, to city voters, to immigrants, Bush would say he was the only one who really understood the megachurches, televangelists, radio show preachers, and Bible thumpers.

The Bushes listened, and it had to have seemed impossible. The Bushes barely hugged each other in public. They came from a tight-lipped, dispassionate brand of Episcopal religion. As Bush thought about the new strategy, he decided that maybe it was a task for his wandering, seemingly aimless oldest son. That namesake son had never really succeeded at much on his own. He had drunk a ton over the years, and he had stumbled into trouble with the law. Maybe this could be his first important political mission—and maybe it could be his own personal political baptism.

With Atwater telling him where to go, the younger George W. Bush began spending weeks traveling from church to church, from Dallas to Houston to Little Rock and beyond, meeting pastors with the largest Baptist and Pentecostal congregations. At each stop, he said that his father was devoted to cracking down on marijuana and pornography; that he was thinking hard about allowing Christian prayers in public schools; that he'd hire church people to take over government jobs.

The more he traveled the South, the more he began thinking of drinking less, of maybe giving up booze altogether. He was beyond weary of the way people constantly compared him to his father—and how they said it was like something out of Shakespeare or Greek tragedy, because by almost every measure he had failed to achieve anything his father had.

Even inside the family he was seen as the prodigal son: he was no war hero like his father. He was a failure in the same oil patch where his father made millions. He was no star at Yale, but just the woozy head of a fraternity that specialized in nasty forms of hazing. He had been trounced in a run for Congress back in the 1970s and mocked for being an effete outsider. He had been arrested for drunk driving in Maine and disorderly conduct in Connecticut. He had been stopped by cops in Princeton, New Jersey, and then ordered out of town.

Now he was going way into the American heartland to meet with thundering preachers and ask them to vote for his father. Maybe, some people said, it was good for him on a deeply personal level.

Maybe he could stand a little Holy Ghost.

CHAPTER 13

Reality Day: The 1990s

JIM MATTOX SEEMED TO BE SUGGESTING that Ann Richards had been doing the business of the state of Texas while being really high on drugs.

His television ads during the Democratic primary race were asking: "Did she use marijuana, or something worse like cocaine, not as a college kid but as a 47-year-old elected official sworn to uphold the law?"[1] Richards, who admitted that she was working on staying sober, coyly responded that over the last ten years she had not consumed a single "mood-altering chemical."

From somewhere in her camp, stories bubbled up about folks seeing Mattox smoking pot when he was a state legislator. And then Richards blasted Mattox for being indicted seven years earlier on bribery charges — but she deftly ignored the fact that Mattox had been acquitted.[2]

By March and April of 1990, national reporters were checking into downtown Austin hotels, excited about watching what several thought was the best political freak show in the nation. As they clutched their coffee cups and walked down Congress Avenue, some were laughing about how they had never seen anything like it. They were pretty much all filing the same story: "For the last month, Texans have witnessed what is widely regarded as the dirtiest campaign in the state's history. In Texas, that means it has been sordid indeed."[3]

Richards smacked not just Mattox but all of her Democratic primary opponents, including former governor Mark White, who began telling people that Richards was worse than one of Adolph Hitler's henchmen. One reporter wrote something he never had before about Richards: "Few expected her to stay above the fray. So scathing was her attack on former Gov. Mark White before the March primary election that he vowed never to support her and compared her to a Nazi. 'What Ann Richards has done would make Himmler blush,' said White, referring to Gestapo leader Heinrich Himmler."[4]

Backed by city voters and plenty of women, Richards swamped Mattox, 56 percent to 44 percent. But the stories about the sordid campaigning kept spreading around the country, like missives from foreign correspondents: "Many Texans described the Democratic race as the roughest campaign they could remember, an unrelenting exchange of charges, negative television commercials and extraordinarily personal attacks between two candidates on a no-holds-barred quest for the nomination."[5]

Beyond the gutter politics, Texas was going to be gaining additional seats in Congress, and political consultants knew that whoever was going to wind up as governor would have a mighty hand in drafting the boundaries of the congressional districts and who would be elected in them. In Austin, the strategists agreed that maybe Richards had actually been helped by playing politics in the sewer, because the upcoming race against her GOP opponent promised to be even more ugly, bloodier, and very strange indeed.

The oilman, rancher, and banker Clayton Williams loved to talk about his affection for Texas A&M University, and at one of his homes, he had a swimming pool built in the shape of the boots worn by members of the school's cadet corps.

His family had roots in the sprawling Big Bend region, an area that matched up nicely with the stereotype of a wide-open and rugged Texas. Williams had played on the high school football team in tiny Fort Stockton, but he was hardly a self-made man from a hardscrabble background: his grandfather was an attorney with a law degree from Harvard, and his father was a county commissioner. Williams wore the finest custom-made cowboy hats, sported hand-tooled boots, and each year seemed to grow more fabulously rich.

He called himself "Claytie," and his wife called him "Sweet Wheat," and he owned a jet, a helicopter, and an almost two-hundred-thousand-acre ranch near Alpine. There was a mansion in Midland and other big spreads scattered around Texas and Wyoming. If friends came to visit, he had crews spray water on the unpaved roads so cars wouldn't get coated with dust. Maybe he was bored, maybe he loathed Ann Richards, but sometimes when people asked him why he decided to run for office, he said that narcotics had taken a toll on his son. Being governor might be the best way to exact revenge and make Texas the epicenter for a big blitzkrieg on drugs. He said that druggies were going to go to prison and learn the "joys of bustin' rocks."[6]

Whatever the real reason, Williams was planning to pour at least $6 million of his own cash into his campaign. He easily secured the GOP nomination. But, now, he was also already suffering from pounding criticism after comparing the capricious weather in Texas to a woman being raped: "If it's inevitable, just relax and enjoy it," he said. After being condemned around the country, Williams apologized and said he had been "insensitive."[7]

With that, the campaign for governor picked up where the primaries had left off—with one regrettable comment after another. Williams essentially admitted to frequenting prostitutes just across the Texas border with Mexico, in the "Boys Town" zones where American teens visited squalid sex-worker compounds south of the Rio Grande, almost as if it was a quaint rite of passage: "It's part of growing up in West Texas. It was a lot different then. The houses were the only place you got serviced. It was kind of what the boys did at (Texas) A&M."[8]

As the race heated up, Richards attracted more attention, money, and support from celebrities inside and outside Texas: Steven Spielberg, Willie Nelson, and even Carol Channing.[9] Williams decided he had to "out Texan" Richards, and he began laying on some ranching references and crowing that he would "head her and hoof her and drag her through the dirt."[10] At one televised Dallas forum, Williams blurted out that Richards was a "liar" and then refused to shake her hand after she had extended it.

The choices were stark: Richards had cut her teeth supporting progressive and liberal politicians and policies. She wanted more minorities in government, and she wanted a woman to have the right to an abortion. She was the last big-time standard-bearer of the liberal Sissy Farenthold–Ralph Yarborough wing of things in Texas. She was a better campaigner than either of her mentors: she was folksier, more down-home, and she could always remind voters that her parents really were from Hogjaw and Bug Tussle.

Williams was a Ronald Reagan–Richard Nixon social and fiscal conservative from a part of Texas where you could still spot pickup trucks with gun racks, Confederate flags, and Day-Glo-orange bumper stickers that said "Fidel Castro Is a Russian Stooge." Nixon had declared his national war on drugs, and Williams wanted the death penalty for Texas dope dealers—and as many agents, guns, and dogs as were needed.

He and Richards lobbed bombs at each other all summer. Williams began suggesting that when she was state treasurer, she was way too cozy with her old business partners. Richards yelled that Williams played fast and loose with the banks he ran. One day, Richards seemed to take a time-out and reflect on the political games: "I tell kids, do not think elected officials are exalted figures—archangels. We're not. We're human beings. But that's not what the public wants—they want us to rise and ascend to Heaven."[11]

The polls had Williams ahead for big portions of the race, so when Richards said she was closing the gap, Williams went all in and announced, "She must be drinking again." When reporters kept pressing him about the long-term impact of his comparing rape to the weather in Texas, he bristled: "If you talk about the weather, you sure get in trouble."[12]

Richards promised a new day, and Williams offered a return to what he said were traditional values. She responded by saying some pieces of Texas history should never be repeated. She traveled to Texas A&M shortly before the election, shook hands, and tried to explain why parts of Texas should remain dead and buried: "Others look wistfully back. That era is gone. The good old days were never what they were cracked up to be. They exist only in memories of those who can't cope with the present or don't know what to do with the future."[13]

Richards won 49.5 percent to 47 percent, and analysts ascribed her come-from-behind victory to events that were impossible to exactly quantify, including the cumulative, corrosive impact of the rape joke by Williams. During her victory speech, she held up a T-shirt that read "A Woman's Place Is in the Dome," with an image of the statehouse in the background. It was heady, with people yelling her name, and Richards soaked it all in. "It looks like, as Barbara Jordan said, 'the people of Texas are back,'" she shouted.[14]

The second female governor in Texas took office in early 1991 after leading a raucous twelve-block "People's March" heading north on Congress Avenue in Austin and straight up the statehouse steps. Ten thousand people attended the inauguration, and Richards wore a white cape made from Texas wool and created by fashion students at Texas Woman's University.[15] For several long minutes, she stared out over the sea of supporters and grinned her trademark, toothy smile. Maybe she was also absorbing the fact that she had followed Ma Ferguson—but this time, she would really be running Texas, and not serving as a proxy for a husband and his political cronies. She had been a homemaker and now was the Lone Star state's forty-fifth governor.

She had campaigned for a "New Texas," and she embarked quickly on an ambitious mission to appoint more minorities and women to state offices, including the first Black regent to the University of Texas system. She championed gay rights, and urged the Texas Rangers to add women and people of color. With her high, silvery hair and a supply of colorful quotes, she continued to draw more national attention. She posed for a magazine cover alongside a motorcycle, mingled with more movie stars and musicians, and grew close to the lauded Texas writer Edwin "Bud" Shrake.

Back at the statehouse, she was also learning to both get along with and suffer the tempestuous Lt. Gov. Bob Bullock. He was a steely-eyed Texas force of nature, someone who had risen through the ranks, and he was known for plowing through five marriages and who-knows-how-many affairs—and for making unwanted advances, including ones aimed at Molly Ivins. He would send her notes and flowers, and sometimes call her a "hairy-legged liberal." One evening, at a political-cum-drinking session at a joint called The Office in Austin, Bullock had tried to block Ivins from leaving the booth they were sharing. She knocked him to the ground and stepped over his sprawled body. Still on his back, he began shouting: "Son of a bitch. Did you see that? I love Molly Ivins!"[16]

There was one thing that Richards understood Bullock was especially good at: he was a master parliamentarian who knew exactly how to make the Texas legislative trains move on time—and in just the ways that could make a governor shine. He had spent so much time below deck that he knew every gear and lever to pull inside the capitol. And he had lived in enough different places in Texas to get a handle on how to force far-flung lawmakers to move together and sign up for his version of the right thing.

Bullock was born in Hillsboro, studied at Texas Tech in Lubbock, and then earned his law degree from Baylor. He served in the Texas House, became secretary of state and state comptroller, and then was elected lieutenant governor. He was an all-around badass—feared, respected, and avoided if you knew he was angry with you. Many believed he was always packing heat and wasn't afraid to fire away if he felt like it.

Richards knew that she'd always be dealing with Bullock as the gatekeeper to the good old boys in the statehouse. He had more than a dash of Pappy O'Daniel in his veins but also a far more cunning understanding of how to move like a stealthy fox inside the Austin henhouse. He also knew how to play to voters when necessary: Bullock loved to step on a stage and shout three words whenever and wherever he could: "God Bless Texas!"

Despite the omnipresent shadow of Bullock, Richards felt empowered to push for controversial measures, including a Texas lottery. Christian forces howled that legalized gambling was going to lead to Texans paying the wages of sin, and the debate grew so intense that some newspapers ordered grizzled political reporters to devote their time, year round, to the "lottery beat." Richards quickly promised that she'd use the money to fund Texas schools, and she made sure to be photographed buying the first lottery ticket, maybe just to prove to wary Baptists that the piece of paper wouldn't turn into a snake.

In the echoing hallways of the state capitol, the grand building that lawmakers proudly noted was taller than the US capitol, representatives and senators were having emergency meetings. Richards was moving way too fast and too insistently. The experts on Texas history told the others that Richards had in her soul a bit of Edmund Davis, the Union soldier who had become governor and then tried to force all manner of progressive moves down the state's throat. Richards didn't let up: she argued for heavier environmental protections and insurance and ethics reforms, and then she went to war with state lawmakers who had crafted a bill that would allow Texans to carry concealed handguns.

"The people of this state do not need to be reminded that weapons of violence produce death to innocent children and adults. I am an avid hunter and believe strongly in the rights of individuals to own guns," she said. "That is not the question here. This legislation will only increase the level of violence on our streets. I have not talked to one law enforcement officer who supports this bill, and I cannot in good conscience ask them to patrol the streets of this state and face additional hazards that this bill will encourage. Frankly, the only outcome of the passage of this bill will be more people killed by gunfire."[17]

She vetoed the bill and said, "I especially want to thank you for choosing to stand by me on this day when we say no to the amateur gunslingers who think they will be braver and smarter with gun in hand."[18]

To some around the state, Richards's gun policies said she was turning her back on a way of life in Texas. Maybe she was too liberal, too progressive. It didn't help that she was supporting Bill Clinton's presidential bid to unseat George H. W. Bush in 1992.

Bush had gone to the White House with the help of that religious mission by his son, and with an infamous ad endorsed by Lee Atwater. It suggested that Democrats had furloughed a Black felon who had gone on to commit rape, armed robbery, and assault. Critics said it was race-baiting and fear-mongering at its worst. Whatever it was, Bush had won the White House in 1988, and he had proved that another Texan after LBJ could go to the Oval Office.

From a distance, Richards almost had to admire what Bush had pulled off. But she also told friends that Bush still wasn't Texan the way she was Texan. She would continue to roast him, and then some, in speech after speech, and she remained convinced that though Bush might have won the White House, he would never have won a race against her in Texas.

In 1992, she jumped at the invitation to serve as the chairwoman of the Democratic National Convention. In Washington, some people were betting she could run as Clinton's vice president, but she told party leaders she wasn't interested. For GOP operatives in Texas, she was the big impediment—and more than a few said she had something to do with George H. W. Bush losing the 1992 race to Arkansas governor Bill Clinton.

In some parts of Austin, it seemed almost unreal that Bush had lost. At least one person was vowing to take Richards down: "Right now she's riding high because she's avoided controversy. People who avoid controversy ride high in the polls. But when the crash comes, she'll fall hard, and it won't be a pretty sight. She's a do-nothing, do-little governor," hissed Karl Rove, a portly and owlish-looking Republican strategist who was opening up a bunker-like political office in Austin and beginning to identify just the right candidates to run against her.[19]

In 1992, a former TV reporter named Kay Bailey Hutchison was named temporary president of the Republican National Convention, and national GOP strategists took note of her as a possible candidate for higher office. A Galveston native, she had become an attorney in Houston, proved her conservative credentials in the Texas House, and then ran for state treasurer—the position Ann Richards had once held.

After Clinton ousted Bush, he named Senator Lloyd Bentsen as his treasury secretary. A special election was held to fill Bentsen's seat, and Hutchison, fueled by big support in Houston and Dallas, won. She was the first Texas woman to become a US senator. But her victory was immediately shadowed by a raid at her old state treasurer office in Austin. Prosecutors indicted her for tampering with records and official misconduct. She was eventually acquitted, and she tried to distance herself from the scandal by campaigning hard for the 1994 Senate race—and she crushed her Democratic opponent by almost 61 percent to 38 percent. Texas had a woman firmly entrenched in the state capitol and another going to Washington.

Richards had made sure that one of the speakers at the 1992 Democratic National Convention was Texas railroad commissioner Lena Guerrero. Born in Mission, not far from the Rio Grande, she had attended the University of Texas at Austin and had been elected to the Texas House, representing parts of Austin. With help from the same political image-makers that had promoted Richards, she was featured in national articles about the changing face of politics in Texas. She became a leader of the Texas Women's Political Caucus, and then *Texas Monthly* lauded her as one of the most influential lawmakers in the state.

Richards named Guerrero to a vacant seat on the railroad commission, where she became the first woman and Latino to serve on the body. Richards was grooming her, and Guerrero seemed poised for bigger things. But suddenly, during her campaign for a full term on the powerful railroad commission, word began emerging that she had lied about being a graduate of the University of Texas—she was nineteen credits shy of her degree. The scandal dominated headlines and news shows for weeks, and it ultimately wrecked her political career. Eventually, people would say she was like another Henry Cisneros, someone who could have gone to the mountaintop in Texas but was waylaid by personal foibles.

Richards glumly accepted the news and tried to concentrate on inroads made by other women around the state. Rose Spector was going to become a Texas Supreme Court justice, the first woman to earn that post. State lawmaker Eddie Bernice Johnson, the pioneering Black politician from Dallas, decided to run for the new 30th Congressional District. She won by an overwhelming margin in 1992—and four other women were

Republican governor George W. Bush (right), who won reelection by a landslide, found a willing confederate in the powerful Democratic lieutenant governor, Bob Bullock. Bullock, who talked up Bush as a potential president, was a bruising backroom operator.

elected to the Texas State Senate, while twenty-four went to the Texas House of Representatives.

In his windowless bunker in Austin, the exceedingly pale Karl Rove was excitedly calling friends and telling them he had finally found his man—someone he thought he could personally reinvent as the electable alternative to Ann Richards. It would take a lot of molding, but George W. Bush, forty-eight, had more than a few essentials—name recognition, his family's vast war chest, and all those hard-earned ties to Christian conservatives from Round Rock to Rockwall, from El Paso to Texarkana.

Rove checked around and was convinced that Bush had straightened up and finally quit drinking. And that Bush could tell a good joke at Rotary Clubs now and then. And that he could fumble his way through a few bits of Spanish. And that Bush's old man, knocked out of the White House by Bill Clinton, had plenty of interest in calling in Texas political favors for his son. The more he weighed it, the more Rove thought it could work.

The younger Bush was born in New Haven, Connecticut, and had attended private academies in Houston and the Northeast. He moved in the same affluent social circles as Molly Ivins, the increasingly famous Texas political columnist. His father had been a big man on campus at Yale, but when George W. went to the same school, he was mostly known for being a sloppy drinker. The first time he appeared in a *New York Times* story was in the late 1960s, and it was about his fraternity branding recruits with pieces of heated metal.[20] At Yale, the father was a baseball star, someone who posed for pictures with Babe Ruth; the son was a scrub who only played one year. The father was a decorated war hero; the son was let into the Texas Air National Guard during the Vietnam War, some said under shady circumstances, and he never saw combat or even left the United States. The father was sent to the Texas oil fields with family money, and he replenished the coffers with millions of dollars. The son was sent to the exact same Texas oil fields, also with family money, but kept coming up empty.

When he tried his only run for office, for Congress in West Texas, he was mocked as a wispy outsider who liked to go jogging when locals went hunting. They called him a latter-day Yankee carpetbagger—someone coming for the oil, but without understanding just how much blood and sweat had been poured into the soil by real Texans.

Even the young Bush knew he needed something, anything, on his resume: "My biggest liability in Texas is the question, 'What's the boy ever done? He could be riding on Daddy's name.'"[21]

Rove realized he could always put cowboy boots on Bush or say he had spent a few years of his childhood in West Texas. He could authentically note that Bush had married a fresh-faced Midland woman with real Texas DNA. But the true stumbling block, of course, was how to package Bush as a man who hadn't inherited virtually everything in his life. And who had been, really, an abject failure compared to his father.

Rove studied Bush more and more, almost like he was in the science lab and building a new chemical compound. Bush didn't read a lot, he wasn't an intellectual, he had no track record in public service. Rove understood full well that in Texas, those shortcomings didn't hold back a lot of candidates. Nobody ever said Pappy O'Daniel deserved the Nobel Prize for physics, or anything else, before he could hold high office in Texas. But the young Bush's business failures just might doom him before he even started running.

As Rove stayed in the lab, trying to figure out ways to gin up Bush's track record, he learned that in the Dallas–Fort Worth region, the Texas Rangers baseball team was going to come up for sale. As the team went on the market, several of elder Bush's business partners and campaign contributors began pooling $86 million to buy the Rangers. And, as they drew up the paperwork, the younger Bush begged in. He scrambled to borrow $500,000 from banker friends in Midland—and the big investors said it would get him 1.8 percent of the team.

Rove was beyond giddy. This was the missing puzzle piece, the way to fill in that blank resume. He didn't care if Bush had only a fraction of the team—he'd begin calling Bush an "owner" of a big-time baseball team. And, well, a business success in an all-American arena.

There was even better news: the media-averse billionaires who controlled more than 98 percent of the Rangers said they wanted Bush to be the public face of the franchise, to talk to reporters because they never really wanted to do it. Bush would stay away from any heavy financial responsibilities associated with the team, but let him offer up some quotes about trades, batting averages, and who was coming up from the minor leagues.

For Rove, it was like the political gods had sent manna from the Texas heavens. Bush would have access to the newspapers, magazines, and airwaves. He'd be in the mom-and-apple-pie business of baseball. Serving the megawealthy, cloistered investment group as an omnipresent cheerleader was right up his alley—he'd done cheerleading in high school. And now he was going to holler to reporters about "his" team and offer them fistfuls of his popcorn.

Friends said Bush seemed happier than ever. Not just because he was finally doing something his father hadn't done, but because, well, he was going to be close to Nolan Ryan, the pitching ace that Bush revered and called a hero. He might not have been as happy about one other task that the ownership group wanted him to perform: Bush would have to go door-to-door convincing neighborhoods and skeptical voters in North Texas to provide massive public funding for a new baseball stadium.

The owners had a ten-year plan. They wanted bond money to pay for a fancier stadium, and then they'd sell the Rangers and the building for an enormous profit. A decade later, Bush turned his initial 1.8 percent investment into a $15 million windfall—after he had dutifully gone door-to-door to sell the new stadium as a boon to local voters in Arlington, outside of Dallas. It was just what he and his father had done back in West Texas—going house-to-house to convince the locals that they were being offered a really good deal.

Rove arranged for reporters to interview Bush as he sat near the Rangers dugout, ate peanuts, and shouted to his favorite players. It was instant, nifty political magic, and Rove was over the moon. "It gives him ... exposure and gives him something that will be easily recalled by people," Rove gushed.[22] Rove picked up the *New York Times* one day, and the full measure of his master plan began to sink in. The paper had begun to routinely describe Bush as "the managing partner."[23]

Rove let the descriptions bake into the stories, including the ones that wondered if another Bush, maybe George W., would one day take his father's place in the political dynasty. It was a theme, a premise, maybe even a hope, that brought journalists over and over again to the baseball stadium to interview the younger Bush. The Kennedys were America's preeminent political clan. But it seemed, to Rove and others, that some voters might not be opposed to another one. Into the 1990s, more and more stories danced around the same idea: was the son going to follow the father?

Rove told Bush that a campaign against Ann Richards wouldn't be easy. The majority of voters still found her appealing. Even the people who loathed her liberal inclinations might vote for her because the Texas economy was soaring. Heading into the 1994 race, one poll showed her approval rating at over 60 percent.

Reporters who were meeting with the Richards camp walked away thinking that her aides really thought Bush was a lightweight, someone who had been gifted with both the silver spoon and the silver foot from his father. He certainly wasn't a tough Texas customer like the ass-kicking Clayton Williams. Richards was being advised by a downtown Austin political consultant known to some as Dr. Dirt: George Shipley was one of the master opposition researchers who specialized in doing the deep dive into an opponent's personal and public history. His team was accumulating dozens of large banker's boxes filled with Bush's financial statements for his oil companies, the details of his baseball ventures, and internal memos noting that researchers should keep looking for news about Bush's criminal record. There were folders devoted to his college years, his marriage, his friendships, his religious beliefs.

As the Richards campaign aides received the intelligence, they seemed more convinced than ever that Bush was a paper-thin opponent; that his time with the Texas Rangers was a political charade; that he still had no record of public service; that he was certainly no war hero, and that he might have been granted admission into the Texas Air National Guard as a political favor to his father ... and as a way to keep him out of harm in Vietnam. (Years later, reporters would scramble to find out if Ben Barnes, when he was lieutenant governor, had arranged for Bush to get that rare, coveted position in the guard.)

Bush's main claim to fame, they decided, was being the namesake son of the former president of the United States. He had the support of oilmen and investors who had adopted the Republican Party in Dallas and Houston—but so had Clayton Williams. He was nowhere as clever a public speaker as Richards. He was definitely not as Texan.

Building to the 1994 election, there was a contented sense that Richards would waltz back into office and keep the last strains of Ralph Yarborough's progressive political dreams alive—and maybe, just maybe, position herself for a run for the presidency.

For many Texans, Austin can seem like a liberal bubble—or an echo chamber where you could hear the same things over and over again. And what political insiders were hearing, repeatedly, was that Ann Richards was going to demolish George W. Bush. But outside Austin—at the rodeo in Llano, at the Dairy Queen in Tye, at the cooperative cotton gin in Roby—it was easy to find voters who simply no longer liked her.

Maybe some never did, maybe some had changed their view when she said she wanted to control their guns. There were rumblings that she had gone "too Hollywood" or "too New York," that she was hanging out with too many people from the West Coast and the East Coast. Or that she was entranced by her own aura and had just moved too far from what was really sacred in Texas.

Meanwhile, Bush really was outworking her. He was there at more small-town chambers of commerce, the Lion's Club luncheons, the Church of Christ picnics, and the volunteer fire department barbecue fund-raisers. He wore the rural Texas political uniform: denim work shirts and blue jeans and ballpark caps. He cracked jokes about the weather. He slapped backs and told Nolan Ryan stories. He never pretended to be intellectual—it wasn't in his repertoire—and for some voters, that had a certain appeal. Bush had spent part of his formative years in Midland, and he actually did know how to talk to the oil-field roustabouts, something that some inside the cloistered Richards orbit in Austin probably hadn't counted on.

Near the November election, emergency meetings were being called by both sides to talk about the polls. The race was now a virtual dead heat—and trending toward Bush. Rove had a feeling this would be one of his biggest coups—and maybe the prelude to a national race. Bush was elected governor with 53.5 percent of the vote; Richards had 45.9 percent. Bush won almost seven out of every ten white voters. Richards won almost eight out of every ten Black and Latino voters.

In Austin, Rove received congratulations from around the country, including from candidates who wanted to know exactly how he had reinvented Bush and how he had beaten a charismatic artist like Ann Richards. Kay Bailey Hutchison also won resounding reelection to the US Senate. Up and down the ballot it was a bellwether moment for the Texas GOP. It marked the first time in Texas that Republicans had the governor's office and both Senate seats.

At Scholz's, the old German beer garden and eatery in Austin, Molly Ivins and Richards sat in the ancient booths and tried to figure out what the hell had happened. Richards's aides were pondering if she really had gotten too far out of touch with the humble populism that had won her the governor's office in the first place. Or maybe it was more than just Richards losing—maybe it was the full realization of the Republican revolution in Texas.

"I may have lost the race," Richards said after the defeat. "But I don't think I lost the good feelings that people have about me in this state. That's tremendously reassuring to me."[24] Friends said, though, that she was stunned to have lost to a member of the Bush dynasty, especially one who wasn't born in Texas and hadn't been elected to anything before.

She had risen to prominence after she lit Bush's father on fire at the Democratic National Convention—her "silver foot" takedown of Bush's old man was still being quoted. She had seen her campaign, her administration, as a bastion of progressive and populist politics in Texas. She had become the steward of a party that had once been the most racist and right-wing in the state's history—but had evolved, through the political spasms of the 1950s and 1960s, into a kind of modern-day version of the Reconstruction-era Republicans.

The end of the Richards regime was stinging inside certain quarters in Austin. It wasn't hard to meet political folks who refused to believe she was through. In time, other developments seemed equally unlikely to her allies: after the sixty-one-year-old packed her things in the statehouse, she became an operative for various firms, including a very private and almost secretive one ironically called Public Strategies Inc. Three months after leaving office, she was hired as a lobbyist for the powerful Washington law firm of Verner Liipfert Bernhard McPherson & Hand, making what one Austin writer said was an estimated $385 per hour representing tobacco companies, railroads, weapons makers, and a company that wanted to fill in one of the largest and most biologically significant wetlands in the Northeast.

The liberal *Austin Chronicle*, once one of her champions, was chagrined: "Times change. So do liberal icons. Four years ago, Ann Richards was an icon, a role model for housewives, recovering alcoholics, divorced mothers, and others who saw themselves as hopeless or helpless."[25]

The publication was unforgiving: "Richards was different. Unlike (Ma) Ferguson, who got into politics after her husband, former Gov. Jim Ferguson, was denied a place on the ballot in 1924, Richards made it all on her own. She was a politician that people believed in. She wasn't born to it, like George W. Bush. She wasn't rich like Claytie Williams or Ross Perot. Richards was a real person. One of us. And now she's one of them, just another lobbyist working for special interests."[26]

One of the patriarchs of progressive causes in Texas was Tom "Smitty" Smith, director of the Texas office of Public Citizen. He said that Richards was "trading on her trust and her reputation as a spokesperson for liberal causes."[27]

After her defeat, she'd retreat to venerable Mexican food joints in East Austin, conferring with her old team. At El Azteca, she would head to a spot hidden from most customers, order the enchiladas, and sometimes pose for a picture with a fan.

One of the open secrets in Austin was that George W. Bush was disinterested in the day-to-day Sturm und Drang of governing Texas, and that he was damned lucky to have a mercurial madman like Bob Bullock as the lieutenant governor to do the hard, detail-oriented legislative bartering, clamoring, and hammering inside the statehouse. Bullock had been a Democrat for years, and he knew exactly the way his party and the GOP had changed in Texas. He loved Texas history, certainly more than Bush, and he felt an almost primordial need to make sure that the state capitol didn't wobble off its axis. He always wanted Texas saluted in better fashion, and one of his grandest plans was to create the ultimate monument to Texas exceptionalism: a huge state history museum that would bear his name.

When Bush became the GOP gubernatorial nominee in 1994, Bullock had leaked word that he would work with him if he won. And now, people who watched the two men said it was surprising to see Bullock so patient and even encouraging. It wasn't in his nature to take the time to walk a political novice through the byzantine briar patches in Austin. Maybe, some said, Bullock was doing it because he feared the worst.

Reporters said that when they visited Bush at his second-floor office in the statehouse, he was playing video golf, or reviewing drafts of his autobiography, which had been written for him by one his aides. She had composed it in three weeks, at her home in Austin. Sometimes he was planning time for real golf at the private Barton Springs Resort in Austin. What he was mostly doing, people said, was biding his time for a run for the presidency in 2000.

As speculation grew, Rove kept the political wheels turning in Texas. There were fund-raising cocktail parties, and more reporters invited from around the nation to do profiles. One of the heads of Random House and Times Books in New York asked me to write the first independent biography of Bush—and I immediately learned how high the stakes had already become.

As I began my work, the journalist Al Hunt granted me an interview about an almost completely unknown incident when a ridiculously inebriated George W. Bush confronted Hunt, his wife, and his small child in a Mexican restaurant in Dallas in the 1980s. They were just settling into their food when a bellowing, abusive Bush showed up at their table and cursed and berated Hunt for his political coverage of the Bush dynasty.

A few weeks after my interview with Hunt, he called me back. He asked if I had contacted Bush about the incident in Dallas. I told him I hadn't yet. He said that Bush had just telephoned him and apologized for the long-ago Dallas fiasco. Hunt was astounded that Bush would suddenly call to apologize, out of the blue, after more than a decade.

Veterans in Austin political circles told me in unblinking fashion that my phones were probably tapped, that someone had heard Hunt telling me about Bush verbally assaulting his family. I scoffed and chalked up what had happened with Hunt as the work of a very careful campaign out to mop up any loose ends from the past: maybe Rove had asked Bush to fork over a list of bad choices he had made, and now Bush was busy calling people to apologize for them.

Not long after, Bush aides began offering to visit my home office, which was filled with a mountain of court documents, police reports, military records, and unflattering bits of news about Bush. One afternoon, two men in gray jumpsuits appeared in my backyard. When I stepped outside to ask them what was up, they said they were doing work on my perfectly working telephone lines. Maybe my friends were right? *Of course not.*

I kept a desk and files at the *Dallas Morning News* bureau across from the governor's mansion, and when I went to pick up my mail, I found stacks of letters addressed to me that were sliced opened and in someone else's office. I went to a coffee shop near the governor's mansion and saw the *Dallas Morning News* bureau chief huddled with a woman who was a longtime aide to both Bill Clements and the Bush campaign. It was, my wife said, probably just a friendly interview. One of my research assistants told me that his car was broken into and his briefcase rifled in Austin. Another researcher saw strangers lingering near her apartment mailbox.

In the summer of 1998, my home phone rang, and Bush's communications director—Karen Hughes, whose father had been the last US official to oversee the Panama Canal zone—told me that Bush wanted to talk to me. I went and sat in the graceful, burnished waiting area in the statehouse. Hughes appeared, carrying a see-through plastic bag that I could tell was filled with Dr. Seuss books. I had a four-year-old daughter and recognized them right away. Hughes was striding in her confident way toward the door leading to Governor Bush's inner sanctum. Throughout his public life, Bush had been plagued by accusations that he was not particularly well read. It was well known that he hadn't written his own autobiography.

Hughes, carrying the Dr. Seuss books, stopped hard and stared at me: "I know what you're thinking!" she shouted, her voice echoing in the grand foyer. "He's not reading these for himself. The governor's going to be reading them to children."

In his office, Bush plunked his black boots—made by the very talented Houston boot maker Rocky Carroll—on his desk. I took out my recorder and pad. He began by asking me what I was working on. Then he began talking about what he *knew* I was working on—in particular, and to my enormous surprise, he began asking about my work contacting the police in Princeton, New Jersey, who might have once detained Bush back when he was drinking hard in college.

He said that he also knew I had been examining his failed oil investments. He added that he never had to work again now that he had sold his tiny share of the Texas Rangers. As he grinned, I looked over his shoulder and could see that Bush had put photographs of his father and grandfather on a shelf behind him. It was as if they were studying him, guiding him, and, of course, measuring him against their own legacies.

Bush asked what else I was working on and called me "Billy Boy." Bush had developed a habit of giving people nicknames; Hughes was "the High Prophet" and Karl Rove was "Turd Blossom" (because wherever Rove went, he stirred up some shit). Bush's media strategist, Mark McKinnon, later told me that Bush had another nickname for me: "Mononucleosis." I took a small semblance of pride in it, thinking that maybe he saw me as a kind of infection or virus that was persistent and hard to shake. That maybe it was a perverse way of saluting me for dogged reporting.

McKinnon laughed and told me that I was "Mononucleosis" because Bush couldn't pronounce my last name.

Bush had inherited the hard-edged conservative tendencies of Bill Clements, John Tower, John Connally, Phil Gramm, and so many others— whether they were running as Democrats or Republicans. Bush appointed pro-business conservatives to state agencies, was a vigorous supporter of capital punishment and the death penalty, and sought ways to bring more Christianity and the clergy into public agencies. He was particularly keen to privatize state social services in Texas and turn them over to faith-based or religious organizations. He made sure pro-oil advocates were on the Texas Railroad Commission, and he wanted "tort reform," specifically a cap on the abilities of law firms to sue large businesses. He wanted to tamp down environmental regulations coming from Washington, especially ones that might roadblock any part of the oil industry. No one on either side of the political aisle was surprised at anything Bush was supporting.

But, there were a few times when he had to go to an ideological crossroads and make far more difficult decisions, including ones that could dent his chances to sell himself across America as a compassionate conservative. Texas was often dubbed the "State of Death" by the media, and during Bush's time in office, dozens of prisoners were executed. In his five years as governor, 154 people were put to death, on average two to three every month.[28]

One death row prisoner, Karla Faye Tucker, attracted special attention because she was scheduled to be the first woman executed in Texas since Josefa "Chipita" Rodríguez in 1863. She was a sixty-three-year-old woman from San Patricio who was hung after being accused of murder—but in 1985, Texas lawmakers had passed a resolution saying that she had been the victim of an unjust judicial process.

Tucker, a sex worker like her mother, had drifted into a scary world of motorcycle gangs and drug dealers and then she hung around big rock groups like the Allman Brothers. She had been convicted of murder for driving a pickaxe into two people during a burglary. For years, she sought a retrial and even a stay of execution, arguing that she had reformed and repented—and become a full-blown, born-again Christian.

Her case attracted national and international attention, and a disparate collection of religious leaders—from the Vatican to the televangelist
Pat Robertson—called for Bush to stop her execution. Bush had enjoyed
the full-throated support of Christian evangelicals, and if he harbored any
hope of moving from Texas and following his father into the White House,
then he would need that base.

On CNN, Robertson was asked why he was so interested in the Tucker
case. Robertson responded, "Because if there was ever a truly rehabilitated inmate, it was Karla Faye. And then the question becomes, is there
no special dispensation we can give to the truly rehabilitated death row
inmate?"[29]

Despite last-minute appeals, Bush let the February 1998 execution proceed, and he turned his attention to his ongoing reelection campaign for
governor. It seemed to plenty of people in Austin that the race was an
afterthought. Bush was running for the White House, that was the real
prize. The governor's race felt like an aside.

The Democrats nominated a sacrificial lamb: Garry Mauro was born
in Bryan, had graduated from Texas A&M, and had gotten his law degree
from the University of Texas at Austin, and then put time in as an aide to
Ralph Yarborough before joining Ann Richards and that cadre of liberals
elected to state office in 1982. He served as the Texas land commissioner
for sixteen years, helped run the Bill Clinton presidential campaigns in
Texas, and made his liberal bonafides clear with his self-penned book,
Beaches, Bureaucrats and Big Oil: One Man's Fight for Texas.

At the Texas Chili Parlor, where lobbyists and consultants sometimes
sat at scarred, old wooden tables and downed Lone Star beers with reporters, there was that strange feeling that the governor's race was over
before it started. That by 1998, the state had changed so much due to an
incredible influx of Republican money and might. That Mauro was more
or less about to march off a cliff.

Another thing was also being bandied about: that Bush's reelection
was being used by Rove to iron out any wrinkles for a presidential bid.
It was a good practice, a way to try the compassionate conservative sales
pitch and see what else might put another Bush in the White House.

That June, a Black man named James Byrd was abducted near the small
city of Jasper. Several white men wrapped his ankles with chains, tied him
to a pickup truck, and dragged him along miles of hot and lonely East

Texas road. Somehow, the forty-nine-year-old Byrd clung to life—until his abductors pulled their truck close to a culvert, chopping off pieces of his body and head.

The men kept driving, the dead carcass bumping on the pavement, until they reached a cemetery reserved for Blacks. Byrd's unrecognizable remains were dumped at the side of the road. A long investigation ensued as police scoured the area searching for pieces of Byrd's body. News crews arrived from around the country, and the long, sordid history of violence against minorities in Texas was revisited. One of the killers was a "cyclops" in something called the Confederate Knights of America. He had KKK tattoos and had been calling for a race war.

In Austin, some state lawmakers began crafting a hate crimes bill, but Bush refused to support the measure, which would have "strengthen[ed] penalties for crimes motivated by race, religion, color, gender, disabilities, sexual preference, age or national origin." Bush argued that there shouldn't be a special, legislated distinction for hate crimes—and that, in fact, all crimes are hate crimes. (In 2001, after Bush left office in Texas, the measure would finally pass.)[30]

Five months after the murder, Texas voters gave Bush a wholesale victory. Mauro was obliterated, 68 percent to 31 percent. Bush became the first Texas governor elected to successive four-year terms. And even before the final votes were tallied, news crews were descending again on Austin to speak to the man many presumed to be one of the key GOP front-runners for the race to the White House. (Other people began arriving in Austin as well: I was contacted by someone who identified himself as an emissary from the Japanese government. He asked if I might be available to meet him and one of his colleagues. We arranged a time to meet at my office in downtown Austin. The men said they were acutely interested in George W. Bush, and they wondered if I would be available to help them learn new, hidden bits about the governor. One of the men reached in his business jacket, pulled out an envelope, and suggested they were willing to pay me. I politely demurred, though relatives told me that I should have peeked inside to see what the going rate was for spying on the governor of Texas.)

By the beginning of 1999, Bush was well into the race for the White House, and it wasn't hard to find people across Texas who wondered if he was even remotely thinking a bit about politics and policies in the state. But in a way, the presidential campaign sharpened Rove's and Bush's focus on core political principles. Rove began taking particular note of an

Austin-based writer and professor named Marvin Olasky, who was touting himself as a reformed communist who had become a solid Christian
conservative.

In 1995, Olasky had taken up the cause of Teen Challenge, a religiously
affiliated organization in Texas seeking to run drug treatment programs.
Olasky's merging of politics and Christianity caught the eye of Rove and
Bush, and he was summoned to a lunch meeting. Olasky was already a
minor hero in some national conservative circles, and was particularly embraced by House Speaker Newt Gingrich, who liked handing out copies of
Olasky's book *The Tragedy of American Compassion* (1992).[31]

After meeting Olasky, Rove decided that they should work harder to
pitch Bush as a gentler kind of Republican—not the one who presided
over the largest number of executions in state history. Not the governor of a place with a long history of segregation—and the lynching of a
Black man named James Byrd in Jasper, Texas. Instead, the idea was to
sell Bush to America as the forward-looking, youthful governor of a New
South state bubbling with high-tech entrepreneurs and booming cities,
and as someone who was friendly to immigrants, the Latino population,
and women's causes.

Mark McKinnon, the Austin ad man, was asked to handle Bush's national image. McKinnon had decided to abandon his usual Democratic
lanes, and he had also decided, quickly, that he had to try to make Bush,
well, something of a cooler conservative—someone who was less fussy
than his father and his mother, Barbara Bush. It was a tough route to
negotiate. Bush once said he had stopped listening to the Beatles at about
the time they stopped playing three-chord songs in the early 1960s. He
didn't particularly care for the psychedelic sounds.

Rove and McKinnon were operating on twin paths: how to claim that
George W. Bush from Texas was a fresh, new, and independent voice while
suggesting to the loyal, deep-pocketed supporters of the family dynasty
that he was never going to rock the boat. Rove and McKinnon were essentially suggesting that they needed to reinvent Bush once again, and this
time make him nationally palatable to new generations; to all those voters
skeptical of "another" Bush; to all the people who associated the family
name with aging GOP patriarchs, like the elder George Bush and Bob
Dole.

If the younger Bush could vault from Texas to the White House, it
would be one of the most unlikely political ascendancies of anyone in the
state. LBJ had become president through fate and circumstance, but also

by paying his political dues for decades as a master of intrigue in Washington. The elder Bush had done the same thing—building his climb to the White House with long years on the front lines. Selling "Dubya" would entail something else.

In Austin, Rove was now being dubbed "Bush's Brain," and he wrote and rewrote the four or five major messages that Bush would repeat in public. Karen Hughes, the communications czar, began standing in the back of rooms where Bush was giving a speech and prompting him by slowly mouthing the lines that he sometimes stumbled through. Then, later, she'd call reporters who were writing their stories about his speech and tell them what Bush had meant to say.

Film crews from the BBC and Japanese television rented rooms in Austin. Writers from Danish and German newspapers arrived. Dozens of expense-account-funded political reporters from every major outlet descended on Texas. Scrambling to get up to speed on Bush's history, many relied on the mainstream political news offerings from the big newspapers and magazines. Wayne Slater of the *Dallas Morning News* gushed that Rove was a "wizard."[32] His paper later added that Rove was "someone of uncommon character who demonstrated both leadership and vision in 2004, who exemplified a trailblazing instinct and ability to navigate adversity."[33] S. C. Gwynne of *Texas Monthly* anointed Rove a "political genius" who "balances work and play fairly well. He reads histories and biographies, collects stamps, loves games like Scrabble."[34]

Outsiders trying to understand the state, and Bush, studied back issues of the *Texas Observer*, searching for more skeptical threads and clues—and the long view of history, the kind that would explain how the Bushes had succeeded in Texas. The tiny investigative publication skipped the horse race coverage, those daily mood swings in the polls that the state's biggest paper, the *Dallas Morning News*, liked to focus on. And it also avoided the glossy hagiography that the state's biggest magazine, *Texas Monthly*, sometimes offered.

Meanwhile, Bush's team was going into overdrive. Media guru McKinnon opened his own bunker in the basement of an old building north of downtown, and across from a city park where every year the hippies in Austin gathered to smoke pot, take their shirts off, and celebrate the birthday of Eeyore, the donkey in the Winnie the Pooh story. I visited McKinnon's underground lair one day and had to find it by going behind some shrubs and down some stairs, and then reaching a metal door that had no outside handle. McKinnon let me inside, where there was a war room of interns and strategists running from fax machines to private offices. Oddly, Frank Sinatra music was wafting through the air. I was told that cell phones didn't work down there, and that that was one of the reasons the bunker was being used by Bush's team.

Every mention of Bush, anywhere, was being scrutinized. Editors and reporters were being called to admonish them about stories they had run or were pursuing. Hughes even wrote me a frothy letter as I finished my biography of Bush for Random House and Times Books. Someone from his office contacted my editor in New York. Rove was controlling who would talk to whom, and the Bush team finally decided to allow me the rare chance to speak with Bush family members, including George W.'s brother Jeb, the governor of Florida. A variety of other relatives—cousins and uncles—also agreed to their first interviews for my long, unauthorized biography.

The impending book was becoming a very small political phenomenon in many state and national outlets, eventually featured on the *Today Show* and all the major networks. It seemed that every scrap of news about Bush, or even just people writing about him, was suitable for coverage. *Texas Monthly* also decided that a Texan writing the first national political biography about Bush was worthy of a story. In a nod to those long-standing accusations that its coverage was overly friendly and protective when it came to famous Texans, it erroneously suggested that Bush family members weren't talking to the author of the book. In fact, they already had—because George W. Bush told them they could.

The misstep pointed to something critical at work inside Texas politics: it said that Bush had a greater hand in his campaign than some of his Texas-based advisors realized, and that he might have felt that local aides, including Karen Hughes, were not ready for the chess moves of a huge, bruising national political campaign. The Bushes were global politicians, and the first son of George H. W. Bush was as instinctive a political animal as anyone in the family. One by one, national GOP strategists were invited by Bush to come to Dallas, Houston, and Austin to plan the battle to retake the White House.

Texas Land Commissioner Garry Mauro vanished in Bush's rearview mirror like roadkill on a long stretch of Ranch Road 152 out in the Texas Hill Country. With his doomed race to unseat Bush went the last upper-level vestiges of the progressive-liberal power movements. For the stragglers in the Ann Richards orbit, it was hard to grapple with the fact that the

Democrat achievements had crumbled so much in just a few short years. But as Bush began his second term in early 1999, he was locked on to matters well beyond weakened Democrats in Austin.

With his less-than-evident knowledge of Texas history, Bush might not have known that he was forever channeling the inventions of Pappy O'Daniel. The old flour salesman had sold himself as a view to the future as well as a protector of the old traditions. When he uncorked his second term as governor, O'Daniel handed out mountains of barbecue to Texans. In 1999, as he embarked on his new term, Bush held a big public picnic with almost a ton of smoked meat—that old-time Texas staple of the working man that was quickly becoming haute cuisine for hipsters.

Later that same evening, Bush put on one of his best pressed suits and hosted a smaller private, intimate dinner for his most important financial supporters. This meal featured gold-tinted tablecloths and napkins, and a room festooned with fresh, dewy roses.[35]

Maybe Bush had mastered how to walk in different worlds. Maybe Karl Rove had shown him the way. Or maybe it was really just his father guiding him again.

CHAPTER 14

Smear Tactics: The 2000s

DOZENS OF PEOPLE WERE DASHING UP the steps of the governor's mansion to escape the cold and reach the bright lights inside. Many of them were dressed for a formal affair, some in fine suits. At least one person was wearing a cheap blazer he had bought on eBay. Tuxedoed waiters served champagne and hard drinks. A seasoned newspaper reporter asked if he could have a glass of bourbon "from General Sam Houston's secret stash in the basement." The Black waiter nodded, offered a small smile, disappeared, and then returned with a tumbler filled with caramel-colored alcohol and three chunky ice cubes. It was December 2000, and a towering Christmas tree was in a corner near a roaring fireplace. A huge antique table was covered with chocolate cakes, cream cakes, and exquisitely designed pastries.

It was supposed to be the night of Bush's coronation, the night he was going to make it clear to the reporters—from the *New York Times* to *Time*—that he was finally going to be president after the long, tortured election of 2000. The race against Al Gore had gone to the wire, to the vote counters in Florida, and finally to the Supreme Court. Bush had huddled with his father and gone over all the possible outcomes, the angles, the moves, and what they would do no matter what happened.

It was, from the outside looking in, a bit like a family drama: the son trying to match the father—the son who had never been the measure of the father was trying to finally get to the same position of power and prestige. It hadn't come easy, but now it was over, and Bush had decided to invite his allies, his insiders, and even dreaded members of the media into the governor's mansion. He was convinced that the media preferred Gore: someone with a longer history of public service, someone who had served in Vietnam, someone who had written his own speeches and books, someone who had mastered particular policy issues—especially, of course, the environment.

Bush gladly agreed to a suggestion that everyone attending his party be invited to have their picture taken with him. At the foot of a burnished wooden staircase, Bush was bobbing on his feet and watching the crowd, especially a tall, blue-eyed woman with a mane of red hair and booming an alcohol-charged laugh. Molly Ivins was still the best-known political journalist in Texas. She was also now the last really big public face of liberal politics in Texas.

She had decided that if she was going to prosper in the land of Lyndon Baines Johnson and the Bush dynasty—in the rattlesnake boil of the Dallas Cowboys, Lee Harvey Oswald, *Friday Night Lights*, NASA, the Alamo, Ross Perot, Howard Hughes, and Bonnie and Clyde—she would write with a pointy cowgirl boot rising to meet some pontificating plutocrat's ass. She had gone after Ronald and Nancy Reagan: "His mind is mired somewhere in the dawn of social Darwinism and she's a brittle, shallow woman obsessed with appearances, but then it was that kind of decade, wasn't it?"[1]

She said one GOP figure's political speech probably sounded better in the original German. She said that Arnold Schwarzenegger resembled a walnut-packed condom. She even occasionally jabbed at her friend Bill Clinton and his sexual proclivities: "With all due respect to the president's private parts, we do have bigger problems in this country."

She didn't spare Bush: "I have known George W. Bush since we were both in high school. We have dozens of mutual friends," she wrote. "Just cut the macho crap. I don't want to hear it ... I grew up with all this pathetic Texas tough."[2]

I went up to Bush, and he seemed startled to see me. I tried a lame joke: "Congratulations. Oh, thanks for helping my book sales." Bush didn't laugh. "Yeah, I did all that for your book." Across the room, Ivins fired up a Marlboro and broke the no-smoking rule inside the home of the governor of Texas.

They had known each other in high school and growing up in the River Oaks part of Houston. They mingled at the same country club parties before he went to Yale and she headed to Smith College. They both had parents who had grown fabulously wealthy from oil. Ivins's father was the price-fixing president of Tenneco, one of the biggest oil companies in the world. Unlike Bush's old man, he wasn't a survivor. Her father had stepped into his backyard one humid evening and raised a gun to his head, and the blast had echoed off the nearby estates.

Ivins bundled up in her winter coat and headed for the beautiful old doors of the Texas governor's mansion. It was cold outside and getting colder. Days later, I was told that someone had heard Bush mutter something that might have sounded like a curse.

Texas was now routinely called a Super State, with Dallas, Houston, and San Antonio bumping onto the list of the ten largest American cities. Rove had followed the demographic changes closely: white voters were still moving to the state, and many were still deciding to self-segregate into those affluent suburbs. The Hispanic population was clearly growing, and Bush had tried to appeal to them in his mangled Spanish.

Every major statewide office had gone to a Republican, and the wholesale victories, up and down the ballot, had as much to do with one Democrat—someone who had decided that before he died he would do all that he could to make sure that Bush succeeded in Texas and beyond. He was still around, in his way, maybe as a ghost attending Bush's coronation party in the governor's mansion.

Bob Bullock had bolted through five marriages and infinite tumblers of alcohol, and had been feared for years in the statehouse. If Cactus Jack Garner was once the most powerful vice president in history, then Bullock was the most powerful lieutenant governor ever to live in Texas. There will never be another Bullock, not in the age of social media and the instant way the foibles and antics of public figures are chronicled. And not in terms of being able to take big-time credit for aiding a less-than-focused governor with an unremarkable record and putting him on the fast track to the White House.

In the spring of 1999, Bullock summoned me to his very comfortable home, dotted with Texas and cowboy memorabilia, near downtown Austin. He was reclining on his bed, surrounded by paperwork, and rambling in non sequitur fashion about some ranchland in Llano—and about whether I was acting like the cartoon detective Dick Tracy, chasing down bad guys. He asked me if I had been tailed on my way to see him, if I had parked in some hidden, out-of-the-way place. He bolted upright on his bed and bellowed, "Y'all want some fried chicken!" And then he collapsed back on his bed, talking about money, his estate, that land in Llano. He focused for a bit and said he was glad that Bush was on his way to Washington and maybe in position to begin surpassing his father's legacy. He seemed, suddenly, emotional and sentimental. The armchair analysts in Austin were saying that the sickly Bullock had begun acting in an even more paternal fashion toward Bush. Maybe Bullock—more entranced than anyone with the curated Texas myths of Texas—wanted nothing more than to see another man from Texas as the leader of the free world.

Bullock remained a Democrat until he died, six months before Bush's party at the governor's mansion. He would have enjoyed being there, if only to harass Molly Ivins, someone he came dangerously close to dating. His support of Bush had suggested to voters, in Texas and around the nation, that Bush was a conciliator, maybe a guy who got along in a nonpartisan way.

In those liberal haunts in Austin, the places where Ann Richards was still revered, some people muttered that Bullock had really just been a sellout—a Democrat who could have derailed George W. Bush anytime he wanted. And, of course, someone who could have changed the course of world history.

Rick Perry had grown up in a cotton-farming family in north-central Texas, in an area filtering out from Abilene and often called "Big Country" by that city's paper. He attended Texas A&M and, after serving in the Air Force, was elected to the Texas House in 1984, selling himself as a fiscally and socially conservative Democratic lawmaker. After an official switch to the GOP, he ran for state agriculture commissioner in 1990 against Jim Hightower, one of the last-standing Texas progressives.

Perry hired Karl Rove to manage his campaign, which often just centered on painting Hightower as a crooked hack. Perry squeaked to a 49-percent-to-48-percent win, served for several years, and then jumped to run for lieutenant governor in 1998. For GOP strategists, he seemed to be generally electable, hardly electric, and an entirely safe heir to Bush's throne.

When Bush stepped down, Perry—dubbed "Governor Good Hair" by

Ivins—was sworn in four days before Christmas in 2000. In his inaugural speech, he made sure to thank those who had made it possible, and he could have gone on for several minutes to salute the long line of Southern Democrats and the New Republicans who had mostly controlled Texas since the end of the Civil War. Instead, he focused on Bush:

> I am particularly humbled today because my predecessor has set
> the bar extremely high. His shadow will loom large over this granite
> building, for it is the shadow of a great man. He is an inspiring leader,
> a trusted friend and our nation's president-elect George W. Bush....
> I stand before you today first and foremost by the grace of God. But
> I also stand before you this afternoon the son of tenant farmers, and
> part of the first generation of my family to attend college.... From
> the border, to the fifth ward of Houston, from the suburbs of Dallas,
> to the farms and fields on the outskirts of a dusty West Texas town,
> there are no second-rate dreams, no second-class citizens.... At the
> dawn of a new day for our friends and neighbors to the south, it is my
> strongly held belief that we have never had a greater opportunity to
> improve the quality of life along the border of Texas.... If the border
> of Texas succeeds, then Texas succeeds.... The border of Texas is not
> the back yard, but the front door to our state and our nation. It is a
> dynamic place enriched by a wonderful people. Its progress, its pros-
> perity, will benefit the whole of Texas.[3]

Perry outlined the matters he promised to address during his time in office and if he was lucky enough to win the 2002 general election: being tough on crime; luring high-tech firms; insisting Texas could go toe-to-toe with California and other places churning out coders, software designers, and computer visionaries. Perry dwelt on technology more than any other issue, insisting there should be more high-tech scholarships handed out in Texas. As he was sworn in, Austin was zooming forward as a Silicon Prairie outpost, with dozens of large and small firms moving in, expanding, and drawing on the resources at the University of Texas. The largest private employer in the Austin area was Dell, and it served as a beacon to other companies—even as state government, programs, and universities continued to float on that usually reliable ocean of oil revenues.

Behind closed doors, Perry was undergoing a bitter divorce from his political Svengali, Karl Rove, despite the fact that he knew he had to immediately focus on the next general election—and that he had to raise money sooner rather than later. Maybe he could get it from those well-heeled techies and venture capitalists he was unsubtly suggesting he would help to set up shop in Texas. The political apparatus in the state had always been an easy two-way street. Oilmen put people in office, including some of their own. Perry seemed to sense that there was a new high-tech fund-raising well to tap, a well he could help build by touting Texas the way it had always been touted—as the low-tax, low-regulation, wonder world of the South.

Perry's campaign to retain his inherited seat really began immediately, though Texas was facing a multibillion-dollar budget shortfall. Some critics were saying he needed to focus on keeping the state solvent instead of the political race, especially since plenty of people had concluded the Democrats were never going to win. The most cynical observers noted that the Democratic candidate, Laredo oilman and millionaire banker Tony Sanchez, was one more lost cause being brought to slaughter—even if Sanchez was willing to outspend Perry in order to become the first Hispanic governor in the state's history. Sanchez, worth an estimated $600 million, spent at least $59 million of his own money on the race. Perry and his supporters poured in as much as $24 million.

The Democrats blanketed the state with ads attacking Perry for refusing to get along with state lawmakers and for vetoing eighty-two bills in 2001. They suggested that he was smothering Texas in partisan gridlock; in fact, Perry had routine success in pushing for standard core conservative policies. The well-funded attacks by Sanchez—a political newcomer most voters had never heard of—seemed to be having some initial impact. Early poll numbers said the race could be tighter than anyone had imagined. A few months before the election, Perry's campaign decided he needed to get rough.

One anti-Sanchez ad depicted men with money-filled suitcases; some said it was an unsubtle reference to the fact that Mexican drug kingpins had tried to launder their cash at banks run by Sanchez. He was never prosecuted or convicted of any crime, but in Austin, some longtime political watchers said they knew what the ads were all about. It was race-baiting, more fear-mongering. And it was meant to scare white people. "That ad really resonated with Anglos," observed a political scientist at the University of Houston. "The general tenor of the Perry advertising has been covert appeals to race," added a University of Texas professor.[4]

Perry crushed Sanchez, 58 percent to 40 percent, and in Democratic circles, there was now a gnawing belief that the Republican revolution would never end.

Harold Simmons was the son of schoolteachers, and he was born in the small northeastern Texas community of Golden. He barreled his way into controlling most of the world's titanium through his ownership of Titanium Metals Corporation. He became a billionaire and began donating millions of dollars to political action committees and defense funds for Republicans accused of breaking the law. He helped pay the legal fees of Oliver North, the military man accused of secretly funneling money to armies trying to overthrow the Nicaraguan government.

Simmons gave an estimated $2 million, maybe more, to the Swift Boat campaign—an organized effort to derail John Kerry, George W. Bush's Democratic opponent in the 2004 presidential race. The plan was to suggest that Kerry had exaggerated his combat record while serving in Vietnam. The attacks on his military service corresponded with investigations launched by several news organizations in 2004 into Bush's own military history. Unlike Al Gore and Kerry, Bush had never gone to Vietnam, and reporters were still investigating whether Bush had been granted special admission into his Texas Air National Guard unit, one that Bush knew would never be sent to the front lines. Reporters were particularly scrambling to find out if someone in Texas politics had gotten him in.

The most infamous investigation was led by a group of Texas political reporters working for CBS and Dan Rather—the Texan who had become a longtime object of derision for members of the Bush family. Their 2004 report suggested there were documents that pointed to Bush having a blemished record in the Texas Guard—and that there were many more questions than answers about whether he lived up to his duties. Very quickly, their review of Bush's career in the Texas Guard was assailed by critics who said the CBS documents were forged and that the CBS reporters in Texas were too close to the Kerry campaign.

The affair became one of the biggest media-centric political stories of the last fifty years, and it would lead to Rather and his Texas team leaving CBS. There was a lengthy investigation into the matter, cochaired by former attorney general Dick Thornburgh, and even a movie about the incident with Robert Redford playing Dan Rather.

In the wake of the incident, and with the help of those millions of dollars from Texas billionaires Simmons and T. Boone Pickens, Bush defeated Kerry in the 2004 election.

Once Bush won, Simmons immediately donated another $100,000 for the inauguration party.

The little family home on a ditch-lined street in Humble, Texas, had no steady running water and no telephone. If Alberto Gonzales wanted to make a phone call, he had to go down the street to a pay-phone booth or a local store. He had an alcoholic father and some troubled relatives, but Gonzales got good grades, attended Rice University, and went on to Harvard Law School. After he graduated, he came back to Houston as a young, hungry corporate lawyer at a prestigious white-collar firm—and one of the few Latinos inside certain upper-echelon, high-dollar legal circles in the city. His big break came when he was assigned to represent the controversial and crooked Enron Corporation. Word circled that he was calm, fastidious, and hardworking. When Bush became governor in the mid-1990s and needed to fill up his staff, he and Rove combed Texas for fierce conservatives who were minorities. Friends in Houston told Bush about Gonzales, meetings were arranged, and he was appointed the governor's in-house general counsel—really, Bush's personal lawyer.

The bespectacled Gonzales proved his loyalty right away: he helped Bush avoid jury duty and having to reveal that he had a hidden criminal record for drunk driving—the kind of black mark that could derail someone with presidential ambitions. As a reward, Gonzales became secretary of state and then was named to the Texas Supreme Court, with Bush leaning on his promotion of Gonzales as proof that he was sympathetic to the concerns of Latinos in Texas.

Bush relied on Gonzales for other things: by routinely suggesting that the governor reject clemency pleas from death-row inmates, Gonzales served as the gatekeeper for the biggest wave of executions in Texas history. His unrelenting and hardened conservatism led to comparisons with Clarence Thomas. Bush's father had appointed Thomas, a Black man, to the Supreme Court, and he proved to be one of the most ardently conservative members in that body's history. His son had found his own minority conservative, Alberto Gonzales, in Texas.

For years, Bush, Rove, and party strategists were committed to using Gonzales to make inroads in the Latino community. The state and the nation were obviously diversifying in enormous ways, and forecasts called for the largest cities and all of Texas to have a majority Hispanic population.

Bush took Gonzales with him to Washington to be his White House counsel, planning to get him a seat alongside Thomas on the Supreme

Court. But Gonzales's career fizzled the more people on Capitol Hill questioned his credentials and whether he was a champion of human rights; there were ceaseless reports that he had called international human rights treaties "quaint," and that his office was more than responsible for allowing the "advanced interrogation techniques"—what critics called torture—taking place on America's watch.

Bush glumly watched as Gonzales's fortunes plummeted in Washington. He had risen far, and fast, and he had hurtled back down almost as quickly. Rove and Bush had hoped they could point to Gonzales as enduring proof that they were advancing Latinos in America. Cynics kept circling back to the idea that all Bush was doing was stealing a page from his father's political playbook.

Gonzales left Washington, his political fortunes in shambles, and came back to Texas to weigh the future. There is always a home back in corporate America for high-ranking administration attorneys. Instead, he wound up teaching in universities, and thinking about writing his autobiography (maybe to counter a full-dress biography that I had written about him).

By 2005, Perry was stunned to learn his approval numbers were falling, maybe as a lingering outgrowth of being painted as an absentee landlord, a do-nothing governor while Texas wrestled with budget woes, school funding challenges, and crime. In Austin, as lawmakers assembled for the legislative session in 2005, Perry was told that his approval rating had dropped to 38 percent. He wasn't the only one poring over the numbers.

Richard "Kinky" Friedman was a singer, writer, and close friend of Willie Nelson's. This is how he tried to explain why he was running for governor against Perry: "Texas has a tradition of singing governors. Pappy O'Daniel's successful race took place in the 1940s. He had a band called the Light Crust Doughboys. I, of course, had a band called the Texas Jewboys. His slogan was 'Pass the biscuits, Pappy.' One of my own most popular, often-requested songs is 'Get Your Biscuits in the Oven (and Your Buns in the Bed).' The parallels are almost uncanny."[5]

Friedman was a fixture in what was left of a particular, quickly dwindling music scene in Austin—a wave of aging artists who had first arrived in the 1970s, emboldened by Willie Nelson's decision to leave Nashville and come swim in Barton Springs. Back then, singers and songwriters moved into wooden bungalows along Lake Austin, maybe grew a little pot out near Kyle and Buda, and listened to the bands at the Armadillo World Headquarters. Friedman had once toured the country, had done a spot

Richard "Kinky" Friedman, a singer turned wise-cracking author and politician, mingles with students and others at Texas State University in San Marcos. During the early 2000s, Friedman sought various offices, including the governorship.

on *Saturday Night Live*, had opened for Bob Dylan, and had sung "How Can I Tell You I Love You (When You're Sitting on My Face)" and "They Ain't Makin' Jews Like Jesus Anymore." He crooned about the Holocaust and mass shootings; his "Ballad of Charles Whitman" centered on the deadly sniper assault at the University of Texas at Austin, one of the signature mass slayings in US history. The National Organization for Women awarded him its Male Chauvinist Pig Award.

"Politics is the only field in which the more experience you have, the worse you get," Friedman said one day. "And I think musicians can better run this state than politicians. And, hell, beauticians can better run the state than politicians.... I want people, in this administration, that don't care about the Republicans and don't care about the Democrats, but care about Texas. That's what I passionately care about."[6]

He said that he wanted to close the Texas-Mexico border until Mexico did something about undocumented border crossings. He had some political appointments in mind: "Willie Nelson, the hillbilly Dalai Lama, also will play a seminal role in my plans. In a Friedman administration, Willie confided to me, he would like to be head of the Texas Rangers. If that's not possible, he'd like to be head of the DEA (Drug Enforcement Agency)."[7]

Friedman added, "Even though the governor of Texas does not do much heavy lifting, this does not mean that he can't do some spiritual lifting. I have a plan to start a Texas Peace Corps, and that is not an oxymoron. I want to fight the wussification of Texas. We didn't get to be the Lone Star State by being politically correct."[8]

He joined the 2006 race as an independent candidate. Former Houston congressman Chris Bell was the Democratic nominee, and state comptroller Carole Keeton Strayhorn was also running as an independent. She had made headlines in Austin a few years earlier when she led a well-publicized tax raid on the famous Antone's nightclub.

The election made national news, often because people were marveling at how weird politics had gotten again in Texas: Friedman won 12.5 percent of the vote—almost 550,000 votes. Perry won 39 percent, Bell 30 percent, Strayhorn 18 percent, and Democrats were left to muse over what would have happened if Perry had faced just a single opponent. At least one thing was clear: Friedman's numbers proved that more than a half million Texans supported a candidate who wanted an unabashed dope smoker like Willie Nelson to head the Texas Rangers—the law enforcement agency, not the baseball team.

Molly Ivins was headed back and forth from her oncologist's office. She had lost her bold mane of red hair but had kept up an almost relentless pace of public appearances on behalf of progressive and liberal politicians in Austin and around Texas. She continued to offer financial support to keep the *Texas Observer* running. In 2007, she passed away after dictating her last column to aides in Austin. The White House quickly released a statement from President George W. Bush. He had decided to take the high road, even though she had mocked him for years and made a mint by doing it: "Molly Ivins was a Texas original.... I respected her convictions, her passionate belief in the power of words."[9]

A few days after she died, her last column appeared in hundreds of newspapers—in New York, California, Illinois, Texas, Florida, and every

Molly Ivins rebelled as a Texas child and as a reporter for the *New York Times* before settling in back home as a sharp-edged liberal commentator, who bestowed the nickname "Shrub" on Republican George W. Bush, her childhood contemporary in affluent Houston.

corner of America: "We are the people who run this country.... We are the deciders.... Raise hell."[10] Around the state you could spot cars with bumper stickers that said: "What Would Molly Say?"

At gatherings to mourn her passing, some inside her tight inner circle were saying that Texas was now firmly in a new age of politics—one where the mainstream media no longer wielded exclusive power; where newspapers were dying; and where voters sought out the news that verified their inherent political beliefs. Some said it was not a place where Ivins would have been comfortable. For years she could rely on big mainstream papers to run her columns and help her reach millions of readers. Friends wondered if she would have been even remotely effective in the modern media world—in the age of tweets and Instagram accounts. When local daily papers were the only regular source of political news for most Texans, she could make or break a candidate's career. Now the old forums and spheres of influence were fading fast.

Two years after her death, an editor at *Texas Monthly* began plotting the creation of a new online-only statewide political publication. Evan Smith, who had an uncanny resemblance to the diminutive right-wing GOP apostle John Tower, was banking on the idea that Texans still wanted to know what went on in the statehouse—that if daily newspapers were dying, maybe a mainstream internet outlet could fill the void.

Several months prior to the 2009 launch of his ambitious political reporting website, Smith announced that T. Boone Pickens was his choice for "Texan of the Year," and that "it is impossible to walk away from a conversation (or three) with Boone without admiring his colorful, remarkable life—or believing his motives are pure."[11] Later that year, Pickens and others, including venture capitalists in Austin, helped underwrite the creation of Smith's new *Texas Tribune*. A handful of the best reporters in Texas joined the publication, and it admirably set about filling the void of political coverage in the Texas capital.

Pickens forked over $150,000 to jumpstart the outlet, and critics quickly wondered how exactly a news operation funded by public figures and business entities, including former Texas lieutenant governor Ben Barnes and a variety of oil and gas interests, was going to work. For decades, Pickens had poured millions of dollars into right-wing political campaigns around the nation. He had given $1 million to Karl Rove's American Crossroads, a committee devoted to funding ultraconservative candidates, and he had bankrolled the Swift Boat campaign.

Pickens wanted a Texan like Bush in the White House, and a better chance, really, to roll forward unencumbered by the lingering ghost of federal intrusion—especially, in Pickens's case, as he was aggressively pursuing a controversial form of extracting oil called fracking, something that would require that a new web of pipelines be rushed into existence without any regulatory roadblocks.

For years, Pickens had toyed with different ways to add to his vast fortune, one that made him one of the wealthiest men in the world. He tried selling water to drought-stricken parts of Texas. He touted coal, and he took a look at whether he could turn a profit in the burgeoning wind and solar energy markets. When he grew either bored or disenchanted, he retreated back to what he knew best—oil and gas. Through it all, Pickens presumed to be able to reach any politician in Texas at any time he wanted.

Bush, for one, was always amenable to hearing from Pickens or his staff. And Pickens kept pouring money into the various Bush campaigns or paying for Bush's inauguration parties. Along the way, Pickens acquired a 65,000-acre ranch in Pampa that at one time was valued at over $200 million and wrote a book called *The First Billion Is the Hardest*. And after he had helped the younger Bush win the White House, Pickens decided to crisscross Texas on a kind of nostalgic farewell tour, a sort of political and autobiographical journey.

Accompanying him and introducing him to forums and banquets and petroleum clubs was Smith, the former editor of *Texas Monthly* and the creator of the newest, largest political reporting operation in Texas. The editor and billionaire traveled the state, with Smith serving as a moderator and narrator guiding Pickens through fond remembrances of his upbringing and career.

In Austin, the last members of the Molly Ivins inner circle debated what she would have said about politics in modern Texas. She had made a cottage industry in mainstream papers by carving up billionaires and the Bush dynasty like Texas Hill Country wild turkeys. A few said that Ivins—whose father was once a titan of the oil industry—would say that there was really nothing new at work. And a few recalled Lyndon Johnson's cynical thoughts about how political history is sometimes recorded and preserved.

"The press helps me," Johnson said one day, his hangdog face no doubt creased by a crooked smile. "The press is one of the best servants I have."[12]

As George W. Bush's approval ratings swooned to record nadirs, a déjà vu feeling cropped up in Dallas, Houston, and Austin: another national leader from Texas was going to come back home beaten down and saddled with suspicions and weariness. But some said it wasn't as bad as when LBJ left public life as a haunted, haggard figure retreating to his lair along the Pedernales River—to walk with his trusty beagles, scooping up pecans that had fallen from the towering trees, or head down the road to the tiny town of Hye to buy peaches from the descendants of the nineteenth-century Germans who had settled in his part of Central Texas.

Maybe more than any political figure in the history of the state, Johnson had advanced a particular national and international image of the "Texas politician"—ballsy, domineering, and more than crafty. He had come to presidential power in the most tragic of circumstances, and then he had presided over a nation torn by riots, war, assassinations, domestic terrorism, and scalding racism. He had pushed for civil rights advances, for some progressive appointments and policies, but the specter of the Vietnam War was his permanent millstone—as was the fact that some still viewed him as the president from the state that "had killed Kennedy."

One of LBJ's oldest and most faithful aides had flown back to Texas with Johnson on the day he abandoned Washington for good: "He was a fellow that wasn't necessarily introspective but that almost demanded having people around," said Larry Temple, the former special counsel to Johnson. "He'd invite himself to people's houses. He had lots of regular visitors."[13]

Bush wasn't going to be abandoning Washington the exact same way

LBJ had—hounded by antiwar protesters chanting "Hey, hey, LBJ, how many kids did you kill today?" But Bush was ending his second term as president with some of the most dismal popularity polls in history—he had a 70 percent disapproval rating—and on the heels of what his critics felt was a Vietnam-like quagmire in the Middle East.[14]

He had shown a swagger at the World Trade Center rubble in the wake of the 9/11 attacks. He had grabbed a bullhorn and shouted: "I can hear you! The rest of the world hears you! And the people—and the people who knocked these buildings down will hear all of us soon." It was his finest public moment, but it was often lost when weighed against the revelations that US forces were torturing prisoners; that the Justice Department had unleashed surveillance on its own citizens; that Bush had done too little before, during, and after Hurricane Katrina, one of the deadliest, costliest disasters in the nation's history.

By 2008, Bush was preparing to spend his postpresidency days back at the limestone "Texas White House" he had built outside of Waco. It was a sprawling, comfortable, architect-designed place with a man-made lake where he could go bass fishing when he wasn't engaging in his new hobby, painting. Bush also bought a second residence, in an expensive, quiet area of Dallas, a modern house backing up to one belonging to the billionaire owner of the Texas Rangers baseball team. It was a neighborhood filled with other billionaires, from Ross Perot to Mark Cuban, including one of Bush's truly powerful financiers, that reticent titanium magnate Harold Simmons.

Back in Austin, Bush's old Texas home made national news: in 2008, a man approached the 152-year-old governor's mansion in the early morning hours of June 8 and tossed a Molotov cocktail toward the stately front doors. The building erupted in flames, and crews raced to douse the four-alarm fire. Governor Perry and his family were not there—they had moved to an affluent, gated community in Travis County while the mansion was being renovated. The plans for the prefire restoration of the mansion included an updated fire-prevention system. The mansion was heavily damaged, almost a total ruin, and reporters wondered if Perry was actually secretly happy. Political insiders said he had never liked living in it, that he thought it was too antiquated, and that he much preferred the newer, lavish home—with its granite countertops, new plumbing, and swimming pool—his family was enjoying. With the fate of the mansion up in the air, Perry settled more deeply into his new community of million-dollar estates. It was near the most exclusive country club in the county—where

Bush, when he was governor, used to play tennis with his father and dignitaries like the president of Argentina.

Six months after the governor's mansion was torched, Bush was out of the White House, heading to Texas and hoping to see his old oil-patch friends, the ones from his hard-drinking bachelor days in Midland. In Austin, political consultants were clucking about how Bush's name had fallen, even in Texas: "It is the name that shall not be spoken," said one longtime advisor for both Democrats and Republicans. "The emotional response from people is almost always negative, never positive. It's a different time and a different deal."[15]

Inside the statehouse, it was even clearer how far his star had plummeted: a Waco lawmaker had introduced a resolution to salute Bush for taking "a principled stance on a wide range of issues of great importance to every American." A Fort Worth lawmaker retorted that it was wrong to salute someone for waterboarding and other torture techniques—a nod to the enormous criticisms suggesting Bush's administration had been defying international protocols by torturing prisoners swept up in the Middle Eastern wars.[16]

Karl Rove studied the landscape and decided that there was only one safe place for Bush to begin his return to private life. Bush would fly to Midland, where there were still dozens of well-connected friends from his rowdy days—from back when he got so loaded he once tried to get onstage with Willie Nelson. It was Laura's hometown, and she was beloved there. The chances of there being protestors, folks angry about how the economy was spiraling down, were virtually nil. The carefully orchestrated touchdown in West Texas was a big success. Almost thirty thousand people gathered to greet him.

Satisfied, Bush then headed to Dallas, where he wanted to see the man he once called his hero, the pitcher Nolan Ryan. Then, in only a matter of days, Bush vanished from the news and disappeared into the cloistered Dallas social scene. No one really knew what he was doing other than mingling with his former partners from the Texas Rangers baseball days, the ones who had opened the golden tent door and allowed him to refashion his public profile.

Newsweek asked me to do a story on what Bush was up to postpresidency. I spoke to a variety of his friends, including Ryan and billionaire Rangers owner Tom Hicks, as well as neighbors around his home in Dallas. "Every time I talk to him or have been around him, he has been very upbeat," said Ryan, who invited Bush to throw out the first pitch at a Rangers season opener. Still, added Ryan, Bush must have begun to think that "you're just another citizen of the United States."[17]

One day Bush made a quick visit to Pershing Elementary in Dallas, close to his home. When he asked children if they knew who he was, they excitedly yelled back, "George Washington." A surprised Bush replied, "George Washington Bush." He tried to explain to the kids that he was, indeed, the former president of the United States.

Meanwhile, Karl Rove was also in Dallas trying to raise money and lay out the plans for Bush's presidential library—it would be the third presidential library in Texas, after the one for LBJ in Austin and the one for Bush's father on the campus of Texas A&M. That latter library/museum featured an apartment on an upper floor where the elder Bushes would sometimes dwell while, below, visitors toured the exhibits and gift shops. In the store, you could buy copies of a memoir "written" by Millie, the Bushes' springer spaniel.

Rove was shaking the financial trees for the "Bush-Cheney Alumni Association," with the goal of preserving the preferred legacy of the latest president from Texas. For a while, its website said, "We were there. And as members of the team, we know the difference between rumor, reality, fact, and fiction. This is our chance to stand up, speak up, and set the record straight."[18] Rove set a fund-raising goal of $300 million and developed a plan to build a library/center at Southern Methodist University. Many people noted that it would be bigger than Bush's father's library at A&M. Bush's family friends contributed generous amounts of money and also formed a sturdy, protective circle around him.

"I know he is working on his book," Hicks told me. "I get the sense that he has the confidence that history will judge him a lot better than the *New York Times*, or the current media, does. I think he feels like he made the best decisions he could make and they weren't all great, but I think he knows so much more."[19]

In 2009, when he was on his surprise visit to little Pershing Elementary in Dallas, a courageous parent approached him under the careful eye of the Secret Service agents. The polite parent wondered if Bush would like to volunteer for the school's annual haunted house carnival.

Bush replied: "I'd make a good ghost."[20]

CHAPTER 15

Total Command: The 2010s

AS BUSH SETTLED INTO PRIVATE LIFE in Texas, new speculation arose about who would be the next politician to emerge from the Bush dynasty. Surely at least one more member of the family was poised for ascension, if not nationally, then at least in Texas. There was already rumbling inside GOP circles that Jeb Bush, the ex-president's younger brother and governor of Florida, would try to run for the Oval Office in 2016. But in Texas, some eyes turned to Jeb's eldest son, George P. Bush.

Born in Houston and a graduate of Rice University and the University of Texas at Austin law school, he was tall, some said charismatic, and deemed an excellent New Age political amalgam by some GOP strategists: his mother was born in Mexico and his father was a Bush. Maybe George P. might appeal to voters in increasingly Latino Texas, as well as the usual evangelical Christian, pro-business, oil-friendly circles that had always been in his family's corner.

He was named by *People* magazine as one of its top eligible bachelors. National reporters flocked to see him, and some of the stories dutifully noted that he had at least one pockmark on his résumé—being arrested, but not charged, for a burglary in Miami when he was eighteen. More than a few profiles brought up a regrettable moment engendered by his grandfather: in 1988, George H. W. Bush, oblivious to the fact that his micro-

Texas Land Commissioner George P. Bush, Republican heir to the Bush pedigree in politics, is the son of Jeb, who served as governor of Florida; his uncle and grandfather were each elected president. He stunned some by becoming an ardent ally of Donald Trump.

phone was on, leaned over to President Ronald Reagan and pointed at George P. and siblings: "That's Jebbie's kids from Florida, the little brown ones."[1]

At the Bush compound in Maine, and at their private retreats in Florida, there was almost always constant talk about the jockeying, the new race, and the new political possibilities. It had been going on for decades, and the Bushes had clearly passed the Kennedys as the nation's longest-running political machine. By the time Bush left Washington in 2009, some political reporters even suggested that one of his daughters would eventually run for office—maybe even in Texas.

The fact that the family was already raising George P. Bush's profile was evident as early as 2003, when he was named the master of ceremonies for his father's gubernatorial swearing-in ceremonies in Florida. George H. W. Bush was studying his grandson very closely, and a thought bumped into his head: "The way he looked, you felt he was in total command.... He likes politics. In my view, this guy will go a long way if he pursues a political path."[2]

For years, George P. lingered on the edges of the political frame, weighing the possibilities, especially in the wake of his uncle's damaged approval ratings. He remained dutifully, continually chronicled by Texas publications wondering when, not if, he was planning to run for office.

And as Rick Perry geared up for a 2010 reelection bid for governor, and with poll numbers suggesting he was going to run away against former Houston mayor Bill White, it seemed finally safe for George P. to go deeper into the waters. He became the Texas Republican Party's deputy finance chairman, and one conservative online publication, *Newsmax*, began taking special interest in him—suggesting he was a key to Republican chances to win over the growing number of Latino voters in the United States.[3]

From a distance, Bush was also a growing admirer of Donald Trump, the New York real estate mogul and investor with deep ties to Florida, where George P. had spent his formative years. By 2014, he decided that he would run for Texas land commissioner. He had no real history of public service or intimate engagement with the General Land Office—the agency tasked with the sale, management, and leasing of millions of acres of state land, as well as overseeing the Alamo.

"I've always had an interest in politics—I can't deny that. I've worked on a variety of campaigns and fought for a variety of conservative causes for a long time," Bush would later say.[4] Very quickly, he began accumulating a multimillion-dollar political war chest.

When Rick Perry decided not to run for a fourth term as governor in 2014, some wondered if the rising Latino population could push a Democrat back into office—and if Republicans had been so wedded to Perry that they hadn't groomed a proper successor. Attorney General Greg Abbott, a native of Wichita Falls and a staunch conservative who had started as a state district judge, emerged as the GOP candidate.

He was paralyzed from the waist down and reliant on a wheelchair after a tree fell on him when he was jogging past a home in Houston. The injury occurred when he was a law school graduate studying for his bar exam. He sued the homeowner, one of the most aggressive divorce attorneys in Texas, and won a judgment estimated at $10 million.[5]

Abbott promised not to veer from the anti-tax, anti-regulation policies that Bush and then Perry had sought as governor. One of Bush's primary concerns as governor had been what he called "tort reform," and Abbott also promised a crackdown on high-dollar civil lawsuits, including ones from trial lawyers seeking big payouts in personal injury cases. Critics, of course, suggested that Abbott was being two-faced, in that he had filed his own massive personal injury lawsuit.

As he prepared for the 2014 race, Abbott described what his days were like as the Texas attorney general: "My job's pretty simple. I go into the office, I sue the federal government, and I go home."[6] By his estimation, he had sued the Barack Obama White House at least twenty-five times since becoming attorney general—challenging the president's so-called Obamacare medical insurance program, filing several lawsuits against Environmental Protection Agency regulations, and rebuffing mandates from the Federal Energy Regulatory Commission.[7]

Some foes wondered if Abbott had squandered a golden opportunity to serve as an advocate for Texans with disabilities. He said he wanted to avoid "public posturing" and that "having known how life was before, you can never get completely comfortable. It's a constant evolutionary process. There's never a magic day."[8]

His opponent, Wendy Davis, was a lawyer and former Fort Worth councilwoman with a steady history of voting as a Republican and even donating money to George W. Bush's presidential campaign. She switched parties, won a Texas Senate seat in 2009, and made a name for herself as someone unafraid to use the power of a filibuster. In 2011, she fought so long against proposed state education budget cuts that a special legislative session had to be called. Two years later, she made national headlines for a history-making moment in Texas politics: a thirteen-hour filibuster in June 2013 aimed at derailing a bill that would make it more difficult for a woman to seek an abortion in Texas.

She was hailed around the nation as a heroine in the right-to-choose movement and as someone who had stood up to the men who held key leadership positions. Her delay tactics succeeded for a bit, and lawmakers had to delay the abortion measure's passage because the legislative session was coming to a close. But another special legislative session was called, and the original measure to restrict abortions passed both chambers.

Three weeks after her stunning filibuster, she announced she was running for governor, and she went on to win almost 80 percent of the vote in the Democratic primary. Her campaign began with a burst of promise but was stalled after reporters suggested that Davis had been offering up some gauzy personal history about her life as a single mother—that she had said she was divorced at the age of nineteen when she was actually twenty-one, that she had been less than clear about how she and her ex-husband shared custody of their children, and that she hadn't explained how her ex-husband had helped pay for her education. Davis charged that the newspaper accounts were trivial, sensationalist, and poor political reporting—the kind that concentrated on small, personal matters rather than the important issues.

"They know they cannot defend their public record, so they're attacking my private life," said Davis. "Greg Abbott and his folks have picked a fight with the wrong Texas gal.... Greg Abbott and his allies have had a stranglehold on power in this state for two decades, and they want to keep it. But now they're hearing all of those voices they shut out and silenced for so long." She added, "You can attack my record. You can challenge my ideas. You can play holier-than-thou with my life story. But I draw the line when it comes to lying about my family." One of Abbott's campaign officials blasted back, saying she "systematically, intentionally, and repeatedly deceived Texans for years about her background, yet she expects voters to indulge her fanciful narrative."[9]

Party insiders around the country were waiting to see if the Texas race would serve as a referendum for future political shifts in the state—and offer some sort of clue to the 2016 presidential race. Democrats clung to the hope that Texas had some reservoir of populism, progressivism, and liberal inclinations—maybe boosted by an influx of newcomers from California, the wild growth of Austin, and a gnawing dissatisfaction with the entrenched Republican presence in the US Senate and every major state office.

If the reservoir was there, it was tiny. Abbott won the race by a margin of close to 59 percent to 39 percent, and with a little more than half of the votes from women. Almost nine out of every ten Black voters in Texas selected Davis, and she also won a majority of Hispanic voters. In his swearing-in address, Abbott said, "Texas has been the blending of cultures from across the globe even before we became our own nation. My wife represents that, as she now has made Texas history as the first Hispanic First Lady in the history of our great state.... Texas is the place where the improbable becomes the possible. Many thought that it was improbable that Texans would overcome total devastation at the Alamo. And yet the unyielding drive for independence that has always filled the hearts of Texans led to victory at the Battle of San Jacinto. And thus began the legend that Texas has become. To this day Texas has been filled with legends who started humbly and succeeded spectacularly."[10]

Sandwiched in his speech, about halfway through his remarks, was a clarion call: "We must do more for the millions of Texans who are tired of seeing our state sovereignty and the rule of law ignored by a federal government that refuses to secure our border ... as governor I will continue my legacy of pushing back against Washington if they spend too much, regulate too much, or violate our state sovereignty. Any government that uses the guise of fairness to rob us of our freedom will get a uniquely Texan response: 'Come and take it' . . . For too long Washington has tried to remake America in its image."[11]

The newly elected Texas land commissioner George P. Bush won 61 percent of the vote in 2014 and made family history by becoming the first Bush to win his first political race. He also found himself fighting a new battle at the Alamo as soon as he took office.

What seemed like an easy and image-burnishing project—his plan to turn the area around the old mission into more of a museum-like, park-like setting—had become a political firestorm. Critics said he was fiddling with the fact that the Alamo always seemed so accessible, so apparent, so in reach of anyone who wanted to visit it. Supporters said he was trying to erase the tawdry, decades-old, retail-and-amusement carnival in the areas around the Alamo, ones that featured a Ripley's Believe It or Not! exhibit and strings of trinket shops hawking coonskin caps. "The circus atmosphere of protesters, 18-wheelers and cement trucks driving through the grounds doesn't give visitors a sense of being somewhere special," Bush said. "Tourists have no idea they're stepping on sacred grounds."[12]

The debate lingered, along with plenty of political gossip that Bush had misfired in thinking that he could promote himself in future elections as the "savior" of the most famous, and infamous, building in the state. When I was a reporter in San Antonio in the 1970s, protesters made occasional attempts to occupy the Alamo, to "reclaim" it in a way that honored its Spanish, Tejano, Native American, and Mexican heritage. The protests were complicated, varied, but often centered on the contention that, for many, the Alamo symbolized a long pattern of subjugation for Latinos and Blacks in Texas; that defining the Alamo as a cradle of liberty was another handed-down version of history that excluded ethnic cleansings, slavery, and fractured treaties.

Another Alamo debate was snaking around Texas: State Board of Education members were exploring the idea of removing the word "heroic" from seventh-grade public school courses that talked about the men who defended the Alamo against Mexican soldiers. And Abbott said that "political correctness" had to end in state schools.[13]

In 2016, Bush began turning his attention to an even thornier issue with true national and international implications. His broad aegis as land commissioner included oversight of the public lands in Texas, including areas hugging the Rio Grande and the Texas-Mexico border—areas looming in the national focus as a presidential candidate named Donald Trump began railing about the people he didn't want coming into the United States from the south. It was entirely fitting and entirely complex in a uniquely Texas way. George P.'s father, Jeb, was running for the presidency against Donald Trump. So was Senator Ted Cruz, who had been elected in 2012 and had become someone to whom George P. Bush, in many ways, owed enormous debts.

Cruz, whose father was from Cuba, had grown up in Houston and attended private schools, before going to Princeton and then Harvard Law School. He developed a reputation as a champion speaker and held a prestigious editorship with the *Harvard Law Review*. He became the first Latino to serve as a clerk to the Chief Justice of the US Supreme Court, and then went into private practice while immersing himself in a variety of conservative causes. Cruz supported the National Rifle Association and aligned himself with attempts to impeach Bill Clinton. Even more than many latter-day Republicans in Texas, Cruz was leaning in a harder right-wing direction—beyond anything any of the Bushes had espoused. Cruz was an uncompromising archconservative, including during his time as a domestic policy advisor on Bush's 2000 presidential campaign.

Groomed and promoted by both Bush and Abbott, Cruz became the first Latino to serve as Texas solicitor general. With deep backing from GOP financial supporters, he won Kay Bailey Hutchison's US Senate seat in 2012 after she stepped down—and became the first Latino senator in Texas history. He was going to Washington as the standard-bearer for some of the most extreme conservative impulses emerging from modern Texas. Sensing that the nation was ready for his brand of right-wing politics, and that groups like the Tea Party were succeeding in promoting hard-core policies, and that the national GOP playing field was wide open, Cruz began crafting his own run for the White House.

As the 2016 presidential race lurched on, George P. watched his father shrivel as he was mocked over and over again on national television by the swaggering Trump, who called him "Low Energy Jeb." He also watched Trump roll over Cruz, who had championed himself as a brilliant orator. Cruz was lambasted by Trump, again and again, as "Lying Ted." And then he watched as Trump simply began to pull away, all while George P. was headed to a personal political crossroads: as the most visible heir to the Bush political dynasty in Texas, he would have to weigh whether to endorse Trump, the "outsider" who ceaselessly ridiculed his father and was also blowing right past a sitting senator from Texas.

And if he backed Trump, George P. would have to do it while Trump was thundering about locking up the border with Mexico—and battling to keep out all those people still chasing their dreams across the Rio Grande. People like George P. Bush's own mother, Columba Garnico Gallo, who was born in the Arperos neighborhood in León, Mexico.

As GOP operatives assessed whether George P. Bush could ever be a viable candidate for governor or the US Senate, there was a lot to consider. Evening news shows were filled with images of immigrant children in detention facilities, separated from their parents. Bodies were found floating in the Rio Grande—one news account showed a dead father with his tiny deceased daughter clinging to his side after a desperate attempt to cross the river.

On one fine spring day toward the end of the decade, my wife and I visited the border area and saw what looked like hundreds of people kneeling alongside an auto parts store outside the city of McAllen. It was another roundup of border crossers, and when we drove into the parking lot, we could see the pleading faces of the detainees and the wary faces of law enforcement. I had been to the exact same area twenty-five years earlier, and I had written a story for the *Dallas Morning News* that was called "Welcome to America" with a subheadline about people being trapped in a "legal massacre."[14]

People who were able to visit detained immigrants and refugees came back with horror stories about the lack of adequate housing, food, and sanitation, and about thousands of people trapped in a legal limbo, scrambling to find the financial and legal means to request asylum. For some, it was like waging war all over again and harking back to the very hallmarks that had created Texas and defined it: that idea of sovereignty, of a state, really a state of mind, unlike any other. And it was one that constantly resisted oversight or regulation except on its own terms.

Despite any misgivings he might have had about what was happening with Mexicans coming to the United States, George P. Bush finally decided to campaign and raise money for Donald Trump. He had studied his uncle in Texas and what had brought him to power. He had studied Rick Perry and what had kept him in office so long. He knew how his grandfather had anticipated the full Republican makeover of Texas and then had ridden that change to the White House. He had to know there really was a persistent political arc in Texas—from the earliest anti-Washington governors to the uncompromising John Nance Garner, from wily John Connally to inflexible John Tower, from George W. Bush to Rick Perry.

"Those are the people I looked up to when I was coming of age politically in Texas," George P. Bush said one day. He was talking specifically about his uncle and his father, but he could have been talking about the men who had carved out the Republican lanes in Texas. He added something else that struck more than a few observers as either unbelievable or painfully poignant.

"Despite carrying the family name, there's nothing written in stone that says I have to run for higher office."[15]

When the field finally cleared in the 2016 presidential race—and when his father had dropped out in an almost humiliating fashion—George P. Bush did what he thought was best. The Texas land commissioner became the first Bush family member to openly advocate for Trump. He sounded defiant: "You know what? You get back up and you help the man that won, and you make sure that we stop Hillary Clinton."[16]

Political reporters raced to summarize it all through the prism of the family's history: "Bush's endorsement was surprising because of the contentious relationship between his father and Trump and because his uncle and grandfather, presidents George W. Bush and George H. W. Bush, haven't endorsed Trump."[17]

Trump won Texas by almost 10 percent and became the tenth straight Republican to secure the state. Democrats parsed the numbers and decided there was a glimmer of hope: when Mitt Romney ran against Obama in 2012, he had won Texas by nearly 16 percentage points. Until the end of the decade, you could still see Trump campaign signs, ones from the 2016 race, hanging on old cedar fence posts not far from where the James and Llano rivers converge—sometimes alongside a Confederate flag.

News from the Texas-Mexico border continued to reverberate around the nation—from stark accounts of drug cartels to the images of fragile-looking families trying desperately to enter the United States. It was as if time had been rolled back, as if the nation was looking at Texas, again, as a place apart. For those who clung fiercely to a view of a noble Texas, one that treasured its independence from Mexico, Washington, and Union forces, it was just more dreaded objectification and intrusion from outsiders. Maybe immigrants were invading. Maybe it was the media trying to capture the place. Trump talked about attempting to corral so-called Dreamers, the children of undocumented immigrants, the ones who lived in fear they'd be rounded up and deported, and it mobilized protests around the state. New political movements and organizations emerged. In the middle of it all, a once relatively unknown congressman decided that he would test the new political awareness in a careful, deliberate way.

The gangly, lanky Beto O'Rourke, who came from a politically influential family, had been an Ivy League–educated punk rock musician before serving on the city council in El Paso. He was omnipresent in the city, willing to give a speech wherever he could, speaking fluent Spanish as he waved his arms and jumped on a table to make his point. He was caffeinated beyond measure, and some people said he parted his hair a bit like Robert F. Kennedy and that he had the same toothy smile. He won a seat in Congress in 2012, was reelected twice, and then decided he could hustle his way into unseating Ted Cruz in the 2018 Senate race.

His quixotic campaign attracted immense national attention, with several stories suggesting that the energized, animated candidate had tapped into big shifts in the voting base of Texas. He lost the race, but it was close enough (Cruz won 50.9 percent to 48.3 percent) for soothsayers to muse that he should go back to El Paso and think about running for governor. Or just skip that step and aim even higher.

San Antonio, more than any city in Texas, is where cultures have collided, coexisted, and compromised since the 1700s; where the Texas legends, at the Alamo and the other missions, often ran the deepest. The identical twin Castro brothers, Joaquín and Julián, were raised in the city, and it was where their father was a public school math teacher and their mother was a neighborhood activist who had worked with La Raza Unida. The Castro brothers had legitimate claim to understanding the ebb and flow of the Texas-Mexico border at a deep, personal level: their grandmother was born in the Mexican border state of Coahuila. In the wake of the Mexican Revolution, she had aimed for Texas in the 1920s.

The Castro boys both attended Stanford and then Harvard Law School, and then worked for the same powerhouse firm of Akin Gump Strauss Hauer & Feld. In 2001, Julián became the youngest member of the San Antonio City Council, at the age of twenty-six. Eight years later, he was mayor. He rocketed to national prominence after President

San Antonio's Joaquín Castro (left) and identical twin brother Julián sit in the Texas House chamber on opening day of the 80th Texas Legislature. Joaquín Castro served five terms in the Texas House before being elected to the US House. Julián won election as mayor of San Antonio and served as US secretary of housing and urban development before unsuccessfully bidding for president.

Barack Obama named him secretary of housing and urban development in 2014—the same position that the once-promising San Antonio mayor Henry Cisneros had held in the Clinton administration. It was, for political wonks in Texas, like fateful theater: another Latino mayor from San Antonio, someone with ties to the city's West Side, someone with an Ivy League pedigree, was in the president's cabinet. And it was clear that the newest HUD secretary was also being groomed for bigger races, maybe in Texas, maybe nationally.

For a few pining Democrats with longer memories, it felt like the days when liberal, populist, and progressive possibilities seemed at hand. Julián's brother Joaquín had secured a seat in the Texas House in 2003 and then gone to Congress in 2013, after crushing his GOP opponent by 30 points. Like his brother, he struck strategists as walking, talking gold. In Austin, wistful Democratic strategists began to talk about how the liberal legacy of Ann Richards, Jim Hightower, Sissy Farenthold, and Ralph Yarborough was dusting itself off—how there had to be a silent majority of pissed-off voters who wanted to ditch the Republicans.

Former US representative Beto O'Rourke, D-El Paso, kicks off his ultimately stunted presidential campaign at a night rally on Congress Avenue south of the Texas Capitol. O'Rourke, fresh off an unexpectedly strong though failed challenge to Republican senator Ted Cruz of Houston, was initially in the top tier of a crowded field of Democrats seeking to deny Republican president Donald Trump a second term.

Back in El Paso, O'Rourke was often not sure exactly what to believe. He was receiving more and more calls from Democratic power brokers around the country. It seemed utterly unlikely at times, but he listened as several began urging him to explore a run for the presidency. The strategists in Austin told their colleagues in Washington that no one had ever campaigned harder than O'Rourke—that during the Senate race against Cruz, he was leaping on chairs in small-town diners all over Texas, giving a rousing, maybe rambling speech, and then hurtling to the next county and city. He was still fresh-faced and could speak Spanish to anyone, and word had circulated that big-time news outlets would love to feature him.

O'Rourke finally decided to roll out his presidential race by agreeing to a splashy story in *Vanity Fair*. The magazine featured a big cover photo of O'Rourke posing with his dog and the words "I want to be in it. Man, I'm just born to be in it."[18]

Somewhere, the late Texas mastermind Bob Bullock was shaking his head. Maybe Cactus Jack Garner was, too. O'Rourke had spent months working triple overtime selling himself as a friend of the ordinary man, the working people, and probably millions who couldn't dream of accessing the glossy people and things featured in *Vanity Fair*. Now it was as if he was being anointed by the luxe, liberal tastemakers. Almost immediately after the story appeared, O'Rourke began to regret it, especially when more and more people said it wasn't just pretentious, it was beyond presumptive—and, worse, a signal that the "elites" had handpicked him.

Bullock might have told him it was the same fatal mistake that Ann Richards had once made. You could almost hear the scary Bullock cackling from wherever he went in the afterlife, saying nothing good would ever come from straying too far from the dust of hardscrabble Texas.

That same year, Julián Castro stood at a podium in Plaza Guadalupe, not far from the home where he had grown up in San Antonio. A mariachi band played. Someone was offering hastily made T-shirts that read, "Julián Castro 2020. One Nation. One Destiny." His mother was looking on, as was his twin brother, who was acting as his campaign chairman.

Telephone poles had flyers and posters glued to them, like something out of the old days when people were being alerted to the fact that Pappy O'Daniel would be bursting into town with promises of a new political tomorrow in his beautiful Texas. It felt like a celebration, almost a full-on party, and parents chased their kids as they tried to grab a balloon.

The West Side of San Antonio had always been among the most resilient neighborhoods in Texas, even when it was horribly neglected and overlooked by generations of city and state leaders. There was a cultural glue unlike in many places, one that kept so many elements bonded: the Catholic churches, the cemeteries that seemed to glow year-round with plastic flowers, the conjunto bands playing at Lerma's nightclub, and even the little icehouses—the small joints where people gathered to hear music, have a cool beverage, and wonder when change was coming.

The crowd cheered as Castro stepped to the microphone. This was the same plaza Pope John Paul II had visited almost twenty years earlier: a visit that people still talked about. It was where so many Texas politicians had come for blessings, prayers, and votes. Castro's beaming mother watched closely as her handsome son stared out over the crowd of people packing the plaza and the surrounding streets.

"When my grandmother got here almost a hundred years ago, I'm sure she never could have imagined that just two generations later, one of her grandsons would be serving as a member of the United States Congress and the other would be standing with you here today to say these words: I am a candidate for president of the United States of America," Castro said, his words echoing around the plaza.[19]

Within a year, his dream was over. He and O'Rourke were both bowing out of the presidential race. They were out of money and out of national support, and they retreated to Texas to think about why some Lone Star candidates, like the Bushes, can manage to translate nationally and others cannot. Doubters began saying they should have concentrated on first winning the governor's seat, or maybe trying for the Senate again. As always in Texas, it was still a jumble of ambitions, choices, and questions.

How would the White House, and who was in it, figure into any bid for high office in Texas? What did the unpredictable swirls around the resolute Rio Grande mean for anyone who ran for office in Texas? What would the oil billionaires want, and whom would they fund? What were white voters in Amarillo and the suburbs outside Dallas thinking? What were Black voters weighing in Palestine and the Third Ward of Houston? What were Latino voters in West Dallas and San Benito going to do?

And what if there were some wickedly catastrophic moments coming to Texas—some unforeseen convulsions that were so sweeping they could change politics like never before?

Epilogue

NEAR A SMALL TOWN WHERE I SPEND a lot of time writing, I grandiosely thought I had a kind of vantage point into several layers of Texas history. I had lived in Abilene, San Antonio, Houston, Dallas, and Austin. And now I wasn't far from where the Comanche had passed through; where white immigrants arrived to take their place; where people cracked open iron mines and later laid down oil pipelines; where acres were cleared for farms and ranches; where railroad tracks came to the frontier; and where there were slaves and segregated schools. It's where some of the last battles in Texas with the Native Americans were fought. It's where so many Texas values conspired and collided: Manifest Destiny, the old West, the ethnic cleansings, the exceptionalism, the individualism, the expansion, and the importation of men in chains.

It was also where that conquering of the land took place—and was still occurring. Into the twenty-first century, a lot of Texas was continuing to be defined by the act of extracting what you can: water, cotton, cedar, and oil. Into the 2020s, it was also the very bedrock of Texas being uplifted. Arguably, the very ground that Texas stood on: sand, millions of tons of eroded rock and silica, was being mined, scooped, and dredged from hills, quarries, creeks, and even the once-wild Llano River, where the Comanche hunted, fished, and worshiped. All across the state, huge trucks were rumbling down country lanes and superhighways, packed to the brim with sand, and delivering it to companies that used it as part of the oil fracking process, or that used it to pour the concrete at the rising skyscrapers in Austin, Dallas, and Houston.

A few people raised a fuss, but it was the newest billion-dollar gold rush in Texas, and it seemed like nothing, really, was going to stop the armies of bulldozers and cement mixers taking up both sides of the narrow two-lane county roads. Every day, mountains of eroded Texas, born from the oldest rocks on planet Earth, were being loaded up and carried away. Investors called it the "new oil." The Spanish had come centuries ago looking for silver. The Comanche came for the buffalo—and to exert their dominance on competing natives. The Mexicans came for land they assumed was rightfully theirs. The Anglos came to make a living and maybe a fortune.

Getting the sand from the rivers and creeks, or from the lands spilling out from Packsaddle Mountain, was going to be a bruising business, a hard-earned and even dangerous enterprise. It would mean fighting the elements, fighting regulations, fighting to control the land. All those things that had been going on in Texas since human beings arrived.

John Nance Garner, the Cactus Jack godfather of all modern Texas politics, once said that playing politics meant that you'd have to bloody your knuckles. He surely knew that there would be new things and even new people to conquer in Texas; that there would always be outside regulations to buck; that there would be polarizing moments along the southern border; and that Texas would always have that notion of being a state like no other.

Beginning in the twenty-first century, some school buildings named after rebel leaders or slavemasters had their names changed; some memorials to Confederate leaders were removed from cities and campuses. The giant monument to Robert E. Lee in Dallas was taken down—and sold for almost $1.5 million to a Texas lawyer. It was moved to a golf course, along the Texas-Mexico border, owned by a Dallas billionaire and oil pipeline operator. In Fort Worth, there was still a long-running debate: what to do with the last dedicated KKK meeting hall in the nation, a place built to seat four thousand men. A weary Texas jury awarded a young Black girl $68,000 after she accused three white classmates of wrapping a rope around her neck and dragging her to the ground.

In 2020, a virus came to Texas, and the state, like the rest of the world, felt under attack. It was the ultimate uncertainty, and one that Texas political leaders couldn't conquer as quickly as they had so many other things. Through the year, the enduring political soul of Texas was revealed in stark, naked fashion: the governor and lieutenant governor insisted that Texas was going to escape the fate of Northern states that had been overwhelmed by the virus. They added that Texans would never be forced to follow all the federal guidelines about how best to fight the virus.

Republican state leaders began to battle local Democratic leaders who wanted to mandate the wearing of masks to prevent the spread of the virus. The lieutenant governor went on national television and said, in essence, that he was willing to die to reopen the economy in Texas if it was shut down as a defense against the virus. Governor Greg Abbott initially refused to issue a statewide order telling Texans to stay at home and slow the spread of the virus. Several mayors and county leaders were livid and began trying to control the virus on their own, through curfews and local orders for people to shelter in place. Willie Nelson seemed right: there didn't seem to be anyone in control in Texas.

A salon owner in Dallas was sent to jail for opening her business in defiance of local lockdown orders. Senator Ted Cruz, Abbott, and others quickly took her side, saying that the woman was being regulated to death—just the way Washington had always treated Texans.

But as the virus snaked into the state, Abbott finally relented and issued what he knew would be a short, temporary, stay-at-home order. He decided to remove it twenty-eight days later. It was one of the shortest stay-at-home orders in the nation. He announced that his temporary order "had done its job," that he was going to let it expire, and that he would permit businesses to reopen everywhere in the state.

"We are Texans. We got this," Abbott declared triumphantly.[1]

In weeks, as bars, restaurants, and businesses reopened, the number of confirmed cases of coronavirus, hospitalizations, and even deaths began to rise. The escalation was breathtaking, from Houston into far West Texas, from meat-packing plants in West Texas to retirement communities along the Highland Lakes. Each day the state began to break records for diagnosed cases of the deadly virus. By the summer, Texas was making international news as an epicenter for the pandemic. For many, it was utterly symbolic: Texas had rebuffed federal guidelines. It had chosen its own destiny during one of the greatest domestic crises in national history.

And then, that same summer, Texas was forced to face its history of deep-rooted racism—how people of color have been treated since the days when slaves were put to work in Freestone County, Dallas County, and Travis County, and since the latter-day lynchings in downtown Waco and the modern-day lynching in Jasper. The death of a Houston man, George Floyd, in Minneapolis ignited a profound nationwide awareness and demand for change. In Texas, there were mass gatherings and protests, sparking fears that the virus would spread further in these large groups.

Dallas raced to dismantle its looming Confederate monument in Pioneer Park, the largest public memorial in the city. Workers in Beaumont spent hours taking down a five-ton obelisk and towering statue honoring Confederate soldiers that had stood for 108 years. One worker said that he was amazed the massive monument had survived all the battering storms over the last century. At Love Field in Dallas, a statue dedicated to the Texas Rangers was removed. The sculpture had been on prominent display for decades and was modeled after the heavily armed Texas lawman that had once enforced segregation in public schools in the 1950s—at the direct order of the governor.

In Llano, county sheriffs said they had received "suspicious inquiries" from a caller in Austin about the Confederate monument at the courthouse. One local leader said that local law enforcement was on alert, as were the game wardens and state police. That leader added that one hundred men from the area had fought in the Civil War, and that at least one still had descendants in the area.

President Trump announced that he would fight to prevent the renaming of military bases, including Fort Hood in Texas (named after Confederate General John Bell Hood). His ally, George P. Bush, still dreaming of following his father and uncle into higher office, thought he had his finger on the pulse of Texas and said "President Trump is the only thing standing between America and socialism."[2]

Meanwhile, even more Black Lives Matter protests and marches were uncorking in Houston, Dallas, Austin, Tyler, Midland, Mason, Edinburg, San Marcos, and even tiny Vidor—where the KKK had a long, entrenched history. (Into the early 1990s, I had a Rolodex filled with phone numbers, sources and contacts. Under the letter "K" I had the name and number for the easy-to-reach state Klan leader living in Vidor.) Around Texas, there was quick, collective soul-searching. Speeches were made, promises were offered by state and local leaders, and there was even a call to end the singing of the "Eyes of Texas" song—a staple of the University of Texas, even though some had complained, for years, that it had racist overtones.

But now, some people said, surely there would be greater inclusion.

Perhaps more monuments to slave owners would come down. The political calculus had to change. *Wouldn't the virus and the social upheavals lead Texas to a long-overdue self-examination? Wouldn't Texas leaders drill down and recognize that states' rights and race informed politics in the Lone Star State from the minute it was formed?*

Skeptics said that this wasn't the first spasmodic reckoning with the past and that Texas would never entirely deconstruct its inherited mythology. It could never start completely afresh and build a new autobiography, because there were too many things that were as deep-rooted and unforgivingly hard as the billion-year-old llanite rocks mined off of Highway 16 near the ghost town of Baby Head.

The indigenous people had been conquered. The enslaved and conscripted people had built the state. It was one thing to issue proclamations, express regret, rename streets, remove statues, even change the courses taught in the public schools—*but what would be the true compensation for the way history and politics was enforced?*

Then, of course, 2020 shuddered to a close with the virus swirling—and with proof that Texas was firmly Republican. Trump won the state, and flags bearing his name remained defiantly on display on narrow country lanes for weeks after Election Day. Sometimes, just below the Trump banners, there was another flag with a single star, a cannon, and the words "Come and Take It"—a nod to the revolution that gave birth to the nation of Texas.

All over the state, pollsters and strategists gathered hastily on teleconference calls to sift through the election returns. Once-optimistic Democrats and progressives talked glumly about the fact that not only had Trump again secured miles and miles of rural Texas, but he also had enjoyed a surge of support among Latino voters along the Mexican border that very few political professionals had predicted. At home in Houston, Ted Cruz weighed how much he would profit on the national stage by backing Trump and the claims that the presidential election was stolen. In Austin, George P. Bush was at peace with his decision to cast his lot with the man who had once publicly besmirched his father. By the end of 2020, insiders were saying it was only a matter of time before Bush tried to run for higher office in a state that supported Trump.

One thing was clear: the Lone Star nation had firmly reminded the rest of the country where many of its citizens stood. Where many of them had always stood: it wasn't a long leap back to the days immediately after the Civil War, when rock-ribbed conservatives seized control and built a bulwark against the progressives, the liberals, and almost anyone else they saw coming from beyond the Red River and the Sabine. Maybe, some said, Texas truly was tied more than ever to the myths and realities of 150 years ago.

Willie Nelson, for one, could have seen them all from his tireless tour bus, but he had retreated to his secluded Hill Country lair. He had lived long enough to hear the tales about the great Galveston hurricane of 1900. He certainly knew about the way a hidden place prophetically called Texas City was almost erased one day in an apocalyptic explosion. He had seen aching tragedies of other kinds: floods that turned placid bodies of water like Bear Creek into roaring beasts; thousands of family farms, like the ones he knew growing up, just withering away. Maybe it had all hardened his views of whatever or whoever was inside the Texas political wheelhouse. Maybe all the bittersweet dreams he sang or heard about as he roamed to yet another low-ceilinged honky-tonk had made him perpetually on guard. Maybe the shimmering heat waves in Galveston, the smothering dust storms in Abilene, the dark blizzards on the prairies near Lubbock—and the lynchings in Waco and Jasper—had left him convinced that it was always going to be a bloody-knuckle world in Texas. He certainly knew that changing political hearts and minds was not easy—and that some things might be doomed to be repeated.

Nelson once wrote a song about the rinse-and-repeat nature of politics and the way fresh promises can fade away when they crash into unrelenting, unforgiving realities: "Delete and fast-forward, my son / The elections are over and nobody won / You think it's all endin' but it's just settin' in."[3]

Acknowledgments

THIS BOOK WOULD NOT HAVE BEEN possible without the wisdom, patience, and support offered by so many people.

Several very talented editors are to be singled out:

Robert Devens deserves special praise for shepherding the work along, offering brilliant advice on ways to view Texas and bring its political history to the page, and being a bastion of good cheer. I have been very lucky, indeed, to work with him.

David Hamrick is saluted for his soaring vision for the grand Texas Bookshelf Series and this work's role in it. I'm beyond grateful he entrusted this idea to me.

The University of Texas Press team has always been among the best in the world of publishing, and numerous colleagues of Robert and David are to be thanked:

The masterful manuscript editor Lynne Ferguson made this book a reality. Enormously intelligent, thoughtful, and supportive, she has saintly wisdom and patience. Nancy Warrington, a brilliant copyeditor, fact-checker, and researcher, rescued this work innumerable times. She is the ultimate editorial lifeguard. Sarah McGavick was both expert and thoughtful. Appreciation and respect to Melissa McGee Tullos for her expert burnishing of the work. And a special thank you to Cassandra Cisneros, Joel Pinckney, Sandra Spicher, and Victoria Millner for their creative and wonderful skills.

Several researchers, reporters, and fact-checkers provided invaluable help:

Katie Lundstrom brought her fierce Midwestern intelligence, a bounty of critical thinking, and a clear-eyed view of the important figures and moments from the past. Kaulie Lewis, who grew up in West Texas, offered a keen knowledge of history, key editorial suggestions, and a thoughtful analysis of how the state has been portrayed. John Savage provided his extraordinary insights, unearthed forgotten moments in time, and served as a wonderful sounding board for how Texas has changed—or not changed. T. Putnam Hill did a deep dive to identify important issues, events, and people at vital historical crossroads. Scott Squires brought his sharp reporting, fact-checking, and editing skills—and worked round the clock. W. Gardner Selby, a good friend and one of the finest political journalists to ever work in Texas, graciously agreed to review the manuscript; offer suggestions and editing; and work diligently to locate dozens of photographs, images, and illustrations of the most important figures in Texas history.

A debt of gratitude to Ashley Mastervich, Wesley Scarborough, Heather Leighton, and Jennifer Murphy for their hard work and sleuthing during some of the earliest stages of this book.

Innumerable writers and historians have done extraordinary work wrestling Texas onto the page. They have created thousands of essential articles, books, and dissertations—and this book would not exist if not for the groundbreaking and passionate work done by them. Many of their names and works are included in the notes for this book.

A nod, too, goes to the unsung chroniclers from defunct periodicals and publications that captured fleeting moments of history: There is a cliché that journalism serves as the first draft of history, but in many instances in Texas, it was the *only* draft of history. There are essential "alternative" histories and accounts to be found in older and smaller publications that served very particular audiences in Texas.

Thank you to the many institutions, organizations, and entities that house important research, especially the Dolph Briscoe Center for American History at the University of Texas at Austin, the Texas State Historical Association, the Texas State Library and Archives Commission, the Texas Historical Commission, the Portal to Texas History, the Texas Digital Newspaper Program, the Houston Metropolitan Research Center, the Dallas Public Library, and the San Antonio Central Library.

Appreciation goes to colleagues from the University of Texas at Austin: the late Lorraine Branham, the former director of the School of Journalism; Glenn Frankel, the former director of the School of Journalism; R. B. Brenner, the former director of the School of Journalism; and Roderick Hart, the former dean of the Moody College of Communication. Special nods to professors Dennis Darling, Nancy Schiesari, Kevin Robbins, and Gene Burd.

Thank you to my colleagues in the Texas Institute of Letters (TIL), including Stephen Harrigan, who was gracious enough to let me read his masterwork of Texas history, *Big Wonderful Thing*, well before it was published.

One late colleague from the TIL, Bob Compton, is thanked for his enduring friendship and help. Bob was a spirit guide for many writers around the nation, and he was a gracious and exceedingly generous person, a fine editor, and a lover of books. A great Texan, he passed away while this work was in progress.

Thank you to Steven L. Davis and his wonderful family for years of camaraderie, cowriting, and adventures. I've been lucky to work with Mr. Davis on two books of history, to benefit from his brilliant writing and research, and to observe his extraordinary efforts during his time as president of the Texas Institute of Letters. Steve long ago recognized and prized diversity, and he has worked mightily to make the state a more inclusive place.

Thanks to my "brother," the late, incomparable Louie Canelakes (and his wife, Bette; his children, Jake, Nicole, and Elizabeth; and his brother, Chris). Mr. Canelakes knew more about Texas than anyone I have ever encountered. In fact, he knew more about anything than anyone I've ever met. He told me once that I was the friend he had waited for his entire life; it was the same thing I thought about him. He was a genius, a prescient saint. His mother, Alex Canelakes, is an equally wise, wonderful, and warm person. His father, James Canelakes, was an extraordinary man.

Thanks to one of the finest writers and thinkers I was fortunate to work with: The late Anne Lang was big-hearted, gracious in the face of personal setbacks, and a consummate reporter and researcher. She was able to draw stories from people in the most empathetic way imaginable. Thanks to an unheralded figure who spent many years accumulating the hidden history of Black Texas: the late Chuck Nevitt. His groundbreaking work, including poring over the defunct *Dallas Express*, inspired me to take a look at the state in different ways.

Thanks to W. Michael Smith, a wonderful writer, researcher, and historian who understands Texas in deep, important ways. I was lucky to profit from his expertise and political insights (Mike has been instrumental in the careers of many luminaries from Texas, including Dan Rather and Molly Ivins—he contributed to their work on state and national politics).

Much appreciation to these writers, reporters, historians, editors, and friends for their help, inspiration: Tina Brown, Sir Harold Evans, Ed Timms, Jacob Payne, Jon Karp, Ryan Sachetta, Oscar Garza, Mike Geffner, Rene Alegria, Kathy Giles, John Wilburn, Mike Maza, Waltrina Stovall, Jan Jarboe, Garcia Milburn, Laura Jacobus, Alan Berg, Rachel Kambury, Jordan Smith, Laura Castro, Brad Tyer, Mike Nahrstedt, Bill Crawford, Dick Tarpley, Gary Morton, Gerald Ewing, Gabino Iglesias, Corliss Hudson, David Kent, Roger Downing, Ron White, Ben Tavera King, Claude Stanush, Michele Stanush, Michelle Smith, Alison Doerner, Steve Euckert, Anne Clevenger, J.B. Hazlett, Lauren Christensen, Jay Root, John Moritz, Jake Dyer, Joe Holley, Laura Tolley, Andy East, Gemma Kennedy, Earnest Davis, John Goodspeed, John Van Beekum, Cary Clack, Brother Leonard Monteleone, Ainslee Embree, Barbara Stoler Miller, Kevin McGowan, Jack Shea, Melissa Houtte, Ellen Kampinsky, Ed Leal, Randy Eli Grothe, Christie Grothe, Rob Tomsho, Lesley Becker, David Leeson, Scotty Ferris, R. L. Griffin, Dinh Phuong, John Hunter, Bill Lodge, Anita Creamer, Beth Nissen, Richard T. Baker, Claudia Feldman, Mike Snyder, Barbara Karkabi, Robert Seale, David Leeson, Earlie Hudnall, Charlie Kilpatrick, Jim Dolan, Steve Levin, Jeff Franks, Shannon Richardson Colletti, Michael Haederle, Wendy Grossman, Tiffany McGee, Darla Atlas, Alison Peck, Kelly Roberts, Chris Coats, Bob Stewart, Kristin Kelch, Moira Bailey, Mindy Marquez, Gabriele Cosgriff, Shermakaye Bass, Steve Barnes, Tim Rogers, Jim Donovan, Robert Seale, Becky Chavarria, John Branch, Buster Haas, Hans-Martin Liebing, Alan Peppard, Bob Hille, John Rawlings, Alberto "Nino Fidencio" Salinas, Ed Leal, Bob Bersano, Ira Hadnot, Elizabeth Franklin, Betty Ewing, R.G. Ratcliffe, Beverly Harris, Harriet Blake, Christine Wicker, Diane Jennings, Marty Primeau, Ross Ramsey, Patrick Beach, Brad Buchholz, Dan Rather, Katie Couric, Brooke Baldwin, Chris Matthews, Mike Roccaforte, Malcolm Walls, John Sinclair, Linda Jones, Bobby "Blue" Bland, David Alvarez, Sister Patricia Ridgley, Donald Payton, Emerson Emory, Will Weisser, Jim Vertuno, Buzz Bissinger, Mario Puzo, Joe Armstrong, Bob Wallace, Douglas Brinkley, James Lee Burke, Gail Sheehy, and David Maraniss.

Thanks to Augustus Maximus and his brother Perseus for their boundless enthusiasm, loyalty, and eternal connection to the things that matter in Texas and beyond.

Thank you to Linda Smeltzer, Martha Williams, and Tom Sheehy. Love to my Minutaglio family in Naples and Rome. Love to Alfred and Mae Minutaglio, my late godparents. And to my late aunts and uncles, Julietta, Antoinetta, Eleanora, and Santo. Love to my brother Robert, and to my late brothers John, Frank, and Tom. Love to my late parents: my mother, Tessie Grilletti Minutaglio, a kind, intelligent, and hardworking saint, and my father, Francesco Xavier Minutaglio, who spent his formative years in Italy, was educated there, and then became a master printer in the United States. (We had a Heidelberg printing press in the basement of our small home, and I like to think I inherited a drop of the ink in his veins.)

My deep love to the true treasures of my life—my extraordinary wife, Holly Williams, and our beautiful, talented children, Rose Angelina Theresa Minutaglio and Nicholas Xavier Minutaglio.

Notes

Prologue

1. "Ten Questions for Willie Nelson," *Time*, May 24, 2010, http://content.time
.com/time/magazine/article/0,9171,1989127,00.html.

2. *Laws of the Republic of Texas, in Two Volumes, printed by order of the secretary of state* (Houston, TX: Telegraph, 1838).

3. Transcription, errors in original preserved, from *Constitution of the Republic of Texas (1836)*, in *Texas Constitutions 1824–1876*, Tarlton Law Library, Jamail Center for Legal Research, https://tarltonapps.law.utexas.edu/constitutions/texas 1836/general_provisions.

4. Bill Minutaglio and Steven L. Davis, *Dallas 1963* (New York: Twelve, 2013), p. 132.

5. Mark McKinnon, "If Washington Wants to Balance Its Books, Congress Could Learn Something from Texas," *Daily Beast*, January 25, 2013, https://www
.thedailybeast.com/if-washington-wants-to-balance-its-books-congress-could
-learn-something-from-texas.

6. This quote comes from Mark Twain, *Pudd'nhead Wilson and Other Tales* (1894).

7. Kristin Gravatt, "Willie," *Y'all: The Magazine of Southern People*, July/August 2005.

Chapter 1: Remain Quietly: The 1870s

1. Gary Cartwright, "Remains of the Day," *Texas Monthly*, May 2008.

2. Henry Louis Gates Jr., "What Is Juneteenth?" http://www.pbs.org/wnet
/africanamericans-many-rivers-to-cross/history/what-is-juneteenth/.

3. "From Texas; Important Orders by General Granger," *New York Times*, July 7, 1865.

4. Charles W. Ramsdell, "Texas from the Fall of the Confederacy to the Beginning of Reconstruction," *Quarterly of the Texas State Historical Association* 11, no. 3 (January 1908): 215.

5. Joyce King, "How Juneteenth Turned Texas' Shameful Slave Legacy into an International Celebration of Freedom," *Dallas Morning News*, June 14, 2018.

6. Carl H. Moneyhon, *Edmund J. Davis of Texas*, Texas Biography Series, Number 2 (Fort Worth: TCU Press, 2010), 113.

7. Scott Stabler, "Free Men Come to Houston: Blacks during Reconstruction," *Houston Review* (now *Houston History Magazine*) 3, no. 1 (Fall 2005): 41–42.

8. Records of Richard Hubbard, Texas Office of the Governor, Archives and Information Services Division, Texas State Library and Archives Commission, Telegrams on Trouble at Sandy Point, July–August, 1877. (This particular telegram was received July 14, 1877.)

9. Thomas W. Cutrer. "Lambert, Will," in *Handbook of Texas Online*, Texas State Historical Association, http://www.tshaonline.org/handbook/online/articles/fla18.

10. Frank X. Tolbert, "When Texas Was a 'Republican' State," *D Magazine*, October 1975, https://www.dmagazine.com/publications/d-magazine/1975/october/when-texas-was-a-republican-state/.

11. Ibid.

12. Edmund Davis, inaugural address of April 28, 1870, Legislative Reference Library of Texas, https://lrl.texas.gov/scanned/govdocs/Edmund%20J%20Davis/1870/IA_Davis_4.28.1870.pdf.

13. Ibid.

14. Joe E. Ericson and Ernest Wallace, "Constitution of 1876," in *Handbook of Texas Online*, Texas State Historical Association, https://tshaonline.org/handbook/online/articles/mhc07.

15. "Census and Census Records," in *Handbook of Texas Online*, Texas State Historical Association, https://tshaonline.org/handbook/online/articles/ulc01.

16. "Texas Almanac," Texas State Historical Association, Texasalmanac.com.

17. John Wesley Hardin, *The Life of John Wesley Hardin as Written by Himself* (Norman: University of Oklahoma Press, 1961), 61–62.

18. Carl H. Moneyhon, "Reconstruction," in *Handbook of Texas Online*, Texas State Historical Association, https://tshaonline.org/handbook/online/articles/mzr01.

19. R. G. Ratcliffe, "Texas versus the Feds," *Texas Monthly*, January 20, 2017, *Burka Blog*, https://www.texasmonthly.com/burka-blog/texas-versus-feds/.

20. Ibid.

21. Moneyhon, *Edmund J. Davis of Texas*, 223.

22. Cartwright, "Remains of the Day."

23. Convention of Colored Citizens in Texas, Brenham, TX, 1873, Colored Conventions.org, and http://coloredconventions.org/items/show/548, accessed December 17, 2018.

24. Douglas Hales, *A Southern Family in White and Black: The Cuneys of Texas* (College Station: Texas A&M University Press, 2002), 90–100.

25. Ibid., 48.

26. Maud Cuney Hare, *Norris Wright Cuney: A Tribune of the Black People* (New York: Ceisis, 1913). This work is a good, general look at Cuney's life and career.

27. "Southern Negro Progress," *New York Times*, August 13, 1893.

28. Hales, *A Southern Family in White and Black*, 96.

29. Ibid., 55–56.

30. "Messages of Gov. Coke," *Collections of the Archive and History Department of the Texas State Library: Executive Series, Governors' Messages, Coke to Ross, 1874–1891* (Austin: Archive and History Department of the Texas State Library, 1916), viii.

31. "Inaugural Address of Governor Coke," in ibid., https://lrl.texas.gov/scanned/govdocs/Richard Coke/1874/IA_Coke_1.15.1874.pdf.

32. Ibid.

33. Dede Weldon Casad, "The Lives and Legacies of Two Texas Governors, Richard Coke and Lawrence Sullivan Ross. Two Governors: A Comparative Study" (PhD diss., University of Texas at Dallas, 2001).

34. Moneyhon, *Edmund J. Davis of Texas*, 223.

Chapter 2: Our Defective Plan: The 1880s

1. Reginald Moore, cited in Megan Gannon, "Century-Old Burials of 95 Convict Slaves Uncovered in Texas," *Live Science*, July 20, 2018, https://amp.livescience.com/63115-convict-laborer-graves-texas.html.

2. Bobby Blanchard, "Texas Has More Than 180 Public Symbols of the Confederacy, with Dozens of Monuments Dedicated after the Civil Rights Era," *Texas Tribune*, August 21, 2017, https://www.texastribune.org/2017/08/21/texas-has-second-most-public-symbols-confederacy-nation/.

3. "From Salem Square to Dealey Plaza to Belo Garden," North Carolina Collection, Forsyth County Public Library, https://northcarolinaroom.wordpress.com/2016/07/15/from-salem-square-to-dealey-plaza-to-belo-garden/.

4. For background on Roberts and his policies, one can consult: Oran Milo Roberts, "Inaugural Address," *Journal of the House of Representatives*, 1st sess., 16th Legislature, January 14, 1879.

5. Oran Milo Roberts, *Our Federal Relations from a Southern View of Them* (Austin, TX: Eugene von Boeckmann, 1892), 128.

6. Ibid., 128–129.

7. Marjory Harper, "Emigrant Strikebreakers: Scottish Granite Cutters and the Texas Capitol Boycott," *Southwestern Historical Quarterly* 95, no. 4 (April 1992): 465–487.

8. "Race War in Texas," *New York Times*, August 18, 1889.

9. "Revised Civil Statutes of the State of Texas," February 21, 1879, 410.

10. *Proceedings of the State Convention of Colored Men of Texas*, Held at the City of Austin, July 10–12, 1883, http://coloredconventions.org/items/show/1128, 15.

11. Hales, *A Southern Family in White and Black*, 34.

12. John Henninger Reagan, "The Fort Warren Letter," *Sons of Confederate Veterans*, http://scv.nyc/the-fort-warren-letter.

13. Richard Heyman, "Mythology Around Confederate John Reagan Gives Incomplete Picture," *Austin American-Statesman*, August 29, 2016.

Chapter 3: Elites and Aliens: The 1890s

1. *The Facts in the Case of the Horrible Murder of Little Myrtle Vance and Its Fearful Expiation at Paris, Texas, February 1st, 1893, with Photographic Illustrations* (Paris, TX: P. L. James, 1893), http://lcweb2.loc.gov/service/gdc/scd0001/20 09/20090812121fa/20090812121fa.pdf.

2. "Another Negro Burned," *New York Times*, February 2, 1893.

3. Ida B. Wells, 1895 pamphlet entitled The Red Record: Tabulated Statistics and Alleged Causes of Lynching in the United States, chapter 3. Reprinted in Southern Horrors and Other Writings: The Anti-Lynching Campaign of Ida B. Wells, 1892–1900, ed. Jacqueline Jones Royster (Boston: Bedford Books, 1997).

4. Robert McNamara, "1893 Lynching by Fire of Henry Smith," August 13, 2017, ThoughtCo.com, https://www.thoughtco.com/1893-lynching-of-henry-sm ith-4082215.

5. James Stephen Hogg, "Message of Governor to the Twenty-Third Legislature on the Subject of Lynch Law," in *Speeches and State Papers of James Stephen Hogg, Ex-Governor of Texas* (Austin, TX: State Printing Company, 1905), 244.

6. "Alien Land Law," in *Handbook of Texas Online*, Texas State Historical Association, https://tshaonline.org/handbook/online/articles/mla01.

7. Donna A. Barnes, "People's Party," in *Handbook of Texas Online*, Texas State Historical Association, https://tshaonline.org/handbook/online/articles/wap01.

8. Charles Allred Cannon, "The Ideology of Texas Populism, 1886–1894" (Master's thesis, Rice University, 1968).

9. Ibid.

10. Ruth Hosey Karbach, "Ellen Lawson Dabbs," in *Texas Women: Their Histories, Their Lives*, ed. Elizabeth Hayes Turner, Stephanie Cole, and Rebecca Sharpless (Athens: University of Georgia Press, 2015), 176–200.

11. Ibid., 193.

12. Ibid., 194–195.

13. Ibid., 176–200.

14. Ibid., 196.

15. Merline Pitre, *Through Many Dangers, Toils and Snares: Black Leadership in Texas, 1868–1898* (College Station: Texas A&M University Press, 2016), 195–205.

16. Colorado County Historical Commission, *Colorado County Chronicles from the Beginning to 1923*, 2 vols. (Austin: Nortex, 1986).

17. Pitre, *Through Many Dangers, Toils and Snares*, 187.

18. Ibid., 199.

Chapter 4: The Bosses: The 1900s

1. Bradley R. Rice, "The Galveston Plan of City Government by Commission: The Birth of a Progressive Idea," *Southwestern Historical Quarterly* 78, no. 4 (April 1975): 365–408.

2. Bradley Robert Rice, *Progressive Cities: The Commission Government Movement in America, 1901–1920* (Austin: University of Texas Press, 1977).

3. Lewis L. Gould, *Progressives and Prohibitionists: Texas Democrats in the Wilson Era* (Austin: University of Texas Press, 1973), 14.

4. Ibid., 15.

5. This quote from Garner has become popular online, though the provenance is unclear. Its proliferation speaks to the way the mythologies of Texas can spread.

6. US Congress, House Committee on Immigration and Naturalization, "Seasonal Agricultural Laborers from Mexico," 69th Congress, 1st sess., 1929, 6–62.

7. Scot D. Bruce, "Woodrow Wilson's Colonial Emissary: Edward M. House and the Origins of the Mandate System, 1917–1919" (PhD diss., University of Nebraska, 2013), 78.

8. "Senators in a Fight," *Iola Daily Register*, July 1, 1902.

9. Sam Hanna Acheson, *Joe Bailey: The Last Democrat* (New York: MacMillan, 1932), vii.

10. Evan Anders, *Boss Rule in South Texas: The Progressive Era* (Austin: University of Texas Press, 1987), 68.

11. Acheson, *Joe Bailey*, 404.

12. "The Twentieth Century," *Texas Almanac*, https://texasalmanac.com/top ics/history/timeline/20th-century-%E2%80%94-1.

13. The themes here are best explored in Anders, *Boss Rule in South Texas*. (Note: His volume is perhaps the definitive look at the boss system in South Texas.)

14. Anders, *Boss Rule in South Texas*, 21.

15. Gould, *Progressives and Prohibitionists*, 40.

16. Ibid., 41.

17. Alwyn Barr, *Reconstruction to Reform: Texas Politics, 1876–1906* (Austin: University of Texas Press, 1971), 242.

18. Gould, *Progressives and Prohibitionists*, 44–45.

19. Betty Trapp Chapman, "Annette Finnigan: Building an Enlightened Community," *Houston History*, March 7, 2012, https://houstonhistorymagazine.org /2012/03/annette-finnigan-building-an-enlightened-community/.

20. A. Elizabeth Taylor, "The Woman Suffrage Movement in Texas," *Journal of Southern History* 17, no. 2 (May 1951): 201–202.

21. Taylor, "Woman Suffrage Movement in Texas," 203.

22. Ruthe Winegarten and Judith N. McArthur, eds., *Citizens at Last: The Woman Suffrage Movement in Texas* (College Station: Texas A&M Press, 2015), chapter 18.

23. George Green, curator, *Walking the Line: The Diverse History of Organized Labor in Texas*, 2017 exhibit, University of Texas at Arlington Labor Archives, Special Collections, Central Library, https://rc.library.uta.edu/uta-ir/bitstream /handle/10106/26620/Labor Exhibit Booklet.pdf?sequence=1&isAllowed=y.

24. Allen, *Chapters in the History of Organized Labor in Texas*, 96.

25. Ibid., 97.

26. Virginia Bernhard, Betty Brandon, Elizabeth Fox-Genovese, Theda Perdue, and Elizabeth Hayes Turner, eds., *Hidden Histories of Women in the New South* (Columbia: University of Missouri Press, 1994), 79.

27. Allen, *Chapters in the History of Organized Labor in Texas*, 222.

28. Garna L. Christian, "The Brownsville Raid's 168th Man: The Court Martial of Corporal Knowles," *Southwestern Historical Quarterly* 93 (July 1989): 45–60.

Chapter 5: Legislative Rest: The 1910s

1. David Martin Davies, "Should Texas Remember or Forget the Slocum Massacre," *Texas Public Radio-Texas Matters,* January 16, 2015, https://www.tpr.org /post/should-texas-remember-or-forget-slocum-massacre.

2. "Refusing to Forget: The History of Racial Violence on the Mexico-Texas Border," a project begun in 2013 as a collaboration between college and university professors "for commemorating the centennial of the period of widespread, state-sanctioned anti-Mexican violence on the Texas-Mexico border (1910–1920)," https://refusingtoforget.org/the-history/.

3. Ibid.

4. Lucia Benavides, "The Texas Rangers Killed Hundreds of Hispanics during the Mexican Revolution," *Texas Standard,* January 22, 2016, https://www .texasstandard.org/stories/texas-exhibit-refuses-to-forget-one-of-the-worst -periods-of-state-sanctioned-violence/.

5. Jim Schutze, *The Accommodation: The Politics of Race in an American City* (Secaucus, NJ: Citadel Press, 1986).

6. Gould, *Progressives and Prohibitionists,* 87.

7. Ibid., 157.

8. "James E. 'Pa' Ferguson Campaign Material," Texas State Library and Archives Commission, https://www.tsl.texas.gov/governors/personality/pferguson -pro-1.html.

9. Ibid.

10. Kurt Terry, "Jesse Washington Lynching," *Waco History,* https://wacohistory .org/items/show/55.

11. "William P. Hobby, 86, Is Dead," *New York Times,* June 8, 1964.

12. "Rangers and Outlaws," Texas State Library and Archives Commission, https://www.tsl.texas.gov/treasures/law/index.html.

13. Green, *Walking the Line,* 12.

14. Kenneth R. Durham Jr., "The Longview Race Riot of 1919," *East Texas Historical Journal* 18, no. 2 (1980): Article 6.

15. "William P. Hobby, 86, Is Dead."

Chapter 6: The Second Coming: The 1920s

1. Charles C. Alexander, *Crusade for Conformity: The Ku Klux Klan in Texas, 1920–1930* (Houston: Texas Gulf Coast Historical Association).

2. Will Guzmán, *Civil Rights in the Texas Borderlands: Dr. Lawrence A. Nixon and Black Activism* (Urbana: University of Illinois Press, 2015), 70.

3. Mike Cox, *Time of the Ranger: Texas Rangers from 1900 to the Present* (New York: Tom Doherty, 2009), chapter 5, "An Asset to Any Law Abiding Community, the 1920s," 100–141.

4. Ibid.

5. Emma Louise Moyer Jackson, "Petticoat Politics: Political Activism among Texas Women in the 1920s" (PhD diss., University of Texas at Austin, 1980), https://search.proquest.com/docview/303071684.

6. Nancy Baker Jones and Ruthe Winegarten, *Capitol Women: Texas Female Legislators, 1923–1999* (Austin: University of Texas Press, 2000); Nancy Baker Jones, "Petticoat Lobby," audio, *Women in Texas History*, https://www.womenin texashistory.org/audio/lobby/.

7. Frank Wagner, "Boll Weevil," in *Handbook of Texas Online*, Texas State Historical Association, https://tshaonline.org/handbook/online/articles/teb01; Fabian Lange, Alan L. Olmstead, and Paul W. Rhode, "The Impact of the Boll Weevil, 1892–1932," *Journal of Economic History* 69, no. 3 (September 2009): 685–718.

8. "Stephen F. Austin Defended Slavery," *New York Times*, July 31, 2018.

9. Texas Public Radio, "Texas Matters: How the KKK Took Control of Texas and How Dan Moody Broke Them," drawn from Patricia Bernstein's book *Ten Dollars to Hate: The Texas Man Who Fought the Klan* (College Station: Texas A&M University Press, 2017), http://tpr.org/post/texas-matters-how-kkk-took-control-tex as-and-how-dan-moody-broke-them.

10. Texas Politics: a project of the Liberal Arts Instructional Technology Services, a unit of the College of Liberal Arts at the University of Texas at Austin, July 14 2018, https://web.archive.org/web/20080402060131/http://texaspolitics. laits.utexas.edu/html/vce/0503.html.

11. Guzmán, *Civil Rights in the Texas Borderlands*, 27.

12. Ibid., 1.

13. *Nixon v. Condon et al.*, 286 US 73, May 2, 1932, https://www.law.cornell .edu/supremecourt/text/286/73.

14. Ramón Rentería, "91 Years since El Paso Physician Tried to Vote and Then Changed History," *El Paso Times*, July 24, 2015 (originally published October 24, 1999).

15. "Did My Family Really Come 'Legally'?" August 10, 2016, American Immigration Council fact sheet, https://www.americanimmigrationcouncil.org/research /did-my-family-really-come-legally-todays-immigration-laws-created-a-new -reality.

16. *Austin Statesman* (1921–1973), March 25, 1923; ProQuest Historical Newspapers: p. 1, accessed through the Austin Public Library.

17. Melita M. Garza, *They Came to Toil: Newspaper Representations of Mexicans and Immigrants in the Great Depression* (Austin: University of Texas Press, 2018). This wonderful work should be consulted by anyone wanting a deeper examination of media depictions of immigrants.

18. Ibid., 3.

Chapter 7: Black Blizzards: The 1930s

1. John Nova Lomax, "Inside Texas's White House," *Texas Monthly*, June 13, 2016.

2. Ross Sterling's "Inaugural Address," January 20, 1931, in *Destiny by Choice: The Inaugural Addresses of the Governors of Texas*, ed. Marvin E. De Boer (Fayetteville: University of Arkansas Press, 1992), 300, https://lrl.texas.gov/scanned /govdocs/Ross%20S%20Sterling/1931/IA_Sterling_1.20.31.pdf.

3. Ibid., 300–301.

4. *Journal of the House of Representatives of the Regular Session of the 42nd Legislature*, Austin, TX, January 13, 1931, 86, https://lrl.texas.gov/scanned/gov docs/Ross S Sterling/1931/SOS_Sterling_1931.pdf.

5. Ibid., 89.

6. Donald Worster, "Dust Bowl," in *Handbook of Texas Online*, Texas State Historical Association, https://tshaonline.org/handbook/online/articles/ydd01.

7. Ibid.

8. "Journal of the Senate of Texas being the Second Called Session of the Forty-Second Legislature," legislative document, September 8, 1931, Austin, Texas, https://texashistory.unt.edu/ark:/67531/metapth307684/m1/629/.

9. Mallory B. Randle, "Work Projects Administration," in *Handbook of Texas Online*, Texas State Historical Association, https://tshaonline.org/handbook/online/articles/ncw01.

10. Quoted in Jacquelyn Dowd Hall, *Revolt Against Chivalry*, rev. ed. (New York: Columbia University Press, 1993), 53; Minutes, Second Annual Meeting, May 17, 1923, Texas Woman's Committee, Dallas, Texas; JDA to Mrs. W. A. Newell, May 5, 1938, Ames Papers (NC); Gould, *Progressives and Prohibitionists*, 262–263; Marguerite Owen to Miss Evelyn S. Logen, December 17, 1924, LWV Papers.

11. Christopher Long, "Dahl, George Leighton," in *Handbook of Texas Online*, Texas State Historical Association, http://www.tshaonline.org/handbook/online/articles/fda86.

12. "President Unveils Statue of R. E. Lee in Brief Ceremony," *Dallas Morning News*, June 13, 1936.

13. Anne Dingus, "John Nance Garner," *Texas Monthly*, November 1996.

14. Emma Tenayuca and Homer Brooks, "The Mexican Question in the Southwest," *The Communist* 18, no. 3 (March 1939): 257–268. Collection of the Dolph Briscoe Center for American History.

15. Alex Wagner, "America's Forgotten History of Illegal Deportations," *The Atlantic*, March 6, 2017.

16. Interview with Emma Tenayuca by Jerry Poyo, Institute of Texan Cultures Oral History Program, University of Texas at San Antonio, February 21, 1987, http://digital.utsa.edu/cdm/ref/collection/p15125coll4/id/1172.

17. Ibid.

18. Richard Croxdale, "Pecan-Shellers' Strike," in *Handbook of Texas Online*, Texas State Historical Association, http://www.tshaonline.org/handbook/online/articles/oep01.

Chapter 8: Beautiful Texas: The 1940s

1. Peter Carlson, "American Schemers: 'Pappy' O'Daniel: Texas Radio Showman Talked His Way into the U.S. Senate," *American History Magazine*, June 2017, https://www.historynet.com/american-schemers-w-lee-pappy-odaniel.htm.

2. The Federal Bureau of Investigation, *FBI Records: The Vault*, "Martin Dies, Jr.," https://vault.fbi.gov/martin-dies-jr/martin-dies-jr-part-01-of-01/view.

3. Robert Caro, "My Search for Coke Stevenson," *New York Times Book Review*, February 3, 1991, 1.

4. Ben H. Procter, "World War II," in *Handbook of Texas Online*, Texas State Historical Association, https://tshaonline.org/handbook/online/articles/npwnj.

5. Willie McNeeley, "Man Tells How It Feels to Be Castrated," *Dallas Express*, October 25, 1941, 1. (Note that this is a self-penned story by the victim.)

6. New York Times, "Texas Whites Lynch Negro," July 18, 1942.

7. Procter, "World War II," in *Handbook of Texas Online*, Texas State Historical Association, https://tshaonline.org/handbook/online/articles/npwnj.

8. Caro, "My Search for Coke Stevenson," 1.

9. James A. Burran, "Violence in an 'Arsenal of Democracy': The Beaumont Race Riot, 1943," *East Texas Historical Journal* 14, no. 1 (1976): Article 8, http://scholarworks.sfasu.edu/ethj/vol14/iss1/8.

10. Langston Hughes, *The Collected Poems of Langston Hughes* (New York: Knopf; distributed by Random House, 1994), 281.

11. Telegram sent by the Ku Klux Klan to Martin Dies on the formation of the House Un-American Activities Committee, 1937, found in Linda Rosenkrantz, *Telegram! Modern History as Told through More Than 400 Witty, Poignant, and Revealing Telegrams* (New York: Henry Holt, 2003), 153.

12. Miranda J. Banks, *The Writers: A History of American Screenwriters and Their Guild* (New Brunswick, NJ: Rutgers University Press, 2015), 74.

13. Michael Kackman, *Citizen Spy: Television, Espionage, and Cold War Culture* (Minneapolis: University of Minnesota Press, 2005), xxiv.

14. Kenneth Dewey Hairgrove, "Sam Rayburn, Congressional Leader, 1940–1952" (PhD diss., Texas Tech University, Lubbock, Texas, 1974).

15. Judith N. McArthur and Patricia Ellen Cunningham, "Cunningham, Minnie Fisher," in *Handbook of Texas Online*, Texas State Historical Association, https://tshaonline.org/handbook/online/articles/fcu24.

16. "Congress has tried more than 200 times to pass an anti-lynching law. This year it could fail again," *Los Angeles Times*, December 5, 2018, https://www.latimes.com/nation/la-na-anti-lynching-law-20181205-story.html.

17. Dan Balz, "The Mystery of Ballot Box 13," *Washington Post*, March 4, 1990.

18. Caro, "My Search for Coke Stevenson," 1.

19. Ibid.

20. Norman Rozeff, "García, Hector Pérez," in *Handbook of Texas Online*, Texas State Historical Association, https://tshaonline.org/handbook/online/articles/fga52.

21. Carl Allsup, *American G.I. Forum: Origins and Evolution* (Austin: Center for Mexican American Studies, University of Texas, 1982), 31.

22. Joe Simnacher, "Hector Garcia: Civil Rights Activist," *Dallas Morning News*, July 28, 1996.

23. Carlos E. Cortés, ed., *Multicultural America: A Multimedia Encyclopedia* (Los Angeles: Sage, 2013), 390.

24. Lawrence Wright, "The Tide Turns," *Texas Monthly*, January 1986.

25. Andrew Glass, "Truman Sworn in as 33rd President, April 12, 1945," *Politico*, April 12, 2018, https://www.politico.com/story/2018/04/12/harry-truman-sworn-in-as-33rd-president-april-12-1945-511037.

26. Drew Pearson, "The Washington Merry-Go-Round," *Northwest Arkansas Times*, January 8, 1953, 4.

27. Maddie Garrett, "Sam Rayburn Leaves Lasting Impact," News12, Fox Media, October 1, 2009, http://kxii.com/home/headlines/63209612.html.

28. Robert Baskin, "Visitor Kennedy, Rayburn Discuss Politics of the Past," *Dallas Morning News*, October 10, 1961.

29. Reed Penney, dir., *Rayburn: Mr. Speaker*, a documentary on former House Speaker Sam Rayburn, http://www.rayburnmrspeaker.com/wp-content/uploads/2014/08/Inventory-Appraisement-of-Sam-Rayburn-Estate.pdf. This is an extraordinary repository of Rayburn history and materials from one of the leading Rayburn experts.

Chapter 9: I Have a Plaintiff: The 1950s

1. Bill Minutaglio, *City on Fire: The Explosion That Devastated a Texas Town and Ignited a Historic Legal Battle* (New York: HarperCollins, 2003), 110–198. Note: This work is meant to serve as an overview history of The Texas City Disaster.

2. Ibid., 199.

3. Joe Nick Patoski, "Boone Pickens Wants to Sell You His Water," *Texas Monthly*, August 2001.

4. Merline Pitre, *In Struggle against Jim Crow: Lulu B. White and the NAACP, 1900–1957 (College Station: Texas A&M University Press, 1999)*, 93.

5. Michael Gillette, "Heman Marion Sweatt: Civil Rights Plaintiff," in *Black Leaders: Texans for Their Times*, ed. Alwyn Barr and Robert A. Calvert (Austin: Texas State Historical Association, 1981), 161.

6. Joe Holley, "Third Ward Mailman Won Case for UT Law School Integration," *Houston Chronicle*, September 23, 2016.

7. Merline Pitre, "White, Lulu Belle Madison," in *Handbook of Texas Online*, Texas State Historical Association, https://tshaonline.org/handbook/online/articles/fwh75.

8. Bill Minutaglio and Steven L. Davis, *Dallas 1963* (New York: Twelve, 2013), 286.

9. Ibid., 285–286.

10. Pitre, *In Struggle against Jim Crow*, 144–145.

11. American GI Forum of Texas and Texas State Federation of Labor (AFL), *What Price Wetbacks?* (Austin, 1953; reprinted in *Mexican Migration to the United States* [New York: Arno Press, 1976]).

12. V. Carl Allsup, "Hernandez v. Driscoll CISD," in *Handbook of Texas Online*, Texas State Historical Association, https://tshaonline.org/handbook/online/articles/jrh02.

13. *Hispanic Americans in Congress, 1822–2012*, H. Doc. 108-225, April 7, 2014, prepared under the direction of the Committee on House Administration of the US House of Representatives, Daniel E. Lundgren, chairman, Robert A. Brady, ranking minority member, by the Office of the Historian and Office of the Clerk, US House of Representatives, 400.

14. "RIP: Judge Albert Peña—Chicano Activist and Leader," *Associated Press*, July 9, 2006, https://doscentavos.net/2006/07/09/rip-judge-albert-pena-chicano-activist-leader/.

15. Bill Minutaglio, "Percy Sutton—The Texas-Bred Politico Is Still the Toast of Harlem," *Dallas Morning News*, August 13, 1995.

16. Paula Allen, "Solemn Pilgrimage Recalls Fiesta's Original Purpose," *San Antonio Express-News*, April 8, 2017.

17. Ricky F. Dobbs, *Yellow Dogs and Republicans: Allan Shivers and Texas Two-Party Politics* (College Station: Texas A&M University Press, 2005), 54.

18. George N. Green, *The Establishment in Texas Politics: The Primitive Years, 1938–1957* (Norman: University of Oklahoma Press, 1984), 122–123.

19. Edward H. Miller, *Nut Country: Right-Wing Dallas and the Birth of the Southern Strategy* (Chicago: University of Chicago Press, 2015), 82.

20. Patrick L. Cox, *Ralph W. Yarborough, the People's Senator* (Austin: University of Texas Press, 2002), 128.

21. Mark K. Updegrove, *Indomitable Will: LBJ in the Presidency* (New York: Crown, 2012), 3.

Chapter 10: The Mink Coat Mob: The 1960s

1. Minutaglio and Davis, *Dallas 1963*, 45, 49, 53–54.

2. Ibid., 59–65, 80.

3. Oval Office recording by Richard Nixon, speaking to Pat Buchanan on November 1, 1972. Richard M. Nixon Presidential Library and Museum, Tape 379, Conversation 379-10.

4. Jack and Christopher Wren Shepherd, *Quotations from Chairman LBJ* (New York: Simon and Schuster, 1968), 72.

5. Interview with Ray Scott, John Nance Garner's caretaker, from the documentary *Cactus Jack: Lone Star on Capitol Hill*, directed by Nancy Schiesari and cowritten by Bill Minutaglio and Nancy Schiesari, 2016.

6. Minutaglio and Davis, *Dallas 1963*, 302.

7. Anthony Champagne, Douglas B. Harris, James W. Riddlesperger Jr., Garrison Nelson, *The Austin—Boston Connection: Five Decades of Democratic House Leadership, 1937–1989* (College Station: Texas A&M University Press, 2009), 50.

8. James Reston, *The Lone Star: The Life of John Connally* (New York: Harper and Row, 1989), 310–315.

9. Elaine Sciolino, "Washington at Work: A Year after Rejection in Senate, Tower Replays Loss of Coveted Job," *New York Times*, April 5, 1990.

10. Thomas H. Kreneck, *Mexican American Odyssey: Felix Tijerina, Entrepreneur and Civic Leader, 1905–1965* (College Station: Texas A&M Press, 2001), 3.

11. Robb Walsh, "Combination Plates," *Houston Press*, August 31, 2000, https://www.houstonpress.com/restaurants/combination-plates-6563946.

12. Eugene Rodriguez Jr., *Henry B. Gonzalez: A Political Profile* (New York: Arno Press, 1976), 39–40.

13. Ibid., 53–54.

14. Brenda Haugen, *Henry B. González: Congressman of the People* (North Mankato, MN: Capstone, 2005), 52.

15. Michael Wines, "A Populist from Texas Who Bows to No One," *New York Times*, March 24, 1994, 18.

16. Armando Navarro, *Mexican American Youth Organization: Avant-Garde of the Chicano Movement in Texas* (Austin: University of Texas Press, 1995), 81.

17. "La Raza Unida Party in Texas," a fifteen-page pamphlet at the University of Texas at Austin, Perry-Castañeda Library, dated May 4, 1970 (a document apparently produced at a MAYO meeting in San Antonio).

18. Bryan Woolley, "High Profile: José Ángel Gutiérrez," *Dallas Morning News*, July 29, 2003, http://www.latinamericanstudies.org/latinos/gutierrez.htm.

19. Ibid.

20. Paul Burka, "Don Yarborough's Texas," *Texas Monthly*, October 2009, https://www.texasmonthly.com/politics/don-yarboroughs-texas/.

21. Ibid.

22. Jack Bass and Walter De Vries, *The Transformation of Southern Politics: Social Change and Political Consequence since 1945* (New York: Basic Books, 1976), 305.

23. Cox, *Ralph W. Yarborough, the People's Senator*, 101.

24. Ibid.

25. Ibid.

Chapter 11: Bitten by the Political Bug: The 1970s

1. William Broyles, "The Making of Barbara Jordan," *Texas Monthly*, October 1976, https://www.texasmonthly.com/politics/the-making-of-barbara-jordan-2/.

2. Barbara Jordan with Shelby Hearon, *Barbara Jordan: A Self-Portrait* (New York: Doubleday, 1979), 110.

3. Ibid., 129.

4. Ibid., 129–135.

5. Ibid., 135–150.

6. History, Art & Archives, US House of Representatives, "Jordan, Barbara Charline," https://history.house.gov/People/Detail/16031.

7. Letter to the Texas Senate from Barbara Jordan, June 10, 1972, https://texashistory.unt.edu/ark:/67531/metapth17419/m1/2/zoom/?resolution=2.596677176323155&lat=2847.6407431636253&lon=684.8703319765556.

8. Max Sherman, ed., *Barbara Jordan: Speaking the Truth with Eloquent Thunder* (Austin: University of Texas Press, 2007), 11.

9. US Congress, "Debate on Articles of Impeachment: Hearings of the Committee on the Judiciary, House of Representatives, 93rd Congress, 2nd sess., pursuant to H. Res. 803," July 24–30, 1974, 110–113.

10. Barbara Jordan, "Speech to the 1976 Democratic National Convention," https://lbj.utexas.edu/news/2012/lbj-professor-barbara-jordans-landmark-speech-1976-democrati.

11. "Interview with Frances Farenthold," by Jack Bass and Walter Devries, *Documenting the American South*, University of North Carolina at Chapel Hill, December 14, 1974, Interview A-0186, Southern Oral History Program Collection (#4007), https://docsouth.unc.edu/sohp/html_use/A-0186.html.

12. Ibid.

13. Vassar News and Events, "Farenthold Conference Honors 'Noble Citizen,'"

May 12, 2015, https://www.vassar.edu/news/stories/2014-2015/150512-farentho ld.html.

14. State Overview, "Frances Tarlton 'Sissy" Farenthold: A Noble Citizen," described as an "online project" that is "presented by the Bernard and Audre Rapoport Center of Human Rights and Justice," maintained by the University of Texas School of Law, https://law.utexas.edu/farenthold/state/.

15. "Interview with Frances Farenthold," *Documenting the American South*.

16. Vassar News and Events, "Farenthold Conference Honors 'Noble Citizen.'"

17. Ibid.

18. Robert Leleux, "Texas (Still) Needs Farenthold," *Texas Observer*, September 21, 2007, https://www.texasobserver.org/2593-texas-still-needs-farenthold/.

19. State Overview, "Frances Tarlton 'Sissy' Farenthold: A Noble Citizen."

20. "Interview with Frances Farenthold," *Documenting the American South*.

21. Ibid.

22. Bill Minutaglio and W. Michael Smith, *Molly Ivins: A Rebel Life* (New York: Public Affairs, 2009), 72.

23. "Interview with Frances Farenthold," *Documenting the American South*.

24. Calvin Trillin, "The Reformer," a magazine piece republished in *Texas Tribune*, December 29, 2010, https://www.texastribune.org/2010/12/29/calvin-tril lins-1972-profile-of-sissy-farenthold/.

25. "Interview with Frances Farenthold," *Documenting the American South*.

26. Ibid.

27. Chuck Doud, "There's humor to be had in suffering," *Madera Tribune* (California), November 16, 2019, citing Frances Farenthold, http://www.maderatribune .com/single-post/2019/11/16/Opinion-There's-humor-to-be-had-in-suffering.

28. Ben F. Barnes and Lisa Dickey, *Barn Burning Barn Building: Tales of a Political Life, from LBJ through George W. Bush and Beyond (Albany, TX: Bright Sky Press, 2006), 193–200.

29. Ibid., 221.

30. Dennis Hevesi, "Dolph Briscoe, Texas Governor in the '70s, Dies," June 29, 2010, https://www.nytimes.com/2010/06/29/us/29briscoe.html?searchResultPo sition=1.

31. "Virginia Múzquiz," *Tejano Voices*, The University of Texas at Arlington Center for Mexican American Studies, https://library.uta.edu/tejanovoices/interview .php?cmasno=127.

32. James C. Harrington, "Power and Responsibility," *Texas Observer*, July 29, 1988, 8.

33. Griffin Smith Jr., "A Question of Balance," *Texas Monthly*, February 1976, 87.

34. Bill Curry, "Texas Republican Governor: Activist, Conservative, Impolitic," *Washington Post*, September 11, 1979, https://www.washingtonpost.com/archive /politics/1979/09/11/texas-republican-governor-activist-conservative-impolitic /3fb98186-6f3a-4ee9-aaf8-f79bf052ba69/?utm_term=.3e33bf406446.

35. Paul Burka, "Remembering Bill Clements," May 30, 2011, *Texas Monthly*, https://www.texasmonthly.com/burka-blog/remembering-bill-clements/.

36. Curry, "Texas Republican Governor: Activist, Conservative, Impolitic."

37. Ibid.

Chapter 12: The Sands Have Shifted: The 1980s

1. Joe Holley, "*Chavez vs. Orendain*—The Texas Farmworkers' Split: The Two Unions Take Different Tacks on Strategy and, Now, Legislation," *Texas Observer*, April 17, 1981, 4–8.

2. Rod Davis, "The Onion Revolt," *Texas Observer*, August 8, 1980, 1–8.

3. Ibid.

4. Terry Fitzpatrick, "Jesus Moya Strikes Again," *Texas Observer*, August 31, 1984, 8.

5. Ibid., 8.

6. Louis R. Beam, "It Is Time," in *Essays by a Klansman* (Hayden Lake, ID: AKIA, 1983), 23–26.

7. Champ Clark, "A Rich, Cool Texan Sets Out to Become President," *People*, February 24, 1975, https://people.com/archive/a-rich-cool-texan-sets-out-to-bec ome-president-lloyd-bentsen-vol-3-no-7/.

8. Nina Butts, "Four Fresh(men) Sing," *Texas Observer*, January 18, 1984, 4.

9. Dan Balz, "Texas Attorney General Praises 'Courage' in Decision," *Washington Post*, December 9, 1982, https://www.washingtonpost.com/archive/politics/19 82/12/09/texas-attorney-general-praises-courage-in-decision/eb507d61-4731 -443c-9fef-45c0c366c1b4/?noredirect=on&utm_term=.aae37a7bd045.

10. Joe Holley, interview with Jim Hightower, "The Mechanics of Victory," *Texas Observer*, May 21, 1982, 7.

11. Ibid.

12. Ronald B. Taylor, "Texas' New-Style Agriculture Commissioner: Jim Hightower Carries His Message of a New Populist Movement Nationwide," *Los Angeles Times*, December 19, 1985.

13. Kathy Whitmire, interview by Jim Barlow, July 14, 2008, Houston Oral History Project, from the Houston Area Digital Archives: http://digital.houstonlibrary .net/oral-history/kathy-whitmire.php.

14. William K. Stevens, "The Houston That Was Loses Its Hold," *New York Times*, November 22, 1981.

15. William K. Stevens, "Woman in the News; Feminist Mayor for Houston," *New York Times*, November 19, 1981, https://www.nytimes.com/1981/11/19/us /woman-in-the-news-feminist-mayor-for-houston.html.

16. Melinda Beck with Stryker McGuire, "Gay Power in Macho Houston," *Newsweek*, August 10, 1981, 29.

17. "The Sands Have Shifted," *Texas Observer*, October 24, 1986, 2, (unsigned editorial).

18. Balz, "Texas Attorney General Praises 'Courage' in Decision."

19. Mark White, "America's Capital Punishment Crisis," *Politico*, May 5, 2014.

20. Paul Burka, "The Strange Case of Mark White," *Texas Monthly*, October 1986, 215.

21. George Slaughter, "White, Mark Wells, Jr.," in *Handbook of Texas Online*, Texas State Historical Association, https://tshaonline.org/handbook/online/arti cles/fwhit.

22. Burka, "The Strange Case of Mark White," 215.

23. Slaughter, "White, Mark Wells, Jr."

24. "Transcript of the Keynote Address by Ann Richards, the Texas Treasurer," *New York Times*, July 19, 1988.

25. Ibid.

26. Bill Minutaglio, "Henry Cisneros Pursues a Dream," *Chicago Tribune*, June 11, 1993, https://www.chicagotribune.com/news/ct-xpm-1993-06-11-9306120138-story.html.

Chapter 13: Reality Day: The 1990s

1. J. Michael Kennedy, "Texas Democrats End Lurid Campaign: Politics: Ann Richards or Jim Mattox Will Be the Gubernatorial Nominee after Today's Runoff. It Caps Possibly the Dirtiest Race in State History," *Los Angeles Times*, April 10, 1990, https://www.latimes.com/archives/la-xpm-1990-04-10-mn-1118-story.html.

2. Brian McCall, *The Power of the Texas Governor: Connally to Bush* (Austin: University of Texas Press, 2009), 96.

3. Kennedy, "Texas Democrats End Lurid Campaign."

4. Ibid.

5. Robin Toner, "Bitter Race in Texas Ends with Richards as Democrats' Pick," *New York Times*, April 11, 1990, https://www.nytimes.com/1990/04/11/us/bitter-race-in-texas-ends-with-richards-as-democrats-pick.html.

6. Mike Shropshire, "Clayton Williams: Texas Crude," *D Magazine*, September 1990.

7. Ibid.

8. Joe Pappalardo, "Trick Town," *Dallas Observer*, May 31, 2001, https://www.dallasobserver.com/news/trick-town-6406505.

9. David Maraniss, "The Texas Two-Step in the Race for Governor," *Washington Post*, October 22, 1990.

10. Ibid.

11. Ibid.

12. Ibid.

13. Ibid.

14. Ann Richards, victory speech, November 6, 1990, user-created video clip, https://www.c-span.org/video/?c4602750/user-clip-ann-richards-victory-speech.

15. Joe Holley, "Austerity Is Message at Today's Texas Inauguration," *Houston Chronicle*, January 17, 2011, https://www.chron.com/news/houston-texas/article/Austerity-is-message-at-today-s-Texas-inauguration-1609268.php.

16. "Special Session: Episode 214: Remembering Molly Ivins," *KLRU-TV*, May 13, 2007.

17. Jan Reid, "Richards Sets Politically Fateful Course on Guns," *Texas Tribune*, October 4, 2012, https://www.texastribune.org/2012/10/04/richards-sets-politically-fateful-course-guns/.

18. Ibid.

19. J. Michael Kennedy, "'92 Democratic Convention: My, How She's Grown: Richards Rises from Footnotes," *Los Angeles Times*, July 12, 1992, https://www.latimes.com/archives/la-xpm-1992-07-12-mn-4291-story.html.

20. "Branding Rite Tied to Yale Fraternity," *New York Times*, November 8, 1967.

21. Eric Pooley with S. C. Gwynne, "How George Got His Groove," *Time*, June 21, 1999.

22. Lois Romano and George Lardner Jr., "Bush's Move Up to the Majors," *Washington Post*, July 31, 1999.

23. Sam Howe Verhovek, "Texas Vote: It'll Be Richards vs. a Bush," *New York Times*, March 10, 1994.

24. Kelley Shannon, "Former Governor Ann Richards Dies," Associated Press story in the *Bryan-College Station Eagle*, September 4, 2006, https://www.the eagle.com/news/state-and-regional/former-governor-ann-richards-dies/article _dcbd99ea-1ae5-5a5f-83a0-4817a7822c0b.html.

25. Ibid.

26. Ibid.

27. Ibid.

28. Helen Prejean, "Death in Texas," *New York Review of Books*, January 13, 2005, https://www.nybooks.com/articles/2005/01/13/death-in-texas/.

29. Debbie White, "Forgiving the Dead Man Walking," *The Christian Broadcasting Network*, https://www.cbn.com/spirituallife/BibleStudyAndTheology/Dis cipleship/Forgiving_The_Dead_Man_Walking.aspx.

30. Natalie Gott, "Texas Senate Passes Hate Crimes Bill," *Washington Post*, May 8, 2001.

31. Graham Vyse, "'Compassionate Conservatism' Won't Be Back Anytime Soon," *New Republic*, March 30, 2018, https://newrepublic.com/article/147694 /compassionate-conservatism-wont-back-anytime-soon.

32. Wayne Slater, "Behind the Scenes in the Latest Attack on Wendy Davis— A Pair of GOP Political Pros," *Dallas Morning News*, March 3, 2018, https://www .dallasnews.com/news/politics/2014/03/18/behind-the-scenes-in-the-latest -attack-on-wendy-davis-in-texas-a-pair-of-political-pros.

33. Wayne Slater, writing at request of *Dallas Morning News* Editorial Board, "Texan of the Year 2004: Karl Rove," *Dallas Morning News*, Dec. 26, 2004.

34. S. C. Gwynne, "Genius," *Texas Monthly*, March 2003, https://www.texas monthly.com/politics/genius/.

35. Claudia Kolker, "The Eyes (and Hats) of Texas Are Upon Him," *Los Angeles Times*, January 9, 2001, https://www.latimes.com/archives/la-xpm-2001-jan-09 -cl-9903-story.html.

Chapter 14: Smear Tactics: The 2000s

1. Ibid., 228.

2. Molly Ivins, "We Do Not Torture," *Memphis Flyer*, November 18, 2005, https://m.memphisflyer.com/memphis/we-do-not-torture/Content?oid=11 23498.

3. "Governor Rick Perry's Remarks after Taking the Oath of Office," December 21, 2000, https://lrl.texas.gov/scanned/govdocs/Rick%20Perry/2000/speech122 101_2.pdf; "Texas Governor Swearing-in," C-Span, December 21, 2000.

4. Jim Yardley, "In Texas, Republican Who Inherited Top Job Is the Winner

Outright," *New York Times*, November 6, 2002, https://www.nytimes.com/2002 /11/06/us/2002-elections-races-for-governor-texas-republican-who-inherited -top-job-winner.html.

5. Kinky Friedman, "Kinky for Governor? Why Not?," *Houston Chronicle*, June 13, 2004, https://www.chron.com/opinion/outlook/article/Kinky-for-governor -Why-not-1955170.php.

6. Morley Safer, "Kinky's Run for Governor of Texas," *60 Minutes*, January 22, 2006, https://www.cbsnews.com/news/kinkys-run-for-governor-of-texas/.

7. Ibid.

8. Ibid.

9. "President Bush's statement on the passing of Molly Ivins," The White House, Office of the Press Secretary, January 31, 2007.

10. Minutaglio and Smith, *Molly Ivins: A Rebel Life*, 306.

11. Evan Smith, "Boone personifies what we love about Texas," *Dallas Morning News*, Nov. 21, 2008, p. 21a.

12. Shepherd, *Quotations from Chairman LBJ*, 72.

13. Bill Minutaglio, "Bush's Afterlife in Texas," *Newsweek*, May 15, 2009, https:// www.newsweek.com/bushs-afterlife-texas-79717.

14. "Presidential Approval Ratings—George W. Bush," *Gallup*, https://news .gallup.com/poll/116500/presidential-approval-ratings-george-bush.aspx.

15. Minutaglio, "Bush's Afterlife in Texas."

16. Reeve Hamilton, "Be It Hereby Resolved: The Texas Legislature Attempts to Pay Homage to George W. Bush," *Texas Observer*, April 1, 2009.

17. Minutaglio, "Bush's Afterlife in Texas."

18. Daniel Libit, "Facebook for Bushies," *Politico*, August 9, 2009, https://www .politico.com/story/2009/08/facebook-for-bushies-025922.

19. Minutaglio, "Bush's Afterlife in Texas."

20. Ibid.

Chapter 15: Total Command: The 2010s

1. Bob Kemper, "'P' Follows 'W' in Dynasty, but Give Him a Few Years," *Chicago Tribune*, August 3, 2000, https://www.chicagotribune.com/news/ct-xpm-2000 -08-03-0008030470-story.html.

2. Brian D. Sweany, "The P. Q&A," *Texas Monthly*, February 2016, https://www .texasmonthly.com/politics/the-p-qa/.

3. Dan Well, "George P. Bush: New Kid on the Political Block," *Newsmax*, July 26, 2010, https://www.newsmax.com/Politics/george-p-bush-texas-hispanics-pac /2010/07/26/id/365654/.

4. Sweany, "The P. Q & A."

5. Theodore Kim, "Accident Set Texas Attorney General Greg Abbott on a Path toward Politics," *Dallas Morning News*, May 31, 2010, https://www.dallasnews.com /news/local-politics/2010/05/31/accident-set-texas-attorney-general-greg-3032.

6. Richard Fausett, "In Texas, Distrust of Washington Collides with Need for Federal Aid," *New York Times*, September 4, 2017, https://www.nytimes.com /2017/09/04/us/texas-storm-federal-aid-abbott-cruz.html.

7. Sue Owen, "Greg Abbott Says He Has Sued Obama Administration 25 Times," *Politifact*, May 10, 2013, https://www.politifact.com/texas/statements/2013/may /10/greg-abbott/greg-abbott-says-he-has-sued-obama-administration-/.

8. Kim, "Accident Set Texas Attorney General Greg Abbott on a Path toward Politics."

9. Jay Root, "Davis Says Critics Picked on 'Wrong Texas Gal,'" *Texas Tribune*, January 28, 2014, https://www.texastribune.org/2014/01/28/davis-says-critics -picked-wrong-texas-gal/.

10. Office of the Texas Governor, "Greg Abbott Delivers 2015 Inaugural Speech," January 20, 2015, https://gov.texas.gov/news/post/greg_abbott_delivers_2015 _texas_inaugural_speech.

11. Ibid.

12. Briana Stone, "Plan to 'Restore the Alamo to Its Former Dignity' Signed by George P. Gush and San Antonio Mayor," *Dallas Morning News*, October 2, 2018.

13. Cassandra Pollock, "Texas Land Commissioner George P. Bush Signs Plan to Overhaul Alamo Plaza," *Texas Tribune*, September 13, 2018.

14. Bill Minutaglio, "Welcome to America," *Dallas Morning News*, May 21, 1989.

15. Sweany, "The P. Q&A."

16. Sean Collins Walsh, "George P. Bush Breaks with Family, Endorses Donald Trump," *Austin American-Statesman*, September 15, 2016, https://www.states man.com/news/20160915/george-p-bush-breaks-with-family-endorses-donald -trump.

17. Ibid.

18. This quote appeared on the cover of the April 2019 issue of *Vanity Fair*, along with a photograph of O'Rourke.

19. Dylan McGuiness, "Castro Launches His Presidential Bid," *San Antonio Express-News*, January 12, 2019, 1.

Epilogue

1. Kathleen Petty, "San Antonio Leaders Urge Continued Social Distancing When State Begins to Reopen on May 1," San Antonio Magazine, April 27, 2020.

2. Tom Benning, "At Least One Notable Bush—George P., the Texas Land Commissioner—will vote for Trump in November, *Dallas Morning News*, June 9, 2020.

3. Willie Nelson, "Delete and Fast-Forward," from the 2017 album *God's Problem Child*, lyrics from https://www.songfacts.com/lyrics/willie-nelson/delete-and -fast-forward.

Photo Credits

p. 17 Image Number 1987/173-023, courtesy of Texas State Library and Archives Commission.

p. 28 Courtesy of Name File Photographic Collection, Rosenberg Library, Galveston, Texas.

p. 43 Courtesy of Texas State Library and Archives Commission (1908).

p. 45 Prints and Photographs Collection, di_02583, The Dolph Briscoe Center for American History, The University of Texas at Austin.

p. 53 Speeches and State Papers of James Stephen Hogg, di_04548, The Dolph Briscoe Center for American History, The University of Texas at Austin.

p. 54 *American Women*, edited by Frances E. Willard and Mary A. Livermore (New York: Mast, Crowell & Kirkpatrick, 1897; republished by Gale Research Company, Book Tower, Detroit, 1973).

p. 59 Smith-Cobb Family Collection, Accession #2755, Box #11, Folder #3, The Texas Collection, Baylor University (1905).

p. 83 Image Number 1975/070-5237a, Courtesy of Texas State Library and Archives Commission.

p. 88 UTSA Special Collections.

p. 99 Prints and Photographs Collection, di_08317, The Dolph Briscoe Center for American History, The University of Texas at Austin.

p. 101 J. T. Canales Estate Collection, The South Texas Archives and Special Collections, Texas A&M University-Kingsville, Kingsville, TX.

p. 106 From the collections of the Dallas Historical Society.

p. 114 By Jenson Studio, Prints and Photographs Collection, e_bte_48, The Dolph Briscoe Center for American History, The University of Texas at Austin.

p. 120 E. A. "Dogie" Wright Papers, di_04828, The Dolph Briscoe Center for American History, The University of Texas at Austin.

p. 122 Courtesy of the Edna A. (Nixon) McIver Family Collection (1910s).

p. 128 Ross Shaw Sterling Papers, di_05549, The Dolph Briscoe Center for American History, The University of Texas at Austin.

p. 140 Fath (Creekmore) Papers Creator, e_rap_0105, The Dolph Briscoe Center for American History, The University of Texas at Austin.

p. 155 John B. Connally; Accession ID: CHA 1989.012. Courtesy of State Preservation Board, Austin, TX. Original Artist: C.J. Fox; photographer: Eric Beggs, 12/92, pre conservation.

p. 159 By Fred Garnatt, Prints and Photographs Collection, e_rap_0046, The Dolph Briscoe Center for American History, The University of Texas at Austin.

p. 162 Sam Rayburn Papers, di_00832, The Dolph Briscoe Center for American History, The University of Texas at Austin (January 8, 1956).

p. 169 Jimmie A. Dodd Photograph Collection, e_jd_0061, The Dolph Briscoe Center for American History, The University of Texas at Austin (June 1948).

p. 171 Courtesy of Mary and Jeff Bell Library Special Collections and Archives, Texas A&M University–Corpus Christi.

p. 177 Sam Rayburn Papers, di_01897, The Dolph Briscoe Center for American History, The University of Texas at Austin (July 18, 1939).

p. 186 Special Collections/Archives Department, John B. Coleman Library, Prairie View A&M University, Prairie View, Texas.

p. 200 Russell Lee Photograph Collection, di_08303, The Dolph Briscoe Center for American History, The University of Texas at Austin.

p. 218 UTSA Special Collections.

p. 220 Image Number 1982/031-002, Courtesy of Texas State Library and Archives Commission (1982).

p. 224 Image Number 1973/54-81, Courtesy of Texas State Library and Archives Commission (1972).

p. 240 The Cactus yearbook of the University of Texas, di_03938, The Dolph Briscoe Center for American History, The University of Texas at Austin.

Index

Page numbers followed by f refer to illustrations.